MAKING CONSTITUTIONAL LAW

MAKING CONSTITUTIONAL LAW

Thurgood Marshall and the Supreme Court, 1961–1991

MARK V. TUSHNET

New York   Oxford
OXFORD UNIVERSITY PRESS
1997

Oxford University Press

Oxford   New York
Athens   Auckland   Bangkok   Bogota   Bombay   Buenos Aires
Calcutta   Cape Town   Dar es Salaam   Delhi   Florence   Hong Kong
Istanbul   Karachi   Kuala Lumpur   Madras   Madrid   Melbourne
Mexico City   Nairobi   Paris   Singapore   Taipei   Tokyo   Toronto

and associated companies in
Berlin   Ibadan

Library of Congress Cataloging-in-Publication Data
Tushnet, Mark V., 1945–
Making constitutional law : Thurgood Marshall and the Supreme
Court, 1961–1991 / Mark V. Tushnet.
p. cm.
Includes index.
ISBN 0–19–509314–3
1. Marshall, Thurgood, 1908–1993.   2. Judges—United States—
Biography.   3. Constitutional law—United States.   4. Civil rights—
United States—History.   I. Title.
KF8745 .M34T87   1997
347.73'26—dc20
[347.30735]   96–25548

9 8 7 6 5 4 3 2 1
Printed in the United States of America
on acid-free paper

For Rebecca and Laura

Preface

My previous work, *Making Civil Rights Law: Thurgood Marshall and the Supreme Court, 1936–1961* (Oxford University Press, 1994), examines Marshall's legal career before his appointment to the federal bench in 1961. The first chapter of this book describes Marshall's route to the Supreme Court from 1961 to 1967. The remainder of the book uses Marshall's experience on the Supreme Court as a vehicle for examining the Court as a whole during his tenure. Treating Marshall and his office as lenses through which we can view the Supreme Court, I locate the Court in the historical and political context of 1967 to 1991. Chapter 3 then deals with Marshall's role on the Supreme Court, the way he ran his office, and his relations with his colleagues. Succeeding chapters take up several controversies that were at the heart of the Court's work and in which Marshall played important parts: race discrimination and capital punishment. As the pages that follow show, the Supreme Court during Marshall's tenure was not regularly shot through with personal conflict, intrigue, or manipulation; to the minor extent those matters arose, Marshall himself rarely participated. Rather, the justices decided cases, they and their law clerks wrote opinions, and the published opinions reflected—on the whole—what the justices were concerned about.

My approach concentrates almost exclusively on aspects of Marshall's role in developing constitutional law. Other aspects of Marshall's Supreme Court work are important to specialists, but providing sufficient background to illuminate his particular contributions would burden nonspecialist readers. (For my treatment of some of Marshall's work in administrative law, see "The Legitimation of the Administrative State: Some Aspects of the Work of Thurgood Marshall," *Studies in American Political Development* 5 (1991): 94.)

The primary sources for this volume are the Thurgood Marshall Papers, Manuscript Division, Library of Congress, and the William J. Brennan Papers, Manuscript Division, Library of Congress, for 1967 through the October 1985 Term. In addition, I consulted the Earl Warren, William O. Douglas, and John Marshall Harlan Papers. Each collection contains many of the same materials, because memoranda and draft opinions were circulated to each justice's chambers. When multiple sources exist, I have cited to the source from which I took notes when the material appeared to me likely to be significant for this work.

I did not systematically interview law clerks, either Marshall's or any other justice's. When Marshall agreed to let me interview him for *Making Civil Rights Law,* he insisted that our discussions avoid his Supreme Court years. In light of this understanding, I was uncomfortable with attempting to interview former law clerks. I also thought such interviews would inappropriately trade on relations that arose for other reasons. Because I was a law clerk to Marshall in the 1972–73 Term, I undoubtedly picked up some information from the former clerks' network, and I have relied on my recollection for a few points, particularly in the prologue and chapters 2, 3, and 9.

Clerks' recollections probably provide less insight than might be thought. Each clerk serves for only a year (occasionally two). Because of their limited tenure, clerks appear to treat as extraordinary some incidents that, in the longer view, are rather routine; for the same reason, clerks are insensitive to the changes in attitudes and operations that occur over longer periods. Finally, they see the Court from the perspective of one chambers only and are notorious for doing their best to make "their" justice look as good as possible. (I cannot, of course, exempt myself from this observation.) A dramatic example can be found in the Brennan Papers. Each Term, Brennan had his clerks prepare "histories" of the Court's important cases. These are not generally available in the Brennan Papers, but a handwritten draft of the history of *Bakke* is available. Written in the first person, but in two hands, the history clearly overdramatizes the events and exaggerates Brennan's role. Similar problems attend Bob Woodward and Scott Armstrong's best-selling book *The Brethren: Inside the Supreme Court.* The accounts in *The Brethren* are factually accurate on nearly every point, but the interpretations come primarily from the law clerks' perspectives and are, again, overly dramatic.

I would like to thank former Dean Robert Pitofsky and Dean Judith Areen of the Georgetown University Law Center and the Woodrow Wilson International Center for Scholars for their support of this project. The staff of the Law Center and the Edward Bennett Williams Law Library were extremely helpful to me as well. L. Michael Seidman, William Eskridge, and Rebecca Tushnet made useful comments on drafts of the manuscript, and Helen McInnis offered important editorial advice. Some passages have been published in "Change and Continuity in the Concept of Civil Rights: Thurgood Marshall and Affirmative Action," *Social Philosophy & Policy* 8 (Spring 1991): 150; "Thurgood Marshall and the Brethren," *Georgetown Law Journal* 80 (Aug. 1992): 2109; "The Supreme Court and Race Discrimination, 1967–1991: The View from the Marshall Papers," *William & Mary Law Review* 36 (Jan. 1995): 473; and "Justice Lewis F. Powell and the Jurisprudence of Centrism," *Michigan Law Review* 93 (May 1995): 1854.

Washington, D.C.   M. V. T.
November 1996

Contents

Prologue: "Things That We Knew but Would Rather Forget" 3

1. "The Right Man and the Right Place": From the Second Circuit
   to the Supreme Court" 9

2. "The Steam Roller Will Have to Grind Me Under":
   Marshall and the Brethren 28

3. "Assumptions About How People Live": Working on the Supreme Court 56

4. "Unless Our Children Begin to Learn Together":
   Desegregating the Schools 68

5. "Vital Interests of a Powerless Minority": Equal Protection Theory 94

6. "Now, When a State Acts to Remedy . . . Discrimination":
   Affirmative Action 116

7. "Compassion in Time of Crisis": The Death Penalty 146

8. "We Are Dealing with a Man's Life": Administering the Death Penalty 163

9. "Some Clear Promise of a Better World":
   The Jurisprudence of Thurgood Marshall 179

Epilogue: "He Did What He Could with What He Had" 194

Notes 197

Bibliography 229

Table of Cases 237

Index 241

MAKING CONSTITUTIONAL LAW

Prologue
"Things That We Knew but Would Rather Forget"

In a tribute to Thurgood Marshall on his retirement from the Supreme Court in 1991, Chief Justice William Rehnquist expressed a common judgment about Marshall's career: "Almost everyone who sits on the Supreme Court is remembered for some contribution to American constitutional law. But Thurgood Marshall is unique because of his major contributions to constitutional law *before* becoming a member of the Court." Three years after he graduated from Howard Law School in 1933, Marshall joined his mentor Charles Hamilton Houston on the legal staff of the National Association for the Advancement of Colored People. Working with the NAACP from 1936 to 1961, Marshall directed a sustained assault on the legal institutions of segregation. As Rehnquist put it in his eulogy to Marshall, "Under his leadership, the American constitutional landscape . . . was literally rewritten." The campaign Marshall directed led to Court decisions that invalidated housing segregation and struck down laws requiring segregated buses and trains. His triumph was *Brown v. Board of Education,* the 1954 decision overturning legalized segregation of the public schools. By the end of the 1950s, Marshall was known as "Mr. Civil Rights."[1]

Marshall left the NAACP in 1961, accepting an appointment to the prestigious federal appeals court in New York. The civil rights movement had changed its focus from Marshall's strategic litigation to sit-ins and demonstrations, and Marshall saw that he had "outlived [his] usefulness."[2] After four years as an appellate judge, Marshall succumbed to Lyndon Johnson's importunings and returned to his role as appellate lawyer, this time as Solicitor General, the U.S. government's chief lawyer before the Supreme Court. He suspected, and many observers believed, that Johnson planned to appoint him to the Supreme Court when the chance arose.

Johnson maneuvered to create a vacancy on the Court and nominated Marshall in 1967. According to Johnson, Marshall was "the right man" for the Court.[3] Johnson wanted to be the president who desegregated the Supreme Court, and

Marshall's role in the legal attack on segregation made him the only real candidate for the position.

The judgment expressed by Marshall's colleagues in their letter to him when he retired, that Marshall's "role in the battle for equal treatment of the races would entitle [him] to a prominent place in that history had [he] never ascended the bench at all," properly acknowledges Marshall's work as a lawyer for the NAACP. Yet it may erroneously suggest that Marshall's contributions to constitutional law through his work as a justice were unimportant.[4]

On the Court, Marshall was a Great Society liberal. Speaking with his law clerks, he referred to Lyndon Johnson as "my President," while Richard Nixon was "your President." Johnson was his president because Johnson combined New Deal liberalism with a deep devotion to the interests of African-Americans that distinguished him from his predecessor John Kennedy.[5] As a New Deal liberal, Marshall supported the expansive use of national power, both legislative and judicial, particularly on behalf of minorities and claims for traditional civil liberties. Along with the professional classes in the New Deal–Great Society coalition, Marshall sought to advance the professionalization of public bureaucracies, including the police, by insisting that officials in daily contact with the public follow rules established by their professional superiors.

Marshall's substantive vision was part of an overall approach to legal decision making. Marshall was a lawyer and judge in the tradition of what legal historian Robert Gordon calls republican lawyering. Republican lawyers, according to Gordon, "illustrate by their example the calling of the independent citizen, the uncorrupted just man of learning combined with practical wisdom." Yale Law School Dean Anthony Kronman describes the lawyer-statesman as a person who is "possessed of great practical wisdom and exceptional persuasive powers, devoted to the public good but keenly aware of the limitations of human beings and their political arrangements."[6]

But, of course, Marshall was an *African-American* lawyer-statesman. Marshall agreed with a Porter pullman who told him that "he had never been in any city in the United States where he had to put his hand up in front of his face to find out he was a Negro." The stories he told his colleagues on the Supreme Court were designed to remind them, in Justice Harry Blackmun's words, that "there is another world 'out there.'" In a note to Marshall in an abortion case, with a copy only to Justice William Brennan, Blackmun lamented, "That 'real world' continues to exist 'out there' and I earnestly hope that the 'War,' despite these adverse 'battles,' will not be lost." One observer believed that in his references to the "world 'out there,'" Blackmun was "shaped in part by his association with Justice Marshall."[7]

As a litigator, Marshall walked into courtrooms throughout the South, facing and then defusing hostility by his easy manner. His professional success rested in large part on the fact that in so many ways he was so much like other lawyers. When Marshall tried a case or argued an appeal, he engaged his listeners in a conversation with them as equals, and they responded to him as an equal. A lawyer who argued against him recalled that "it is a credit to him that he could be cordial when . . . there was no hotel, restaurant, or restroom open to him" near the courthouse. Describing his first day at an Oklahoma murder trial, Marshall wrote that he was introduced to the court and "the building did not fall and the world did not come to an end." The court personnel, he said, were "very nice and explained that this was their first experience in seeing a Negro lawyer try a case—first time they had seen such an animal." He courageously faced down a threatened lynching and then transformed this experience into a humorous story that he recounted at least once a year to his law clerks. His good-humored use of this otherwise quite grim tale was typical. If told by someone else, Marshall's stories might have been depressing, a law clerk observed. Marshall's remarkable good humor made it possible for him to transform the circumstances that shaped him.[8]

Like many lawyers, Marshall simply enjoyed being with other people. He was happy to relax after work over drinks. He was a legendary storyteller, in precisely the way that great trial lawyers are storytellers. As Justice Anthony Kennedy put it, Marshall's "gift of story-telling" was "an essential part of his professional greatness."[9] As a storyteller, Marshall was not above modifying his account of real events a bit to give his stories a better punch line. Those who heard him describe his voice modulations and his ability to adopt accents appropriate to the story at hand.

According to Justice Sandra Day O'Connor, "It was rare during our conference deliberations that [Marshall] would not share an anecdote, a joke or a story; yet, in my ten years on the bench with him, I cannot recall ever hearing the same 'TM' story twice." For Kennedy, Marshall's "stories prove[d] that his compassion and his philosophy flow from a life and legend of struggle." As Justice Byron White said in tribute, "Thurgood could tell us the way it was, and he did so convincingly, often embellishing with humorous, sometimes hair-raising, stories straight from his own past." Marshall saw his role as educating not only the public but his judicial colleagues as well, because their experiences were more limited than his. With Earl Warren's departure from the Court in 1968, Marshall was the only justice with a wide range of experience in national politics. Even more, Marshall had "encountered prejudice on a sustained basis" and explained to his colleagues, who had not, what it meant.[10]

Marshall took on an even more important task as the Court moved away from the vision that inspired him. As White put it, Marshall "would tell us things that we knew but would rather forget; and he told us much that we did not know due to the limitations of our experience." O'Connor's tribute to Marshall said that he routinely "made clear . . . the impact of legal rules on human lives."[11]

United States v. Kras, decided in 1973, dramatically illustrated Marshall's ability to bring the real world into Supreme Court opinions.[12] The Court upheld a statute requiring that people who wanted to go bankrupt and discharge their debts pay a $50 filing fee, which was challenged by a man who alleged that he could not afford the filing fee because he needed all his money to pay the medical expenses for his gravely ill child. As Justice Potter Stewart wrote in his dissent, the Court in effect held that "Congress may say that some of the poor are too poor even to go bankrupt." Blackmun's opinion for the Court cast some aspersions on Kras's allegations that he could not afford to pay the filing fee and noted that the fee could be paid in monthly installments at a rate of about $1.50 per week, "less," Blackmun wrote, "than the price of a movie and little more than the cost of a pack or two of cigarettes." Marshall responded with real feeling. He could not agree, his opinion said, "that it is so easy for the desperately poor to save $1.92 *each week* over the course of six months." The Court suggested that "weekly savings of less than $2 are no burden," but, Marshall's opinion continued, "no one who has had close contact with poor people can fail to understand how close to the margin of survival many of them are." Sudden illnesses might wipe out their savings: "[A] pack or two of cigarettes may be . . . a luxury indulged in only rarely. The desperately poor almost never go to see a movie, which the majority seems to believe is an almost weekly activity." In a passage described by one former law clerk as "[a]ngry with the majority's callous indifference," Marshall concluded, "It is perfectly proper for judges to disagree about what the Constitution requires. But it is disgraceful for an interpretation of the Constitution to be premised upon unfounded assumptions about how people live."[13]

Marshall's attention to the way people live played roles both small and large in the Court's decision-making process. When the Court decided in 1981 to uphold Ohio's practice of placing two prisoners in cells designed for only one, Justice Lewis F. Powell inserted a footnote saying, "Many persons not confined in prisons, and not always compelled by poverty, would welcome comparable sleeping quarters" to those in the Ohio prison. Marshall replied indignantly,

> I know of no one who would voluntarily spend most of his time with only 30 square feet to call his own, unless compelled by poverty or by the State. It is perhaps unnecessary to add that no one would contend that the conditions in which the poor are forced to live represent our nation's standards of decency.

Powell tinkered with the sentence, but in the end he omitted it from the published opinion.[14]

Marshall's concern for the lives of the poor was more important in the abortion cases. Blackmun's first cut at the problem in 1972 sharply restricted state power to regulate abortions in the first trimester but allowed states to "restrict abortions to stated reasonable therapeutic categories." Powell suggested that the state's power should be limited until the fetus reached viability, on the theory that the state's interest in preserving the life of a fetus that was by definition capable of living on its own was "clearly identifiable, in a manner which would be generally understood." Blackmun was sympathetic to Powell's suggestion and noted in particular the "practical aspect" that "there are many pregnant women, particularly younger girls, who may refuse to face the fact of pregnancy and who, for one reason or another, do not get around to medical consultation until the end of the first trimester." But, Blackmun said, after the first trimester, states "may well be concerned about facilities and such things as the need of hospitalization." His draft said that states had no power to regulate abortions during the first trimester. If he simply shifted the line to viability, that approach would leave decisions about hospitalization "to the attending physician."[15]

Marshall's closest ally and friend on the Court by 1973, Justice Brennan, shared Powell's concerns and believed that Marshall's voice might carry special weight. After discussions among Brennan's and Marshall's law clerks, Marshall sent Blackmun a "crucially important letter." Citing "the difficulties which many women may have in believing that they are pregnant and deciding to seek an abortion," Marshall worried that Blackmun's "earlier date [the first trimester line] may not in practice serve the interests of those women." But, the letter continued, Marshall shared Blackmun's "concern for recognizing the State's interest in insuring that abortions be done under safe conditions." He suggested modifying Blackmun's general approach: Instead of barring state regulations before the first trimester and allowing extensive regulation after that, the opinion should allow state regulations "directed at health and safety alone" between the end of the first trimester and viability. Brennan then sent a letter bolstering Marshall's suggestion. Blackmun immediately decided to accept the new approach, and, as Powell's biographer puts it, "Marshall's compromise became law."*16

Marshall was particularly alert in reminding his colleagues about issues of race. Shortly after his appointment to the Court, all his colleagues voted to uphold a lower court order barring segregation in prison. White drafted an opinion describing in some detail when segregation might be used to preserve order, and Marshall responded, "I would respectfully suggest that we merely uphold the judgment. (PERIOD)," which the Court did. When Chief Justice Burger's office grouped two cases together to indicate they were related, Marshall objected: "The only similarity . . . is that they both involve Negroes—nothing else." Explaining to his colleagues his refusal to attend the 1980 dedication of the University of Maryland's law library in his name, Marshall told them, "I am very certain that Maryland is trying to salve its conscience for excluding the Negroes from the University of Maryland for such a long period of time."17

The 1977 case of *Moore v. City of East Cleveland* involved an ordinance that had the peculiar, and probably unintended, effect of barring a grandmother from maintaining a household with her two grandchildren. As Justice John Paul Stevens wrote, "Something smells about this case," and a majority struggled to work out a theory under which the ordinance was unconstitutional. During the conference discussion, Stewart said that the ordinance "followed [the] growth of [a] middle class all white satellite of Cleveland when blacks took over." Its "purpose was to preserve middle class status [and] prevent ghettoizing." Marshall responded that he did not accept Stewart's "emphasis on [the] Negro or emigrants from ghetto." For Marshall, and eventually a majority of the Court, the ordinance was invalid because a "family unit protected by the Const[itution]" was "being broken up." When Burger indicated that cities could define "families" as "parents and their offspring," Marshall replied, "I have seen too many situations where a strong grandparent literally held the family together and was responsible for the educa-

---

* David Garrow calls Marshall's letter, which I drafted, "as momentous as anything that had been written during *Roe*'s entire development." Garrow, *Liberty and Sexuality*, 583. My recollection is that the letter was only one among a number of communications Blackmun received, urging him to accommodate the "practical aspect" of the abortion problem. If there was to be some accommodation, it almost necessarily would have been along the lines Marshall's letter suggested. Perhaps, however, the fact that the precise suggestion came from Marshall mattered to Blackmun.

tion and upbringing of decent, law-abiding youngsters, to agree that the 'nuclear' family is the basic building block of our society." The nuclear family, Marshall wrote, was "a middle class norm that government has no business foisting on those to whom economic or psychological necessity dictates otherwise."[18]

According to one law clerk, Marshall asked questions at oral arguments "for the purpose of reminding the litigants and the Court about the real context . . . of the cases before them." An observer wrote that his questions to counsel at arguments before the Supreme Court were "built around the theme that you are ignoring the obvious [which is], in Marshall's view, . . . what really happens between the cops and a criminal suspect in a squad car, or the way social workers really treat welfare clients." Marshall was "reticent" at oral argument, asking few questions, but when he intervened he tried to get at what he saw as the basic human problems in the cases. Blackmun said that Marshall "would appear formidable on the bench and almost sullen." But his questions had a point.[19]

In *Florida v. Bostick,* police officers were "working the buses," boarding interstate buses, and asking the passengers for "consent" to a search of their bags for drugs. Terrance Bostick allowed the search, which did turn up cocaine. Defending the officers' action before the Supreme Court in 1991, Florida's lawyer said that the searches were consensual because the passengers could have gotten off the bus even though the officers were armed and blocking the aisles. Knowing the answer in advance because of his familiarity with the record, Marshall asked the lawyer, "Was the defendant in this case by any chance a Negro?" According to Marshall's law clerk, the attorneys for Florida "all turned red and shuffled their feet" before answering, "Yes." Adhering to his long-held view that "I don't leave [the] Fourth Am[endment] at home when I leave," Marshall dissented when the Court reversed the lower court's decision that the search was unlawful, although his opinion did not mention Bostick's race. Marshall's emphasis on the real-world setting led O'Connor to revise her majority opinion significantly; instead of finding that Bostick had consented to the search, the opinion sent the case back to the lower court to decide whether he had consented.[20]

Abraham Lincoln's First Inaugural Address appealed to "the better angels of our nature." Marshall's colleagues believed that he did so as well. In conversations he would grumble about the perilous course his conservative colleagues were setting and then express concern for the health of one of them. He was, according to O'Connor, "eternally at peace and perpetually at war."[21]

1

"The Right Man and the Right Place"
From the Second Circuit to the Supreme Court

President John F. Kennedy wanted to demonstrate his commitment to the interests of African-Americans without incurring enormous political costs. Appointing African-Americans to prominent positions was a more promising strategy than proposing substantive civil rights laws and regulations. Early in the Kennedy administration it became clear that Marshall was an obvious candidate for an important judgeship. Referring to Marshall's role in *Brown v. Board of Education* and his stature in the civil rights movement, prominent African-American corporate lawyer and civil rights adviser William T. Coleman wrote the White House in May 1961 that "it would be a good thing if the President would so recognize and reward the man who has done more to move us to a democratic society not based upon race than any other person." Coleman added that "the first reaction of a politician might be that such an appointment would infuriate the South" but that "realistically, the South would be happy. Thurgood Marshall sitting in New York would handle no matter which would adversely affect the interest of the South. In addition, it would remove him from active combat in the racial segregation cases."[1]

Louis Martin, the Democratic National Committee's liaison to the African-American community, believed that Marshall's appointment would be a good sign that Kennedy's "heart was in the right place." When Martin ran into Marshall at a New York airport, Martin asked if Marshall would be interested in a judgeship. Marshall replied that he would like an appointment to an appellate court but not a federal trial court. According to Marshall, he was told that Attorney General Robert Kennedy said that it was a district court position "or nothing." Marshall responded, "All I've had in my life is nothing. It's not new to me."[2]

Attorney General Kennedy was initially unenthusiastic about the possibility of putting Marshall on the court of appeals. The nomination, Kennedy believed, would create problems with Senator James Eastland of Mississippi, an arch-segregationist who as chair of the Senate Judiciary Committee would control the confirmation process. Kennedy tried to persuade Marshall to take the district court position, but Marshall refused. After a few weeks, Kennedy decided that something could be worked out, and Martin informed Marshall that "what they had talked about was OK." Interpreting this comment as an offer of an appointment as a federal trial judge, Marshall replied that he thought he lacked the temperament to be a trial judge because he lost his temper too easily. Because Marshall had an easygoing nature, his reply was probably Marshall's diplomatic way of saying he believed he was entitled to a more prestigious appointment.[3]

Martin then told Marshall that he would be appointed to the Court of Appeals for the Second Circuit, which covered New York, Connecticut, and Vermont. Aside from the Supreme Court, the Second Circuit was probably the most important appellate court in the federal system in the 1960s, and the appointment satisfied Marshall. The organized bar in New York initially raised questions about Marshall's fitness because he lacked experience with the corporate law questions that the Second Circuit frequently decided. Indeed, Bernard Segal, chair of the American Bar Association's Committee on the Federal Judiciary, which made informal recommendations to the Department of Justice on potential nominees, told the attorney general's office that Marshall would be rated "Not Qualified" for the district court. Burke Marshall, the assistant attorney general for the Civil Rights Division, assured the attorney general that Marshall was the most experienced lawyer ever considered for the appeals court and that Marshall would develop expertise in corporate law as he had in everything else he had dealt with.[4]

Marshall's nomination on September 23, 1961, was hailed by the *New York Times,* which praised President Kennedy's "good judgment" in naming the fifty-three-year-old Marshall to the court and Marshall's "high intelligence, his scrupulous respect for the law and the judicial qualities evident even in his briefs and pleadings." The nomination was likely to be controversial, and Congress's imminent adjournment made it unlikely that Marshall would be confirmed by the Senate. President Kennedy gave Marshall a recess appointment, allowing him to begin work before he was confirmed, and Marshall was sworn in on October 23. Administering the oath of office to Marshall, Chief Judge J. Edward Lumbard may have been alluding to the controversy about Marshall's experience when he said that "few, if any, members of the American bar have had so varied an experience" in court as Marshall. He quoted former New York bar leader and 1924 presidential candidate John W. Davis's statement after the oral argument in *Brown* that "he could not remember a more effective adversary appearing against him. And he added: 'This fellow is going places.'" Lumbard concluded, "Here he is."[5]

Kennedy sent Marshall's nomination to the Senate again on January 15, 1962. Ordinarily the Senate Committee on the Judiciary would have scheduled immediate hearings on the confirmation of a recess appointee. In Marshall's case, though, nothing happened—at least in public. A hearing scheduled for April 16 was postponed, first until April 24 and then until May 1. By then Marshall had been sitting as a judge for more than six months. In early April 1962, Republican Senator Kenneth Keating of New York called the delay inexcusable and said that the subcommittee considering Marshall's nomination was stacked against him. The subcommittee's chair was Democratic Senator Olin Johnston of South Carolina; the other members were Democratic Senator John McClellan of Arkansas, and Republican Senator Roman Hruska of Nebraska. Neither Johnston nor McClellan attended their subcommittee's initial hearing. Introducing Marshall, Senator Keating addressed those who thought Marshall's appointment merely satisfied a special interest group, saying that Marshall "will serve on the federal court as a lawyer and an American, not as the special pleader for any group or segment of our society."[6]

The first day of hearings adjourned; only the formalities had occurred, leading observers once again to criticize the delay and to ask "the President or Attorney General to take steps to right this wrong." Keating continued to chastise the subcommittee for giving Marshall "the runaround." The hearings resumed on July 12, focusing on a 1956 suit by the Texas attorney general against the NAACP and the Legal Defense Fund (LDF). That suit challenged a contract between the NAACP and Heman Sweatt, the plaintiff in one of the NAACP's major desegregation cases. The NAACP promised to support Sweatt during the litigation. This financial support was a clear violation of standard rules of legal ethics. Marshall denied knowing about the improper contract and said that he had only "cooperative" relations with the local lawyers who got the LDF into ethical trouble because "you cannot supervise a man and require him to do what you want on a couple of thousand dollars a year."[7]

Senator Keating called the questions about Marshall's ethics "a waste of time" and urged the attorney general to pressure the Southern Democrats who were delaying the confirmation vote. Senators Hruska and Everett Dirksen joined their Republican colleague in his criticism. Throughout July, other senators, now including some Democrats, joined Keating in attacking the subcommittee. Finally, Democratic Senator Thomas Dodd of Connecticut threatened to take the confirmation out of the subcommittee's hands. A third day of hearings was set for August 8; although Senator Johnston refused to hold a full day of hearings, he said he hoped to complete the subcommittee's hearings by mid-August. In fact the hearings were strung out through the entire month: When Senator Mike Mansfield, the Democratic leader of the Senate, delayed the opening of the Senate until noon one day to allow the subcommittee to meet, Johnston did not schedule a meeting; Johnston later postponed a session because the whole Senate was voting; and one session was cut short at noon when Johnston left to catch a plane.[8]

When the subcommittee did meet, its time was consumed with further nitpicking about the practices of the NAACP's legal staff. Marshall was asked, for example, about a letter in which he said that "we have to . . . attempt to get someone as an intervenor" in a Louisiana desegregation suit—arguably a violation of ethical norms that prohibited lawyers from generating litigation—and about whether as head of the LDF in New York he had practiced law in New York without a license from that state. The subcommittee also examined Marshall's membership in the National Lawyers Guild, from which he resigned in 1949, and other allegedly subversive organizations. The hearings concluded with testimony about Marshall's role in producing the brief in *Brown*, which, his critics on the subcommittee said, was designed to reveal rather than conceal the historical truth. Senators Keating and Philip Hart, Democrat of Michigan, accurately captured the tone of the hearings when they called the questioning "ridiculous" and "un-lawyerlike."[9]

Meanwhile the political maneuvering over the nomination intensified. Marshall's supporters believed that the subcommittee would recommend against confirmation. By the end of August they were prepared to short-circuit the subcommittee and have the full Judiciary Committee vote on the nomination; they counted eleven committee votes in favor of Marshall and only four against him. Partisan politics began to play a role, too, as Democrats became concerned that Senator Keating, a Republican, was taking the lead on the Marshall nomination and was being aided by his Republican colleague from New York, Senator Jacob Javits. In response to a news-conference question, President Kennedy said he had assurances that the Senate would have a chance to consider the nomination before it adjourned. He also expressed his irritation at the publicity Keating had been receiving by pointing out that Keating had not tried to get Marshall appointed to a judgeship during the Eisenhower administration. Kennedy demonstrated the administration's support for Marshall by having Deputy Attorney General Nicholas Katzenbach or one of his aides escort Marshall to the hearings each morning. They attempted to make sure that photographs of Marshall included Katzenbach, as well as Senator Keating or Javits, but the publication of pictures showing only Marshall and a Republican senator continued to infuriate President Kennedy.[10]

The subcommittee hearings ended on August 24, but there was no indication of when a vote would occur. Preliminary votes were announced, then postponed. Finally, on September 7 the full Judiciary Committee bypassed its subcommittee and voted 11–4 to recommend Marshall's confirmation. No further delays occurred despite Senator McClellan's suggestion that he might filibuster on the floor of the Senate. The Senate confirmed Marshall's nomination by a vote of 54–16 on September 12, 1962, eleven months after Marshall had begun to sit as a judge. His opponents were all Southern Democrats, though Senators Estes Kefauver of Tennessee and Ralph Yarborough of Texas voted in favor. After Marshall took his seat, Simon Sobeloff, who had been President Eisenhower's solicitor general before his appointment to the federal appeals court in Baltimore, wrote Marshall, "Though you had to endure some inconvenience, it was inevitable that the opposition would sputter out. At that you were delayed less than I was. Our common admirers in the Senate held me up a year and a day."[11]

Marshall expressed confidence in the ultimate outcome throughout the confirmation hearings, probably because he understood the politics of the situation. In the midst of the political maneuvering, Warren Weaver of the *New York Times* noted that delays in confirmation might be "politically satisfactory" to both sides once Marshall was confirmed. Southern Democrats could say they had tried their best but were frustrated by the Judiciary Committee's majority, and Northern Democrats and Republicans could point to their extraordinary efforts on Marshall's behalf. Indeed, that had been the scenario from the beginning. Senator Eastland had assured Attorney General Kennedy that the Senate would be allowed to vote on Marshall's confirmation once the Southern Democrats had milked the nomination for its political benefit to them. The hearings and delays were simply political dramas intended to have no effect on the outcome.* Eastland's assurances had to be kept secret, of course, if the charade was to have any political benefits. Yet that very secrecy created political difficulties for President Kennedy, who saw his initiative in nominating Marshall taken from his hands by Senator Keating's criticisms of the confirmation delays.[12]

Marshall sat on the Second Circuit from 1961 to 1965. On the whole he enjoyed being a judge. In his first year, while the confirmation struggle was occurring, he found the job more wearing than he had anticipated, as he, his law clerk, and his secretary moved from office to office, borrowing rooms from judges whose decisions Marshall would ultimately have to review. As he hoped, the job allowed him to spend more time with his family, and it provided him with a far more comfortable income than he had earned before. Yet becoming a judge changed Marshall's life in ways he found less attractive. The judges on the Second Circuit typically had close contact with the practicing Wall Street bar before their appointments, and they developed a strong tradition of refraining from substantial continuing contact with the bar. In addition, Marshall was concerned that he not bring discredit upon the African-American community and therefore was rigid in his break with his previous activities. As a result, Marshall found himself leading an almost monastic life, quite in contrast to the active life as a lawyer that had suited his gregarious personality. In some ways, according to one of his early law clerks, Marshall found himself "imprisoned" in a job he had to take but for which he was not temperamentally suited.[13]

Further, Marshall was not entirely comfortable with his colleagues on the Second Circuit. His colleagues took criticism more personally than Marshall thought appropriate. Marshall, in contrast, was quite tolerant and "not quick to take personal affront," and he reserved his anger for situations he deeply cared about. He could not understand, for example, why a colleague with whom he played poker broke off their game for a year simply because Marshall disagreed with him about one case.[14]

During his years on the Second Circuit, Marshall wrote more than 130 opinions, in cases ranging from workers' compensation problems to complex tax deals to important constitutional issues. The caseload of the Second Circuit, like that of most federal appellate courts, was so heavily loaded with relatively routine cases that Marshall did not have many opportunities to develop a distinctive jurisprudence. A fairly strong assumption that trial judges correctly decided their cases further limited those opportunities.[15]

Early in his Second Circuit work, Marshall seemed uncomfortable in business and tax cases, largely because of his unfamiliarity with their technical details. His ability to grasp the essence of a case by reading a transcript, though, meant that he could understand what the lawyers were trying to accomplish and what the basic issues generating disagreement were. In a rather tepid letter to Coleman comment-

---

*A more dramatic version of the political aspects of the nomination is that Senator Eastland, desiring an appointment for his friend Harold Cox, told Robert Kennedy, "Tell your brother that if he will give me Harold Cox, I will give him the nigger." Quoted in Revesz, "Marshall's Struggle," 240. Revesz persuasively questions the accuracy of this version.

ing on Marshall's appointment, Frankfurter said that perhaps "nine-tenths" of the Second Circuit's business was "wholly outside of [Marshall's] professional experience," but "I do not think it requires a genius to master the law." The "industry and wholesale devotion in the service of the kind of intelligence that Marshall undoubtedly possesses" will "in due time" make him "a good judge." Marshall's first law clerk, Ralph Winter, once referred to Marshall's "unfortunate experience with your first law clerk" in a complex tax case, which nonetheless drew a letter from Professor Ernest Brown of the Harvard Law School, a leading tax scholar, saying that the opinion reminded him of "Learned Hand [a great judge of the Second Circuit] at the height of his powers." As Winter put it, "He certainly has more confidence in [the opinion] than you and I ever did."[16]

Marshall knew that to earn the respect of his colleagues, he had to do well in all the types of cases presented to the court. Marshall quickly established a close relationship with Judge Henry Friendly, an Eisenhower appointee widely regarded as one of the country's best appellate judges. Friendly had been a leading Wall Street lawyer, and his background in corporate law made him the perfect mentor for Marshall in these areas. Marshall respected Friendly as a giant in his field of corporate law but did not concede any power to dictate a case's disposition to Friendly; indeed, Marshall got particular pleasure out of circulating an opinion that led Friendly to change his position. During the first months of Marshall's service, Friendly saw things somewhat differently. He wrote his friend Felix Frankfurter, "TM seems easily led. I do not have the feeling that he realizes the difficulties of his job and is burning the midnight oil in an effort to conquer them. . . . All this makes life fairly easy for him, save when he is confronted with a difference of opinion, and then he tosses a coin." Friendly was "alarmed by Marshall's willingness to arrive at quick decisions on issues he does not understand."[17]

The picture was different seen from within the chambers. There Marshall was interested in identifying the crucial issues in cases, at quite a detailed level, and in figuring out the proper resolution of those issues. He was less concerned about the particulars of drafting an opinion whose language reflected all the nuances of the issues. Rather, he talked to his law clerks about the opinions before he had the clerks draft them and guided them in resolving the issues.[18]

As a judge, Marshall understood that the Warren Court was transforming the constitutional law surrounding the criminal process. Sympathetic to that effort, Marshall sought to push it forward where he could, though he by no means automatically agreed with defendants' claims that their constitutional rights had been violated. Rather, he attempted to draw out the reasonable implications of Supreme Court decisions even if the Court had not yet done so. After the Supreme Court decided in *Mapp v. Ohio* that illegally seized evidence should not be admitted in criminal trials, for example, the Second Circuit held, over Marshall's dissent, that *Mapp* should not be applied to overturn existing convictions. Marshall's dissent argued that refusing to apply *Mapp* was inconsistent with the fundamental idea that the Constitution defined rules of law independent of decisions of particular courts.[19]

Marshall's most revealing criminal procedure opinion was *United States ex rel. Hetenyi v. Wilkins.*[20] Hetenyi was tried in New York's courts for murdering his wife. The jury convicted him of second-degree murder, but that conviction was reversed on appeal. Hetenyi was tried again, and this time the jury convicted him of first-degree murder. That conviction also was reversed on appeal. A third trial resulted in a conviction for second-degree murder. Hetenyi then sought relief from the federal courts. He argued that his constitutional rights were violated when he was prosecuted for first-degree murder after the initial jury had implicitly rejected that charge by convicting him of the lesser offense of second-degree murder.

Ordinarily a defendant in this position would say that the prosecution was barred by the double jeopardy clause, which provides that no one shall "be subject for the same offense to be put twice in jeopardy of life or limb." In 1833 the Supreme Court held that the Bill of Rights, including the double jeopardy clause, applied only to prosecutions in the federal courts. Hetenyi, prosecuted in the state courts, could rely only on the Fourteenth Amendment's due process clause, which says that no state may "deprive any person of life, liberty, or property, without due process of law." In the 1930s and 1940s the justices of the Supreme Court argued among themselves and in their opinions over the extent to which the due process clause "incorporated"—that is, made applicable to the states—the protections of the Bill of Rights. By the 1960s the Court's position was that the due process clause incorporated some but not all of those protections. A protection was applicable if it was "of the very essence of a scheme of ordered liberty" or was a "fundamental principle[] of liberty and justice." Notably, these phrases come from a 1937 case in which the Court held that the double jeopardy clause was not incorporated in the Fourteenth Amendment.[21]

Marshall's opinion in *Hetenyi* agreed with the defendant's contentions. It noted that the Supreme Court was currently "refashioning" this dimension of constitutional law and argued that cases squarely contrary to Hetenyi's position had been "tarnished by the gradual but certain evolution of our constitutional understanding of justice and fairness." The courts, Marshall wrote, must be "faithful to the evolution of our societal values" and should reject opinions rendered "during th[e] lull in the Supreme Court's concern for constitutionally protected human rights." His opinion argued that the "basic core" of the double jeopardy standard had been incorporated into the Fourteenth Amendment and that even under the weakest definition of the core the second prosecution of Hetenyi on a charge that a jury already had rejected violated his right to fair treatment. Anticipating the Supreme Court's continued expansion of the incorporation doctrine, Marshall endorsed the use of national judicial power to limit what states could do.

The Supreme Court almost immediately decided to consider whether the due process clause incorporated the double jeopardy clause. Although the Court's majority avoided a decision, a dissenting opinion by Justice Abe Fortas, which Chief Justice Earl Warren and Justice William O. Douglas joined, cited *Hetenyi* with approval. In 1969 the Court's decision in *Benton v. Maryland* incorporated the double jeopardy clause; a year later the Court adopted the rule barring prosecution for a greater offense after conviction for a lesser one, as Marshall had held in *Hetenyi*. The Court's opinion in *Benton* was written by Justice Thurgood Marshall.[22]

Civil rights issues reached the Second Circuit only occasionally during Marshall's service there. The civil rights movement focused primarily on the South. Federal statutes prohibiting discrimination in employment and housing were adopted late in Marshall's term on the Second Circuit, and the general revolution in public consciousness about vindicating rights through litigation had not proceeded very far. By the mid-1960s, though, the civil rights movement began to move north, and Marshall wrote two interesting civil rights opinions.

Reverend Milton Galamison organized a protest against the New York World's Fair of 1964. The protestors staged a "stall-in" that blocked traffic on New York's bridges and disrupted its subway operations to draw attention to discrimination in housing, education, jobs, and law enforcement. They were prosecuted for violating a number of New York laws against disorderly conduct, obstruction of railway cars, unlawful assembly, and the like. Galamison then sought to use a procedure called removal, which would transfer the trial of the criminal cases from the state courts to the federal courts. This procedure was developed during Reconstruction, as Congress became concerned that Southern courts were unfairly enforcing ordinary criminal laws against African-Americans. Unfair enforcement did not mean, of course, that the defendants had not violated the law, so Congress wanted to provide a forum in which the charges could be resolved fairly. That forum was a federal court.

The civil rights removal statute in effect in 1964 had two provisions: Removal was possible in cases in which the defendant was "denied or cannot enforce in [the state court] a right under any law providing for the equal civil rights of citizens" or in which the defendant acted "under color of authority derived from any law providing for equal rights." The first provision simply transferred the trial to the federal court; the second gave defendants a complete defense to the criminal prosecution. [23]

Marshall dissented from Judge Friendly's opinion rejecting removal, despite Marshall's discomfort with disruptive protests, which dated from the sit-ins of 1960–61. [24] A note to his colleagues called his dissent "the opposite of . . . short and concise." [25] The dissent argued that removal was proper if defendants had engaged in self-help to protest unlawful discrimination. Judge Friendly addressed this issue by saying that protests—exercises of free speech rights—were not covered by laws providing for equal rights. For Marshall, this approach ignored the historical setting in which Congress enacted the removal provision and the "tremendous[] importan[ce]" of peaceful protests in the constitutional scheme. Thus, when defendants "sought to effectuate the mandates of the Equal Protection Clause . . . and did so in a way protected by the Due Process Clause" and the First Amendment, removal should be available. This approach, Marshall said, would give the provision an appropriate scope without opening the door to removal of all cases in which defendants raised free-speech claims, as the majority feared.

Both sides in *Galamison* offered powerful opinions. The outcome undoubtedly reflected Friendly's skepticism about Galamison's efforts and about the propriety of expansive removal. As Friendly stated:

[T]he pain of decision is exacerbated when one choice may somewhat impair expectations entertained by persons of good will whose objectives we admire, and the other, in our view, would do violence to institutions and relations we hold equally dear, the continued efficient functioning of which has far greater long-run importance to minorities than the special relief here sought.

His use of "somewhat," "objectives" (rather than "methods"), and "special" seem to signal Friendly's skepticism. Marshall may have been unenthusiastic about Galamison's methods, too; in speeches he made a few years later, Marshall called civil disobedience "often necessary" but insisted that "he who advocates civil disobedience must be aware of its import" and said that "you just can't build yourself by disobeying the law" and destroying property. He was, however, deeply concerned to make sure that federal remedies were available in civil rights cases, which surely dominated his assessment of *Galamison*.[26]

That concern also informed his dissent in *Ephraim v. Safeway Trails, Inc.*, which the majority treated simply as a case about the liabilities of interstate carriers but which "struck a visceral note" with Marshall.[27] Florence Ephraim, an African-American woman, bought a bus ticket from Safeway Trails for a trip from New York to Montgomery, Alabama. Safeway did not operate beyond Washington, D.C., and therefore sold her a combination ticket for a through trip on a number of additional carriers. When Mrs. Ephraim reached Raleigh, North Carolina, she had to change buses. On boarding the new bus and asking what seat to take, she was told by the bus driver, "Lady, on this bus you sit anywhere." After other changes of buses and drivers, the trip reached Georgia, where the carrier was Southern Stages. When a white woman boarded the bus and found no seats at its front, the driver asked Mrs. Ephraim and another rider to move to the back of the bus. They refused. At a later stop in Georgia, the driver got out and returned with an armed police officer, who ordered Mrs. Ephraim to move to the rear. When she refused again, the officer told her to leave the bus, pushed her down the aisle, clubbed her, and continued to beat her, leading to a two-day hospital stay.

Mrs. Ephraim sued Safeway Trails in a New York federal court, which awarded her $5,000 in damages. The Second Circuit's opinion reversing the award rested on the "well settled" rule that "an initial carrier [like Safeway Trails] may not be held liable for the torts of a connecting carrier [like Southern Stages]," unless Safeway had been at fault. Marshall's dissent pointed out that Mrs. Ephraim, "in order to obtain redress, would be relegated to traveling back to the areas where she had been subjected to the brutal beating by law enforcement officials." The only law review comment on the case perceptively but ponderously praised Marshall's dissent for the "intriguing" suggestion that "a court in examining a plaintiff's opportunities for recourse should focus its attention not merely on the narrow outlines suggested by legal doctrine but also on the practical realities which may prevent an apparently good theoretical basis of recovery from ever maturing into an actual remedy."[28]

In some ways Marshall's most famous case on the Second Circuit was among the least important legally. In 1964 the comedian Lenny Bruce faced prosecutions all

over the country for his act's allegedly obscene content.[29] In New York, Bruce
tried to get a federal court to keep the state from enforcing its criminal obscenity
law against him. Acting as his own lawyer in a situation that even the best lawyer
would have found difficult, Bruce fumbled the procedures, and the federal trial
court rejected his efforts. Bruce appealed to the Second Circuit, where he faced a
panel including Marshall and Friendly.

To show that his act was not obscene, Bruce launched into a performance. He
talked about the misuse of Christian symbols and then performed part of his act
that dealt with race and justice. He said he had never "heard any outward hostility" from Negroes. But, he said, he was "going to hear it," because "there's going
to be a vote, and a change." Soon "you'll see an all-black jury and a black judge."
Then Bruce continued in the stereotyped voice of an outraged white liberal,
"How'm I gonna get a fair shake when they're all black?" To which he replied,
"You're not." In the equally stereotyped voice of an African-American, Bruce
continued, "Your're full of shit, you liberal! I'm tired of talking to you people." He
ended again in the liberal's voice, "They gave me twenty years for raising my
voice—those niggers!" According to an observer, when Marshall heard that, his
"head jerked up and he nearly dropped a pen from his hand."[30]

Bruce thought he lost his case when he went too far for Marshall. The appeals
court did reject Bruce's appeal, but he never really had a chance. Bruce's legal
claims were extreme in the trial court; only under extraordinary circumstances
would a federal court bar a state from continuing a prosecution it had already
begun. His case in the appellate court was even weaker, for there the issue was
only whether the trial court had abused its discretion in refusing to issue a temporary order against the state prosecution. Bruce's performance could not have en-
deared him to Marshall, but it had no effect on the case's outcome.[31]

Marshall had a reputation as a solid though unspectacular appellate judge after
four years on the Second Circuit. The next stage in his career opened with Lyndon
Johnson's victory in the 1964 presidential election. Fervently committed to civil
rights, Johnson wanted to be the president who named the first African-American
Supreme Court justice. Marshall was the natural candidate, but the way had to be
cleared.

The process began when Archibald Cox, a Harvard law professor, who had
been named solicitor general by President Kennedy, submitted his resignation.
Cox wanted to continue as solicitor general but believed that he should have the
incumbent's endorsement. That would occur, in Cox's eyes, when Johnson refused to accept the resignation. Johnson saw his opportunity, however, and surprised Cox by accepting the resignation. Johnson immediately asked Marshall to
become solicitor general, calling Marshall "a patriot of very high ability." He told
Marshall that he wanted the public to see an African-American arguing cases for
the government of the United States in the Supreme Court. The *New York Times*
praised the nomination: "It is impossible to consider the appointment . . . apart
from its symbolic aspects." When "Negroes are pressing for the last full measure of
legal equality," selecting "the best-known Negro attorney as the Government's
chief lawyer dramatizes the nation's commitment to equal rights." The *Times*

observed that the fact that Marshall would be the first African-American to serve as solicitor general "presumably . . . played a part" in his decision to leave the court of appeals. The editorial said, "It is doubtless his hope—as it is our expectation—that his service as Solicitor General will bring nearer the day when the appointment or election of Negroes to any position will be free of any special symbolic significance."[32]

The *Times*'s closing comment alluded to widespread speculation that Marshall's appointment as solicitor general presaged his appointment to the Supreme Court when the opportunity arose. At his confirmation hearing, Marshall said he accepted the appointment because "the President of the United States told me that he thought that I was the best person at the time to represent the United States as Solicitor General and asked me to do it." Marshall later said Johnson expressly stated that the appointment was "not a stepping stone to anything else . . . including the Supreme Court." Marshall also said that although he believed Johnson's assertion, Johnson "seldom did things off the top of his head." Indeed, as Nicholas Katzenbach, attorney general under Johnson, said, it is inconceivable that Marshall would have given up his lifetime appointment to the Second Circuit unless he had "read Johnson that way." Yet Marshall also regarded a request from the president, particularly from Lyndon Johnson—who supported the Civil Rights Act of 1964, the Voting Rights Act of 1965, and the civil rights movement's hope that "we shall overcome"—with an old-fashioned patriot's respect. His decision to accept the office was not very calculating.[33]

When he retired from the Supreme Court, Marshall said that his job as solicitor general was "the most effective job" and "maybe the best" job he ever had, including even his position on the Court itself. As solicitor general, Marshall was "in the dead middle of everything that's legal and you have your two cents to put in." Marshall supervised the development of the government's legal position in a wide range of legal fields, and he often had the last word on what that position was. On the Supreme Court, Marshall was only one of nine justices, whereas as solicitor general, Marshall's two cents mattered.[34]

When Marshall was solicitor general, he headed an office with three assistants and six or seven additional lawyers. The solicitor general's most important role is to represent the United States before the Supreme Court.[35] The office submits almost all the government's briefs, and members of the office, including the solicitor general, are the oral advocates in most of the government's Supreme Court cases.[36]

One of Marshall's assistants called him "a benevolent Solicitor General." He managed the office with a loose hand. The solicitor general traditionally relied heavily on the office's talented staff. The staff prepared cover memoranda on materials prepared by other departments and made recommendations that the solicitor general typically followed. Briefs followed a similar course, though with more supervision within the office: a draft from the part of the government affected, rewriting by an attorney in the office, and supervision by an assistant. Cox looked draft briefs over rather closely; more interested in oral advocacy, Marshall accepted the briefs as they came to him. Much of the office's work, then, was delegated to the assistants and to the staff.[37]

When disputes arose between Marshall's staff and lawyers elsewhere in the Justice Department, Marshall called the lawyers into his office and listened to them present their positions. Then, often making some sort of joking comment, he announced which one he agreed with. Marshall's judgments about what position the government should take were typically sound, even when he rejected staff recommendations.[38]

For some on the staff, Marshall suffered by comparison with Cox, in large part because the staff attorneys had the same academic orientation that Cox had and because, as relatively young lawyers, they were unaccustomed to Marshall's special strengths. Some thought he was detached and uninterested in the office's work. Others appreciated his willingness to delegate most of the important work to them, grasp the essence of the legal problems they were dealing with, and retain final control. Marshall generated a great deal of loyalty among these subordinates. They "came to appreciate Marshall's instinctive earthy responses" to the questions his staff posed him. They were loyal to Marshall because they agreed with him and because of who he was—not merely the solicitor general of the United States and the head of their office, but Thurgood Marshall, whose contributions to constitutional law they admired and who was likely to become the first African-American justice of the Supreme Court.[39]

Marshall's ability to get along with people at all levels served him well as solicitor general. When he had to tell officials that the office would not support their positions, he was able to convey that he sympathized with them and understood their positions but that he simply disagreed with them. His authority rested on his self-confidence and his relationship with President Johnson as much as on his legal power. Still, Marshall's personality itself made him easy to take. He managed to charm the irascible head of the draft system, Lewis Hershey, when he refused to back up one of Hershey's legal positions and, according to one of Marshall's assistants, got Hershey to leave "with a smile and not a frown."[40]

Ordinarily, Marshall's staff rejected the positions taken by lawyers elsewhere in the government only when the underlying issues were rather technical. Disagreement was rare when issues that implicated important questions about law and politics arose. The U.S. government was in an important sense unified when Marshall was solicitor general. There were few disagreements between the presidency and Congress, and even fewer within the executive branch, on the matters of concern to the solicitor general's office. As solicitor general, Marshall was a team player, supporting Johnson's political appointees when he could.

Marshall helped resolve an extremely sensitive issue regarding electronic surveillance, or bugging. The problem originated in a 1954 memorandum to the Federal Bureau of Investigation by Attorney General Herbert Brownell. Brownell approved bugging in "internal security matters" involving "espionage agents, possible saboteurs, and subversive persons." When Robert Kennedy became attorney general, an FBI agent briefed him on the bureau's wiretapping activities. Kennedy continued to authorize the use of wiretaps. Wiretapping differed from bugging, however: Wiretapping involved placing a device on a telephone line to overhear conversations over the line, whereas bugging involved placing an electronic device in a room to overhear all the conversations in the room. Kennedy was not told that the FBI used bugging, though lower level officials in the Justice Department knew it was occurring and assumed that Kennedy learned about it during his regular FBI briefings. [41]

In May 1966 Marshall informed the Supreme Court that the FBI had bugged a hotel suite maintained by Fred Black, a lobbyist implicated in an influence-peddling scandal and under indictment for tax evasion. After the indictment, FBI agents overheard conversations between Black and his attorneys and passed on information from those conversations to Justice Department officials handling the prosecution, though without revealing that its source had been a bug. The Court asked Marshall for a memorandum describing, among other things, the authority on which the FBI relied for its activities. [42]

Director J. Edgar Hoover insisted that the FBI had received specific authorization from Kennedy. Kennedy claimed that he had authorized wiretaps but not bugs and had not even known that the FBI was bugging anyone. Explaining what had happened was a delicate matter because both Hoover and Kennedy had important political support. Hoover engaged in detailed negotiations with Nicholas Katzenbach at the Justice Department through a number of intermediaries including Marshall, who was ultimately responsible for presenting the government's position to the Court. Marshall met and swapped jokes with Hoover and eventually told the Court that "under Departmental practice in effect for a period of years prior to 1963 and continuing into 1965, the Director of the FBI was given authority to approve the installation" of bugs. By using the passive voice and failing to date precisely when authority had been given, Marshall's memorandum satisfied Hoover without pinning the blame on Kennedy. Although Kennedy was not completely satisfied with this resolution, he eventually came to think that Marshall had done the right thing in using ambiguous but revealing language. [43]

Marshall's appearances as an oral advocate for the United States illustrated most of the strengths and weaknesses of his overall performance as solicitor general. According to Marshall's chief assistant, Ralph Spritzer, Marshall was at his best as an oral advocate "when he could say a homely truth, and could speak with passion and personal commitment." Often the government's positions were full of compromises and shadings, and Marshall's style was sometimes not well suited to those positions. While Marshall was solicitor general, the office won slightly fewer cases than Cox or Marshall's successors, probably because he was representing the government in a Court that was interested in developing limitations on government power. [44]

Marshall argued eighteen cases during his two years as solicitor general, a significantly smaller number than Cox had argued and a somewhat smaller number than average. The reason probably was that the mix of cases in which the United States participated included fewer cases in areas with which Marshall was familiar. Only six of Marshall's cases involved civil rights or broad questions of constitutional law; the rest involved business matters. Marshall took on the business cases in part because he thought it was his responsibility as the solicitor general and in part because he had been stung by statements in a *New York Times* article asserting that he had not performed well as a judge in business cases. Spritzer helped pick the business cases Marshall would argue; precisely because Marshall was unfamiliar with the area, they needed to find cases in which the legal issues were not highly specialized.

Even so, Marshall occasionally had difficulty. He prepared for oral argument by discussing the case with the attorney who had written the brief and tried to respond to questions from the Court in a relatively informal way. Marshall's approach served him well when the questions could be answered by his stating what good common sense would tell a person about a major issue of social or legal policy. In many of the business cases, however, he could not be effective using the only style of oral advocacy with which he was comfortable. In one case, for example, he explained his inability to answer a question by saying, "I had no experience in that field," and was uncertain of the position the government had taken in analogous cases. In another, his adversary recalled that Marshall responded to questions from Justice Abe Fortas by reading answers that the staff attorney sitting next to him had just written out; when pressed by Fortas to explain one of those answers, he replied, "I am handing them up to you just as I get them." In still another case, the lawyers on the other side concluded from Marshall's "uninspired" oral argument that he was "either fundamentally unfamiliar with labor law or a poor oral advocate."[45]

These criticisms of Marshall's performance must be placed in a broader context. The business law issues, though important to the development of national law, did not deeply engage the Warren Court's passions. Oral arguments in these cases sometimes consisted of dull readings of prepared arguments by the advocates on both sides, with the justices occasionally interjecting some relatively minor questions. Second, and probably more important, the office of the solicitor general was more often than not trying to defend a relatively novel position, taking the middle ground between more traditional claims asserted by other adversaries.[46]

For example, in 1967 the Court had to decide whether the creation of the Penn-Central Railroad by means of a massive merger of most rail lines in the Northeast was consistent with federal law. The merger's opponents argued against it on many grounds. One was apparently minor. They argued that the merger should be blocked because some small railroads were not going to get adequate financial protection once the merger occurred. The initial drafts from the Justice Department agreed with the opponents: Instead of upholding the merger, the Court should send it back for full-scale reconsideration by the Interstate Commerce Commission. Louis Claiborne in Marshall's office thought that the merger itself was legal but only if the small railroads were protected. To protect them, though, the Court need not block the merger entirely. It could approve the merger in principle but send the case back to the commission for proceedings narrowly focused on the small railroads.

After extended discussions within the cabinet, Johnson decided to honor a promise that Robert Kennedy had made as attorney general not to oppose the merger. The cabinet wanted Marshall to support the merger completely.[47] Claiborne still believed the smaller lines had to get some protection. Although he was "obviously unhappy with the situation," Marshall backed Claiborne up, saying that he had better be "damned sure you're right." From the White House's point of view, Marshall compromised: The government was not going to oppose the merger entirely; it would ask only that the Interstate Commerce Commission work out the details of protecting the small railroads. As Claiborne saw it, however, he and Marshall were completely vindicated. The politicians in the White House, concerned with completing the merger, misunderstood the legal points involved in protecting the small railroads. Unlike the politicians, the lawyers were uninterested in whether the merger should occur or not; they only wanted to guarantee that the small railroads were protected.[48]

Marshall argued before the Court that the merger was lawful in general but that the commission had erred in allowing the merger to go through before it decided what protection to give the small railroads. This position, sensible as it might be, had little foundation in the law before the Penn-Central case itself, and figuring out how to delay the merger for only a short time—by sending the case back to the commission or by holding it in the courts—was not easy. It is not surprising that Marshall had difficulty in defending the position against skeptical questions; any solicitor general would have had similar difficulties. The Court in the end adopted the position Marshall asserted.[49]

Another example is *Linn v. United Plant Guard Workers,* a libel suit against a union for statements made during an organizing campaign. The legal issue was whether federal labor law barred states from enforcing their libel laws in such situations. Linn, the plaintiff, argued that state libel laws protected general interests in reputation, which could be impaired by statements in organizing campaigns as much as by statements in newspapers. The union replied that enforcing libel laws in hotly contested union elections would severely limit its ability to organize. As Marshall said at the oral argument, "Indeed, some of us know some labor leaders that if you prevent them from cursing, you would take all their free speech away from them." Marshall urged the Court to adopt a middle position: Extreme statements could be the subject of libel suits but less extreme ones, even though libelous under ordinary state law standards, could not be. The oral argument revealed that implementing this position would not be at all easy, and Marshall's answers to questions were not entirely satisfying. Nonetheless, once again a sharply divided Court adopted a position quite close to the one Marshall presented, although the Court expressly disagreed with the precise formulation Marshall offered.[50]

Of course, Marshall was more engaged with cases within his area of expertise, and he was enthusiastic about supporting efforts to push the boundaries of existing constitutional doctrine. In *Harper v. Virginia Board of Elections,* for example, the Court considered the constitutionality of Virginia's poll tax. The Voting Rights Act of 1965 directed the attorney general to bring an action to declare the poll tax unconstitutional; the Department of Justice responded to that direction by presenting its position in an amicus brief in the *Harper* case. The most obvious line of attack on the poll tax was that it interfered with the right to vote. Unfortunately for this argument, the Supreme Court consistently held that the Constitution did not create a general right to vote in state elections; rather, according to the Court, the Constitution limited the grounds on which a state could limit voting, for example, by barring a state from disfranchising African-Americans or women. Notwithstanding this doctrinal difficulty, Marshall's oral argument stressed that a poll tax should be unconstitutional because the ability to pay such a tax had no relation to the voter's capacity to understand political issues or even to the state's desire to raise revenue; as Marshall put it, "I don't know of a single tax in this world that's stayed the same rate, not for 75 years." He returned repeatedly to the fundamental unfairness of a poll tax in the modern world. The Court's decision in *Harper*, striking down the poll tax, did not adopt Marshall's argument that the right to vote was indeed guaranteed by the Constitution, but it invoked the themes of unfairness and economic inequality he had raised.[51]

A final difficulty in evaluating Marshall's oral advocacy as solicitor general can be seen in the oral argument in *Miranda v. Arizona*. The Court considered four separate cases with the limits on the use of confessions in criminal cases. One involved a federal bank robbery prosecution. Previous decisions hinted that the Court might rule that statements made to the police alone, without the presence of counsel, could not be admitted in a subsequent criminal trial. Marshall noted that if the Court required counsel at questioning, it would have to guarantee that the lawyers be effective, which might mean obstructing all questioning.[52]

The Department of Justice was anxious that the Court not adopt an absolute bar to questioning. At a conference with Marshall in the attorney general's office, Attorney General Katzenbach and the head of the department's Criminal Division expressed their strong view that the United States should give some ground by arguing that the police should be allowed to question suspects as long as certain warnings were given—which was FBI practice anyway. Marshall accepted the consensus without trying to impose his own position, which appeared to some of his subordinates to be less protective of suspects' rights. He was, he said, not "too optimistic about the outcome."[53]

At the oral argument, Marshall insisted that the FBI warnings were adequate. The questions from the justices made it clear, however, that the outcome that most concerned the Department of Justice—prohibiting questioning without a lawyer present—was simply not in prospect. Most of the argument involved exchanges in which the lawyers were essentially conduits for questions the justices posed to each other about whether warnings should be required. In a sense, Marshall won the case before the argument began, although ultimately the Court adopted a set of warnings that went beyond the FBI practice. Fifteen years later, Marshall still insisted that "[the] FBI rules should have been adopted in toto by *Miranda*."[54]

Overall, Marshall as an oral advocate was like Earl Warren. He had a powerful physical presence and gave the appearance of integrity, strength, commitment, and sound common sense. When those things mattered, he was quite effective. And those things mattered a great deal to many on the Warren Court, who plainly liked Marshall as a person, as solicitor general, and as a representative of African-Americans in the United States. Because the Court was "susceptible to his strengths," as one of the lawyers in the office remarked, he could speak directly to questions of fairness and justice. He was, in short, a near perfect match for the Warren Court.

Lyndon Johnson nominated Marshall on June 13, 1967, to be the first African-American justice of the Supreme Court. Moving personnel like chess pieces, Johnson created a place on the Court for Marshall. Ramsey Clark was the son of Justice Tom Clark, appointed to the Court in 1949. Ramsey Clark served in the Department of Justice as head of the Lands Division and as deputy attorney general. When Johnson moved Nicholas Katzenbach from attorney general to undersecretary of state in September 1966, Ramsey Clark became acting attorney general, a position he held for almost six months as Johnson tested his loyalty. Johnson finally nominated Ramsey Clark at the end of February 1967. Because of the government's role before the Supreme Court, his appointment as attorney general created the potential for serious conflicts of interest if his father heard government cases in the Supreme Court or for serious problems of understaffing the Court if Justice Clark withdrew from all government cases. Justice Clark therefore submitted his resignation, as Johnson probably expected.[55]

Johnson wanted to appoint Marshall to the Court. Johnson did hesitate briefly when his wife suggested that he could "fill the vacancy with a woman" because he had already "done so much" for African-Americans. He also thought a bit when his old friend Abe Fortas suggested that Marshall was not as intellectually capable as other African-Americans who ought to be considered, such as William Hastie, then sitting on the court of appeals in Philadelphia. When asked about Marshall's intellectual abilities, Katzenbach assured Johnson that Marshall would never "discredit" the Court. He stated forcefully that if Johnson appointed an African-American to the Supreme Court, it had to be Marshall, a great hero to African-Americans and liberal lawyers. Johnson had Ramsey Clark call Marshall to the White House without telling Marshall what the meeting was about. Johnson then told Marshall he was nominating Marshall and planned to announce it immediately. Marshall asked for time to call his wife, Cissy, but Johnson preempted him, picking up the telephone and calling her himself. They then went to the Rose Garden, where Johnson made a brief statement: "He deserves the appointment. . . . I believe that it is the right thing to do, the right time to do it, the right man and the right place."[56]

When Marshall's nomination was announced, the *New York Times*'s editorial echoed its comments on his nomination as solicitor general: The nomination was "rich in symbolism." The editorial conceded that there were judges "whose judicial work has been far more outstanding" and asserted that Marshall had not shown Cox's "intellectual mastery" as solicitor general. But, it said, "apart from the symbolism, Mr. Marshall brings to the Court a wealth of practical experience as a brilliant, forceful advocate." Southern senators "accepted [the nomination] . . . in silence"; only Strom Thurmond spoke against it. Otherwise, there was "hardly a ripple of adverse comment." Joseph Kraft of the *Washington Post* did observe that Marshall "will not bring to the Court penetrating analysis or distinction of mind," but that was the worst the mainstream media had to offer. More extreme views came from the rightwing journal *Human Events* and from journalist James Jackson Kilpatrick, who had helped construct Virginia's program of massive resistance to desegregation. According to Kilpatrick, writing in the conservative

National Review, Marshall would quickly join the "horseblindered liberal ideologist faction."[57]

Recalling his experience when nominated to the Second Circuit, Marshall began intensive preparation for the hearings. His staff gathered and reviewed transcripts of previous confirmation hearings for Supreme Court nominees and developed questions they believed he would be asked. In addition, his staff learned that Professor Alfred Avins, a legal scholar who had written extensively on the intentions of the framers of the Thirteenth, Fourteenth, and Fifteenth Amendments, was advising Senator Thurmond. In response, they reviewed Avins's articles.[58]

Marshall's confirmation hearings were not as difficult as the Second Circuit hearings, but they were not entirely easy either. At one level, the hearings raised interesting questions of constitutional theory. At another level, though, they were once again a form of political theater, with Senators McClellan, Sam Ervin, Jr., of North Carolina, and Thurmond playing to their audiences back home; as a result, the interesting questions were not seriously examined.

McClellan was concerned primarily with Marshall's views on criminal justice issues, because as he saw it the problem of crime threatened the nation's "internal security." Because of that concern, McClellan said, he had to "inquire into the philosophy of those who are nominated to this high position. I want to know what their thinking is and what their attitude is." Marshall responded to McClellan's questions about *Miranda* by saying that the government's brief, which had argued against the imposition of any broad warning requirements, expressed his "personal views"; he refused to discuss the Court's decision itself, because he believed that whatever he had to say about *Miranda* would have implications for cases the Court would hear. Marshall's position on *Miranda,* whether limited to his endorsement of the FBI's warnings or expanded to include what the Court had required, was entirely consistent with the liberalism of the 1960s that saw professionalization of the police as the best way to control abuses of public power and eliminate discriminatory law enforcement practices.[59]

The next two days of questioning saw extended exchanges between Marshall and Ervin, who began by reading a series of quotations about the Constitution's general meaning and about the proper methods of interpreting it. Marshall characterized the Constitution as a "living document . . . written with a broad stroke" and therefore not properly subject to interpretation based on a narrow view of original intent. A large part of the discussion concerned the Fifth Amendment and *Miranda.* After rejecting Ervin's position that the Fifth Amendment's words made it clear that the Constitution permitted unregulated police questioning, Marshall said it could be interpreted only by relying on prior decisions. At that point, however, the problem he faced the day before resurfaced: The relevant precedent from 1967 on police questioning was *Miranda,* and Ervin understandably thought it appropriate to discuss the case's implications, in light of Marshall's reliance on precedent as a basis for interpreting the Constitution. Marshall tried to avoid this line of questioning by saying that such cases would come before the Court and that "we know, you and I, that you are talking about a matter which was in the *Miranda* cases." Pressed by Ervin, he did agree that *Miranda* was the first decision of the

Court to say that the Constitution required a specified set of warnings—hardly a major point.[60]

Ervin's theme was that the Supreme Court had been making law, not discovering it, and he illustrated this proposition by criticizing the Court for refusing to apply some of its criminal procedure decisions to cases that had already resulted in sometimes extended periods of imprisonment. This, he said, demonstrated that the Court was not applying rules that had always been in the Constitution: If the rules had always been in the Constitution, it would be patently unfair to continue to imprison people on the basis of convictions that violated those rules. Citing his Second Circuit dissent on this question, Marshall agreed with Senator Ervin. Marshall and Ervin then engaged in a fairly extensive discussion of whether there was a difference between changing the words of the Constitution and changing their meaning. Throughout the discussion, Marshall firmly asserted his own positions and stood up well against questions from a senator widely regarded as a constitutional expert.[61]

The next day of hearings was consumed in a bizarre series of questions by Thurmond, who relied entirely on questions Avins prepared for him. The questions ranged from the rather general—"Do you believe that the Civil Rights Act of 1866 was constitutional before the ratification of the Fourteenth Amendment?" to which Marshall responded, "I am in the middle on that. I researched it when the school cases were up, and I consider it unimportant because the amendment was adopted and they were reenacted"—to the ridiculously specific—"What purpose did the framers have, in your estimation, in referring to the incident involving former Representative Samuel Hoar in Charleston, South Carolina, in December 1844, as showing the need for the enactment of the original version of the Fourteenth Amendment's first section?" To questions of the latter sort, Marshall responded disdainfully, "I haven't the slightest idea." He did agree that Thurmond's evidence was relevant to the proper interpretation of the Fourteenth Amendment, though never dispositive. Thurmond's dependence on Avins, and the obvious fact that he was not seriously interested in Marshall's answers except for purely political purposes, came out when Senator Edward M. Kennedy somewhat puckishly asked Thurmond to rephrase one of his complex and detailed questions; Thurmond repeated the question word for word, and when Kennedy pressed him for a paraphrase, Thurmond refused to do so, expressing some irritation.[62]

The hearings concluded on July 24, 1967, with almost nothing having been said by Marshall's supporters, who were confident of victory and understood the political purposes of the show being put on by the Southern senators. By a vote of 11–5, the committee recommended Marshall's confirmation. After six hours of speeches, the Senate confirmed Marshall's appointment to the Court on August 30 by a vote of 69–11, with all of the negative votes cast by Southern Democrats.[63] It was, as the *Washington Post* reported, an "occasion for self-congratulation." The next day Justice Hugo Black, the Court's senior associate justice and an Alabaman, administered the oath of office to the first African-American appointed to the Supreme Court.[64]

2

"The Steam Roller Will Have to Grind Me Under"
Marshall and the Brethren

The Supreme Court in 1967 was the "right place" and the "right time" for Marshall in part because it was the heyday of the Warren Court. When Marshall took his seat on the Court at the start of the 1967 Term, he might have expected to participate in a continuing series of liberal decisions. Chief Justice Earl Warren, appointed by President Dwight Eisenhower in 1953, and Associate Justice William J. Brennan, appointed by Eisenhower three years later, had become the leaders of the Court's liberal wing. They were regularly joined by Justices William O. Douglas and Abe Fortas and less regularly by Justice Hugo L. Black. Douglas and Black, appointed to the Court by Franklin D. Roosevelt, were old New Dealers; Fortas began his legal career as a New Deal lawyer and became a Washington insider and close adviser to Johnson, whom Fortas supported wholeheartedly. With Marshall, the Court had a solid bloc of five liberal justices.

The Court's conservatives were led by Justice John Marshall Harlan, who was Judge Friendly's predecessor in leading the Second Circuit before coming to the Supreme Court in 1955. Potter Stewart, a moderate Republican appointed by Eisenhower in 1958, ordinarily joined Harlan. Justice Byron White, Kennedy's first Supreme Court appointee, regularly supported expansive national power and civil rights but joined the conservatives on most issues of criminal procedure.

Although Marshall's appointment confirmed and extended the liberal domination of the Supreme Court, it turned out to be the last victory. Within a few years Warren was gone, replaced by Warren Burger. Over the next decade, Republican presidents appointed increasingly conservative justices, and constitutional law changed from the weapon for liberal social engineering in which Marshall believed into a solid guardian of the status quo.

The Warren Court's decisions responded to the interests of the New Deal and Great Society coalitions: organized labor, African-Americans, and liberal intellectuals. Those coalitions gradually disintegrated during the 1970s. As historian William Berman puts it, they had been held together by the Democratic party's ability "to serve as the champion of both corporate America and social decency." Stable and sustained economic growth made it possible for the Democratic coalition to satisfy the demands of working-class Americans and of African-Americans through a social welfare system financed by progressive taxes. Changes in the position of the United States in the world economy destroyed this "growth coalition." The "new politics of austerity all but precluded legislative deals that included benefits for the rich, the middle class, and the poor alike." Two other commentators observed, "In the context of slow and erratic growth, . . . a gigantic squeeze began to develop on social spending. This . . . constrained [the Democrats'] ability to deliver the social benefits that had long secured them a real mass base."[1]

By the early 1970s, the Democratic coalition began to fracture into interest groups competing with each other for their shares of a no-longer-expanding economic pie. The Warren Court's agenda of expanding rights exacerbated the Democrats' difficulties. Paying for the rights articulated by the Court meant increasing taxes. In journalist Thomas Edsall's words,

> Insofar as the granting of rights to some groups required others to sacrifice tax dollars and authority, to compromise longstanding values, to jeopardize status, power, or the habitual patterns of daily life, this new liberalism became, to a degree, a disruptive force in American life, and particularly so within the Democratic party.[2]

The party's leaders were unable to develop a program that would unite the declining labor movement, African-Americans, environmentalists, and feminists, in part, political scientists Thomas Ferguson and Joel Rogers argued, because the party's leaders also needed to satisfy the requirements of its supporters in the business community.[3] Racial antagonisms that had been suppressed in the coalition's programs of general social welfare resurfaced. Republican leaders saw their opportunity to exploit these emerging divisions within the Democratic coalition. The political outcome was a shift in the presidency from Democratic to Republican control. Marshall saw a Democrat in the White House for only six of his twenty-four years on the Court.

The Republican challenge to Democratic political control was partly intellectual. Conservatives began to articulate policy alternatives to the Democratic agenda that had dominated political discourse. One of their intellectual arenas was constitutional law. Conservative scholars developed critiques of the culture of rights they associated with the Warren Court. The rights the Warren Court protected, conservatives argued, were not grounded in the nation's constitutional traditions and contributed to the social fragmentation that so troubled many voters.

The Warren Court's justices turned out to have few resources to turn back these challenges. The Warren Court's vision had important egalitarian elements in it, yet the Court's place in the American political system made it impossible for the Court to deliver consistently on its egalitarian promises. Occasional decisions embracing egalitarian views were accompanied with decisions incompatible with those views. As a result, the Warren Court could easily be tarred with the charge of being "unprincipled" or "political."

The Warren Court could not supply any alternative ideology, however. Its constitutional theory was founded on the New Deal experience, when the Supreme Court obstructed Congress and state legislatures seeking to address pressing economic issues through social welfare legislation like minimum wage laws. President Franklin Roosevelt transformed the Court after 1937. The new Supreme Court aggressively protected individual rights, and Marshall contributed to that project as a litigator. But the justices no longer thought they had any basis in the Constitution for telling legislators that their economic and social programs were unconstitutional.

The Democratic coalition could have been held together by a unifying economic vision. Occasionally, liberal justices provided glimpses of such a vision. In 1972, for example, Marshall wrote a dissent resting on the proposition that everyone had a right to a government job unless the government had a good reason not to give the applicant a job.[4] Marshall also developed a way of understanding the Constitution's guarantee that governments may not deny people "the equal protection of the laws" that suggested how the courts might insist that governments pursue economic and social programs that benefited workers and the less well-to-do.[5] But these were only mild hints, usually in dissent and always in tension with the more openly stated lesson the Court learned after the New Deal, that social and economic matters were for legislatures to work out.

The Warren Court's academic supporters provided less assistance than conservative theorists provided their side. Occasional suggestions that the Constitution required an expanded welfare state and redistribution of wealth either failed to provide enough detail, and so seemed utopian, or were overly programmatic, and so seemed vulnerable to skepticism about the efficacy of social engineering. As the Warren Court faded, liberal academics became entirely defensive, criticizing the Court for changing course without providing much in the way of an argument for the Warren Court's path.

The Court could not provide the glue needed to hold the Democratic coalition together. Indeed, the Court exacerbated the divisions that were tearing the Democratic coalition apart when it handed out occasional victories to one or another of the interest groups struggling within the coalition. As Edsall writes,

> Instead of being seen as advancing the economic well-being of all voters, including white mainstream working and middle-class voters, liberalism and the Democratic party came to be perceived, in key sectors of the electorate, as promoting the establishment of new rights and government guarantees for previously marginalized, stigmatized, or historically disenfranchised groups, often at the expense of traditional constituencies.[6]

The Democratic coalition was further fractured by the issue of race. As economic conditions changed, working people came to see themselves as competing for shares of a fixed pie rather than attempting to secure a larger share of an expanding pie. Race provided a convenient focus for this competition. According to sociologist Jonathan Reider, for example, "Opposition to [affirmative action programs] sprang from the self-interest of vulnerable whites, whose hold on middle-class status was precarious. Integration threatened white ethnic monopolies on labor markets, the civil service, unions, and municipal power."[7] Whatever liberal justices did in the 1970s and 1980s would compound the political difficulties of the coalition that provided essential support to them. Marshall's position on issues of race ironically contributed to a political process that made it increasingly difficult for him and his liberal colleagues to achieve victories.[8]

By the early 1970s, Republicans dominated the presidential arena and provided an articulate alternative to the Warren Court's jurisprudence. Given the chance, Republican presidents appointed relatively conservative justices to the Supreme Court. With nearly every new appointment, liberals believed that the achievements of the Warren Court were in grave danger. Yet, although the Court gradually drifted to the right, the shift was less dramatic than some had feared and others had hoped. In 1983 a collection of scholarly essays was titled, *The Burger Court: The Counter-Revolution That Wasn't*. A later assessment was called, *The Center Holds: The Power Struggle Inside the Rehnquist Court*.[9] Those titles conceal the dramatic changes in constitutional law from 1967 to 1991, even as they accurately suggest a measured pace of change. On questions of race, for example, the law when Marshall left the Court was markedly more conservative than it had been when the Warren Court's justices were in control.[10] How Marshall and his colleagues, both liberal and conservative, adapted to the pace of change is an important part of the story of the Court during Marshall's tenure.

Earl Warren was, to his colleagues, the "Super Chief." His leadership kept disagreements over the law from becoming personal. Warren's experience in California politics and as a national political figure made him the kind of lawyer-statesman with whom Marshall was comfortable. Marshall, Warren, and Brennan were gregarious men who established working relations by recounting anecdotes and telling jokes. They all wanted to interpret the Constitution to promote justice and were willing to leave to others the details of the arguments linking just results to the Constitution's words and the Court's precedents. Warren expressed this perspective in his celebrated question to advocates who presented the Court with legalistic arguments: "Yes, but is it fair?"[11]

Marshall's approach was slightly different. He was a litigator influenced by Dean Houston's idea of law as an instrument of social engineering. Combining that with a trial lawyer's perspective, Marshall believed that the right answers to legal questions yielded sensible solutions to practical problems. A judge who identified those solutions found the law at the same time. Seeing the judge's job in this way, Marshall took advantage of what everyone agreed was his greatest strength, the soundness of his judgment.

Marshall's appointment to the Court suggested bright prospects of a Court working in harmony to promote liberal constitutional values. Acknowledging that Marshall was "more qualified [for the Supreme Court] . . . than many of his predecessors" and paying tribute to Marshall's "skill and industry," conservative columnist James J. Kilpatrick lamented the appointment because it would "upset the rough balance of liberalism and conservatism that recently has prevailed upon the high tribunal" and would place "the judicial activists . . . in full control." Even the Warren Court's conservatives—moderate Republicans John Marshall Harlan, a leading New York corporate lawyer, and Potter Stewart, a Yale-educated judge from a prominent Cincinnati family—fit comfortably within the Warren Court's way of doing business.[12]

Marshall's opinions during his first years on the Court provided some modest confirmation of Kilpatrick's prediction but less than Kilpatrick might have expected. Marshall's first opinion extended the Court's holdings that required counsel be provided in criminal cases to a Washington procedure in which formal sentencing was deferred pending the defendant's completion of probation. Initially, both Brennan and Black were reluctant to require counsel in that setting, but in the end they joined Marshall's brief opinion. In a memorandum to Marshall, Black wrote that he had been persuaded by the opinion to change his vote and said that "it gives me much pleasure, therefore, to agree to this, your first opinion for the Court, written with brevity, clarity and force."[13]

In *Frank v. United States,* Marshall wrote for the Court, which denied a jury trial to a person convicted of criminal contempt.[14] The Court had already held that juries were required in all cases involving anything other than a "petty offense," and it had held that criminal contempt was a petty offense only if the defendant received less than six months in jail on conviction. Frank received a sentence of three years' probation for criminal contempt. The question for the Court was whether the period of supervision was so long that the Constitution required a jury trial even though Frank was not sentenced to jail at all. Initially, Marshall voted against reviewing the conviction, but after argument he voted, with the majority, to require a jury trial. The difficulty the majority faced was that defendants convicted of petty offenses, that is, those for which the longest jail term could be six months, could also receive probation for three years. Marshall's draft opinion distinguished the petty offenses on the ground that there was no statutory limit on the time a defendant *could* receive if sentenced for criminal contempt.

This opinion was, as Marshall put it, "effectively detonated by Byron [White's] dissenting opinion." White pointed out that under Marshall's theory, people like Frank were entitled to jury trials because there was no set limit to the jail sentence they could receive, whereas people sentenced to exactly the same period of probation under statutes limiting their potential time in jail to six months would not be entitled to juries. This reasoning, according to White, came close to violating fundamental ideas about equal treatment. After Fortas changed his vote "with a request to Brother Marshall for papal indulgence and Panther forgiveness," Marshall lost a majority for his opinion.* Marshall then changed his vote and wrote the Court's opinion denying Frank a jury trial.[15]

Three important opinions in Marshall's first years placed him in the center of the Warren Court's liberalism. None was controversial within the Court. In *Benton v. Maryland,* Marshall had the opportunity to apply the Constitution's ban on double jeopardy to the states. As a circuit judge in 1965 deciding the *Hetenyi* case, Marshall had been forced to adopt a rather convoluted approach to set free a defendant who had to defend himself twice. With the power of the Supreme Court

---

*Fortas's notes were often effusive: In withdrawing his vote from a Brennan opinion, Fortas said, "With great pleasure, I join Justice Marshall's eloquent and irresistible dissent." Fortas to Brennan and TM, March 27, 1968, Marshall Papers, box 48, file 1 (Johnson v. Massachusetts).

behind him, Marshall held directly that the double jeopardy ban applied to the states, citing *Hetenyi* in a footnote on a collateral point.[16]

Stanley v. Georgia, decided in 1969, was an obscenity case. The defendant was convicted of possessing obscene materials in his house. All the justices agreed that Stanley's conviction could not be upheld, but they initially found it difficult to select a theory. Warren thought the conviction should be reversed because there was no showing that Stanley had known the materials were obscene. Brennan "ha[d] trouble bringing possession into [the] First Amendment" and eventually wrote a concurring opinion finding the conviction invalid because the materials had been seized during an illegal search. Harlan and Black offered the theory that Marshall adopted in his opinion for the Court. As Harlan put it, the "state can't make a crime out of what an individual draws or paints in the privacy of his own room." For Marshall, "Th[e] right to receive information and ideas . . . is fundamental to our free society. . . . [A]lso fundamental is the right to be free, except in very limited circumstances, from unwanted governmental intrusions into one's privacy." Stanley was

> asserting the right to be free from state inquiry into the contents of his library. . . . If the First Amendment means anything, it means that a State has no business telling a man, sitting alone in his own house, what books he may read or what films he may watch. Our whole constitutional heritage rebels at the thought of giving government the power to control men's minds.[17]

Finally, *Amalgamated Food Employees v. Logan Valley Plaza* gave Marshall a chance to revisit the state action problem he addressed as a litigator in *Shelley v. Kraemer*. A union established a picket line at a supermarket located in a large shopping mall near Altoona, Pennsylvania. The mall owners got a state court to enjoin the picketing. The union argued that this injunction violated its members' free-speech rights. The mall owners replied that they were simply attempting to protect their rights as property owners and that there was no state action, because the injunction simply vindicated their right to keep trespassers off their property. Marshall's opinion for the Court began by noting that had the picketing occurred on city streets, the union's constitutional claim would unquestionably be valid. In addition, Marshall relied heavily on a 1946 decision holding that courts could not limit picketing on the streets of a company-owned town. For Marshall, modern realities meant that shopping malls had to be considered just like the streets of a traditional downtown shopping area.[18]

An incident during Marshall's first year on the Court illuminates Marshall's personal style and his understanding of the law. An Ohio juvenile court found Buddy Whittington a delinquent after a short hearing. The judge found probable cause to believe that Whittington had committed second-degree murder. Whittington appealed the determination that he was a delinquent to the Ohio Supreme Court and, after losing there, appealed to the United States Supreme Court. Two months after the Ohio courts finished with Whittington's case, the Supreme Court made a major decision about the procedures juvenile courts must use in cases that might end up with the juvenile in a state institution. The procedures in Whittington's case probably did not satisfy the new standards, but before the Supreme

Court could consider the merits of his claim, it had to face a question regarding its own power. The statutes regulating the authority of the Supreme Court say that it can review only "final judgments" of state courts. Was the juvenile court's determination that Whittington was a delinquent a final judgment? The court had not ordered Whittington to jail, and indeed after the Supreme Court decided to review his case, the juvenile court ordered that Whittington be tried in an adult court for the murder. Yet, after the finding of delinquency Whittington ran the risk of being placed in a state institution or a foster home, and the Ohio courts treated the delinquency determination as reviewable.[19]

After hearing argument in the case, the justices asked Fortas to research the "final judgment" question. At the Court's conference on April 5, 1968, when *Whittington* came up again, what Douglas called "a rather interesting discussion" occurred.[20] Fortas was absent from the conference because he was at the White House advising President Johnson on how to deal with the disturbances in Washington that had broken out after the assassination of Martin Luther King, Jr., the night before. Warren summarized Fortas's research, and "before the Chief Justice had hardly finished, Marshall broke in to state his views at length." Douglas continued, "He is a fine individual, but extremely opinionated and not very well trained in the law. His report was rather on the side of wasting a lot of time and in a lot of idle talk and irrelevant conversation."*

When Marshall spoke again, he said that "[i]t can be [a] final judgment if we want it to" and that the Court should "let them clean their own laundry." Douglas was puzzled by this last comment, but the outcome of the case makes it clear what Marshall meant. The Court issued an unsigned opinion drafted in Marshall's chambers that sent the case back to the Ohio courts for them to decide what effect the juvenile court's decision to send Whittington to trial in adult court had; if that decision essentially washed out the delinquency determination, the judgment would not be final, but if the delinquency determination remained in effect, it would be final.

On June 26, 1968, President Lyndon Johnson announced that Earl Warren would retire, effective "at [the] pleasure" of the President. Johnson accepted the resignation "effective at such time as a successor is qualified." Johnson nominated Abe Fortas to be Chief Justice and named Homer Thornberry, a federal judge in Texas and another old friend who had served in the House of Representatives, to fill the seat that would open with Fortas's promotion. Believing that their nominee would win the 1968 presidential election, Republicans sought to keep Johnson from naming a new Chief Justice. They argued that Warren had resigned in the peculiar manner he used so that he could influence the choice of his successor and that Fortas was tainted by cronyism with Johnson, whom Fortas had continued to

---

* Douglas did not suggest that anyone else had been troubled by Marshall's intervention. Nor did he note that Marshall might have been disturbed by King's assassination, although Douglas wrote another memorandum to the files the same day mentioning that "a good deal of Washington, D.C. was on fire as a result of the race riots," in the course of criticizing the Court as "timid and hesitant" in an important civil rights case. Memorandum to files, Douglas Papers, box 1423, file: Argued Cases, No. 645 (Jones v. Mayer).

advise after his appointment to the Court. More damaging was the disclosure that Fortas accepted a special law school lectureship financed by people who were likely to have cases before the Court and designed for him alone. After a motion to end Republican delaying moves received fewer than the required sixty votes, Fortas asked that his name be withdrawn.[21]

Richard Nixon's successful 1968 campaign included pledges to turn the Supreme Court away from its liberal orientation. He nominated Warren E. Burger to be Chief Justice. As a judge on the federal court of appeals in Washington, Burger had a reputation as a conservative, especially on criminal law issues. Then, in 1969, additional investigations into Fortas's financial affairs produced information that induced him to resign.[22] Nixon sought to use the opportunity this resignation presented to further the Court's transformation and to strengthen the Republican party's position in the South by nominating a white Southerner. He nominated Clement Haynsworth to the vacant seat. Haynsworth, a respected federal judge from South Carolina, was caught in the backlash of the Fortas affair. Labor unions and civil rights organizations opposed his nomination, partly because they disagreed with his conservatism and partly to deny Nixon a victory in his Southern strategy. Minute scrutiny of Haynsworth's finances turned up some rather petty matters in which, Democrats contended, Haynsworth had sat in cases in which he had a direct financial interest. Haynsworth voted in favor of the Deering-Milliken company's position in a bitter labor dispute while he was a director of a company that provided food vending service to three of Deering-Milliken's plants, and he concurred in a decision awarding several thousand dollars to the Brunswick Corporation, in which Haynsworth held 1,000 of the 18 million outstanding shares. Politics and extreme sensitivity to ethical questions combined to defeat Haynsworth's nomination by a vote of 55–44.[23]

Nixon then peevishly turned to another conservative federal judge, Harrold Carswell. Carswell was almost universally regarded as unqualified for the Supreme Court. When Carswell was called mediocre, a defender, Senator Roman Hruska of Nebraska, replied: "Even if he is mediocre there are a lot of mediocre judges and people and lawyers. They are entitled to a little representation, aren't they, and a little chance?" Reporters discovered that Carswell had defended segregation in 1948 and had helped incorporate a racially discriminatory private club. In the end, Carswell's nomination too was defeated. Declaring that the Democrat-controlled Senate made it impossible to name a Southern conservative to the Supreme Court, Nixon then nominated appeals court judge Harry Blackmun of Minnesota, who was rapidly confirmed in 1970.[24]

The transformation of the Court seemed complete after Hugo Black and John Marshall Harlan resigned from the Court for reasons of health shortly before the October 1971 Term began.[25] Harlan was a moderate conservative, and Black, by the time of his retirement, was no longer the consistent champion of all liberal causes. Nonetheless, their replacements, Lewis F. Powell and William H. Rehnquist, were substantially more conservative. By 1972 the Supreme Court was no longer the Warren Court, although it had not really become the Nixon Court.

Douglas retired in 1976, replaced by John Paul Stevens, a moderate Republican. A second wave of change hit the Court in the 1980s, with a series of appointments by President Ronald Reagan. When Stewart retired in 1981, Reagan took the opportunity to nominate Sandra Day O'Connor to be the first female justice. Burger's retirement in 1986 allowed Reagan to acknowledge Rehnquist's contributions to the Court's gradual change by promoting him to Chief Justice. Reagan then strengthened the Court's conservative wing by nominating Antonin Scalia to fill the seat Rehnquist's nomination opened up. In 1988 Anthony Kennedy joined the Court, replacing Powell. Although the Court did not repudiate central Warren Court decisions, by 1989 it could fairly be called the Rehnquist Court to symbolize its transformation.

The Court drifted to the right more slowly than many expected in large part because Burger's leadership was a continual irritant that impeded the more conservative justices from forming a coherent bloc. Perhaps the best that could be said of Burger was that he looked the part of the Chief Justice. His colleagues at the Court repeatedly had to ask themselves whether Burger was merely a bumbling administrator or rather a Machiavellian manipulator. On reflection, they generally concluded that he was the former, but the mere fact that the issue never went away kept tension high throughout Burger's tenure.

News stories about the new "Nixon-Burger Court" suggest one source of tension in Burger's early years. Nixon had campaigned in favor of changing the Court's direction dramatically. Insiders wondered "what effect the Court's new composition will have" on the law. Harlan, White, and Stewart, who disagreed with some of the Warren Court's major decisions, nonetheless were concerned that large doctrinal changes in a short period would fuel the public belief that the Court was a mere captive of political forces. Black worried to Harlan that it was "bad practice for the Court to ask counsel to discuss whether old cases should be overruled." In 1972 White opposed a Burger suggestion that some recent double jeopardy cases be overruled even though White himself had dissented in those cases:

> I doubt that we should lightly overrule or put aside a rule of constitutional law fashioned in accordance with those institutional procedures contemplated by the Constitution and Congress. A judgment reached in this fashion is entitled to at least some period for clinical observation before it is interred. It may be that experience will prove it as wise as its authors expected. On the other hand, it may prove improvident, in which event it will receive a timely enough burial.[26]

The question of how fast change would occur became particularly pressing after Black and Harlan retired. A significant number of important cases were argued before Powell and Rehnquist took their seats. The justices decided that, as a rule of thumb, they would request reargument in cases in which the "bob-tailed Court" of seven justices divided 4–3. The Court's liberals remained suspicious, however. Late in the Court's Term, Stewart "expressed his outrage at the high handed way things are going, particularly the assumption that a single Justice if CJ can . . . hold up for nine months anything he chooses, even if the rest of us are ready to bring down 4–3s." In one case, written by Stewart, in which the justices voted to hand down a 4–3 decision, Douglas became concerned that Burger was withholding his vote as part of a "strategy to have [the case] reargued." Burger replied, "If there is any 'strategy' to reargue this case, I have not heard of it. Perhaps it is only 'in the eye of the beholder'!" After Douglas expressed his concern about Burger's delay, Burger tried again: "I assume you read my brief note as an effort to relieve our pressures with a bit of flippancy. (Vera [Burger's wife] tells me I'm not very good at being flippant and that sometimes it is taken otherwise.)"[27]

Burger could not defuse suspicions about his motives so easily. Sometimes he suggested a strained reading of a case's facts to allow the Court to produce a conservative result, which Marshall and others derided as "reaching out." After years of working with Burger, Powell found Burger "heavy-handed and insensitive." He was incredulous when Burger simply appropriated a couple of footnotes from a Powell draft dissent, without even asking Powell's permission, and then responded to Powell's complaint with a "cheery note telling Powell to 'Relax!'" Burger's presentations at the justices' conferences were long-winded and vague, and he was "too self-important . . . and too self-engaged." Blackmun resented being "taken for granted" as a "Minnesota Twin" of his old friend Burger and was annoyed that Burger assigned few important opinions to him. Eventually, Blackmun found some of Burger's reactions to suggestions "petulant," and he disliked Burger's imperiousness. Rehnquist once was "amazed" when Burger allowed an opinion to come down before Rehnquist had made "last minute changes" in his dissent: "I realize there can be slipups and misunderstandings," Rehnquist wrote, "but it does seem to me that this opinion was put out with too much haste and without any adequate notification to those who presumably had a right to be notified." Burger sometimes got under Stevens's skin as well. In one case Burger inserted a footnote in a dissent criticizing the majority's "haste" and its "strain[ing] to reach out" to decide a constitutional issue. Stevens was outraged, and pointed out that the only ones who had voted to hear the case in the first place were the dissenters; it hardly made sense for them to criticize the majority for "reaching out."[28]

Although Burger tried to be sensitive to his colleagues' personal needs, even here he could fail. Burger scheduled a special conference to deal with administrative matters in April 1972. After the conference had been set up, a favorite aunt of Marshall died, and he asked Burger to reschedule the conference. Burger agreed. Then, when former Supreme Court justice and South Carolina governor James F. Byrnes died, Burger rescheduled the conference again so he could attend Byrnes's funeral. He set the conference for the time Marshall was attending his aunt's funeral. Marshall was furious; as he saw it, Burger had thought the funeral of a leading segregationist more important than the funeral of a member of Marshall's family.[29]

Suspicions of Burger erupted in the abortion cases, first argued before a seven-justice court in 1971. The cases came from Texas and Georgia. Texas had an old statute, allowing abortions only to save the woman's life. Georgia had a more modern one, allowing abortions when approved by a hospital committee. The challenges were based on two theories. Each had problems. Under the first theory, statutes restricting the availability of abortions were unconstitutionally vague because they allowed abortions to save the woman's life but did not tell doctors clearly enough when such threats existed. The difficulty was that only a year earlier the Court had upheld the District of Columbia's abortion statute, which allowed abortions to save the woman's life or health, against a vagueness challenge. How could Texas's narrower statute be less clear? Under the second theory, abortion statutes were unconstitutional because they violated a woman's right of privacy. The difficulty here was that the constitutional basis of the right of privacy was uncertain, and the scope of any such right was undefined.

At the conference on the cases, the vote was clear but the theory was not. Only White would have upheld both statutes. Blackmun appeared to reject the privacy theory and seemed to approve Georgia's statute. The Texas statute, however, did not "go far enough to protect doctors." Burger's diffuse statement of the case rather clearly indicated that he did not find the Texas statute vague and suggested that he rejected the privacy theory as well. Douglas, Brennan, and Stewart supported the vagueness attack on the statutes, and Marshall agreed, although he indicated support for the privacy theory as well.[30]

When he is in the majority, the Chief Justice is entitled to give the job of drafting an opinion to another justice in the majority. Otherwise, the most senior associate justice in the majority assigns the opinions. As Douglas counted the votes in the abortion cases, he was the senior justice in a majority to strike down both statutes, with Burger dissenting in both cases. He was outraged when Burger assigned the opinion to Blackmun, even though Douglas himself had planned to give Blackmun the opinion. Douglas sent Burger a note objecting to the assignment. Burger replied, "[T]here were, literally, not enough columns to mark up an accurate reflection of the voting" in either case. He had marked no votes, believing that the outcome would "stand or fall on the writing." Burger suggested that the cases were "quite probable candidates for reargument." That suggestion, plainly inconsistent with the standard that only cases divided 4–3 would be reargued, heightened the liberals' suspicions of Burger. Blackmun eventually circulated opinions relying on both the theories to strike down the statutes. Douglas and Brennan did not find them terribly persuasive, but they were willing to go along. A strong dissent by White shook Blackmun's confidence, however, and he moved for reargument. Douglas drafted a stinging dissent from the reargument order, chastising Burger for actions that "no Chief Justice in my time would ever have taken." In the end, Blackmun and the liberals prevailed, but Burger's "disingenuous" actions kept them on edge.[31]

Burger's actions in the abortion cases turned out to be part of a pattern but not one of manipulation to achieve conservative results. The pattern, rather, was of ineptitude. He listed one case for reargument because there was a 4–3 vote; Brennan corrected him that the vote was 5–2, and Burger apologized for basing his conclusion "on recollection." Burger misinterpreted a conference consensus for a "narrow" resolution of a voting rights case, thinking the majority wanted to vacate a broad decision rather than, as the votes were, to affirm the decision with a narrower theory. Once Burger erroneously listed a case for further discussion after four justices had already voted to grant review. After a while, Burger plaintively sought his colleagues' understanding: "Sometimes a change [in votes] is made directly to Bill Rehnquist [acting as secretary] either sotto voce or while the conversations going on impede communications."[32]

The Chief Justice opens the Court's discussions of its cases by summarizing the issues and indicating his views. Burger's case statements were rambling. He spent too much time on preliminary details, often said too little about the central issues, and frequently failed to say what he thought. He would "pass" on voting, later circulating a memorandum indicating where he eventually settled. Sometimes Burger's haziness occurred in cases with few ideological overtones. In one minor case, Brennan's clerk summarized the votes: "[N]ow you have: HLB, JMH[,] BW & Whatever on WEB." Brennan scribbled, "Since TM is out, that gives us four, so to h—— with it (him)."[33]

Burger kept the liberals' suspicions alive when he "passed" in cases that divided liberals from conservatives. When the Court revisited the issue of shopping malls and the First Amendment, Douglas initially assigned the opinion to Marshall, relying on Blackmun's "very tentative" vote to affirm the protestors' claims. Burger immediately replied, "The vote was not 5–4 as I had reserved and not voted at all. . . . I will assign the case in due course if I vote to affirm." Douglas sent Brennan a note, "The CJ would rather die than affirm." Two weeks later Blackmun decided to reverse, as did Burger, who said he "continue[d] to find the case a very difficult one."[34]

Burger's practices in assigning opinions were also a persistent source of irritation. In 1985 Brennan assigned two cases to himself, telling Burger in a note that none too subtly criticized Burger for giving Brennan too few cases, "Together with the two I assigned myself last week, this brings my total assignments to six, which at least approximates the total assignments to some of my other colleagues." When Burger assigned an opinion to Blackmun as the "least persuaded" and "the need periodically for the 'good of the soul' and what Judge Hutcheson called 'intellectual discipline,'" Blackmun responded irritably that he was not the least persuaded and would write an opinion consistent both with the majority's views and with Blackmun's earlier dissents in related cases. But, Blackmun said, "All this has nothing whatsoever to do with your references to the 'good of the soul.'" He would keep the opinion, he said, to avoid a repetition of earlier experiences, when he received no opinion assignments.[35]

Burger believed as well that his role as Chief Justice gave him the obligation to write the Court's opinions in what he regarded as its most important cases. The results were often not happy.[36] Burger thought, perhaps correctly, that the Court's opinion should be written by the Chief Justice when the Court voted to require President Nixon to comply with a court order in the Watergate affair that he turn over tapes made in his office. Burger believed that the president ought to have a somewhat broader executive privilege than most of his colleagues did. In addition, the case was decided under great time pressure. Different justices prepared pieces of a final opinion. Burger had to stitch those pieces together and, in the process, gave his views about executive privilege more prominence than a majority thought proper. The justices managed to get the opinion into a form they all could agree with after extensive negotiations. But, once again, Burger mishandled his colleagues.[37]

Part of Burger's difficulties occurred because he was sometimes obtuse about legal analysis and was unwilling to leave things in his clerks' hands. Occasionally, Burger's difficulties with legal analysis led him to propose decent solutions to novel problems, but more often they forced his colleagues to wrestle with him to get an acceptable legal analysis into the opinions.

Thornton v. Caldor presented the Court with a constitutional problem it had not faced before 1985.[38] A Connecticut statute provided that no one could be forced to work on "his Sabbath," leaving it up to each worker to decide which day that was. Only Rehnquist disagreed with the conclusion that the statute was an unconstitutional establishment of religion. *Lemon v. Kurtzman,* a 1973 Burger opinion, stated the Court's general test for deciding when the establishment clause was violated. That decision, however, had been widely criticized among conservative legal theorists. Burger's first draft in *Thornton* did not cite *Lemon.* Powell was "puzzled" over the omission. He and Brennan believed that Burger's opinion would signal a retreat from the Court's commitment to *Lemon.* Although Burger did not believe that *Lemon* provided "the test [for] all seasons," he eventually included it in a stripped-down opinion. Burger's instincts here were better than Powell's and Brennan's. The central problems of establishment of religion arise when a majority tries to use the political process to advance its own religious commitments. The Connecticut legislature, in contrast, was trying to accommodate individual religious views by easing the pressures they felt from their employers. Whatever the result in *Thornton* should have been, it clearly called for a more elaborate analysis than *Lemon* offered.[39]

More often, Burger's fuzzy legal analysis was troublesome. His difficulties occurred in the small and the large. Once he proposed to reverse a state supreme court's interpretation of its own state's statute, a legally impossible result. Frequently, his first drafts rambled, failing to distinguish between quite different approaches to the legal problems at hand. He wrote "sloppy" opinions, according to one Brennan law clerk, and his colleagues were accustomed to seeing in his opinions what Powell called "dicta that no doubt you intend to condense or discard."[40]

Often, too, Burger simply did not understand what was at stake. He was sometimes "not on the same 'wave length'" after discussions with his colleagues. Upholding a search after a controlled delivery of drugs in which the police had lost control briefly, Burger did not see why his colleagues cared so much about changing his initial formulation, that the loss of control was irrelevant unless it was "more probable than not" that the drugs were removed during the period when the police lacked control, to the more stringent requirement that there be "no substantial likelihood that the contents have been changed." He overreached in saying that a sexually suggestive speech by a candidate for high school office "has no claim to First Amendment protection" and got O'Connor to join his opinion only after he omitted the statement. His first draft in *Bowsher v. Synar,* which struck down the Gramm-Rudman budget limitation program in 1986, concerned his colleagues because it "cast doubt on the constitutionality of independent agencies." Saying that the draft was "a 'rush job,'" Burger replied to a flurry of memoranda that he did not disagree with any of them: "[T]he essence of the problem is whether we skin the tiger from the neck to the tail or vice versa. Either way suits me."[41]

A minor 1979 case encapsulates Burger's performance as Chief Justice. The issue in *Kentucky v. Whorton* was whether a state court violated the Constitution in failing to instruct the jury on the presumption of innocence. Kentucky's supreme court held that the instruction always had to be given, and that failing to give it would never be "harmless error." When the case got to the Supreme Court, the justices all agreed that the state court had to be reversed, but they disagreed about the theory. The majority believed that a trial judge did not have to give the instruction in every case, if the trial was nonetheless fair under the "totality of the circumstances." Three dissenters thought that the judge always had to give the instruction but that omitting it might sometimes be harmless error.

The two theories are not that different from an appellate court's point of view. But they are quite different to a trial judge. The dissenters' theory meant that a trial judge should always give the instruction, but convictions would not always be reversed if the judge failed to give the instruction. The majority's theory meant that sometimes a trial judge need not give the instruction at all. Burger did not understand the differences and assigned the opinion to Stewart. Stewart wrote back that he actually held the minority view and planned to dissent. He genially offered to write the majority opinion, too. After a majority signed on to that opinion, Stewart just as genially circulated an opinion dissenting from the one he himself had written.[42]

Burger himself may have offered the most cogent comment on his leadership. *Vorchheimer v. School District* was an attack on Philadelphia's use of separate academic high schools for young men and young women.[43] Rehnquist was absent from the hearing because of illness, and the Court's initial vote was 4–4. Burger tried to persuade his colleagues to have the case reargued after Rehnquist recovered, saying that the Court should not "evade[ ]" the constitutional question and certainly anticipating that Rehnquist would vote to allow the "separate but equal" schools. His efforts failed, and Burger wrote Blackmun, "I find it difficult to cope with four unregenerate, unreconstructed 'rebels'! In which case I conduct as orderly a retreat as possible."[44]

Burger's failings were hardly the only reason for the slowness of change on the Court. William J. Brennan became the Court's central figure. Brennan persuaded Blackmun and particularly Powell that the Warren Court's values of nationalism, equality, and individual dignity were closer to the nation's constitutional commitments than the values Rehnquist stood for. Brennan's willingness to be reasonable when his more conservative colleagues indicated to him that they would not go as far as Brennan wanted made him particularly effective in cobbling together the five votes needed to make constitutional law. When Brennan managed to pull a fractured Court together in a routine 1990 case, after O'Connor had tried and failed with two different approaches, Scalia praised his effort: "It is humbling to learn that such an obviously correct answer was lying before us all along." Engaged in a tug-of-war with Brennan during Scalia's first term to get Scalia's vote in an important case that raised questions about the power of the national courts, Powell nonetheless said that Brennan's opinion "advances [his thesis] with the skill of a great advocate."[45]

Brennan's skills went beyond advocacy. His colleagues regularly consulted him for strategic advice. Stevens wondered whether "it would be poor tactics" to circulate an opinion in a case in which Burger had said he had problems but had not indicated what they were; Brennan told him that sending the opinion around might "help the Chief reach his decision." Brennan suggested that Douglas try a different approach in one case because it was "more palatable" and "more likely to command a majority." Even when dissenting, Brennan offered advice to the author of majority opinions. When Rehnquist wrote to uphold a military regulation barring an Orthodox Jew from wearing a yarmulke while serving as a military psychiatrist, Brennan tactfully suggested that Rehnquist avoid describing the psychiatrist's practice as an "idiosyncracy," which, Brennan said, "might inadvertently, but deeply, offend our Jewish friends." Rehnquist immediately agreed.[46]

Brennan also made constant gentle efforts to induce O'Connor and Powell to take his side. He circulated draft opinions to them before sending the drafts to the rest of the Court; he negotiated over language in letters that were not sent to other justices. He accommodated their suggestions repeatedly, sometimes diluting his own position significantly, to avoid losing control of the opinion and risking that another author would be far less careful to preserve anything Brennan valued. One exchange with O'Connor suggests Brennan's approach to these matters: It ended, "We have a deal."[47]

Powell and Brennan "frequently" "exchange[d] views privately," working out their difficulties without exposing them to the rest of the Court. Each gave the other "precirculation look[s]" at drafts. When Brennan added a footnote quoting Powell in an opinion, Powell responded with a personal note, "You are a scholar and a gentleman—and a generous one!" Early in Powell's tenure, Brennan drafted a separate opinion supporting Powell's decision restricting a college's ability to regulate student political organizations but sent it to Powell before circulating it because "the last thing I want to do is upset your applecart." Later Powell did "major surgery" on a criminal procedure opinion "to meet [Brennan's] views." Powell got along so well with Brennan because Powell saw Brennan as another "gentleman" who was entirely reasonable in his approach to constitutional law. Brennan got along so well with Powell because Brennan understood how to persuade Powell to move away from his instinctive conservatism to what Brennan and ultimately Powell regarded as a more reasonable and moderate position. By 1987 Powell felt comfortable in noting to Brennan, in a relatively minor case, that "we are on the side of righteousness."[48]

Brennan paid less attention to Marshall in correspondence. Marshall and Brennan were friendly though not intimate outside the Court; they both were pleased when Marshall's grandson was named William in honor of Brennan. They worked closely together on the Court but primarily through conversations rather than correspondence. Brennan rarely wrote Marshall in the cajoling way he did when writing Powell or O'Connor, largely because he needed to work on them and he did not have to work on Marshall. By 1987 Brennan sent a note to Marshall saying, "You and I are in dissent (so what else is new?)." He did know what mattered to Marshall, however. Asking Marshall to draft a dissent in a double jeopardy case, Brennan specifically referred to the *Hetenyi* case that Marshall had written as a circuit judge.[49]

Shortly before his retirement in 1990, Brennan came close to apologizing to Marshall for undermining *Miranda v. Arizona* in a Pennsylvania case.[50] Highway patrol officers arrested Inocencio Muniz for driving while intoxicated. They took him to the police station and asked him his name, address, age, height, date of birth, and the date of his sixth birthday. *Miranda* required police officers to warn people in custody that they have a right to a lawyer and that their answers to questions can be used against them. The officers did not give Muniz these warnings before they asked the questions, and the Pennsylvania courts suppressed the videotape showing Muniz answering them. Rehnquist and three other justices believed there was nothing wrong with any of the questions. Most were routine "booking" questions. The question about Muniz's sixth birthday, they thought, did not reveal anything about the inner workings of Muniz's mind; it was, instead, a check on how well he could do "a simple mathematical exercise," a test of his "mental coordination" just like other tests of physical coordination. The other justices disagreed about the sixth-birthday question; they concluded that it did call for "testimony" by Muniz because the prosecution expected to rely on the difficulty Muniz had answering to support its case.

Brennan took the case for himself. He had to write an opinion upholding the booking questions while invalidating the sixth-birthday one. He did so by creating a new exception to the *Miranda* rule for booking questions. O'Connor pushed Brennan to expand the new exception. Worried that O'Connor might "lead the revolution" and deprive Brennan of "control over the breadth of the exception," Brennan turned to the brief filed by the United States and, in a footnote, quoted language limiting the scope of the exception. That satisfied O'Connor, but Brennan became concerned that Marshall, who planned to dissent, might point out that the new exception's narrow scope was inconsistent with the reasons for creating it. A dissent doing that, Brennan feared, might revive O'Connor's concerns. Laying these concerns out in a letter to Marshall, Brennan said, "I am prepared to take my lumps for recognizing the exception" but asked, "Is there any way we can get together on this?" After Marshall showed him a draft of the proposed dissent, Brennan was relieved. "Thanks, pal, for permitting me to glance at your dissent," he wrote. "I think it is quite fine. . . . If Sandra had gotten her hands on this issue, who knows what would have been left of *Miranda*." Marshall went along with Brennan's request to "reword[ ] a few passages" to "help contain the exception" by indicating that the exception should be read narrowly.[51]

Brennan's persuasive skills would not have retarded the Court's drift to the right had not Powell been open to persuasion. Powell understood himself to be a centrist. His former law clerk, J. Harvie Wilkinson, who was appointed to the federal bench by President Reagan, summarized Powell's self-understanding by describing Powell as offering "a perspective grounded in realism and leavened by decency, conscientious in detail and magnanimous in spirit, solicitous of personal dignity and protective of the public trust." He saw himself as attempting to steer the Court down a middle path between the liberalism of Marshall and Brennan and the conservatism of Rehnquist and Burger.[52]

Powell brokered a deal in 1975 when the Court took up a number of cases dealing with the government's power to search near the borders. Rehnquist was concerned that Powell's opinions, barring border patrol officers from stopping cars during their "roving patrols," might limit the power to stop and question people at established checkpoints. Powell thought Rehnquist's objections were misplaced and suggested some "minor language changes," which Rehnquist "rejected as inadequate." Rehnquist offered "counter-proposals that were quite lengthy." Powell negotiated with Rehnquist, who had been "conferring" with Burger, White, and Blackmun "with inconclusive results." Powell worked out language he found acceptable, which he then sent to Brennan, Stewart, and Marshall. As Powell saw it, the new language would satisfy Rehnquist while leaving open the questions on which the liberals might disagree. After a meeting in Brennan's office, the liberals signed on to Powell's compromise, and Rehnquist had to go along.[53]

Powell thought Marshall ill-suited to deal with much of the Court's work. In Powell's biographer's words, Marshall "faced too many problems that did not yield to analysis by anecdote," and his "tendency to see every issue in bright lines and stark contrasts seemed crude and escapist" to a justice like Powell who saw himself as a centrist. Marshall "held [Powell] at a distance" as well, because he saw Powell as speaking for the white South. Marshall resented the narrowness of the perspective suggested by widespread statements that Nixon was trying to find a Southerner for the Court; as far as Marshall was concerned, there already was a Southerner on the Court.[54]

Powell's working relations with Marshall were relatively formal. Occasionally, Powell sent Marshall a personal note praising an opinion. In general, however, Powell sought out Marshall only when he needed Marshall's vote. From 1980 to 1982, the Court struggled over two cases involving Richard Nixon. Morton Halperin sued Nixon and former Secretary of State Henry Kissinger for their actions in putting him on the White House "enemies list" and wiretapping his telephone. Halperin claimed that these actions violated his free-speech and privacy rights. In a parallel case, Ernest Fitzgerald, a civilian employee of the U.S. Air Force and a whistle-blower, contended he had been fired because he was not "loyal" to the administration. Fitzgerald sued Nixon, former Attorney General John Mitchell, and Nixon aides Bryce Harlow and Alexander Butterfield, claiming that they had violated the First Amendment.[55]

The first question in the lawsuits was whether the president and high executive officials were protected against suits like these even if they *had* violated the First Amendment. Under well-established law, some officials—judges and legislators—had such an absolute immunity, because, the Court believed, the threat of being sued might keep those officials from exercising their best judgment about good public policy. Other officials, however, had only a "qualified" immunity; they could be sued, but they would be liable only if they had acted in bad faith.

The Court reached the case involving Nixon and Mitchell first. Rehnquist disqualified himself because he had been Mitchell's direct subordinate when

Mitchell was attorney general. White, joined by Brennan and Blackmun, supported giving the president only a qualified immunity. Powell forcefully urged that presidents had to be absolutely immune from suit if they were to carry on the important work of governing, and he was joined by Burger, Stevens, and O'Connor. With Rehnquist out of the case, however, Powell needed one more vote. Surprisingly, Marshall voted in favor of absolute immunity at the conference. Burger assigned Powell the opinion.

Powell discovered two rather different ways to rule in Nixon's favor. One would reject Halperin's suit by finding absolute immunity. The other would reject it by finding no basis in law for a damage action like Halperin's. As Powell worked on the opinion, he decided that the second approach was better; Halperin's right to sue was logically prior to the question of Nixon's immunity. Stevens agreed, but Burger, Rehnquist, and O'Connor insisted on a decision dealing with presidential immunity. Powell therefore developed a second version, dealing with that question. Marshall, however, thought that Powell's immunity opinion went too far in protecting the president no matter what he did. Over the next few months, Powell sent Marshall notes in other cases, asking him for comments on a precirculation draft and personally thanking him for changes in an opinion. Powell's efforts to reach Marshall on a personal basis may have been too transparent, in light of the way they had dealt with each other in the past. Eventually, Marshall "altered [his] views somewhat on presidential immunity" and decided to go along with White's approach, which produced "considerable bad blood" between Marshall and Powell, according to Marshall's law clerk Stephen Carter. The next year the Court took up Fitzgerald's case and, with Rehnquist participating, gave the president absolute immunity, with White writing a dissent that Marshall joined.[56]

In the first years of Burger's tenure, the Court gained four new members: Burger himself, Blackmun, Powell, and Rehnquist. All found the work of the Court more difficult than they had expected. Lewis Powell had been a successful corporate lawyer and activist in bar politics, but he was unacquainted with many of the issues on the Court's docket. He was "overwhelmed by work" in his first term because of his unfamiliarity with the range of the Court's work. He told his colleagues in one early criminal procedure case that he had "no real feel for the applicable law." The sheer number of cases to be processed also made the job hard. The new justices came to the Court believing they had to be "hands on" judges, deeply involved in all aspects of their chambers' work. They tried to read all the applications for review, draft their own opinions, and read the drafts from other justices closely. They soon found it impossible to continue that course. After starting with the view that he should draft his opinions, characteristically with numbered paragraphs, Blackmun found himself criticized from inside and outside the Court for his slow work. In January 1971, Hugo Black complained to Blackmun that the Court was "further behind in handing down opinions at this time of year than we have ever been since I became a Justice, more than 33 years ago." Blackmun replied that his first year has been "a very difficult one for me personally," because he had to vote and write opinions when "each . . . case[ ] is a new decision for me, and is not ground which I am covering for the second or even the third time." Like Powell, Blackmun turned over the opinion drafting to his law clerks. [57]

The new Court settled down a bit after a few years. The justices each found a comfortable working style. When Douglas retired in 1975 after suffering a severe stroke, President Gerald Ford delegated the job of choosing a successor to his attorney general, Edward Levi. Levi wanted to remove the nomination process from the political contention that Nixon's nominations had produced. He made an entirely professional choice: John Paul Stevens, a moderate Republican antitrust lawyer whom Levi knew from Chicago, where Stevens had been serving as a federal appellate judge. [58]

One political scientist referred to Stevens as the "Lone Ranger" of the Court, because he regularly developed legal arguments that no other justice shared. He found Burger's heavy-handedness harder to deal with than his colleagues did. Stevens's idiosyncracies, including his "habit of citing himself frequently," annoyed Marshall. Next to a Stevens opinion beginning "Any student of history who has been reprimanded for talking about the World Series during a class discussion of the First Amendment knows that it is incorrect to state that a 'time, place, or manner restriction may not be based upon either the content or subject matter of speech,'" Marshall wrote, "Is he for real[?]" On another Stevens draft, Marshall noted, "Is he bragging or complaining[?]" When Stevens drafted a sentence saying that the Court had ignored a question Stevens posed, Marshall scribbled, "What nerve!! Gee ain't I great!" These comments, confined to the chambers, did not affect Marshall's ability to work with Stevens. After being persuaded by a proposed Scalia opinion in a 1987 case involving a prisoner's rights to fair procedures, Stevens abandoned the dissent he planned and Marshall took it over. Eventually, Stevens, saying "I cannot vacillate any further," joined Marshall anyway. [59]

As a candidate for the presidency, Ronald Reagan promised to nominate a woman to the Supreme Court. Stewart's 1981 retirement gave him the chance. After canvassing the possibilities, Reagan's advisers narrowed the list to two. Reagan interviewed Sandra Day O'Connor, a state court judge from Arizona who had been Rehnquist's law school classmate and had been a state legislator as well. Reagan found O'Connor's politics and personality congenial and nominated her as the first woman to sit on the Supreme Court. After a period in which her stilted diction was the subject of an occasional joking comment, O'Connor loosened up, to the point that she could change her position with the observation, "As the saying goes concerning Texas juries, they believe in justice, but they aren't dogmatic about it." O'Connor saw herself as a moderate, but her interest in states' rights, contrasting sharply with Brennan's nationalism, meant that she disagreed with Marshall and Brennan on many of the issues they cared most about. "She doesn't want to hurt people's feelings," Marshall said, but "if you cross her, she'll kick you . . . as hard as anybody."[60]

Burger retired in 1986, to head a commission sponsoring celebrations of the Constitution's bicentennial in 1989. President Reagan rewarded Rehnquist's service as a leader of the Court's conservative wing by nominating him to succeed Burger. Reagan nominated Antonin Scalia, an extremely conservative appeals court judge who had played a major role in constructing modern conservative legal thought, as the new associate justice. Scalia's nomination was uncontroversial. Rehnquist's was not. Liberal interest groups took the nomination as an occasion to publicize their disagreements with the direction in which the Court was moving. They also raised questions about Rehnquist's participation in a Republican program to challenge voters in Arizona, which they charged was designed to discourage minority voters. With a Republican majority in the Senate, the result was preordained, although Rehnquist's opponents managed to produce thirty-three votes against his promotion.

His colleagues found Rehnquist a superb Chief Justice, particularly after their experiences with Burger. Rehnquist ran the conferences with an iron hand. His statements of the cases were crisp, and he marched through the docket as if his most important concern was getting the meeting over. He pressed the justices to circulate opinions quickly and to vote as soon as opinions were circulated. In 1989 he told the justices that, in assigning opinions, he would "put more weight than I have in the past" on whether a justice had failed to circulate a majority opinion that he or she had been assigned, whether a dissenting justice had failed to circulate a dissent within four weeks of the proposed majority opinion, and whether the justice had failed to vote in cases when both majority and dissenting opinions had been circulated.[61]

Some justices were bothered by Rehnquist's pressure to get the work done. Stevens responded to Rehnquist's proposal about opinion assignments by "applaud[ing] your efforts to emphasize the value of getting our opinions out quickly," but he was concerned that "too much emphasis on speed can have an adverse effect on quality," a concern that Brennan and Scalia shared. Stevens, with his idiosyncratic views, also observed that sometimes the first dissent ended up failing to address issues that another dissenter wanted to deal with; the second dissenter, having waited to see how the first would draft the opinion, would then have to start working. And, perhaps more important, Stevens pointed out that Rehnquist's proposal might "enhance . . . the incorrect impression that the majority votes as a 'block'": If a proposed majority opinion received five votes quickly, its writer would be eligible to get another assignment before those who dissented from the draft were, with the result that members of such majorities would get a disproportionate number of majority opinions assigned to them.[62]

Rehnquist's skill in keeping the peace within the Court led Marshall to say only two years after Rehnquist's promotion that he "is going to be, if he isn't already, a damn good chief justice." As one liberal observer of the Court said, it was as if Rehnquist "took charm pills." His notes to colleagues on their opinions were as genial as possible. Joining a Marshall opinion in 1982, Rehnquist wrote, "If this were November rather than June, I would prepare a masterfully crafted dissenting opinion exposing the fallacies of your . . . discussion. Since it is June, however, I join." Similarly acceding to a Marshall result he probably found uncongenial, Rehnquist wrote, "I yield to superior firepower—and perhaps superior reasoning—and join your opinion" allowing a prisoner's lawsuit to go forward. Consoling Marshall over some changes Marshall had been forced to make to accommodate others, Rehnquist said, "I have been in the same boat in other cases" and encouraged Marshall to change the opinion, "though of course I reserve the right

. . . to object to any insidious footnotes that you may drop." Marshall went along with Rehnquist's friendly request to tone down a discussion of some cases in which Rehnquist dissented: "Just because I dissented . . . doesn't mean that I have a right to object to their citation . . . but it does somewhat dampen my enthusiasm." Rehnquist was genial even in responding to dissents, once telling his colleagues in the majority, "Since I think, *mirabile dictu,* that Bill Brennan's dissent does raise some legitimate undecided questions," he would revise his opinion. And, immediately apologizing for a sharp response to Brennan in a case about the rights of the mentally handicapped, Rehnquist attributed his reaction in part to the Valium he was taking to alleviate his back pain.[63]

Rehnquist was confident enough of the strength of his personal ties with Marshall to circulate an opinion calling a footnote in a Marshall dissent a "bizarre" position that "only a cynic or an ignoramus" could take. Brennan at least was puzzled by the opinion, but Marshall wrote "Ignore!!!" on Rehnquist's opinion. The next day Rehnquist told his colleagues, indirectly, that the opinion was a joke: "You may not know it," he wrote, "but today is the 274th anniversary of the Battle of Pultowa. . . . On the anniversary of that battle, we Swedish-Americans try to look around for something kind and considerate we can do for our friends and colleagues. This year, I have decided that my 'Pultowa Day' act will be to withdraw the concurring opinion which I circulated yesterday."[64]

Personal relations were one thing. Positions on constitutional issues were another. Rehnquist did everything he could to push the law in a conservative direction. As a journalist put it, Rehnquist was "a one-man strong right wing." Rehnquist regularly stood firm when requested to "downplay" the conservative implications of his drafts. When Brennan asked for a conference discussion in a case in which Rehnquist already had five votes, Rehnquist objected to what he thought would be a pointless effort to refight a battle he had already won. Marshall called Rehnquist's response "the like of which I have not seen before." "If there are five votes to start a steam roller," Marshall continued, "then the steam roller will have to grind me under. I will not move out of the way."[65]

The steamroller could, however, grind Marshall and the liberals under, when the votes were there. *Barnes v. Glen Theatre,* decided during Marshall's final year on the Court, involved an Indiana statute against public indecency, which the city of South Bend claimed allowed it to ban theaters with nude go-go dancers.[66] A majority found that the statute did not violate the theater's free-speech rights, and Rehnquist took the opinion for himself. He faced a doctrinal problem. Well-established free-speech law was very skeptical of statutes designed to suppress speech because the speech's content leads people to think things the legislature does not want them to think. Rehnquist's first draft acknowledged that South Bend was trying to suppress erotic dancing because it *was* erotic. The regulation, that is, was based on content in exactly the way free-speech law said was most questionable. Rehnquist tried to explain how erotic content was connected to bad conduct, but no one else found his analysis persuasive. Scalia circulated a separate opinion "quite as damaging," according to Marshall's clerk, as Rehnquist's. No one else liked that one either. Eventually, Rehnquist got fed up and sent around another opinion. Where his first draft said the regulation was based on content, this one expressly said that it was not. And, because the regulation was not based on content, the city could use it without the strong evidence it would have needed under standard free-speech law for content-based regulations. Rehnquist's flexibility led him to adopt in his second draft a position he found "difficult" in his first. The bottom line, however, was the same. The regulation did not violate free speech. The second version got enough votes to fly, which was apparently all Rehnquist wanted.[67]

If Rehnquist calmed the Court down, Scalia irritated it. At one point or another during his first years on the Court, Scalia annoyed every other justice, even the mild-tempered Rehnquist. Powell thought Scalia's "volubility" was "bad manners." Believing that a justice could vote responsibly only after seeing both sides, Scalia routinely waited until proposed majority opinions and dissents were both circulated, which kept some decisions in suspense longer than Rehnquist liked. His draft opinions were full of sharp criticisms of his colleagues' work, and although he sometimes toned them down before publication, the opinions remained pointed, "almost uncivil" in Powell's eyes. Changing "Such a regime is too extravagant to be believed" to "That is not the regime the Constitution establishes" made a slight difference, but justices who read the first version knew what lay behind the second. And Scalia's way of putting his objections was bothersome. When Brennan added a note to an opinion to accommodate White, Scalia said that the note "goes over the edge." Despite the fact that he needed Brennan's vote to get a majority opinion in another case, Scalia's response to Brennan's suggestions was, "I have no idea what" the suggestions mean.[68]

The personal notes Scalia occasionally passed to his colleagues were not enough to smooth over all the feathers he ruffled. Acknowledging that Brennan and Marshall would be unable to join a draft dissent in a drug-testing case, Scalia urged that they write only a short separate dissent, in which they would say they dissented in part "for the reasons given in Justice Scalia's extragavantly good opinion—or something like that." But even Scalia's attempts at humor often had an edge, as when he referred to his "usual and seemingly inimitable practice of trying to accommodate all suggestions."[69]

Scalia gave more attention to details than most of his colleagues believed warranted. They accommodated him but found his insistence on minor changes a persistent irritant. "Although I really do not share your concerns," Stevens responded to one suggestion, he decided to make the change. In another opinion, Stevens went along with Scalia's request to omit the phrase "not without some misgivings," but, he said, "the mere fact that two or three Justices have no misgivings does not make the sentence inaccurate because I have a distinct recollection that several of us at Conference did express misgivings." When Stevens criticized a Scalia opinion for "overstat[ing]" original intent, Scalia refused to accept Stevens's proposed changes and ended up writing a dissent rather than a majority opinion. O'Connor refused to join a Scalia opinion until he omitted a phrase making fun of the possibility that defendants could object if "elderly ladies" were excluded from juries. In a case involving searches of public employees' workplaces, O'Connor found it impossible to accommodate Scalia's rigid position.[70]

When Scalia pressed White to focus more precisely on the facts of a search-and-seizure case, White called Scalia's approach "not cost-free in terms of time and effort" and asserted that "we have enough to do around here" anyway. When Scalia said that "it seems quite clear" that the Court lacked jurisdiction in another search case, White responded testily, "I am as confident as you are the other way that we have jurisdiction."[71]

Blackmun, too, got impatient with Scalia. When Scalia called a footnote in a Blackmun draft "strange," Blackmun retained it with slight modifications, saying that Scalia "read too much into" it. In another case Blackmun accommodated some suggestions from Anthony Kennedy, but, Blackmun said that if the changes did not satisfy Scalia, "his position is more extreme than I am willing to adopt." Trying to deal with competing suggestions from Scalia and Kennedy, Blackmun was told that his effort did not solve Scalia's difficulty but rather "aggravate[d] it." A flurry of letters around a 1988 Scalia draft sharply criticizing a court of appeals for ignoring what the Supreme Court had said illustrates how suspicious Blackmun was of Scalia. Blackmun "withheld" his vote "because the tone of the opinion has disturbed me." Responding to Blackmun's reference to the old barroom sign "Don't shoot the piano player; he's doing the best he can," Scalia said, "I think we have here a piano-player who doesn't play our requests," but he made some modest changes in tone. Blackmun got his back up and responded that he would never join the opinion if he thought it was too critical, because he had sat as a court of appeals judge "too long . . . to feel otherwise." Scalia was puzzled at Blackmun's reaction: "I am hurt that you chose to interpret what was meant to be a confession of error to be a criticism." While Blackmun clearly had misunderstood Scalia's intention, the misunderstanding rested on Blackmun's general suspicions of Scalia.[72]

In his first years on the Court, Scalia shifted the way the justices wrote about the use of legislative history in interpreting statutes. Scalia strongly opposed doing so, arguing that the statute itself, not what any member of Congress said about it, was the law. Most of his colleagues had a less hard-edged view of the question. In 1989 Stevens asked Scalia to insert a "rather general statement" that the Court was satisfied that a particular statute's text was an accurate reflection of its drafters' intent. Scalia responded, "I could not possibly say [that] because I truly have no idea whether that is so." O'Connor told him, "[Y]ou go too far in discounting the intent of the drafters," and Blackmun, too, was "uncomfortable with a literalist brand of statutory interpretation." The case divided the Court sharply, and Scalia gave in a bit, saying that his initial approach "seems not to be a way to win friends and influence people." Even so, Stevens refused to join the opinion, objecting to Scalia's "unwillingness to seek any guidance at all" from drafting history. In another case, Scalia lost his majority after long discussions about statutory interpretation, because Blackmun found Brennan's approach "more in line with my view of the use of legislative history."[73]

Scalia pushed his point of view on any appropriate occasion. He tried to get Stevens to change the phrase "we are unwilling to ignore" legislative history to "we nonetheless consider" it, saying that he was indeed willing to ignore legislative history but would sometimes consider it if others wanted to. When Scalia asked Brennan to change "Congress plainly did not intend" a particular meaning to "[the] Act cannot reasonably be interpreted" that way, Stevens was suspicious: "[I]t does seem to me rather strange to be unwilling to acknowledge that a search for congressional intent is an entirely appropriate part of our approach to statutory construction." Scalia called this "an unnecessary disagreement," saying that it was fine with him for the Court to refer to congressional intent. But Scalia's campaign had an effect. When Marshall drafted an opinion in 1987 saying that "legislative history is not legislation," Brennan asked him to drop the phrase because it might suggest "a more restrictive approach" than Brennan thought appropriate.[74]

Scalia's peremptory tone often annoyed Marshall. When a Scalia opinion called Marshall's analysis in a 1987 environmental case "utterly unique, not to say bizarre," Marshall replied, "I am rather puzzled by the tone of Nino's concurrence. As far as I can tell, our difference is a semantic squabble without any practical consequence. . . . I can think of absolutely no . . . case that would come out differently" based on Scalia's approach. Scalia took out the word "bizarre" and toned the concurrence down a bit, after which Stevens and O'Connor joined his opinion. In another case involving access to government information under the Freedom of Information Act, Scalia wrote Marshall a long letter, again peremptory in tone, referring to "damaging dicta" in Marshall's opinion, saying, "the principle [of the opinion] goes much too far," and suggesting two changes. Marshall accepted one but not the other. After Scalia circulated a concurring opinion making the same points, often in the same language, Marshall gave in. Scalia then withdrew his opinion, with a handwritten note: "I am very sorry for having raised any problems so late in the Term. I owe you one." After another such flap, Marshall revised his opinion, saying, "I do not believe that my language is anything but an accurate statement of the law, but if you would prefer an alternative formulation, I do not have strong enough feelings to object." Blackmun observed, "Often, over the years, I have been amused by how excited we tend to get at times against a circulating opinion. This case was an example."[75]

In 1991 Scalia's actions in *County of Riverside v. McLaughlin* led Marshall to his pithiest comment on his colleague.* The Court had to decide how promptly states had to bring people they arrested in front of a judge.[76] O'Connor led a majority to the conclusion that states ought to have forty-eight hours, particularly if, as in California, the initial appearance before the judge allowed defendants to see more of the prosecutor's case. Saying that "there is considerable confusion" in the case, Marshall asked Scalia to draft a dissent. Scalia's draft made two points: States had to bring people in front of a judge as promptly as possible, which every authority agreed could be done within twenty-four hours, and they could not justify delay by saying that defendants had been given some special protections like added discovery of the prosecutor's case. Scalia was willing to give states some leeway and insisted only that defendants be brought in front of a judge within thirty-six hours. The opinion insisted, however, that states could not "trade-off . . . promptness and additional procedural protections."[77]

---

* A law clerk once wrote Marshall, "I think Justice Scalia's dissent (for a change) is worthy of your vote. . . . Put another way, should you join the schmuck in *Schmuck?* (Just kidding, of course)." Paul to TM, undated, Marshall Papers, box 482, file 6 (Schmuck v. United States).

Kennedy initially voted with O'Connor, but Scalia's opinion led Kennedy to think that he might broker a compromise. Writing to O'Connor and Scalia, Kennedy asked whether O'Connor could say that there was a presumption that hearings could be held within thirty-six hours and that administrative reasons—but not any special procedures that were said to benefit defendants—might justify another twelve-hour delay. He noted that his position was not that different from Scalia's. Agreeing with that characterization, Scalia thought he could persuade Kennedy to convert the dissent into a majority opinion. He was "not flexible," Scalia said, on the thirty-six-hour limit. Kennedy agreed with Scalia on the dissent's two main points and, Scalia implied, ought to join it as is. Kennedy opposed what he thought were Scalia's "wooden requirements" and, rebuffed by Scalia, stood by O'Connor. She tinkered with her opinion, making it clear that forty-eight hours was an absolute limit, suggesting that individual defendants could challenge shorter delays on a case-by-case basis, and insisting that states delay as little as possible when they offered special procedures.[78]

A week and a half later, Scalia told O'Connor he was prepared to join her opinion. The other dissenters would not; Stevens said that O'Connor's forty-eight-hour period was too long, and Blackmun pointed out that O'Connor's opinion continued to maintain that a trade-off between prompt hearings and special procedures was appropriate. "OK, OK," Scalia replied. "I shall stand by those courageous and unusual enough to have joined my dissent. I shall circulate a brief revised dissent shortly—24 hours." A month later Scalia circulated the new dissent. It insisted that the Constitution required hearings within twenty-four hours—not thirty-six, as he had said before. Although Scalia had been prepared to join O'Connor's opinion a few weeks before, now he claimed that it endorsed an outrageous violation of the Constitution. Referring to the abortion cases, Scalia wrote, the Court "creates rights that the Constitution does not contain and denies rights that it does." O'Connor's opinion "eliminates a very old right indeed." Stevens was annoyed enough at Scalia's opinion that he proposed his own succinct dissent: "For the reasons stated at pages 7 through 10 of Justice Scalia's opinion, I respectfully dissent," and Marshall wrote a one-paragraph dissent referring to but not joining Scalia's. On the top of Scalia's final version, Marshall wrote, "Nuts!!!" He was frustrated that Scalia's refusal to accommodate Kennedy meant that the Court would allow hearings to be delayed an extra twelve hours. But he was also commenting on Scalia's tone of outrage at an opinion he had been prepared to join.[79]

Blackmun echoed Marshall's comment in *Riverside,* though more delicately, in a note to Scalia refusing to make some changes Scalia wanted, punning in Italian: "Nino," Blackmun wrote, "hai una grande testa, ma sei anche un gran testardo."* Scalia replied, "I don't know what 'testardo' means, but I'm sure that . . . it's nice." Perhaps: A rough translation is, "Nino, you're a smart guy, but boy are you stubborn."[80]

---

*Another note written the same year and again with a pun in Italian was, "Questa scalata non é degna di un Scalia. Scendi e vedrai piu chiaro"—roughly, though more obscurely, "This high-falutin' stuff is unworthy of a Scalia. Descend and you will see more clearly." Blackmun to Scalia, June 19, 1991, Marshall Papers, box 532, file 7 (Pauley v. Bethenergy Mines).

Scalia's appointment had been relatively uncontroversial because it was unlikely to change the Court's ideological composition. Powell's retirement in 1987 was different. By then, Powell had become the Court's stabilizing center, far more conservative than Brennan and Marshall but not aggressively pushing the Court to the right. President Reagan took the opportunity to try to complete the Court's transformation by nominating Robert Bork, probably the nation's most prominent legal conservative. Liberal interest groups mounted a furious lobbying campaign against Bork, which Marshall later called a "travesty." In Marshall's eyes, Bork was a serious person, a former solicitor general and court of appeals judge like Marshall, who had not been treated seriously by the Senate. The Republicans had lost control of the Senate in the 1986 elections, and Reagan was weakened by the ongoing Iran-contra scandal. Bork's nomination was defeated by a vote of 58–42. Reagan then proposed to nominate Douglas Ginsburg, a former Marshall law clerk who had served in the Reagan Justice Department and briefly on the court of appeals but decided against doing so when Ginsburg acknowledged that he had smoked marijuana with some of his law students at Harvard.[81]

Reagan finally settled on Anthony Kennedy, a California lawyer and lobbyist who had been named to the court of appeals by Gerald Ford in 1975. Kennedy's low-key conservatism did not provoke liberal opposition to his nomination. During his first week on the Court, Kennedy cast a key vote, which shaped Marshall's view of his new colleague. In 1976 the Court had held that a federal statute dating from 1866 prohibited discrimination in private transactions, including house sales and employment. That decision was controversial from the outset. Critics had argued that it was unnecessary, because more recent civil rights statutes adopted better approaches to race discrimination, and legally unsound, because it distorted the understanding Congress had in 1866 to reach a result that people found comfortable a century later. Suggestions for overruling the 1976 decision surfaced repeatedly inside the Court.[82]

Brenda Patterson sued the credit union that employed her for race discrimination. She claimed that her white supervisor had harassed her on the job, had given her bad job assignments, and had failed to give her chances at promotion and training that he made available to her white colleagues. She used the 1866 Civil Rights Act rather than more recent statutes because she had a better chance to get substantial damages under the older statute. The trial judge ruled that the 1866 act did not cover racial harassment on the job, and the court of appeals affirmed. The 1866 act gave African-Americans the "same right" to "make and enforce" contracts that whites had. Patterson's claim rested on the argument that the racial harassment she suffered made her employment contract different from the ones whites had, so she was not being allowed to "make" the same contract they had.[83]

Several justices were skeptical about the scope of Patterson's argument. But the Court's conference on the case centered on a different issue: Should the 1976 precedent be reconsidered? Rehnquist thought it should. White, who had dissented in the earlier case, agreed, as did O'Connor, Scalia, and Kennedy. Because the question of overruling the precedent had not been briefed or argued, Rehnquist drafted an order directing the parties to address overruling the precedent. Blackmun and Stevens wrote stinging dissents, calling the Court's decision "neither restrained, nor judicious" and suggesting that the public would see the Court's action in political terms. Rehnquist added a paragraph addressing the dissents, saying that the mere fact that the 1976 precedent helped civil rights litigants was irrelevant: "We think this is what Congress meant when it required each Justice or judge . . . to swear to 'administer justice without respect to persons, and do equal right to the poor and the rich.'" Kennedy particularly admired this paragraph and told Rehnquist that "the dissents do not sit well with me, and are most disappointing." Next to that statement, Marshall wrote, "Wow." Although Marshall, with his usual generosity, thought Kennedy "an honest, decent guy," he also found Kennedy a rigid conservative, "to the right of Rehnquist."[84]

When the case was reargued, Kennedy indicated a surprising inclination to rule for Patterson. His commitment was weak, however, and Kennedy took the opinion over after Brennan failed to work out a legal theory that would satisfy him. Refusing to overrule the precedent, Kennedy's opinion nonetheless ruled against Patterson, holding that what happened while a contract was in force did not affect a person's right to "make" a contract.[85]

In June 1990, at the end of Kennedy's first term, Brennan announced his retirement. Marshall suffered from Brennan's retirement. Brennan had been on the Court in what liberals understood as good times and bad, from the time in the late 1950s when, liberals thought, the Court came close to capitulating to McCarthyite assaults, to the high point of the Warren Court from 1962 to 1968, and then to the travails liberals experienced during the Burger and Rehnquist years. He had a sense that things would always work out well in the end. Brennan's cheerfulness, even when cases came out wrong, offset Marshall's sometimes assumed but sometimes real curmudgeonly persona. Even more, Marshall's hearing and eyesight problems made it particularly difficult for him at the conferences, where for the first time in his tenure on the Court he was first in line to present the liberal point of view. Turning eighty-two a month after Brennan's retirement, Marshall was, in his own words, "getting old and coming apart." Starting in January 1991, a few months into his first term after Brennan's retirement, Marshall discussed retiring with his doctor and his wife. They all agreed that the time had come for him to leave the Court. Marshall announced his retirement on June 27, 1991.[86]

The Court that Marshall left in 1991 was very different from the one that he had joined in 1967. The disintegration of the New Deal and Great Society coalition made it impossible for the Court to stay on the path charted by the Warren Court. Even so, much had been preserved: No one could be executed in 1991 who could not have been executed in 1967; the police could not engage in searches in 1991 that the Court had barred them from conducting by 1967; no woman or her doctor could be prosecuted in 1991 for obtaining or performing an abortion that she could have obtained in 1967.

One reason that the Court merely drifted in a conservative direction without vigorously repudiating Warren Court precedents was strong internal pressure to avoid the appearance that short-run changes in the Court's composition produced large changes in constitutional law. These concerns were most urgent in the early 1970s, with the formation of the Nixon-Burger Court, and the mid-1980s, as the

Reagan-Rehnquist Court took shape. As Paul Gewirtz, one of Marshall's law clerks, wrote in a proposed 1972 dissent that was never circulated:

> If the pronouncements of this Court on the meaning of fundamentals vary back and forth from year to year, the whole notion of fundamentals disappears. . . . We cannot exist as an institution if recent doctrine is always up for reconsideration, if every case becomes the occasion for some intimation that prior doctrine is questioned. We become too much a court of political appeal, not a court of law.[87]

The pressure could sometimes be overcome, of course, but it operated as a check on more drastic action. Byron White was the most important justice to voice this view, because he regularly did so when his colleagues knew that he disagreed with the precedents he was following. He had opposed some drastic changes early in Burger's tenure. A decade later White made the point again:

> I have been strongly opposed to the notion that the dissenting Justices in a particular case should feel free to consider overruling that case as soon as a new Justice with similar views arrives on the scene. . . . If that were the usual policy, the law would be in a shambles and the Court's authority severely diminished. . . . At least there should be some sound reason for overruling such as experience over a period of time.[88]

White's position acknowledged that more substantial changes in the Court's composition, taking place over a longer period, would justify changing the law. These institutional concerns ensured that change would occur at a measured pace.

The differences between 1967 and 1991 lay more in the constitutional vision animating the Court than in the results in any one or two cases. In 1967 Marshall could have expected the Court to continue on a path that would have provided a constitutional basis for even more of the liberal program than had been laid by then. Instead, within a few years of Marshall's arrival, the Court simply stopped moving down that path.

Marshall believed that realizing the nation's aspirations required continued movement. Having offered the nation the possibility of a liberal constitutional order, the Court abandoned its promises. When he retired, Marshall responded to a question about the liberal and conservative reaction to his retirement by saying, "President Roosevelt and Churchill both died and the war went right along." The struggle for justice would continue too. African-Americans were better off in 1991 than in 1967, but "so are the white people, better off since I sat on the Court." But, Marshall said in response to a different question, "I don't look back, I look forward." What he saw did not encourage him.[89]

3

"Assumptions About How People Live"
Working on the Supreme Court

Justice Lewis F. Powell described the Court as "nine small, independent law firms." Most of its work was done within each justice's chambers and then circulated to the rest of the Court. During Marshall's tenure, the justices engaged in relatively few person-to-person discussions of their positions on constitutional questions and almost none on broad questions of constitutional interpretation. As Rehnquist put it in 1981, "All of us know that we have some individual discussions now, but they tend to be on a two or three person basis." In part the justices' discussions were few because they had difficulty enough in handling the Court's workload. Burger's ineffectiveness as a manager meant that case discussions at the conferences were truncated. His colleagues were impatient by the time Burger had finished his rambling descriptions of the cases. Rehnquist managed the conferences more efficiently, but he simply wanted to get the votes recorded and the conferences over.[1]

Some justices, including Warren, Burger, and Brennan in his later years on the Court, prepared "talking papers" as the basis for their conference presentations.[2] Marshall did not, until his last years on the Court, when his eyesight deteriorated.* Conference discussions began with the Chief Justice's presentation and continued in order of seniority. As a result, until Brennan's retirement Marshall spoke no earlier than fourth, after the Chief Justice, Brennan, and White. When his turn came, at least three other justices had spoken, ordinarily from strongly opposed perspectives. Marshall's approach to constitutional law led him to be rather short at the conferences. Unlike some of the justices who came to the Court after him, Marshall felt no need to stake out a distinctive position or define himself and his views to his colleagues. Most of the time his views were close

---

*In late 1986, Senator William Proxmire raised questions about justices' use of official cars and drivers to transport them from their homes to the Court. Marshall used a Court police officer for that purpose, and Rehnquist, "after some rather lengthy negotiations," got Proxmire to agree that "home-to-office transportation" was legal. Legal Office to Marshal Wong, Nov. 20, 1986, Marshall Papers, box 407, file 5; TM to Rehnquist, Jan. 5, 1987, box 406, file 5, Marshall Papers; Rehnquist to conference, Sept. 17, 1987, box 435, file 2, Marshall Papers.

enough to Brennan's that he did not think it a productive use of his colleagues' time for him to spell out minor differences that mattered little in the end. He used his time at the conferences to mention the real-world dimensions of the Court's cases. When a majority voted to uphold an army ban on religious headgear in 1986, Marshall said, "I know how important this cap is to [an] orthodox Jew." In a complex case involving federal payments for aid to education, Marshall summarized the basic point: "The poor children should not suffer." He objected to a federal statute denying education aid to students who failed to register for the draft because the statute "operates against the poor." Supporting a 1983 majority vote to strike down an ordinance against loitering, in part because it gave police too much discretion to choose whom to arrest, Marshall pointed out, "Negroes face this situation every day in the street."[3]

To Marshall, the details were less important than broader themes. When the details mattered, they would be hammered out in opinions rather than in very short conversations during the conferences. And, for most of his tenure, Marshall was the most liberal justice, unlikely to influence any of his colleagues on the details anyway.

Each of the Court's law firms consisted of the justice and the law clerks. Marshall relied heavily on recommendations from judges and former law clerks in selecting his new clerks. Although Marshall sometimes joked that after assembling all the law clerk applications with the best on top, he would pick the ones on the bottom, Marshall's clerks were regularly regarded within Court circles as among the strongest as a group.[4] The people who recommended clerks to Marshall were interested in ensuring that the law clerks would be compatible with Marshall as well as up to the task. These people had little difficulty satisfying that twofold requirement, for Marshall was a hero to the large body of liberal law students during his tenure, many of whom were among their classes' best students.[5]

The law clerks formed a "clerk grapevine," as Powell called it, that let the justices know the thinking in other chambers. Marshall's clerks were particularly close to Brennan's, informing Marshall about Brennan's plans, but they usually were plugged into the whole network of clerks. Their information could assure Marshall that an opinion was likely to get Powell's vote or that it was unnecessary to prepare a dissent from a denial of review in a death penalty case because other justices would vote to hear the case.[6]

The law clerks also helped Marshall prepare for oral argument. During his first decade on the Court, Marshall had his law clerks write short memoranda describing the issues raised by petitions for review. Because the memoranda dealt with every petition for review, they usually were no longer than a page or two. Marshall then used these same memoranda to prepare for oral argument. A quick study, Marshall found the two-page memoranda enough to orient his reading of the briefs. Later, Marshall shifted his practice, joining other justices in having the clerks prepare more extensive "bench memos" dealing only with the cases the Court decided to hear.[7]

The clerks' role in drafting opinions was far more important. Most justices relied heavily on their law clerks to draft opinions by the time Marshall arrived at the Court. Justice Louis Brandeis reportedly said that "the reason the public thinks so much of the Justices of the Supreme Court is that they are almost the only people in Washington who do their own work," but within a few years of Brandeis's retirement, justices like Pierce Butler, James Byrnes, and Frank Murphy had their clerks draft "almost all of [their] justice's written work." By 1967 Brandeis's view did not provide an accurate description of the Court's internal processes.[8]

The degree to which individual justices relied on law clerks to produce draft, or even final, opinions varied among the justices. By the late 1960s, Brennan occasionally drafted opinions in some minor cases but relied on his clerks for drafts in the major ones. Burger sometimes circulated his own drafts, which his law clerks then had to wrestle into shape; one of Marshall's clerks commented "Read this and weep" on a draft Burger dissent, referring to its incoherence and not its position. Most justices outlined the main points of an opinion to their law clerks. That was often sufficient to shape the final opinion. As one of O'Connor's clerks said, "Even when you're sitting down to draft an opinion, the Justice has told you what to write. Even if the Justice isn't going to change a word, you're already pretty limited in what you can do." Justices edited the drafts they received, and, again, the degree of editorial supervision over the drafts varied. Some justices went over the drafts in detail; others inserted paragraphs into what their law clerks had produced.[9]

Rehnquist had his clerks "do the first draft of almost all cases" in his chambers, and sometimes he left those drafts "relatively unchanged." Laurence Tribe reported that "a number of opinions [he] worked on" as Stewart's law clerk "are really almost exactly as [he] drafted them," including one of Stewart's most celebrated opinions. Although Burger denied it, his "law clerks wrote his opinions, . . . and everyone knew it." Powell dictated suggestions to his clerks to add paragraphs or footnotes on particular points; as his biographer recorded, "Powell kept several clerks busy on opinions that he in an important sense 'wrote,' even when he never put pen to paper." In one case, Brennan wrote to his clerk, "I've made some suggested changes for you to consider. Incorporate what you agree with on the copy on which you are working." In another, Brennan's law clerk sent a memorandum about a draft the clerk had circulated, saying, "You are one of the few main players who hasn't seen 'the Brennan position' as I had been spreading it about." All the justices relied heavily on their law clerks, particularly for working out details; as legal scholar Bernard Schwartz said in his discussion of the Burger Court's processes, "The Justices normally outline the way they want opinions drafted. But the drafting clerk is left with a great deal of discretion on the details of the opinion, particularly the specific reasoning and research supporting the decision."[10]

Describing the drafting process is misleading if it suggests that the law clerks were real decision makers. Like his colleagues, Marshall made the decisions. Law clerks could recommend a course of action, but Marshall made up his own mind. One law clerk took "one shot at laying out why [a Rehnquist opinion] is correct before starting to work on a dissent" but ended up writing the dissent, which no other justice joined. Marshall wrote "NO!!!" on the first page of an O'Connor draft and adhered to that position despite his law clerk's statement that her approach was better than the dissenting position of Burger, which the clerk called "distressingly illegitimate."[11]

Marshall relied heavily on his law clerks for drafting once he decided what to do, and he probably edited their work less than most of his colleagues did their clerks' work. "His instructions were clear, he gave the marching orders, but he gave us leeway on how to get there," according to one clerk. He insisted that the clerks' drafts convey the passion he felt. Marshall returned a draft to one clerk several times "for failing to express in a properly pungent tone his understanding of the case."[12]

The leeway the clerks had, and their inexperience, sometimes led them into mistakes that Marshall had to correct. When Powell said that many people "may be more than a little astonished" by a clerk's footnote mentioning research asserting that Jewish prisoners in Nazi concentration camps adopted the values of their guards, Marshall immediately removed the footnote. More subtly, he replaced the phrase "I do not believe the Constitution permits this," which suggests that the Constitution's meaning depends on a justice's beliefs, with "the Constitution does not permit this," making the Constitution objective. The law clerk who drafted *Kras,* the case involving bankruptcy fees, initially wrote, "It may be easy for judges with life tenure and guarantees against a reduction in salary to think that weekly savings of less than $2 are no burden." Able to convey the anger that animated the opinion more gracefully, Marshall changed the phrase to, "It may be easy for some people to think . . . ."[13]

Marshall chose his law clerks carefully, because they had a special responsibility in dealing with his traditionalist streak.* Marshall knew that his deepest views were sometimes different from the more traditional ones he initially expressed, and he relied on his clerks to remind him when he went astray. The clerks would tell Marshall that he "couldn't" vote with Rehnquist or that he "had to" join a Blackmun opinion. The locution was inept, as Marshall regularly reminded his clerks, but the sentiment was correct: Marshall did want his law clerks to tell him that he really did not want to do what he first said. When his law clerk Martha Minow wrote a bench memo in a case dealing with a federal statute with a "Bill of Rights" for the handicapped and said that "the Bill of Rights is more than a hortatory statement," Marshall wrote "baloney" in the margin. But, when Rehnquist later circulated a draft denying that the statute created enforceable rights, Marshall responded with a letter saying that Rehnquist's view was "untenable" and that the statute was not merely "hortatory."[14]

All went well when the law clerks understood their role in reminding Marshall of his fundamental views. Sometimes, however, the clerk responsible for a case agreed with Marshall's initial impulses and began working on an opinion that, in the end, Marshall rejected. The difficulties were sometimes compounded because, although Marshall liked to argue, he did not like personal confrontations and was sometimes indirect in the instructions he gave; one law clerk referred to "reading tea leaves" in trying to figure out Marshall's position. Marshall found it difficult to

* See Chapter 9 for a discussion of Marshall's traditionalism.

direct the clerk to stop working on an opinion when a law clerk supported a position Marshall knew in his heart he should not have taken. Often these opinions simply sat on Marshall's desk, until the clerk realized that Marshall did not want the opinion to get out of the chambers.[15]

In 1973, after Marshall voted to uphold a tax credit for tuition paid to nonpublic schools, his law clerk developed a fairly elaborate argument reaching that result, but Marshall eventually voted with Powell and the majority to find the scheme a violation of the Constitution's ban on establishments of religion; the draft opinion never emerged from the chambers. And just before Marshall's retirement, a law clerk "thought" Marshall "gave [him] the go ahead to continue" working on a dissent, but Marshall joined the majority and abandoned the clerk's twenty-three-page draft.[16]

In the presidential-immunity case, law clerk Stephen Carter left his successors a fairly bitter memorandum describing Marshall's "switch at the last minute." As Carter described the case's history, Marshall voted for presidential immunity at the conference and was "adamant" in adhering to that vote. After seeing Powell's draft, which Carter said gave the president a broad immunity "based in part on what we considered a slipshod use of history and in part on a functional analysis," Marshall "instructed me (by implication) to begin work on a separate memorandum." According to Carter, Marshall "did not inform the Conference . . . , preferring to play his cards close to his vest." Carter worked hard on an opinion offering the president some immunity, but Marshall eventually changed his vote. "Consequently," Carter wrote, his work "went for nought." Carter was willing to infer an instruction to draft an opinion because he was more sympathetic to the claims for presidential immunity than Marshall turned out to be, and probably more sympathetic than Marshall was from the outset, despite Marshall's initial vote.[17]

The Court's political composition made assignments to write opinions for the majority a source of tension. A rather strong institutional norm required that the Chief Justice ensure that each justice write appoximately the same number of Court opinions. New justices typically had somewhat fewer than the average number of opinion assignments. The Court's composition had changed by the time Marshall settled in to the job, and he was considerably more liberal than the Court. As law professor Geoffrey Stone wrote, "Marshall found himself a member of an ever-dwindling, ever more frustrated liberal minority. He found himself waging a trying and for the most part unsuccessful holding action against what he must have perceived as an increasingly conservative and hostile majority. It has been a difficult and disappointing experience."[18]

The change in the Court's political coloration severely limited the opportunities Marshall had to write majority opinions in major cases. In his first term on the Court, Marshall wrote ten majority opinions, slightly fewer than the average of thirteen for all justices. In his second term, Marshall wrote thirteen majority opinions, slightly more than the average of eleven. In the course of the next five terms, when the composition of the Court changed substantially, Marshall rather consistently wrote somewhat fewer opinions than the average. Sometimes Burger assigned him majority opinions in cases in which his conference vote reflected Marshall's traditionalism, and Marshall had to decline the assignment after he settled on the liberal position he was more comfortable with. Perhaps more important, Marshall's majority opinions tended to be in technical statutory areas such as tax law rather than in the areas of civil rights and constitutional law. Justices and law clerks referred to cases in the first area as "dogs" or, as Brennan referred to one group of them in a note to Marshall, "happy, happy Indian cases." (Once when Douglas asked Brennan's advice on assigning opinions, Brennan replied, "I think Lewis [Powell] will surely like to write in an Indian case.")[19]

Brennan as senior associate justice had the authority to assign opinions when there was a liberal majority. He rarely gave Marshall assignments in these cases. Some of Marshall's clerks thought Brennan took too many of the important cases for himself. The composition of a liberal majority, however, was more important in dictating opinion assignments. Strategically, opinions had to be assigned to the "least persuaded," to lock in a liberal vote from someone who might otherwise shift to the other side when a proposed dissent was circulated. Marshall was rarely in that position.[20]

Every justice was occasionally assigned a majority opinion in which his or her views were more extreme than the rest of the majority's. Sometimes justices seized the opportunity to circulate opinions more consistent with their own views than with the conference vote. That strategy was sporadically successful, because justices gave each other a fair amount of leeway on what they described as matters of style. Sometimes, however, the more extreme opinions would not fly. In a 1983 employment discrimination case, for example, Rehnquist circulated a draft that would have made it more difficult to establish discrimination in connection with managerial jobs than with mechanical ones. Marshall circulated a dissent severely criticizing the distinction as "untenable" and "unwieldy." O'Connor and Powell, the "least persuaded" here, said they would concur only in the judgment. Rehnquist recast his approach to salvage a majority opinion, reaching the same result but focusing entirely on the precise facts of the case. In another case two years later that involved claims that a judge was biased, Stevens diplomatically told Rehnquist that his draft "indicates that your recollection of the conference consensus is a little different from mine" and proposed some language that was more generous to litigants challenging judges, which Rehnquist adopted. In another employment discrimination case, Brennan avoided a broad ruling limiting the ability of job applicants to challenge hiring practices by drafting an opinion finding that the controversy had become moot, contrary to the conference discussion.[21]

The justices' reactions to these aggressive drafts varied depending on who circulated them. Suspicions about Burger's intentions and the concern about the sloppiness of his legal analysis made many justices very careful in reading Burger's drafts. When Burger drafted an opinion in 1971 affirming a conviction in a free-speech case "to discourag[e] these 'eager beavers' who thrust constitutional issues on us prematurely," Stewart took the case away from Burger with a powerful dissent. In 1977 Stewart, Brennan, and Marshall got Burger to omit a section of an opinion that criticized the claim that barring people from covering over New Hampshire's license plate motto "Live Free or Die" was a form of symbolic speech.

After Burger made "inadequate changes" in a criminal procedure opinion in 1984, Powell "undertook to cooperate with him" and got Burger to adopt a substantially different standard. "I think our basic objective has been obtained," Powell wrote Brennan, Marshall, Blackmun, and Stevens.[22]

The justices were accustomed enough to these aggressive drafts to have some settled practices about them. As Rehnquist somewhat testily told Scalia in 1990, if the justice who was assigned an opinion ended up rejecting the conference vote, the drafter should notify the rest of the Court about his change of position, explain it in a memorandum, and see if the opinion should be reassigned. The justices prodded the drafter to change the opinion when they believed a draft went beyond the proper scope of the majority's agreement. In a 1974 case involving the scope of a person's privilege to withhold information that might be incriminating, Marshall voted with the majority to deny the privilege and was assigned the opinion. His draft described the privilege in a way that offered broader protection for a person's writing and possessions than his colleagues wanted, and Rehnquist, Powell, and Stewart all pushed him to delete the language. In a procedural case, Marshall modified his first draft to accommodate Brennan, then returned to his original position when White and Powell pointed out that Marshall's initial draft "was in accord with the vote." Writing in 1981 to limit the scope of a federal statute dealing with youthful offenders, Marshall wanted to criticize the federal prison system for failing to follow the underlying liberal policy of the statute even if they had not violated its terms, but his colleagues would not let him. *Berkemer v. McCarty* involved two episodes in which a suspect was questioned. The conference vote was to find that the second episode did not violate the suspect's constitutional right. Marshall's first draft dealt only with the first episode, thereby limiting his approval of the police conduct, but he had to redo the opinion to meet his colleagues' demands.[23]

Like everyone on the Court, Marshall would ordinarily accommodate requests to modify these aggressive drafts. He would stick with his initial drafts when he had the votes. Even when his clerk suggested that Stevens had "a valid point," Marshall noted in response, "We have 5 votes." With six votes in hand, he told O'Connor that he "would prefer not to make further adjustment" in one opinion. When O'Connor and Scalia criticized a Marshall draft for relying on an opinion Scalia said had been "effectively overruled," Marshall resisted and eventually had his way when Rehnquist joined a slightly modified opinion. In a gender discrimination case, Marshall noted "Wait" on a letter from Scalia suggesting changes; a month later, Marshall decided to leave the opinion as it stood, ending up with a plurality opinion only. When Kennedy suggested a new footnote in an opinion, Marshall reduced it to a citation, and Kennedy replied, "I suppose half a loaf (or even a single slice) is better than none."[24]

Not surprisingly, however, Marshall was occasionally irritated by his colleagues' responses to his aggressive drafts and even more so when they tried to preempt one by telling him what to do before he circulated an opinion. In 1976, when Marshall was assigned to write an opinion recognizing a prisoner's limited right to decent medical care, Marshall got annoyed at a flurry of memoranda from his colleagues insisting on limiting the right fairly severely. Marshall reported the various positions that his notes indicated the justices had taken and said that he drafted the opinion "with an effort to get some place in between all of this without abandoning my position in toto." In a similar case in which Marshall was assigned an opinion in tension with his broader views on church-state relations, Marshall resisted strong suggestions from Powell and Rehnquist to cite a case in which Marshall had dissented; Powell then wrote a separate opinion discussing the earlier case in some detail. [25]

Ideological critics such as Terry Eastland, who served as a speechwriter in the Department of Justice during the Reagan administration, criticized Marshall and some of his colleagues for their heavy use of law clerks, saying that "relying on clerks is a cheat on democratic government." Coming from a speechwriter, this was a little odd. Eastland coupled this criticism with a hint that Marshall was lazy, and something more than a hint was conveyed by the cover of the issue of the *National Review* in which the article appeared, a drawing purporting to show Marshall asleep on the bench. The *National Review* or Terry Eastland would not have liked Marshall under any circumstances, and Marshall may have decided that the people whose opinions he valued needed no more demonstration of his ability than the opinions coming from his chambers. [26]

Eastland's criticism echoed Powell's observation that Marshall sometimes seemed to him disengaged from the Court's work. Powell expressed incredulity that, in a brief conversation, Marshall had seemed to indicate that he did not know the details in one part of an important dissenting opinion that Marshall had circulated. Blackmun reported that, as Marshall's hearing became impaired, he would sometimes lean over, ask, "Harry, how did Brennan vote?" and then simply repeat Brennan's vote himself. [27]

In fact, throughout his tenure Marshall paid close attention to the Court's work. Draft opinions are covered with his short comments. Sometimes they were overall appraisals: "Not bad!" on a Rehnquist draft; a pessimistic "This will not fly!!!" on a proposed reversal of a criminal conviction; "on and on and on!!!" on a twenty-one page draft dissent from Stevens; a caustic "unadulterated BS!!" and "Wow" on draft dissents by Rehnquist and Burger in a school prayer case. Sometimes they were substantive. The notes might suggest the main lines of a separate opinion. Or they might warn, "Look out," for an opinion's treatment of precedent or ask, "What about the death penalty cases?" next to a discussion of a proposed limit on life sentences that were disproportionate to the offenses. In a case challenging a state law allowing churches to veto applications for liquor licenses in their neighborhood, Marshall noted on Burger's proposed opinion, "?? Church + state. I like plain old due process." His attention went to small matters as well. He refused to read a document that one side had sent to the Court after argument, because it was "[n]ot a joint submission." He noted on a memorandum from Rehnquist discussing whether to allow an army lawyer to argue in uniform, "What possible reason can there be for wearing a military uniform to argue in this civilian court?" When O'Connor circulated an opinion in a complex case in which she had told the conference she was "not sure" she understood the case, Marshall wrote on her draft opinion, "Wait for dissent to be sure," and later joined Brennan's separate opinion. [28]

Inside the chambers, Marshall clearly was on top of the Court's work, at least until the very end of his tenure. Critics persisted in suggesting that he "was not ideally suited to his . . . role as a Justice." Even a journalist sympathetic to Marshall wrote, "In American universities and law schools, the opinions of Thurgood Marshall aren't ranked with those of John Marshall or Louis Brandeis."* The image persisted in part because Marshall's engagement occurred inside his chambers. His colleagues, particularly in their first years with him, sometimes thought that Marshall was dominated by his law clerks, because they saw his traditionalist streak in conference corrected after his return to his chambers. Most came to understand that was how Marshall himself chose to work. As in the prisoner medical-care case, some of his more conservative colleagues occasionally may have refused to cut him the slack they gave other justices because of their concern about his involvement in the Court's processes, but, like Eastland's, their concerns were more fundamentally grounded in disagreement with the positions Marshall took. Marshall did little to combat the sense that he was disengaged, in part because he knew it was not based on reality and in part because he suspected it was based on racism. His critics had an image of what a justice should be like, of how intensely involved a justice ought to appear to be in the Court's work. Marshall did not share that image. When Burger rather pompously conformed to it, Marshall delighted in pricking the balloon, sometimes greeting Burger with, "What's shakin' Chiefy baby?"[29]

Marshall's role in prodding the Court to pay attention to the constitutional law regarding race culminated in his successful campaign to overturn *Swain v. Alabama,* a 1965 decision written by Byron White. Robert Swain was an African-American accused of rape in Talladega County, Alabama. No African-American had ever sat on a trial jury in Talladega County. Some were occasionally called for jury service, but prosecutors routinely exercised their right to exclude people without giving a reason—peremptory challenges—to exclude African-Americans. Six were called for service in Swain's case, but all were struck, and the all-white jury convicted Swain and sentenced him to death. White's opinion refused to examine the prosecutor's motives for using peremptory challenges, because that would "establish a rule wholly at odds with the peremptory challenge system."[30]

As Marshall pointed out, scholars questioned *Swain* from the start. Ordinarily, *no* government official—no bureaucrat, no judge, no governor—can make the life of an African-American worse simply because of that person's race. Yet, under *Swain,* prosecutors could deny African-Americans the right to serve on juries for just that reason and could create juries that might not give African-American defendants fair consideration. Eighteen years after *Swain,* Marshall decided that

---

*This comment underestimates the importance of Marshall's opinions in law school curricula. The two leading casebooks on constitutional law, for example, include about twenty Marshall opinions, roughly the number of opinions they have from Potter Stewart. (The count is rough because deciding whether to call an excerpt an "opinion" or not is a matter of judgment.) The other justices who served with Marshall for an extended period have more opinions in these casebooks. In part, that occurs because casebook editors favor majority opinions over concurrences and dissents, and Marshall was the author of relatively few significant majority opinions.

the time had come to overturn it. Dissenting in 1983 from a denial of review in a New York case, Marshall crafted an ingenious legal "end run" around *Swain,* which he argued, found no violation of the Fourteenth Amendment's equal protection clause. But, Marshall said, the Sixth Amendment gave defendants a right to trial by an impartial jury, which was violated when African-Americans were excluded from juries because of their race.[31]

Only Brennan joined Marshall's dissent, but Stevens wrote an unusual separate statement, which Blackmun and Powell joined. Stevens did not disagree with Marshall's legal analysis but said that he wanted more lower courts to consider the question before it would be time for the Supreme Court to reconsider *Swain.* A little more than four months later, Marshall returned to his campaign. A Mississippi prosecutor used all eight of the possible peremptory challenges to remove African-American jurors in a death penalty case. Marshall's dissent from the Court's denial of review answered Stevens's concerns by noting that five members of the Court "suspect[ed] that . . . rights are being regularly abridged." It was, Marshall thought, an abdication of judicial duty, especially in a capital case, to put off dealing with the issue.[32]

Seven months later, Marshall brought the issue up again, saying that it was "one of the gravest and most persistent problems facing the American judiciary today." Meanwhile, a lower court judge, ruling in the same New York case that Marshall had first used to attack *Swain,* found that race-based peremptory challenges did indeed violate the Constitution. Judge Eugene Nickerson, a respected trial judge, agreed that it was "unusual, to say the least," for a lower court judge "to reexamine a Supreme Court case squarely on point." But, Judge Nickerson wrote, Stevens's opinion invited lower court judges to do so. Nickerson relied on the equal protection clause. The court of appeals affirmed his result but shifted the ground to the Sixth Amendment, as Marshall had suggested.[33]

That decision was enough to get the Supreme Court to reconsider *Swain* in *Batson v. Kentucky.* Batson was charged with burglary; the prosecutor used peremptory challenges to remove all four African-Americans from the jury. When the justices discussed the case, they had to decide whether to rely on the equal protection clause or the Sixth Amendment. Because the equal protection clause was centrally concerned with race, that seemed the cleaner route, but using it would have required the Court to overrule *Swain.* The Sixth Amendment theory, however, might reach quite broadly, because it required an "impartial" jury that was a cross section of the community. That theory therefore focused on the composition of the jury that actually was seated, rather than the reasons for a lawyer's decision to exclude someone from the jury. As Brennan put the problem, the equal protection analysis "would be narrower and more closely tailored to the problem" and "would also avoid potentially serious difficulties in defining what groups should be cognizable under the fair-cross section requirement." A strong requirement that a jury be a cross section of the community might lead to arguments for proportional representation on juries.[34]

After a confused presentation of the competing legal theories by Burger, Brennan urged his colleagues to decide the case on equal protection grounds and overrule *Swain.* White agreed, saying that he did not think the Sixth Amendment approach "can possibly work." Marshall went along, but he wanted to go even further and ban all peremptory challenges. How could anyone tell, he worried, "whether [a] strike is racially motivated"? All that mattered to Marshall was to be clear on whether the Court's theory would be equal protection or the Sixth Amendment, not the precise manner in which an equal protection theory would be articulated. Both Blackmun and Powell agreed that the Court should overrule *Swain*. By this time it was clear that *Swain* was doomed, and the justices started to discuss whether their rule would bar defense attorneys from exercising race-based peremptory challenges. Because *Batson* did not raise that issue, however, the discussion was inconclusive.[35]

Powell wrote the Court's opinion finding a constitutional violation. Marshall prepared a separate opinion congratulating the Court for its "historic step," but he pointed out that the Court's analysis would not end racial discrimination in jury selection. Under the Court's analysis, Marshall said, defendants had to establish a "prima facie" case that an African-American was excluded because of his or her race. But they would be hard-pressed to do so "unless the challenges are . . . flagrant." And, when prosecutors were questioned about their reasons for excluding jurors, it would be easy for them to "assert facially neutral reasons," which the courts could hardly "second-guess." Such reasons might not be outright lies, because the ban on race-based challenges "requires [prosecutors] to confront and overcome their racism on all levels." Without being consciously aware of it, prosecutors might say that they excluded a juror as "sullen," when they would not have found a white juror with exactly the same demeanor similarly sullen.[36]

Brennan was concerned about Marshall's opinion. Praising the opinion as "a powerful warning of the ways in which the Court's opinion may be evaded . . . and as an eloquent reminder of the lingering problem of unconscious prejudice," Brennan thought the opinion "might inadvertently help an unscrupulous prosecutor." He worried that "we might accidentally lose some of the ground that you and I have fought long and hard to attain" and suggested some changes in Marshall's opinion to avoid narrow readings of the Court's holding. "You may well be right," Brennan told Marshall, "that the goal the Court seeks to achieve . . . can be circumvented by prosecutors and lower courts, yet, shouldn't we at least make it as difficult as possible for them to do so?"[37]

A few days later, Marshall replied, declining Brennan's suggestions. "I see no reason to be gentle in pointing . . . out" that the Court's "approach will by its nature be ineffective in ending racial discrimination in the use of peremptories." He "doubt[ed] that pulling my punches would make the situation any better." A month later, before the opinion was announced, Marshall circulated a newspaper series from Dallas with the headline, "Race Bias Pervades Jury Selections." When the opinion was announced, Burger and Rehnquist dissented. Marshall scrawled "NO!!" in the margin next to Burger's assertion that the Court's opinion would undermine all peremptory challenges. Marshall disagreed with Burger's assessment of the majority opinion but also disagreed with Burger's desire to preserve peremptory challenges. Marshall's experiences as a trial lawyer convinced him, though not his colleagues, that racial discrimination could not be eliminated unless the Court took the large step of eliminating all peremptory challenges. Once again, he reminded his colleagues of "the difference between the law on paper and the law in action" and, as Harvard law professor and Marshall law clerk Randall Kennedy put it, demonstrated his "commitment to speaking his mind even at the price of isolation in the short run."[38]

O'Connor's tribute to Marshall eloquently described how Marshall's stories "personally affected" her. After Marshall's retirement, she wrote, she sometimes caught herself "looking expectantly for his raised brow and his twinkling eye, hoping to hear, just once more, another story that would, by and by, perhaps change the way I see the world." Recounting one of Marshall's stories about a death penalty case, O'Connor noted, however, that she "disagreed with Justice Marshall about the constitutional validity of the death penalty." O'Connor's tribute captures the difficult position Marshall found himself in. Except for his first few years on the Court, Marshall was at the margins of the debates within the Court. He was, O'Connor said, "a man who knew the anguish of the silenced and gave them a voice." The conservative Court on which he served listened and then pretty much went on with its business.[39]

4

"Unless Our Children Begin to Learn Together"
Desegregating the Schools

From Lyndon Johnson's perspective, Thurgood Marshall was the right man at the right time for the Supreme Court not only because he was the nation's most prominent African-American lawyer but arguably because he was the lawyer most qualified for a position on the Supreme Court. Marshall stood for the law as the African-American's best hope for progress when the civil rights movement had turned from the courts to social protest activities in the streets. Marshall wholeheartedly endorsed the domestic programs of the War on Poverty as Johnson's solicitor general. Perhaps more important, he criticized Martin Luther King, Jr., for "leading the movement in the wrong direction" by linking the movement for African-American advancement to opposition to the Vietnam war. He opposed the black power movement, saying that he was "afraid our young people are getting the wrong people to be their heroes" and that "if you believe like Mohammed Ali that every man who is black is right, then I am against you."[1] Marshall was, of course, acting as a player on the administration's team in making these speeches, but they reflected his own views as well. Marshall continued to hope that constitutional law would promote civil rights as the Supreme Court confronted questions of school desegregation during his tenure, but the Court's decisions increasingly suggested that Marshall's hopes were misplaced.

Marshall regularly spoke optimistically of the coming era of desegregated education after the Supreme Court invalidated school segregation in *Brown v. Board of Education*. Very little desegregation had occurred in the Deep South by the time he left the NAACP in 1961, however. The Supreme Court stayed away from desegregation cases after announcing its "all deliberate speed" formula in 1955. Its hesitation arose in part from concern over the political limits on the Court's ability to insist on substantial desegregation in the Deep South and in part from Justice Felix Frankfurter's misplaced belief that the Court could induce desegregation by appealing to the "better" class of white Southerners. In the Deep South, however, deliberation meant inaction.

By the late 1960s, the justices had become impatient with the Deep South's recalcitrance. They also benefited from a changed political environment: The enactment of major civil rights acts in 1964, 1965, and 1968 demonstrated that the nation as a whole had the political will to support more aggressive action against segregation. The Civil Rights Act of 1964, in particular, gave federal executive officials substantial weapons, through the threat of cutting off federal funds for segregated schools.

Ironically, the fundamental issues changed just as the Supreme Court became willing to take up the question of desegregation once again. The decade of resistance transformed the meaning of desegregation in ways that became clear only after Marshall took his seat on the Court. The new meaning of desegregation, in turn, suggested that the constitutional problem of segregation was no longer confined to the South. A new era of resistance began as desegregation efforts moved north.

In *Green v. New Kent County,* decided in 1968, the Court took the first major step in giving desegregation a new meaning.[2] It invalidated a county's freedom-of-choice desegregation plan allowing students to choose the school they wished to attend. New Kent County, outside Richmond, Virginia, was a rural county with little residential segregation. It had two high schools, and a neighborhood school plan would have led to substantial integration. While the freedom-of-choice plan was in effect, no white students chose to attend the previously black school, and only 15 percent of the African-American students chose to attend the previously white schools. As Justice Brennan told his colleagues, the "purpose of *Brown* [was] to break down segregation." As he saw it, "[t]here are alternatives that will do it," and the board therefore could not "ignore" the neighborhood school plan in favor of a freedom-of-choice plan. When the opinion was about to be announced, Chief Justice Warren sent Brennan a note, "When this opinion is handed down, the traffic light will have changed from *Brown* to *Green*. Amen!"[3]

Green's unanimity concealed serious analytic problems that later cases brought into the open. The Court had never really resolved for itself, much less for lower courts, what "desegregation" meant. It might mean the elimination of race as the basis for pupil assignments, whether that basis was openly stated or studiously concealed. Or it might mean the accomplishment of a substantial degree of biracial attendance in most schools. Judge John Parker of South Carolina posed the question in a phrase that became the rallying cry for desegregation opponents: "[T]he Constitution," Parker wrote, "does not require integration. It merely forbids discrimination," by which Parker meant "the use of governmental power to enforce segregation."[4]

One main strategy for resisting desegregation involved pupil assignment policies that supposedly assigned students to schools without regard to race.[5] As implemented, however, these policies were "gerrymanders," accomplishing racial separation without explicitly relying on race. The justices came to believe that these policies were merely facades behind which race discrimination continued. The question then arose: Were other responses to the Court's rulings similar facades? *Green* seemed to say they were. Even though students nominally made individual decisions to attend particular schools, the Court held, the pattern of results showed that the freedom-of-choice plan perpetuated race discrimination.

Although it did not say so openly, *Green* suggested that a board could not adopt a freedom-of-choice plan in good faith, at least when the plan's result reproduced the segregated conditions that existed before 1954 and when a reasonable alternative was available that would have produced more integration. This point could easily be made in *Green*'s factual setting: Students of both races would have attended each high school in substantial numbers if the school board assigned students to neighborhood schools. On this interpretation of *Green,* the degree of actual integration simply signaled that race discrimination still affected school board decisions. The Court never said, however, that it relied on the pattern of results to support an inference of bad faith; perhaps the justices still recollected Frankfurter's belief that school boards represented the best in the white South and could be nursed along if the Court expressed enough sympathy with their problems. With the Court reluctant to talk openly about bad faith, the next step was almost inevitable (and unobservable): A low degree of actual integration became more than a signal but, instead, a demonstration that the Constitution continued to be violated.

According to *Green,* the freedom-of-choice plan was a "deliberate perpetuation of the unconstitutional dual system." School boards, it said, now had an "affirmative duty to take whatever steps might be necessary to convert to a unitary system in which racial discrimination would be eliminated root and branch." That duty could be satisfied only by a plan that "prove[s] itself in operation."[6]

Justice Black initially voted to uphold the freedom-of-choice plan in *Green,* but he eventually joined the majority. Black never believed that white Southerners would accept substantial biracial attendance at schools.[7] All he wanted was for white Southerners to demonstrate their adherence to the constitutional antidiscrimination norm by acting in good faith to eliminate race as a basis for public decisions. By blurring the line between using the pattern of results as a basis for inferring bad faith and using the pattern as a basis for an independent determination of unconstitutionality, *Green* posed problems for Black—and, it turned out later, for other justices.

The Court's next confrontation with desegregation remedies saw more strains among the justices, this time caused by Chief Justice Burger's inept handling of the Court's work. His colleagues slapped Burger down, but the changing composition of the Court began to have its effect.

The issue in *Alexander v. Holmes County Board of Education* was simply one of timing, not of what sorts of plans boards had to propose.[8] The Court of Appeals for the Fifth Circuit, with jurisdiction over desegregation cases in the Deep South, endorsed the guidelines developed by the Department of Health, Education, and Welfare for determining when federal funds could be denied school districts, and the court took them to indicate what the Constitution required as well. In July 1969, the appeals court ordered the department to submit desegregation plans for thirty-three Mississippi school districts, to take effect in September. Pursuing its Southern strategy, the Nixon administration moved to delay the order's effective date. At the end of August the court of appeals agreed, postponing the date for submission of plans until December. Because it was unlikely that plans submitted in December could be implemented in the middle of a school year, this decision would have delayed desegregation until September 1970—fifteen years after *Brown II*.

The civil rights plaintiffs asked Black to override the Fifth Circuit's last order and thereby restore the September date. Because the issue was only one of timing, Black was sympathetic. But, writing as a single justice, he refused to overturn the "deplorable" order of the court of appeals. He urged the plaintiffs to seek review by the full Court, to "do away with [the 'all deliberate speed' formula] completely."[9]

The Court granted the plaintiffs' petition for review on October 9, 1969, and heard argument in the case only two weeks later. After the argument, Black told his colleagues that he had always opposed the "all deliberate speed" formula and would not again endorse it. Black would have insisted on immediate desegregation; Brennan thought that no more than two weeks should be allowed for compliance with desegregation plans to be submitted immediately, while John Marshall Harlan would have been even more flexible. These were not large differences, however. The justices agreed that Burger would draft an order announcing the Court's conclusion.[10]

Burger met with Harlan and White to block out the order.[11] The first draft was circulated on October 24, the day after the Court's conference. Burger drafted a short opinion instead of a simple order. It began with a comment that "the Attorney General [had] urged" ending segregation before the beginning of the 1970 school year. It gave the court of appeals until mid-November to enter its order regarding "interim relief"—not much sooner than that court's initial December 1 deadline. The deadline for implementation was vague: "at the earliest possible time and date" after the court's action. Burger's cover note said that he had avoided specifying "any 'outside' date"—that is, a statement that the boards should act no later than some date—"because of the risk that it could have overtones which might seem to invite dilatory tactics."

None of Burger's colleagues thought he had done what they wanted, and most started to work on separate draft orders. Harlan objected to the comment about the Department of Justice: "I think it undesirable to blink the fact that the Government stands in opposition to the central and only issue in the case before us." Brennan's order would have said that "'all deliberate speed' is no longer constitutionally permissible" and that the court of appeals should immediately order what was needed to achieve immediate termination of any dual school system based on race or color. Black carried through on an earlier threat to dissent if anyone wrote an opinion rather than a brief order. His proposed dissent criticized Burger's order because it "revitalizes the doctrine of 'all deliberate speed.'" It would be "disastrous" to continue "for one more day" an unconstitutional dual school system. "The time has passed for 'plans' and promises to desegregate."[12]

Marshall "attempt[ed] [a] compromise," continuing to refer to "interim" relief and requiring only "reasonable means for achieving . . . immediate termination." Marshall's draft, though, was tighter than Burger's, setting an "outside date": Schools had to be desegregated by December 31, 1969. Marshall wanted the

Court to insist on *complete* desegregation by a specific date. In exchange, he would not insist on "immediate" desegregation, which his colleagues seemed to think meant desegregation in late October.

On October 27, the justices met again. Burger had revised his proposed order, which now would require desegregation "forthwith"—the term Marshall urged the Court to adopt when he argued *Brown II* in 1955. Burger's continued insistence on keeping his comment on the administration position bothered the other justices. Burger promised to circulate another revision, which came around late the same afternoon. Burger was never one to discern subtle differences between his position and those of his colleagues. His cover note said that he had been helped by Marshall's draft, "which was very much like what I had initially submitted." In fact, the proposed order differed significantly from Marshall's. True, it did repudiate "all deliberate speed," and it specified that the schools should "begin to operate as a unitary system" in November. It omitted Marshall's trade-off, however, setting no date for the completion of desegregation.

Even worse, Burger failed to appreciate that his colleagues wanted a crisp order to make it completely clear that the courts could no longer tolerate any further delays. To accomplish their intention, the justices wanted to issue only an order, with no opinion. As Black had put it, "There has already been too much writing and not enough action in this field. Writing breeds more writing, and more disagreements, all of which inevitably delay action." Despite these expressions, Burger circulated a draft opinion with the third revised order.

Burger's sense of the case's importance is suggested by the fact that he proposed to follow the extraordinary procedure in *Cooper v. Aaron,* the Little Rock school desegregation case, in which the Court's opinion listed the names of the participating justices. He could not have known, of course, that some members of the Court had had misgivings about that procedure even in *Cooper* itself.[13] His draft opinion was so lame, however, that it could only have confirmed his colleagues' impression that Burger had an inflated sense of his own stature inside the Court and out. Although his colleagues wanted a clear endorsement of immediate desegregation, Burger would have had them say, "In the circumstances we have no doubt that this will present problems and difficulties," because the desegregation plans were drafted under severe constraints of time and lack of information. The draft opinion also said that the justices "hope[d]" that the "heavy burdens on pupils and teachers alike will . . . be more than offset by the fulfillment now to some of these pupils of promises long unkept." The concluding sentiment was worth expressing, but its rhetorical force was undercut by the statement about "problems and difficulties"; the draft read as if the Court were being reluctantly dragged to endorse immediate desegregation notwithstanding its problems, rather than as if the Court were finally coming around to vindicating fundamental constitutional rights. Brennan read the draft as an attempt by Burger "to save Nixon" from a confrontation with the Court: Nixon, the draft's tone suggested, had correctly understood how difficult desegregation would be, although perhaps his administration had ultimately come down on the wrong side of a hard question.

Brennan thought the draft opinion "obscured" the message that "all deliberate speed" was dead. Black objected to specifying any dates at all, believing they would give lawyers the chance to seek further delay beyond the deadline by citing new information not available to the Court. Black also thought that no one really believed desegregation would occur by a specific date. The best the Court could do, Black thought, was use the word "immediate" and leave the rest to the lower courts.

Next Brennan circulated a revised order, and Stewart sent around a draft opinion. Brennan thought the Court should state its message "in the briefest and plainest possible words." His draft order began with a short statement that desegregation according to "'all deliberate speed' is no longer constitutionally permissible. The obligation of every dual school system is to desegregate now." The court of appeals should have "directed that each school system begin immediately to operate as a unitary system within which no person is to be barred from any school because of race or color." These phrases survived into the final order. Black and Douglas signed on to this draft. Harlan did, too, although he said that he would have preferred to specify an "outside date" as Marshall had, to prevent "dilatory tactics."

Stewart's draft opinion said that "further delay . . . will not be tolerated" and specified an "outside date" of November 15, 1969. Not surprisingly, Harlan indicated that he could join Stewart's opinion. Having counted the votes, Marshall knew that it was "impossible to get unanimity on cut-off dates" and on that assumption was willing to join Brennan.

Burger, too, could count. He met with Brennan and basically adopted Brennan's draft, recirculating it under his own name on the afternoon of October 28. In light of all that had happened, it suggests something about Burger's obtuseness that his cover memorandum said that the final draft "returns to what I proposed to the Conference except (a) the preamble is altered and (b) the dates are omitted."

Although only a few days had passed since oral arguments, the justices were now impatient to get the order issued. After all, what had divided them was a dispute over just how immediate "immediate" desegregation would have to be, and those who wanted the schools to start the process right away thought that every day of delay undermined their position. Harlan went along with the Brennan-Burger revision because the divisions had been reduced to "pure semantics." Both White and Stewart had "substantial misgivings" about the order, taking it to suggest that "all deliberate speed" had been abandoned only to be replaced by an equally defective standard of "as soon as possible." The order was issued on October 29.

Two things stand out about the Court's deliberations in *Alexander*. The justices were divided by differences in their understanding of what it meant to abandon "all deliberate speed" in favor of immediate desegregation. On the surface it seemed as if the differences were over timing, but underneath they were over the meaning of desegregation. Black and Burger thought that "immediate desegregation" meant, "Do *something* right away to eliminate segregated schools." They rejected a cutoff date in part because they assumed that school boards would begin to do something at the latest date possible, that is, the cutoff date. They rejected a cutoff date as well because they knew that when the cutoff date arrived, plaintiffs would ask what exactly had been done. And they were confident that by late 1969 the patterns of racial attendance at schools would not be that much different from what they were in early 1969, no matter what the school boards had done. Black's misgivings about *Green* meant that he would not be terribly troubled, as long as he was sure that the school boards had indeed done something in good faith.

In contrast, Burger, not having participated in *Green*, may have taken it quite seriously. Given *Green*'s apparent insistence on results, the prospect loomed of saying that the results achieved by "immediate desegregation" were inadequate and that even more aggressive steps to desegregate would have to be taken. Sensitive to the Nixon administration's legal and political strategy, the Chief Justice could not have been happy.

Harlan and Marshall had the same understanding, but for them the cutoff date was affirmatively desirable precisely because it would force the Court to face up to the ambiguities about what desegregation meant. They believed that the Constitution demanded that school boards fully abandon the racial criterion for student assignment and do so in good faith; that is why they went along with *Green*. They might eventually have divided over how often a pattern of results demonstrated the existence of bad faith, but in *Alexander* that issue was not before them. A cutoff date meant that "desegregation" had to be completed by a specified date. When that date arrived, the Court would have to decide what desegregation meant.[14]

Ever the politician, Brennan sought the middle ground, which in this case meant perpetuating ambiguity. The differences between Brennan and Burger were largely rhetorical: how to convey the sense that the Court really did mean "immediate" desegregation even though it did not know what desegregation really meant. Rhetoric mattered in the charged political setting of 1969, with the administration for the first time since 1955 asking to slow the desegregation process. Indicating even indirectly that the Court was roughly in line with the Nixon administration's position would have given rise to the view that "immediate" meant "some time soon," and Burger alone wanted that.

For all this, the Court's internal discussions of *Alexander* were rather restrained. In part, of course, that resulted from the compressed time frame. With justices and clerks churning out one draft in the morning and responding to drafts from other chambers in the afternoon, there was little time to focus on personal relations or feelings. But in part the restraint occurred because the justices were learning about Burger's managerial style. When Burger's cover memoranda repeatedly showed that he failed to understand what the other justices were concerned about, the inference that he really did not understand was far stronger than the inference that he was a Machiavellian manipulator seeking to sneak an endorsement of the Nixon administration's position past his colleagues.

This pattern was to repeat itself, most notably in *Swann v. Charlotte-Mecklenburg School District,* decided after a long debate inside the Court in April 1971.[15] The Court unanimously endorsed extensive transportation remedies—busing—in a school desegregation case. In *Alexander* a dispute about the timing of desegregation remedies concealed a disagreement about the meaning of "desegregation"; in *Swann* a dispute about the scope of those remedies concealed the same disagreement.

The problem originated with *Green.* Suppose a board acted in good faith to eliminate race as a criterion for student assignment, for example by assigning students to the schools nearest their homes. In New Kent County, a neighborhood schools policy would have produced substantial integration because there was little residential segregation. What about a neighborhood school policy in a system with substantial residential segregation? The easy way out would have been to find that school boards adopting such policies were acting in bad faith. But the history of neighborhood school policies was so well established that it would have been a true slap in the face to tell Southern school boards that their prior resistance to desegregation barred them from adopting a neighborhood school policy that educators throughout the country regarded as educationally sound.

Green pointed in two directions. One was that results indicated good or bad faith. The other was that results were the measure of continuing constitutional violations. A Memphis case gave the Court a chance to choose between these two meanings. The plaintiffs sought more extensive relief than the trial court ordered. The court of appeals refused to grant the new relief, finding that the city would achieve a "unitary system" in which segregation had been completely eliminated as soon as it complied with the district court's orders. *Alexander,* it said, was therefore inapplicable to Memphis. According to Brennan's law clerks, the case "was heralded in the press as an occasion for the C[our]t to decide what is required for a school system to be unitary."[16]

When the plaintiffs sought Supreme Court review in 1970, the initial vote to grant review was 4–3.[17] This vote was misleading, however: Only Burger really wanted to take the case "to clear up what seems to be a confusion, genuine or simulated," about *Green.* Brennan "wanted the C[our]t to avoid reaching the issue" because "[t]here was always the risk that any realistic definition . . . would have appeared to be a retreat from Brown [and] that any other type of definition would have been simply impractical (given the views of whites)." Harlan, Stewart, and White were uncertain enough that they waited to see what Brennan might produce. He drafted a proposed per curiam opinion vacating the court of appeals decision, which Stewart and White approved with minor changes. Brennan adopted a position that time would show was strategically the best the liberals could do as the Court's composition changed. He focused on the district court's finding that the system was still segregated. That finding, he argued, was supported by substantial evidence and should not have been rejected by the court of appeals. With such a finding in hand, *Alexander* remained relevant to Memphis.[18]

Burger concurred in the result, but he was not happy. "At some point," he wrote, "we should resolve some of the basic practical problems including whether any particular racial balance must be achieved as a constitutional matter, to what extent school districts and zones may or must be altered and to what extent busing is compelled as a constitutional requirement." As it turned out, his colleagues did not want to resolve those basic questions in *Swann* either.

The Charlotte-Mecklenburg school district was one of the largest in the country, as a result of the consolidation of the city and county districts in 1960.[19] By 1965 only token desegregation had occurred in the district: A handful of African-American students attended schools with a white majority, and a smaller handful of whites attended black-majority schools. Prodded by local activists and concerned about federal pressure, the school board developed a desegregation plan that would have closed some African-American schools in the county area, created neighbor-hood school assignments, and allowed "freedom of choice" for students able to provide their own transportation. Federal district judge J. Braxton Craven ap-proved the plan in 1965, finding that the board had no duty to "increase the mixing of the races" in the school population.[20]

Green changed the legal landscape, and the NAACP's lawyers reopened the case in 1968. Although more desegregation had occurred by then, more than two-thirds of the system's African-American students still attended all-black schools. Relying on the interpretation of *Green* that imposed an affirmative obligation on school boards to eliminate segregation "root and branch," district judge James McMillan concluded that *Green* required—or, as it turned out, at least allowed him to require—more substantial steps. In 1970 he adopted a proposal initially designed by one of the plaintiffs' experts. The plan involved pairing African-American and white schools, attendance zones extending from the city outward to the suburbs and the county, and—as a result—substantial student busing. The aim, Judge McMillan wrote, was to achieve ratios of whites to African-Americans in each school that roughly approximated the ratio in the entire district.

The court of appeals affirmed the parts of McMillan's order dealing with junior high and high schools, but it remanded the parts dealing with elementary schools. According to the court of appeals, the Constitution required district judges to enforce "reasonable way[s] of eliminating all segregation," but requiring as much busing as Judge McMillan's order did in elementary schools was not reasonable.

The justices voted unanimously to hear the plaintiffs' challenge to the reversal of the elementary school order and stayed the effect of the court of appeals deci-sion. As a result, McMillan's order would be implemented while the Court consid-ered *Swann*. The case attracted substantial public attention, and the Court put it on an accelerated schedule, hearing argument on the Court's first day of oral argument during the 1970 Term.[21]

As in *Alexander*, the impetus to question *Green's* meaning came from Burger and Black, while the impetus to evade the answer came from Brennan and Stew-art. As he had in *Alexander*, Burger evoked the Court's traditions, this time suggesting that because the case was as important as *Brown*, the justices should simply discuss it without taking a vote. He wondered whether "any particular demo[graphics] are either required or prohibited" by the Constitution. For him, *Brown* created "a right to be free from discrimination," and the "[r]acial composi-tion of a unit" helped provide "evidence of discrimination." He was bothered by what seemed to him the "rigidity" of McMillan's use of racial ratios. Black reit-erated his view that "[i]t's foolish to think that this question will be solved in our own or our children's lifetime." As he consistently had done, Black was resigned to a rule of purely formal nondiscrimination: "[T]here was to be no legal discrimina-tion on account of race." A neighborhood school policy did not violate that princi-ple.[22]

To varying degrees, all the other justices disagreed with these points. As they stated their positions, a consensus apparently emerged. Rigid racial ratios were not required and probably were impermissible. Some one-race schools might remain even in fully desegregated districts. Marshall noted, "There's no such thing as freedom of choice for Negro children in the South." Overall, the justices agreed, district judges had a great deal of discretion to determine what was needed to eliminate segregation. The proper question was whether McMillan's order was within that broad range of discretion. And, they agreed, it was. There were some differences on the margin: Harlan and recently appointed Harry Blackmun would have preferred an opinion providing some detailed guidance about the proper exercise of discretion, and Blackmun was "worried about continuing judicial surveillance"; Brennan argued that *Green* required substantial integration. The tenor of the discussion was that McMillan had not erred and that the court of appeals should not have modified his order.[23]

Again, Burger's peculiar view of his role impeded the development of an opinion. Burger believed the Chief Justice should speak for the Court in such an important case even though his statements to his colleagues strongly suggested that he disagreed with McMillan. He therefore drafted a "memorandum" to serve as the starting point for a Court opinion. He counseled his colleagues to defer writing separately "until we have exhausted all other efforts to reach a common view." In "emphasiz[ing] the importance of our attempting to reach an accommodation" and making his draft the starting point, Burger gained some strategic leverage: His colleagues would have to move toward him by suggesting places in his draft that should be modified. Once again, it was easy for his colleagues to suspect Burger's motives. And, once again, Burger's motives were almost certainly not Machiavellian: He was trying in his fumbling way to play the role he believed a Chief Justice should play.

Burger's draft ended up remanding the case to McMillan, but it was hardly an endorsement of what McMillan had done. For example, Burger narrowly construed *Green* and wrote that "some of the problems we now face arise from viewing *Brown I* as imposing a requirement for racial balance, *i.e.*, integration, rather than a prohibition against segregation." Although hardly inaccurate, this statement was a red flag to those who recalled Parker's similar statements, and Brennan scrawled "No" next to this passage on his copy of Burger's draft.[24] Prodded by arguments that lower courts could consider the policies pursued by government agencies other than school boards—siting decisions by public housing authorities, for example—in deciding whether the "prohibition against segregation" had been violated, Burger confined his focus to school boards. He would not use desegregation as a tool for larger schemes of social engineering: "The elimination of racial discrimination in public schools is a large enough burden. . . . Too much baggage can break down any vehicle."

Then Burger turned to the trial judge's discretion to order a remedy. Here, too, the tone was grudging: "Populations, pupils or misplaced schools cannot be moved as simply as earth by a bulldozer, or property by corporations." McMillan's order, the draft opinion said, had "strong intimations" that he insisted on "fixed mathematical racial balance." Although racial composition might be "one relevant step," it could not be a rigid requirement. Nor could a district judge insist that all one-race schools be eliminated. District judges could change attendance zones and order busing, but they had to be cautious. These were "not impermissible tool[s]." The aim was to "achieve as nearly as possible that distribution of students and those patterns of assignments that would normally have existed had the school authorities not previously practiced discrimination." Exactly how that might be determined was obscure, but "reasonable" determinations by district judges would suffice. On busing, the draft emphasized that "the age of the students" was an important consideration in deciding how much travel time should be required. This consideration seemed to suggest that the court of appeals was right to reverse the busing order for elementary students while affirming the one for students in upper schools, but the draft nonetheless remanded the case to Judge McMillan.

Everyone else on the Court disagreed with the tenor of Burger's draft. Marshall sent Burger a draft opinion saying explicitly at every point that McMillan had not abused his discretion. Harlan had already sent him a draft opinion saying that "racially identifiable school[s]" were inconsistent with *Brown I*. District judges could use "a remedial criterion based on results" to determine whether segregation had been eliminated, and Harlan would explicitly have endorsed "mathematical racial balancing." Douglas responded to Burger's draft by insisting that it misinterpreted McMillan's order. The judge had not required "racial balance," Douglas wrote. Further, he would not ignore discriminatory actions by other government agencies in dealing with segregated schools.

Brennan was stern. Burger's draft was, in places, "wrong." It had a negative tone when what was needed was a "positive" opinion. Brennan pushed for "specific[]" and "positive guidelines." As he had said in conference, the goal was "to achieve substantial integration." In seeking that goal, district courts could "take race into account in assigning pupils," they could use racial ratios as "a goal or rule of thumb," they could use all the techniques McMillan had used, and they should regard busing as "only an incident of the remedial techniques . . . and [it] should not be viewed as a separate issue."

Stewart expressed "serious reservations" about some parts of Burger's draft, in particular that the draft suggested that a school board might not be allowed to seek racial balance in its schools. But, like Burger, he would not have used a school desegregation case to get at the effects of housing discrimination. He was less certain than Douglas and Brennan that McMillan had used racial ratios merely as a starting point or rule of thumb. He thought that McMillan might erroneously have believed that it was impermissible to have racially identifiable schools, even those resulting from housing patterns. As Stewart saw it, these were modest qualifications to his overall position, that McMillan had been largely correct and that Burger's draft was too grudging in acknowledging the district judge's remedial powers. The qualifications, though, helped stiffen Burger's resistance on these points as he yielded on others.

After showing a proposed opinion to Brennan and Marshall, Stewart sent it to Burger. Although Stewart would not have recognized "a substantive constitutional right to attend a school having a particular racial mixture," once a substantive constitutional violation had been established—as it had been—the only question was whether the district judge's remedial order was within his discretion. Stewart then shifted gears, addressing the claim that *Brown* and *Green* required no more than that school boards ignore race in making student assignments. That claim supported pure neighborhood zoning. But, Stewart wrote, "[v]iewed as a remedy for decades of self-imposed segregation, colorblind neighborhood zoning . . . is closely analogous to the 'freedom of choice' plans" in *Green*. Where neighborhood zoning would reproduce the prior pattern of racial separation, it was "not enough to meet the affirmative remedial duty of the local board." After going through a list of possible remedies—most of which McMillan had used—Stewart described them as "an appropriate part of . . . the district judge's inventory of means to the end of disestablishing the dual system."

Burger misunderstood the messages he was getting. As he put it in the cover memorandum he sent around with a revised draft, he knew that "some points [his colleagues had made] were in conflict with [his] own position." He apparently believed that he could firm up what seemed to him support for *his* position by stating it even more clearly and thereby weaken the position of those who disagreed with him. That belief misread the comments he had received. Any sensitive reader would have understood that the justices Burger might have counted on—Harlan and Stewart in particular—were politely but firmly disagreeing with him. The politeness was the form, the disagreements the substance; Burger apparently believed that the disagreements were marginal and that the politeness indicated fundamental agreement on his central points.

Burger's second draft did little to accommodate his critics. He did adopt Stewart's point that school boards could assign students to schools in appropriate ratios "to prepare students to live in a pluralistic society." But, he wrote, federal courts had "no such roving, at-large powers."* And, responding to suggestions from Stewart and Brennan, Burger endorsed the use of plans that allowed any student to transfer from a school in which he or she was a member of the majority to one in which he or she would be in the minority. Instead of saying that altering attendance zones was "not an impermissible tool," the new draft called it "a permissible tool." Finally, the opinion would have made a general statement approving busing in appropriate cases. Picking up a sentence from Stewart, Burger wrote, "Desegregation plans cannot be limited to the walk-in school."

Otherwise, the second draft was even more critical of McMillan's order than the first. Early on, it reiterated the statement about integration being distinct from prohibiting segregation and then strengthened it, stating that "the term integration nowhere appears in any opinion dealing with pupil segregation."† Burger added a new paragraph emphasizing the limits of judicial action under the Constitution:

> In policy and program the authority of the political branch—Congress, the states and school authorities—is broader than that of the courts. . . . Much that a majority or even all of this Court might consider desirable and proper lies beyond our power to command and we serve that Constitution best if that is our guide.

* This qualification probably can be best understood as the result of Burger's style of opinion drafting. Typically, his law clerks wrote first drafts. Then Burger would insist on inserting particular lines that captivated him, even if they did not fit terribly well with the remainder of the opinion. These insertions ordinarily were relatively unthinking, almost spontaneous reactions to the drafts, and they would pop in and drop out of opinions without being significant.

† Black's opinion in United States v. Montgomery County, 395 U.S. 225 (1969), did use the term, but that was a teacher desegregation case.

The opinion continued to assert that desegregation decrees were different from traditional judicial orders. To modify his opinion further, Burger said, would "go beyond what at least five are prepared to accept."[25]

Burger may have hoped that this draft would pick up votes from Black, Stewart, Blackmun, and perhaps Harlan. Brennan and Douglas, however, met with Stewart and convinced him that Burger's approach was inadequate. They argued again that McMillan had *not* used rigid mathematical ratios; rather, he used them flexibly, as Stewart believed they could be used. Interpreting McMillan's order to avoid "doctrinaire" adherence to "a rule of 'racial balance,'" Stewart decided that he should vote to approve the order without qualification.

Burger learned that Stewart was likely to abandon him. He went to Stewart's chambers and said that he, too, had decided to affirm McMillan's order fully. This, Stewart said, left him "completely boxed in"; if Burger circulated a draft affirming McMillan's order, Stewart would have to go along. Burger's next try abandoned the contrast between desegregation cases and other traditional equity cases. The little essay on the courts' role disappeared as easily as it had appeared. The Parker-like statement contrasting integration and desegregation disappeared from its place early in the opinion, only to reappear later in Burger's discussion of mathematical ratios. There Burger wrote that ratios may be "an appropriate starting point in shaping a remedy." A starting point only, however, because "[t]he Constitution, of course, does not command integration; it forbids segregation." No particular racial balance had to be maintained permanently. Busing, the new draft explicitly said, was "within [the district] court's power to provide equitable relief." The conclusion continued to use the term "reasonable," but now it explicitly said that "we are unable to conclude that the order of the District Court is not reasonable, feasible and workable."

The bottom line was at last where a clear majority believed it should be. The question for the rest of the Court, then, was whether they should worry about the opinion's tone or sign on because the result was a rather clear affirmation of the *power* of district courts to order extensive remedies in segregation cases and a somewhat grudging affirmance of the use of that power in *Swann*. If, as many believed, *Swann* presented a case at the extreme end of the spectrum of desegregation cases, finding that McMillan's order was not an abuse of his discretion would indicate that similar orders were even more clearly appropriate in less-extreme cases. And, of course, no one on the Court had seriously contended that district judges *had to* enter orders like McMillan's, a position which is about all that Burger's draft really disapproved.

With the discussions at this point, those who wanted a stronger position nibbled away at Burger's opinion. Marshall wanted Burger to remove the line that one vehicle could carry only so much baggage and expressed concern about a transfer policy that might "result in the more affluent and educated Negro parents using the plan and leaving the poor Negroes stuck in the all-Negro school."[26] Douglas wanted Burger to remove the passage saying that courts in school desegregation cases should not concern themselves with discriminatory actions by other public agencies even if those actions contributed to "disproportionate racial concentrations in some schools."

Brennan continued to push for more extensive revisions, which would eliminate the "hazard" that a grudging tone might "arrest the trend" in the South
toward acquiescence in *Brown.* Burger's draft, according to Brennan, "express[es]
a sympathy for these local boards that I don't think is warranted. . . . [A]ny tone
of sympathy with local boards having to grapple with problems of their own making
can only encourage continued intrans[i]gence." Brennan was particularly exercised by Burger's statement contrasting desegregation and integration: "To revive
[that contrast] again would I think only rekindle vain hopes." These all were, as
Brennan acknowledged, matters of "tone. . . . But as our experience with 'all
deliberate speed' proved, tone is of primary importance."

Harlan also objected to matters of detail. He thought that a test seeking to
determine the distribution of students that would have existed if segregation had
never existed "cannot offer any real guidance." Harlan offered a revised section of
the opinion dealing with racial balance. In the course of reorganizing Burger's
draft, Harlan dropped the statement about desegregation and integration that
bothered Brennan so much.

At this point most of the controversy within the Court had ended. Burger still
lacked formal agreement on his opinion, but his third draft was enough to make it
difficult to organize an alternative. Two additional redrafts made largely stylistic
changes. Much of the grudging tone had been eliminated in the third draft. The
redrafts brought parts of the opinion that had been untouched earlier into rhetorical agreement with the remainder, further firming up the approval of the district
court order. For example, the opinion no longer referred to the irrelevance of
action by other government agencies; instead it referred to "all the problems of
racial prejudice," which might refer to purely private prejudice beyond the reach
of the Constitution. Nonetheless, the "one vehicle" sentence remained to the end.
And, with the votes in hand, the Chief Justice refused to delete the suggestion that
busing elementary school children was more troublesome than busing older ones.[27]
Burger's memorandum with his final draft had a beleaguered tone: "I believe I have
demonstrated a flexible attitude, even down to using words of others when I saw no
real difference and preferred my own." He did not "prefer all of these changes" but
wanted a unanimous opinion. But, he threatened, if the opinion did not receive a
unanimous endorsement, "I will naturally restore my own choice of language" in
an opinion that could get five votes.

At the end, everyone was tired of negotiating an opinion acceptable to all. The
process was hardly a pitched battle, however. Burger started out with a fuzzy set of
ideas about busing, which overlapped to some extent with the views of some of his
colleagues but which, to the extent that they had any substance, were rather
different from the majority's. Burger's fuzzy thinking led him to believe he could
write an opinion for the Court. Then Burger discovered the differences between
his views and the majority's as his drafts set down the ideas in necessarily more
precise terms. Once again, though, the fuzziness helped. As Burger modified his
opinion, he could tell himself that he was simply substituting other justices' words
for his own while retaining the same underlying ideas. Most of his colleagues
would have been surprised at that characterization. But, precisely because Burger
never thought that he was really changing his position—and perhaps he was not,

because he never really had a position to begin with—the division within the Court never became heated.

After Black and Harlan were replaced by Lewis F. Powell and William Rehnquist, the Court permanently divided on the issue of desegregation. The new justices shared Burger's unease with extensive judicial involvement in desegregation, and Powell could bring his experience as chair of the Richmond school board from 1952 to 1961 (the perspective of the white South in the early years after *Brown*) to counter Marshall's experience in attempting to bring about desegregation (the perspective of the African-American South). What is most striking about the Court's internal deliberations is how uncontentious they were. The justices expressed their views, the votes were taken, opinions were drafted, and the justices joined one or another side—and that, basically, was that.

A telling example is the case in which the Court's tradition of unanimity in desegregation cases broke down during Powell's and Rehnquist's first year on the Court. *Wright v. City of Emporia* involved a city-county district that was two-thirds African-American.[28] Invoking Virginia's school consolidation statutes in 1969, the city sought to separate from the county system. That would have increased the African-American percentage in the county system to 72 percent, while creating a city district that was roughly evenly divided racially. Again, Burger attempted to preempt discussion by circulating a memorandum upholding the division, but Stewart responded with a draft that quickly got the necessary five votes. The majority held that the separation of the city and county schools would unconstitutionally interfere with desegregation. As Marshall saw it, "[t]here wasn't 'root & branch' disestablishment" of the prior segregated system, and until that occurred, the city could not "separate out [the] segments." The four justices appointed by Richard Nixon dissented. The case made so few ripples within the Court, however, that even Bob Woodward and Scott Armstrong, journalists looking for the best stories about the Court under Warren Burger, did not mention it.[29]

Green's emphasis on desegregation plans that worked inevitably suggested that the Constitution was violated unless there was substantial integration. *Swann* established the power of district judges to accomplish substantial integration through extensive remedies. The cases together forced the question of de facto segregation onto the Court's agenda. In doing so, they also forced the Court to take up the question of segregation in the North. Political support for desegregation equally inevitably eroded as the Court attempted to deal with those questions. Nixon's Southern strategy, appealing to concerns in the South over desegregation, became a successful national strategy. As support for desegregation waned because courts began to affect white Northerners, the Court's decisions gradually abandoned aggressive efforts to desegregate the schools, both North and eventually South. The change occurred slowly, and not every decision was against desegregation. The trend, however, was clear. Marshall and his liberal colleagues reconciled themselves to it, taking comfort in the small victories they sometimes managed to achieve.

The Denver school case, which reached the Court in 1972, was the Court's first extended confrontation with Northern segregation.[30] Although Denver had never adopted a formal policy of segregating students by race, the plaintiffs alleged that other school board policies were designed to separate the races. They pointed in particular to the board's actions in an area known as Park Hill, where the African-American population was expanding. The board used mobile classrooms in Park Hill to deal with increasing enrollments without having to assign African-American children to "white" schools, and it allowed parents to choose the schools for their children in areas in which the racial composition was changing, but not elsewhere. By the time the case got to the Supreme Court, all the justices agreed that the school board had attempted to keep the schools in Park Hill all black. The issue that divided the Court was whether the board's actions in connection with Park Hill justified a remedy reaching throughout the Denver school system to include areas in which no one contended there had been direct decisions to maintain segregation. Schools in many of those areas were racially identifiable, as the courts put it, but that resulted primarily from the residential segregation typical of the nation's cities, North and South. Could the courts use the "hook" of the board's intentional segregation in Park Hill to justify an order that included busing throughout the city?

The trial judge ordered a limited remedy, and the court of appeals affirmed the trial judge but ordered a stay of the order's implementation. The plaintiffs' first move was to get the Supreme Court to allow the trial judge's order to go into effect. "Three cheers & hurrah," Douglas wrote Brennan when the Court voted to vacate the stay. Black, however, thought the district court was "wrong as a matter of constitutional law" because, as he saw it, segregation in Denver was based on residential segregation alone.[31]

When the justices discussed the case, Burger called it "not the typical *Brown* case." The liberals focused on the implications of Park Hill for the entire district. Brennan and Stewart thought that the "import" of the findings about Park Hill shifted the burden to the school board to show that it had *not* engaged in segregation elsewhere in the city. As Marshall put the point, it was hard to see "how [the] school board can be good for one section [and] not for the other." This was a minimal position, designed to attract a fifth vote from Blackmun, who clearly was ambivalent about what to do.[32]

The liberals had an alternative. They would have liked to do away with the distinction between segregation resulting from school board policies (de jure segregation) and segregation resulting from residential segregation (de facto segregation). Douglas restated a point he had persistently argued, that "[w]hat has been called de facto is in most cases de jure," because of government housing polices, for example. More important, Powell said that the "[d]istinction between de jure [and] de facto can't be defended constitutionally or logically."[33]

Rehnquist was startled by Powell's statement and immediately responded that it "[n]ever occurred to [him] to reject [the] distinction." But Powell's intent became clear as the justices worked with the case. Brennan drafted an opinion "within the framework established by our earlier cases." It found that the board's acts to segregate Park Hill meant that it had to show that segregation elsewhere in Denver's schools did *not* result from intentional discrimination. If it failed to carry that burden, Brennan indicated, the district judge could order full-scale remedies, including busing. Powell responded with an alternative: Do away with the distinction between de jure and de facto segregation, but sharply confine the remedies in both situations to maintain neighborhood schools. This solution would have extended the courts' reach into the urban North, while making their regulation of school boards much less intrusive.[34]

Brennan leaped at the chance to eliminate the distinction and offered to rewrite his opinion to do so. But he refused to "retreat from [the Court's] commitment of the past twenty years to eliminate all vestiges of state-imposed segregation in the public schools." The key vote was Blackmun's, and he waited for more than a month before joining Brennan's initial opinion. Although agreeing with "both parts" of Powell's proposal, Blackmun said, he decided that the Court did not have to deal with them in the Denver case.[35]

Powell renewed his effort in 1979. He wanted to use the Dallas desegregation case to "rethink[] . . . the role of the federal judiciary in public education."[36] A district court had ordered the city to adopt a desegregation plan that involved substantial student transportation, although the court tried to preserve some aspects of geographical zoning. The court of appeals sent the case back to the district court for a determination of whether it could reduce the "large number of one-race schools" that remained. At first there were not enough votes to hear the city's appeal, but Powell's proposed dissent from denial of review persuaded the Court to hear it. Powell believed that the orders that lower federal courts were entering contributed to "resegregation" because whites fled city school systems undergoing desegregation.

As in a number of desegregation cases, Marshall took himself out of the case because the National Association for the Advancement of Colored People or its branches, former clients, were named plaintiffs.* After argument, the justices were evenly divided. Burger said that "[b]ussing isn't going to work," but Blackmun thought that reversing the court of appeals "would set back *Brown*."[37] The usual consequence of an even division is an order affirming the lower court with no accompanying dissent. But to avoid even the modest implication that four justices believed the court of appeals correct, Burger proposed to dismiss the writ as improvidently granted. That disposition made sense because the court of appeals had not actually directed the elimination of one-race schools, and it was premature to assume that the district court would actually do so. It also meant that Powell could publish a dissent.

To head Powell off, Stevens asked whether it was "appropriate to invest a substantial amount of work in the preparation of opinions" when the Court was evenly divided.[38] Again, this strategy fooled no one. Even Burger knew what was going on, and he jokingly changed his vote to affirm a court of appeals decision wildly inconsistent with the positions he had taken through the 1970s. That way,

---

* In 1984 Marshall changed his position. He told his colleagues that he no longer thought it necessary to disqualify himself in all cases in which the NAACP was a party. He had severed his ties with the NAACP forty years earlier, and was "uninvolved in [its] internal working." As with the relations between a judge and his or her former law firm, "[t]ime therefore has erased the ties" he previously had with the NAACP. Marshall to conference, Oct. 4, 1984, Marshall Papers, box 353, file 9.

Burger said, there would be no problem with Powell's writing a dissent.[39] In the end, the Court dismissed the writ as improvidently granted, and Powell published a long opinion setting out his views, which Stewart and Rehnquist joined.

A testy exchange between Burger and Brennan prodded Blackmun into action in the Denver case. District judges in Richmond and Detroit had ordered "inter-district busing," in which students from the suburbs would be bused into the center cities, and students from the cities would be enrolled in suburban schools. Demographic changes in the cities of the North, including large-scale African-American migration and the relocation of white families to the suburbs, coupled with widespread practices of residential segregation, meant that "desegregation" confined within a city's limits could not produce many schools with a substantial number of white children. Advocates of urban desegregation pressed the courts to accept the idea that they could respond by including suburban school districts in the desegregation program.[40]

The Detroit case attracted a great deal of national attention, because it showed that whites in the North might not be able to escape what they saw as the problems of integrated schools by relocating to the suburbs. As his actions in *Swann* showed, Burger was never enthusiastic about busing, and he believed the Court could use the Richmond and Detroit cases to cut back on busing as a remedy for segregation. The justices tracked what was happening in the Detroit case, and on May 30 Burger told Brennan that he wanted to defer decision in the Denver case until the court of appeals decided the Detroit case; the Denver case, Burger wrote, "should go over to the next Term." Brennan responded sharply that Burger's "concern is premature," because no one could know what the court of appeals would do in the Detroit case. Blackmun cast his vote with Brennan later that day.[41]

Meanwhile the Court was struggling with the Richmond case, which ended up making no law at all. In 1972 Judge Robert Mehrige directed that Richmond, Virginia, and its suburbs jointly participate in a desegregation plan that would have involved transporting students across established district lines. Mehrige believed this was a natural extension of *Swann:* If neighborhoods were not sacrosanct in the effort to eliminate the vestiges of segregation, why should school district boundaries be? The court of appeals, however, reversed Mehrige's order, and the Supreme Court decided to review the Richmond case while it was still dealing with the Denver case.

Powell could not participate in the Richmond case because of his service on the Richmond school board. Stewart agreed with Brennan's position in the Denver case, but now Stewart finally "got off" the bus, as he put it. For him, "this is simply a Richmond District law suit [and] ought to stay within Richmond lines." The initial vote found the Court evenly split. Again, the liberals tried to pull out a victory by redefining the issue. As White put it, the question was simply "a matter of remedy." He read the court of appeals decision to rely on a flat rule that district courts were "disempowered to disregard county lines," and he thought that was wrong. The Court should define a constitutional standard identifying when a district judge could override district lines, and it should send the case back to the lower courts to apply that standard. Blackmun initially thought he could "go along" with that approach. He had started out, he said, in opposition to "forcing disregard of district lines," but he had come to think that there was "much to be said for [a] metropolitan remedy."[42]

The Richmond case was argued on Monday, April 23, 1973. Ordinarily, the Court would have announced its even division quite soon after argument, perhaps as early as April 30. In the Richmond case, however, the announcement was delayed. White's approach "intrigue[d]" Blackmun, and he wanted to see whether White could come up with a persuasive elaboration of the approach. White suggested remanding the case to Mehrige and quickly drafted a "quite narrow" opinion with three elements. It relied heavily on the principle approved in *Swann*, that district judges had extremely broad discretion in devising appropriate remedies for prior segregation. It would have found that transportation across existing district lines *could be* an appropriate remedy. All the justices agreed that cross-district remedies might be appropriate if the city and its suburbs "colluded" in some formal way to maintain segregation (for example, by agreeing that a suburb could annex a part of the city, removing from the city a white residential area that might be part of a city desegregation order). But, White suggested, such remedies might also be ordered even if no formal collusion occurred. Finally, the opinion would have held that Mehrige erred because he sought to achieve racial balance through his cross-district remedy.[43]

The strategy behind this draft was clear. Blackmun insisted on reversing the particular order Mehrige entered, but perhaps he could be persuaded to approve cross-district remedies in principle. Rehnquist criticized White's approach as relaxing the "collusion" requirement too much, and the Chief Justice wrote that Mehrige had "embarked on an 'end run' around *Swann*," seeking to achieve racial balance in the Richmond and suburban schools. Even White thought his proposal was "not as good as I thought when I wrote it (true so often, isn't it)," but he thought it might be better than a 4–4 division. The criticisms of White's opinion were enough to keep Blackmun from joining White. The announcement that the Court was evenly divided was made on May 21, 1973, a month after oral argument.[44]

The Richmond case highlights how the Burger Court dealt with segregation cases: The Court's liberals made modest efforts to carry their program along; when those efforts failed, no one thought much about them. In some ways, this attitude merely reflected the state of collegial interaction in the late 1970s and into the 1980s. By then there were relatively few true exchanges about cases and proposed opinions. A justice would circulate a draft, and the notes joining the opinion would roll in.

Marshall, of course, had a different view of the cases. At the conference on the Richmond case, he said, "If [the] local school board [and the] local [district judge] agree as we said in *Brown*, we should buy it." As Marshall saw it, *Brown* had insisted that the underlying problems of desegregation were intensely local, which is why the Court stayed away from desegregation cases for so long. The Court had let local courts delay desegregation. Now, when local courts were implementing effective remedies, the Court should let them go ahead. When White circulated his proposal, Marshall said, "After worrying with the law, the precedents, and my conscience, I now find myself willing to agree" with White's approach. He was so grudging because the liberal victory White sought came at the cost, necessary but hardly to be welcomed, of abandoning the Court's willingness to let these cases be worked out locally.[45]

The issue of interdistrict remedies returned to the Court in the Detroit case a year later, but with Powell participating, the case was over before it began. Burger tried to use the case for a general attack on busing, but he could not get Stewart and Blackmun to go along. As usual, Burger simply "folded" fundamental objections to his appoach into a draft that got increasingly disjointed.[46]

Burger eventually got the point. His opinion for the five-justice majority held that remedies for intentional segregation had to be confined to the boundaries of the school districts that engaged in the unconstitutional segregation. The opinion criticized interdistrict remedies as focusing on "racial balance" rather than unconstitutional actions leading to segregated schools and emphasized the country's "deeply rooted" tradition of "local control over the operation of schools." According to Burger, an interdistrict remedy in the usual case of urban segregation could "be supported only by drastic expansion of the constitutional right" at issue, a transformation of a right to be free of discrimination into a right to attend schools in which there was racial balance.[47]

Burger's struggle to work out a decent opinion delayed circulation of his draft for three months. It came around at the end of May. Taking the chance to tweak Burger, and perhaps reminding him of his earlier suggestion that the Denver case be held over for another term, Marshall requested that the Detroit case be put over because he did not have time to write the dissent so late in the term. That year, however, the Court stayed in session a month longer than usual to deal with President Nixon's effort to resist production of tapes he had made in the White House, and Marshall's attempt to delay the decision, probably not serious in any event, failed.[48]

Marshall's long dissent, which was joined by Douglas, Brennan, and White, began by noting that "after 20 years of small, often difficult steps" toward the "great end" of "equal justice under law," the Court's majority "today takes a giant step backwards." For him, the Court's approach "emasculat[ed]" the equal protection clause and relied on "superficial" grounds to abridge "the right of all of our children, whatever their race, to an equal start in life and to an equal opportunity to reach their full potential as citizens." His opinion pointed both to the past and to the future: "Those children who have been denied that right in the past deserve better than to see fences thrown up to deny them that right in the future. . . . Unless our children begin to learn together, there is little hope that our people will ever learn to live together."

Much of Marshall's opinion recited the findings the district judge had made, to counter Burger's characterization of the case as one in which the judge simply wanted to achieve what he believed to be a desirable racial balance in the schools. The opinion's detailed description of the proceedings and findings in the lower courts demonstrated sensitivity to the fluid way in which complex litigation develops. Because state authorities had substantial legal responsibility for operating Detroit's schools, Marshall argued, a remedy reaching beyond the city and into the suburbs did not distort a system of true local control that had been operating smoothly and without effect on segregation in Detroit. Marshall's sense of practical reality led him to insist that Detroit and its suburbs really were "a single community" and that the majority's attempt to separate the city and the suburbs relied on mere formalities in state law. Under these circumstances, the opinion said, "school district lines . . . will surely be perceived as fences to separate the races when . . . white parents withdraw their children from the Detroit city schools and move to the suburbs in order to continue them in all-white schools." The opinion also pointed out that segregation in the schools and residential segregation interacted: "The rippling effects on residential patterns caused by purposeful acts of segregation do not automatically subside at the school district border."

The Court proceeded on the assumption that there had been a violation of the Constitution; for Marshall, once such a violation was established, the trial judge had broad discretion to develop an effective remedy to desegregate the Detroit schools. And desegregation meant "ensur[ing] that Negro and white children in fact go to school together." Thus, for Marshall, the key fact was that a "remedy" confined to the city of Detroit could not "effectively desegregate" the city's schools. In saying that, "in the final analysis," desegregation meant that "Negro and white children in fact go to school together," Marshall's opinion exposed the ambiguity about the meaning of desegregation that had plagued the litigation after *Brown:* If *Brown* meant only that governments could not take race into account in assigning students to schools, the majority, following the analysis that Judge John Parker had adopted, was obviously correct; if *Brown* meant that the Constitution contemplated some substantial degree of actual integration, as Marshall believed in *Brown* and after, and as some of the Court's decisions suggested, Marshall was right in urging that only an interdistrict remedy could produce desegregated schools.

Addressing the "basic emotional and legal issue[]" of busing, Marshall argued that a metropolitan plan would probably not significantly increase the number of students riding buses to school, although he conceded that "some disruption" was inevitable. The opinion concluded with a paragraph on what Marshall believed to be the underlying reason for the majority's action, "a perceived public mood that we have gone far enough." But, Marshall said, "racial attitudes ingrained in our Nation's childhood and adolescence are not quickly thrown aside in its middle years." Even "strident" public opposition should not divert the Court. "In the short run, it may seem to be the easier course to allow our great metropolitan areas to be divided up each into two cities—one white, one black—but it is a course, I predict, our people will ultimately regret."

The Court sent the Detroit case back to the lower courts to develop a remedy confined to the city limits, which Marshall called "a solemn mockery" of *Brown.* The trial court modified student assignments within the city, but at the center of its new remedy was a group of educational programs including special training for teachers and remedial reading classes and modifications of testing for students. The city's school board accepted these programs; for the board the only question was how much of the cost would be shouldered by state agencies. The state agencies, however, objected both to the payment and to the underlying educational programs and appealed to the Supreme Court. Burger wrote the Court's 1977 opinion upholding the educational remedies and the allocation of costs to the state.[49]

Powell thought the case "a 'sport' in every respect." It was, his concurring opinion said, "largely a friendly suit" between the plaintiffs and the Detroit school board, which "have now joined forces apparently for the purpose of extracting funds from the state treasury." Powell's opinion provoked Marshall into writing his own concurrence, which said that what was "most tragic" about the case was that it was "in no way unique." It was "unfortunately, not unusual" that Northern school boards segregated African-American students, and it was to be expected that the students' academic development would be "impaired by this wrongdoing." Unlike Powell, who thought it odd, and somewhat reeking of conspiracy, that the city's school board did not object to the educational remedies, Marshall expressed hope that other school boards would similarly acknowledge their "responsibility for the injuries that Negroes have suffered."[50]

To some extent, Marshall and Powell were talking past each other, with Powell stressing the practical dimensions of the way in which the case was presented to the Supreme Court and Marshall stressing the practical dimensions of the educational process in Detroit. Yet, to a greater extent, Marshall understood that Powell's rhetoric about the "uniqueness" of the case evoked concerns about Northern desegregation that, as Marshall's brief opinion forcefully stated, ought to be rejected.

The careful balance between the Court's two sides continued through the 1970s. In *Dayton Board of Education v. Brinkman*, a firm majority voted in 1977 to reverse a court of appeals decision directing the trial judge to order more extensive transportation remedies in a Northern case.[51] As Stewart saw it, the lower courts relied too heavily on the mere fact of racial imbalance. They should have focused more tightly on "how the segregative school board actions contributed to increased imbalance." Powell said that he had "always been disturbed about compelling cities with racial concentrations due to demographic considerations . . . to break them up."[52]

When Rehnquist circulated his draft, Brennan wrote that he was "disturbed by the tone of your opinion," which he found "unnecessarily harsh." Somewhat disingenuously, Brennan said that he would "rather not" write separately and "probably won't if you can see your way to remove the chastizing tone." Rehnquist would have none of this and politely replied that he would "certainly give" specific suggestions "careful consideration." Brennan responded with "suggestions for softening the vigor of your criticism" of the court of appeals, but, he wrote, he would "certainly understand why you may conclude that I'm asking too much."[53]

Justice John Paul Stevens supported Brennan, but in the end Rehnquist kept some quite strong criticisms in his opinion; eliminating them, he told his colleagues, would "somewhat alter[] the focus of the opinion."[54] The published opinion called one district court conclusion "of questionable validity" and said that the district court's remedy "was certainly not based on an unduly cautious understanding of its authority"; the court of appeals "simply had no warrant in our cases for imposing" a systemwide remedy where only three particular violations were found, and "imposed a remedy . . . entirely out of proportion to the constitutional violations," because it was "vaguely dissatisfied with the limited character" of the district court's remedy.[55]

And, after all, why should Rehnquist have done much? Stevens ended up concurring, and Brennan concurred in the result. Their separate opinions tried to map out the findings the lower courts should make to justify the systemwide remedy. Their opinions were functional dissents strategically cast as concurrences. Rehnquist understood that his opinion's tone had to be stern to send a message that might in the end be more important than the precise holding.

The case returned to the Court two years later, after the lower courts made the findings Stevens and Brennan asked for, and now Stewart agreed. The court of appeals, he said, was not "a rogue elephant." Powell and Rehnquist, discovering they had been outmaneuvered, thought the "time has come for a major reclarification on remedy," but—as had been true since *Swann*— they did not have the support of a majority. As Marshall put it, the Court could not reverse the lower courts "without gutting" *Swann* and the Denver case.[56]

During Marshall's tenure the Court did not definitively resolve a question that cropped up in *Swann* and, even more, in later Northern segregation cases: To what extent can courts in *school* segregation cases rely on *residential* segregation to justify awarding relief? Some residential segregation resulted from government actions, such as locating segregated public housing projects in white and African-American neighborhoods, thereby perpetuating their racial identifiability. Some residential segregation resulted from segregated education itself, since parents selected where to live based on what type of schools were nearby. In the latter case, the law could treat residential segregation itself as a vestige of school segregation. Continued patterns of racial separation in the schools might then result in the first instance from residential segregation but more remotely from school segregation in the past. School boards might have an affirmative duty to respond to the effects that residential segregation had on schools as another vestige of school segregation.

That issue lurked in a case decided during Marshall's final term on the Court. The Court's main concern in *Board of Education of Oklahoma City v. Dowell* was with the standard for determining when a district court could end its supervision of a school desegregation case.[57] The court of appeals applied a stringent standard, allowing termination of the decree only if continuing it would be a "grievous wrong." After the conference discussion of the case, it was clear that a majority wanted to reverse the court of appeals. Beyond that, however, things were less clear. Some wanted to signal that it should be relatively easy for district courts to terminate decrees; others wanted to specify a clear standard for termination; still others thought that situations varied so much that it would be unwise to provide much specific guidance to lower courts.

Rehnquist drafted an opinion that, he said, "decides only one of the principal questions," holding that the court of appeals standard was too stringent and remanding the case for further consideration. The draft included a footnote referring to residential segregation's effects on school segregation, but the footnote simply directed the lower courts to consider that question anew on remand. White urged Rehnquist "to say expressly that on remand, residential segregation should not be treated as a vestige of the prior illegally segregated school system." Justice Sandra Day O'Connor immediately protested: "I cannot go along with anything that even remotely suggests the resolution" of the residential segregation issue. As she saw it, even Rehnquist's footnote "sends unwarranted signals" on the question, but "[u]nfortunately we do not appear to have a Court for any particular solution." Rehnquist spoke with O'Connor and then told White that he planned to leave the footnote as it was, "not saying anything more about it."[58]

O'Connor's militancy in this exchange is striking. As Rehnquist pointed out, she was one of the five justices who had voted to reverse the court of appeals, over three dissents.[59] She seems to have been concerned that resolving the residential segregation question would have taken the Court too far down the road too quickly. In contrast, a more gradual movement, in a succession of cases, might be acceptable.

The contrast between large and gradual changes in the law may best explain the absence of contention over desegregation cases in the 1970s and 1980s. As long as the Court was moving slowly, though from the liberals' point of view in the wrong direction, it would have been unproductive to raise the stakes within the Court. The votes to change the law were there, and, as the failed effort to shift Blackmun's vote in the Richmond case shows, the votes were unlikely to disappear. Under those circumstances, the Court's liberals could do no more than keep the pace of change moderate. Converting division into contention would not have helped.

During Marshall's tenure the Court frequently addressed what remedies could be used in school segregation cases. It only occasionally dealt with cases in which the basic issue was whether unconstitutional discrimination against African-Americans had actually occurred, and Marshall wrote few opinions about that question. When he did, the opinions were dissents, opinions for less than a majority of the Court, or concurring opinions. In *Memphis v. Greene*, decided in 1981, Marshall's discussion of the question of discrimination demonstrated his sense of the practical reality that formed the context for abstract legal issues.[60] The case involved a street closing in Memphis. The street went through Hein Park, a residential area of Memphis in which all the homes were owned by whites. A large city park, with a golf course, the city zoo, picnic areas, and other recreational facilities, was at the southern end of the street. The northern end intersected heavily traveled avenues. The area north of Hein Park was predominantly African-American. Homeowners in Hein Park persuaded the city to close the northern end of the street, so that traffic through their residential area would drop significantly. African-American residents of the city challenged the street closing as a form of race discrimination, pointing out that closing the street meant putting up a barrier precisely at the boundary between a white residential area and a predominantly African-American one and also meant that African-Americans who wanted to use the city park would have to find more inconvenient ways into the park, while white residents of Hein Park would be able to use the park as usual. The court of appeals said that the street closing was a "badge of slavery, . . . one more of the many humiliations which society has historically visited upon blacks."

As Marshall's law clerk put it, "[T]here must be more to this case than meets the eye. . . . It seems terribly unlikely that a federal appellate court would order such relief unless there is a 'smoking gun' lurking somewhere in the record."[61] Not having discovered a smoking gun, the majority found that the closing did not violate the Constitution. Stevens's opinion began by noting that the lower courts had made an unchallenged determination that the closing was not intended to discriminate against African-Americans. Rather, the city's decision rested on the typical concerns in street-closing cases: residents' desires, management of traffic flow, and "safety and tranquillity." Acknowledging that the closing would inconvenience some drivers, the majority found that the impact could not "be equated to an actual restraint on the liberty of black citizens that is in any sense comparable to the odious practice" of slavery. The inconvenience, as Stevens called it, was "a function of where [the drivers] live and where they regularly drive—not a function of their race." He concluded, "[P]roper respect for the dignity of the residents of any neighborhood requires that they accept the same burdens as well as the same benefits of citizenship regardless of their racial origin."

Marshall's dissenting opinion indignantly opened by saying that the case was "easier than the majority makes it appear."[62] As Marshall saw it, the case involved closing the main street between "an all-white enclave and a predominantly Negro area" to serve purported interests of "safety and tranquillity," which he said were "little more than code phrases for racial discrimination." He offered an interpretation of the case's facts counter to the majority's, incorporating—as the opinion put it—"a dab of common sense": "The picture that emerges . . . is one of a white community, disgruntled over sharing its street with Negroes, taking legal measures to keep out the 'undesirable traffic'. . . ." For Marshall, when residents of Hein Park referred to "undesirable traffic," he understood them to mean not that the amount of traffic was undesirable but that the people driving the cars were. Marshall cited testimony that putting up a barrier to block access to the street would "serve as a monument to racial hostility." African-Americans, in short, were "being sent a clear, though sophisticated, message that because of their race, they are to stay out of the all-white enclave . . . and should instead take the long way around."

The most emphatic statements in Marshall's opinion rejected Stevens's effort to minimize the street-closing's impact. What to Justice Stevens was mere "inconvenience," Marshall described as a "plain and powerful symbolic message" that African-Americans "are being told in essence: 'You must take the long way around because you don't live in this "protected" white neighborhood.'" He thought that "it defies the lessons of history and law to assert that if the harm is only symbolic, then the federal courts cannot recognize it," adding quotations from *Plessy v. Ferguson* and *Brown v. Board of Education* to drive the point home. "The message the city is sending to Negro residents . . . is clear, and I am at a loss to understand why the majority feels so free to ignore it." For him, putting up a barrier "at the behest of a historically all-white community, to keep out predominantly Negro traffic" was a clear violation of the guarantees of equality. It is difficult to avoid hearing resonances in this opinion of the experiences Marshall and other African-Americans had in finding that they were such "undesirable traffic" that they could not remain in some towns in the South overnight.

Powell's biographer John Jeffries asserts that the outcome of the Detroit case "produced a regime of schizophrenic contradiction: Bus the cities but not the suburbs." As Jeffries writes, "[A] divided Court chose to fight only where the battle could not be won."[63] Their efforts in the Richmond and Detroit cases showed that Marshall and his allies on the Court preferred to fight where the battle might be won, but they could not command a majority consistently enough to create a body of law that held out some hope for a solution. Ironically, their occasional victories only perpetuated tension over the issue of desegregation and contributed to the strengthening of the Republican coalition whose victories in presidential elections made further liberal victories on the Supreme Court increasingly unlikely.

5

"Vital Interests of a Powerless Minority"
Equal Protection Theory

The Fourteenth Amendment was ratified in 1868. Five years later, the Supreme Court "doubt[ed] very much whether any action of a State not directed by way of discrimination against the negroes as a class, or on account of their race, will ever be held" to violate the amendment's equal protection clause. In 1927 Justice Oliver Wendell Holmes called arguments based on equality "the usual last resort" in constitutional litigation.[1] By 1967, however, the Court had suggested that the equal protection clause might provide the basis for more vigorous judicial review in the service of equality in areas other than race. The Court's hints never quite developed into a full-fledged doctrine. The majority struggled to work out a way to deal with cases that seemed to raise troubling questions about equal treatment. Marshall's opinions offered a coherent alternative to the majority's approach. Geoffrey Stone, University of Chicago law professor, said that Marshall's approach "has clearly dominated the attention of judges and academics who have attempted to make sense of the realities of the court's jurisprudence."[2] By the time he left the Court, Marshall's analysis made more sense of what the majority had done than the majority's own analysis. The Court said it rejected Marshall's approach, but in reality the Court adopted the approach, though not the conclusions Marshall drew. The issue of affirmative action attracted more public attention, but the Court's struggles with the general theory of equal protection were the background against which it dealt with that issue.

The Court initially shied away from invalidating statutes as violations of the equal protection clause because the justices knew that every statute treated some people differently from others. A vigorous jurisprudence of equal protection threatened the ability of legislatures to legislate at all. In an early case, for example, the Supreme Court upheld a New York city ordinance barring privately operated buses from displaying advertising on their sides even though delivery trucks could do so.[3] The city council, the Court said, had the power to classify businesses and treat those in one class, the delivery trucks, differently from those in the other, the buses.

94

In the years before 1937, the Supreme Court did have an aggressive jurisprudence under the Fourteenth Amendment. It invalidated many important pieces of Progressive-era legislation designed to regulate the economy. For example, the Court held that laws setting minimum wages and maximum hours violated the Fourteenth Amendment's due process clause.[4] When the Court invoked similar theories to invalidate laws enacted as part of the New Deal's response to the depression of the 1930s, it faced a firestorm of political criticism. President Franklin D. Roosevelt tried to persuade Congress to enact a statute allowing him to appoint several new justices. Although Roosevelt's court-packing plan failed in Congress, the Court soon changed course.

By the 1940s the Court was dominated by justices who thought aggressive judicial review of economic regulation improper. When New York's regulation of advertising returned to the Court in 1949, Justice Douglas wrote for the Court upholding it again. The city council, he said, "may well have concluded that those who advertise their own wares on their trucks do not present the same traffic problems" as those who let others hire space on the sides of trucks. A few years later, Douglas again explained why the courts should move slowly: "The problem of legislative classification is a perennial one, admitting of no doctrinaire definition. Evils in the same field may be of different dimensions and proportions, requiring different remedies. Or so the legislature may think."[5]

The approach Douglas took came to be known as "rational basis" review. Courts should respect legislative judgments about treating groups differently, even if the groups might seem quite similar. Judges should uphold legislation as long as they could imagine some reason for thinking that the problem posed by one group was different from that posed by the other. Judges might not be persuaded that the traffic hazards posed by advertising on trucks owned by the advertisers were much less than the hazards posed by advertising on rented trucks, but they should uphold New York's law if they did not think the distinction completely irrational.

The rational-basis test represented the New Deal's jurisprudence. New Deal liberals had seen their political successes in legislatures thwarted by activist courts. Their jurisprudence was designed to protect their legislative victories. Courts, they concluded, should not interfere with the outcome of legislative struggles among contending interest groups. Soon, however, the justices came to understand that questions of equal treatment were often more serious than Holmes suggested. Plainly the issues of race that the Roosevelt Court confronted involved questions of equality, and the justices began to understand that prejudice against African-Americans was just one of many types of unfair discrimination the courts should respond to.

In 1938 Justice Harlan Fiske Stone began to articulate a general approach to questions of equality. A footnote in a case involving claims by corporate interests suggested that the Court would be more alert when the claim was that legislation discriminated against "discrete and insular minorities," who might not be able to use the ordinary political processes to overcome discrimination.[6] A 1942 Douglas opinion added another element to the emerging law of equality. *Skinner v. Oklahoma* involved a statute that required the sterilization of defendants convicted of certain crimes.[7] The defendant challenged the statute as a violation of the constitutional ban on cruel and unusual punishment, which brought into the case the aura of Nazi programs of euthanasia that hovered over it. Finding that challenge a difficult one, however, Douglas relied on an equality argument. The statute required sterilization for specified crimes but did not require it for other crimes: chicken stealing but not embezzlement, for example, even though "the nature of the two crimes is intrinsically the same." Douglas said that the punishment dealt with "one of the basic civil rights of man," because marriage and procreation were "fundamental to the very existence and survival of the race." When fundamental rights were involved, the courts had to give "strict scrutiny" to laws treating people unequally, which meant that the laws had to be justified by very strong arguments. The reason for believing that chicken stealing was somehow more genetically linked than embezzlement—so that sterilizing chicken stealers would foreclose more crime by their children than sterilizing embezzlers would—was not strong enough to satisfy this requirement.

Before the 1960s the Court rarely invoked the "strict scrutiny" test except in cases involving explicit racial discrimination. The justices learned several lessons from the New Deal experience. They believed that aggressive judicial review invited retaliation and threatened the Supreme Court's independence. That inclined them to accept a theory of general judicial restraint. They also believed, however, that the Progressive and New Deal periods showed that the political interests they sympathized with could indeed win legislative victories. Judicial restraint, therefore, did not threaten the interests with which the justices sympathized.

Faced with a happy congruence between the political values they held and a theory of general judicial restraint, the justices did not have to worry. When they occasionally discovered areas in which legislatures seemed unsympathetic to interests they valued, the justices struggled to develop a way of intervening against legislatures without abandoning some semblance of judicial restraint. To some, the equal protection clause was a convenient doctrinal tool for that task. The justices were not ruling out legislation entirely when they found that a statute violated the equal protection clause. All they were demanding, the doctrine said, was equal treatment: Oklahoma could continue to sterilize habitual chicken thieves as long as it was willing to sterilize embezzlers as well.

In the long run, this strategy to reconcile judicial activism and restraint could not have succeeded. Even in the Oklahoma case, for example, critics could fairly ask why the Court thought chicken stealing and embezzling were "intrinsically the same." The strategy might work, however, as long as political circumstances were favorable, for the Court would not actually face the retaliation it feared.

The Court appeared ready to develop a doctrinal framework for equality by the time of Lyndon Johnson's Great Society legislation. The Great Society agenda connected race and poverty. According to its proponents, the Great Society's programs to reduce economic disparities would simultaneously reduce racial tensions. Instead of working *against* the political system, therefore, aggressive judicial review would be part of the national government's efforts to reduce inequality. Without the threat of retaliation to caution them against exercising the power of judicial review too frequently, liberal justices no longer felt attracted to a general theory of judicial restraint. As they saw things, a big Court was a natural part of a big government.

By the late 1960s, it seemed possible that the doctrinal structure of the constitutional law of equality would adjust to these perceptions. Perhaps poor people were not precisely a "discrete and insular minority," but they certainly appeared to be at a disadvantage in the political process. Their claims were asserted on behalf of important elements in the political constituency of the Great Society. Indeed, their claims were often asserted *by* lawyers for the legal services programs that received Great Society funds.[8]

As in many areas of constitutional law, the replacement of the Warren Court by the Burger Court cut short the full development of the doctrinal structure whose outlines had begun to emerge in Marshall's early years on the Court. It became unnecessary to construct a constitutional framework for equality with the passing of the Great Society impulse. Indeed, Republican appointments to the Court after 1970 revived the threat of retaliation. The liberals who remained on the Court could no longer see themselves as one branch of a coordinated national government dedicated to reducing economic disparities. The Republican appointees, of course, saw no need to work out a constitutional theory of equality. As the New Deal liberal justices had done before, the Republican appointees found themselves in the happy situation in which their political interests coincided with a general attitude of judicial restraint.

Claims by women for constitutional protection made that attitude less than fully satisfying. The justices found themselves searching for a new constituency to support them as the Great Society's political coalition disintegrated. The claims of middle-class women in particular resonated with the political experiences of some of the Republican appointees. Justice Powell said, for example, that his position on abortion was powerfully influenced by conversations with his daughters, and it clearly was affected by his social class—"well-educated, non-Catholic, upper-class."[9]

The Burger Court developed a jurisprudence of gender discrimination. In doing so, however, it had to reconcile what it was doing about gender discrimination with what it was doing about other forms of discrimination. Only Marshall developed a satisfactory solution to that problem. The rest of the Court struggled to get out of the doctrinal morass to which the justices' conflicting impulses led them.

All these developments were driven by the justices' concerns over reaching the right results within a doctrinal framework they found comfortable. The inside story of the Court's evolution is that there are no deep secrets hidden in the archives: The justices' opinions fully reveal what they worried about and how they reached their decisions.

The Oklahoma sterilization case called for strict scrutiny when laws impaired the fundamental interests of some while protecting those same interests for others. The doctrinal problem was to identify what *fundamental interests* were. An easy solution would have been to define fundamental rights in terms of rights protected directly by the Constitution. That would not work, however. *Police Department of Chicago v. Mosley,* a 1972 Marshall opinion, showed that there is no reason to rely on notions of equality to explain why restrictions on constitutional rights are improper.[10] Chicago prohibited picketing near schools, except in cases involving labor disputes. Mosley conducted a lone vigil protesting the use of affirmative action hiring at a high school. Marshall relied on the equal protection clause to find that "selective exclusion from a public place" was unconstitutional. The opinion noted that the equality claim was "closely intertwined with" free-speech interests. Marshall relied on the equal protection clause because of a doctrinal difficulty: The Court had never squarely held that picketing, whether in labor disputes or otherwise, was itself protected by the First Amendment. If it was protected by free-speech principles, selective restrictions on picketing would violate the First Amendment. Marshall was able to insist on a high level of justification for the city's ordinance without resolving the underlying doctrinal problem by relying on the equal protection clause and invoking the concept of "fundamental rights."

The fundamental-rights cases posed doctrinal problems, then, because the attractive definition of fundamental rights as constitutional rights generated analytic problems. In addition, the important fundamental-rights cases actually involved rights the Court had not held protected by the Constitution. Even in the early 1970s, for example, no case held that anyone had a constitutional right to procreate. The Court, therefore, could not define fundamental rights in the equal protection context simply as constitutional rights. But why should the courts decide which values were truly fundamental, in a society in which some people regarded some values as fundamental while others thought them only modestly important?

Voting was the value on which the Court could most easily agree, and Marshall's 1972 opinion in *Dunn v. Blumstein* set the course.[11] Over the sole dissent of Chief Justice Burger,[12] the Court held unconstitutional Tennessee's rule that people could vote in state elections only after they had resided in the state for a year. Marshall's opinion was his first to provide a version of his distinctive approach to equal protection cases: To decide such a case, the opinion said, the court must "look . . . to . . . the character of the classification in question; the individual interests affected by the classification; and the governmental interests asserted in support of the classification." Tennessee's residency requirement was based on recent interstate travel and affected the "opportunity" to vote and therefore, according to Marshall's opinion, could be justified only by a "substantial and compelling reason." The opinion cautioned, though, that this approach "d[id] not have the precision of a mathematical formula. The key words emphasize a matter of degree."

No one really disputed that voting was fairly called fundamental in a democratic society. Other interests were more divisive. Welfare rights cases were the turning point for the Court's majority. Welfare rights lawyers argued that the Constitution required the states to expand their public assistance programs.[13] This effort was decisively defeated by the Supreme Court in *Dandridge v. Williams,* a 1970 decision that articulated the approach the Court would take during the remainder of Marshall's time on the Court.[14] Following federal regulations, Maryland established a "standard of need" for recipients of public assistance. The idea behind the federal requirement was to identify what people needed and, presumably, give it to them through the welfare system. Most recipients of public assistance in Maryland did receive the amounts defined by the need standard. To control costs, Maryland imposed an upper limit on the amount any family could obtain. As a result, large families received less than the needs of the members added together. For example, the needs of the members of Williams's family added together came to $296 per month, but Maryland's upper limit on payments was $250. Williams argued that Maryland's absolute upper limit violated the equal protection clause because it failed to take into account the real needs of large families.

Justice Stewart wrote the Court's opinion. "In the area of economics and social welfare," the opinion said, legislation simply had to have a "reasonable basis." To adopt a more stringent standard "in the social and economic field" would set the courts free to strike down laws they thought unwise or bad policy. Stewart acknowledged that most of the cases using the "reasonable basis" standard involved regulation of business, while *Dandridge* involved "the most basic economic needs of impoverished human beings." But, he said, there was "no basis for applying a different constitutional standard" despite "the dramatically real factual difference." For the majority, a test requiring more of the state than that it have a "rational basis" for what it did would invite the courts to "second-guess state officials charged with the difficult responsibility of allocating limited public welfare funds among the myriad of potential recipients" and to impose the judges' own views about "intractable economic, social, and even philosophical problems."

Marshall's vigorous dissent criticized "the Court's emasculation of the Equal Protection Clause as a constitutional principle." Under Maryland's system, it said, "persons who are concededly similarly situated (dependent children and their families), are not afforded equal, or even approximately equal treatment," because some received all they needed while others did not. For Marshall, the majority "avoid[ed] the task" of justifying this unequal treatment by "focusing upon the abstract dichotomy between two different approaches," the reasonable-basis approach and the fundamental-rights approach. Yet, the opinion said that "this case simply defies easy characterization" in those terms. The reasonable-basis test was developed, as the majority said, in cases involving business regulation and might be explained, Marshall wrote, by a "healthy revulsion from the Court's earlier excesses in using the Constitution to protect interests that have more than enough power to protect themselves in the legislative halls." In contrast, *Dandridge* involved "the literally vital interests of a powerless minority." For Marshall, it was insufficient to say only that the case "falls in 'the area of economics and social welfare.'"

Marshall offered his alternative, echoing his opinion in *Dunn v. Blumstein:* "[C]oncentration must be placed upon the character of the classification in question, the relative importance to individuals in the class discriminated against of the governmental benefits that they do not receive, and the asserted state interests in support of the classification." Here "the stuff that sustains . . . lives" was at stake, and the distinction between large and small families was not "one that readily commends itself as a basis for determining which children are to have support approximating subsistence and which are not." Marshall pointed out that, even if the state was trying to encourage employment, limiting the assistance given to large families did nothing to encourage those in smaller families to find work. Tweaking the majority, he concluded that "were this a case of pure business regulation, these defects would place it beyond what has heretofore seemed a borderline case." But, of course, Marshall's central concern was that the case did not involve "a gas company or an optical dispenser" but "needy dependent children."

Dandridge articulated what came to be known as the *two-tier* approach to equal protection. In the upper tier, the courts gave state laws "strict scrutiny" and asked for "compelling" justifications for treating one group differently from another. In the lower tier, all that was required was a rational basis for the unequal treatment. Cases fell into the upper tier if they involved a "suspect classification" like race or other "discrete and insular minorities" or if they involved "fundamental rights." *Dandridge* suggested that the Court would not be generous in defining fundamental rights and obviously rejected Marshall's standard of relative importance as a basis for defining fundamental rights.

Marshall continued to elaborate his sliding-scale approach. Under it, courts were to arrive at a constitutional judgment by balancing the competing interests, sensitive to the impact of state laws on individuals and the difficulties states had in carrying out their necessary tasks. Over the next decades, the sliding-scale analysis clearly did a better job of explaining the Court's behavior than the two-tier analysis. The sliding-scale approach remained vulnerable to Stewart's charge that a directive to courts to "balance" competing interests left the judges free to impose their vision of the good society on legislatures. That, however, did not really distinguish Marshall's analytic approach from the Court's behavior, more flexible in practice than its doctrine suggested.

The Court's next substantial confrontation with fundamental questions of equal protection doctrine led it to try to pin down the meaning of fundamental rights more precisely. It also attempted to identify and limit the suspect classifications that shifted cases into the upper tier. *San Antonio Independent School District v. Rodriguez,* decided three years after *Dandridge,* rejected a constitutional challenge to school finance systems based primarily on local property taxes. At the Court's conference, Blackmun said he did not "think we can effectively legislate quality education." Powell, recalling his experience on the Richmond school board, thought that upholding the constitutional challenge would lead to "a complete restructuring of local [and] state gov[ernmen]t" and concluded that "education is not a fundamental interest requiring application of [the] compelling interest test."[15]

Powell's opinion for the Court found that property-tax financing systems did not discriminate against a suspect class, the poor, because the relative poverty of people residing in districts with low property tax rolls did not make them "completely unable" to obtain an education.[16] As he had said at the conference, education was not a fundamental interest in the two-tier system. Unequal school financing did not result in "an absolute deprivation of the desired benefit" but led only to a lower quality of education than was available in other districts.

For the majority, fundamental interests were those "explicitly or implicitly guaranteed by the Constitution," not those that were "important" in terms of "societal significance." It would not find that there was an implicit constitutional right to education, although it did suggest that the Constitution might be violated if states provided no public education at all. Powell rejected the argument that education was so closely related to the right to free speech and the right to vote that a right to education was a predicate for the effective exercise of those constitutional rights. The difficulty, according to Powell, was that the courts had neither "the ability [n]or the authority to guarantee to the citizenry the most *effective* speech or the most *informed* electoral choice." He noted that "the logical limitations" on the approach he rejected were "difficult to perceive," because it could equally well be argued that "the basics of decent food and shelter" were also necessary predicates for the effective exercise of political rights.

Marshall again criticized the majority for trying to squeeze all equal protection cases "into one of two neat categories which dictate the appropriate standard of review." His dissenting opinion provided a detailed review of the Court's cases which showed, to his satisfaction and to that of most commentators afterward, that the Court "has applied a spectrum of standards" depending, in his view, "on the constitutional and societal importance of the interest adversely affected and the recognized invidiousness of the basis upon which the particular classification is drawn." Recalling the problem in *Mosley,* the opinion noted that calling interests fundamental only if they were protected by the Constitution would make the "fundamental interests" branch of equal protection law "superfluous," because "the substantive constitutional right itself requires" strict scrutiny of the state's justifications. And, the opinion said pointedly, "I would like to know where the Constitution guarantees the right to procreate, or the right to vote in state elections."*

Marshall conceded that "the process of determining which interests are fundamental is a difficult one." He argued that the "task in every case should be to determine the extent to which constitutionally guaranteed rights are dependent on interests not mentioned in the Constitution." As the connection between the specific constitutional right and the interest at stake became closer, the interest became more fundamental "and the degree of judicial scrutiny . . . must be adjusted accordingly." Calling the *Rodriguez* dissent "Marshall's greatest opinion," Cass Sunstein, law professor and a former clerk to Marshall, observed, "*Brown* was a case about education," and Marshall believed fervently that "equality of opportunity . . . entailed, first and foremost, a right to equal prospects in education."[17]

According to his law clerk Elena Kagan, the case Marshall "cared most about" during the 1988–89 Term was *Kadrmas v. Dickinson Public Schools,* and Marshall insisted on a "properly pungent tone" in the opinion she drafted.[18] The Court upheld a North Dakota statute allowing school districts to impose a fee for bus service to and from schools. Justice O'Connor's opinion for the Court refused to apply "heightened" scrutiny to the statute, saying that "doing so would require us

---

* Powell struggled to respond, explaining the Court's 1942 decision in *Skinner* by citing the 1973 abortion decision, issued only a few weeks before *Rodriguez,* and using earlier cases to show that the Court had indeed recognized an implicit constitutional right to "equal treatment in the voting process."

to extend the requirements of the Equal Protection Clause beyond the limits recognized by our cases, a step we decline to take." Marshall's dissent began with a quotation from his opinion in *Rodriguez* and criticized the Court for "continu[ing] the retreat from the promise of equal educational opportunity." For him, the case "involves state action that places a special burden on poor families in their pursuit of education." As he saw it, charging a fee for bus service in remote rural areas was "no different in practical effect from imposing a fee directly for education." And, obviously, charging a fee "necessarily fell more heavily upon the poor than upon wealthier members of the community." Quoting *Brown,* the opinion stressed "the vital role of education in our society":

> A statute that erects special obstacles to education in the path of the poor naturally tends to consign such persons to their current disadvantaged status. By denying equal opportunity to exactly those who need it most, the law not only militates against the ability of each poor child to advance herself, but also increases the likelihood of the creation of a discrete and permanent underclass.

The opinion ended by saying that the Court "displays a callous indifference to the realities of life for the poor." The case was, for Marshall, a revisit to *Brown,* and its promise that education would be "the only route by which [the poor] become full participants in our society."[19] The Court, Marshall believed, betrayed that promise in *Rodriguez* and *Kadrmas*.

When fundamental interests interacted with poverty, Marshall's sliding-scale approach allowed him to explore the matters that most concerned him. Congress adopted the so-called Hyde Amendment, named for pro-life Republican Representative Henry Hyde of Illinois, which barred the use of federal Medicaid funds for abortions. The Court upheld the constitutionality of the Hyde Amendment in 1980, applying the two-tier approach.[20]

The outcome of *Harris v. McRae,* the Hyde Amendment case, may well have been inevitable, given the political climate surrounding the abortion issue. When the justices discussed the case, they focused primarily on whether the Hyde Amendment was significantly different from an earlier restriction on public funding for abortions, which the Court had also upheld. Burger said that he "never regarded *Roe* as creating [a] new const[itutional] right but only [as] a limitation on [the] state." Powell, reiterating his approach from *Rodriguez,* thought that, although there was "no const[itutional] right to any medical care, . . . since some was provided equal protection [was] implicated, although the test was the weak rational-basis standard."[21]

Justice Brennan wrote the primary dissent, but Marshall wrote separately. His dissent concluded by saying that denying public assistance to poor women who needed abortions as a medically necessary procedure would have "a devastating impact on the lives and health of poor women. I do not believe that a Constitution committed to the equal protection of the laws can tolerate this result." His opinion focused on two points. He again criticized the Court for the "relentlessly formalistic catechism" of its two-tier approach. He said that the case was "perhaps the most dramatic illustration to date of the deficiencies" in the two-tier approach; "legislation that imposes a crushing burden on indigent women can[not] be treated with the same deference given to legislation distinguishing among business interests." Applying his own approach, Marshall stressed the "grotesque choices" facing a poor woman denied public funding for a medically necessary abortion: She could have an illegal abortion or attempt to bear the child, which would "significantly threaten her health and eliminate any chance she might have had 'to control the direction of her own life.'" Further, the affected class "consists of indigent women, a substantial proportion of whom are members of minority races." "In these circumstances," the opinion said, "I am unable to see how even a minimally rational legislature could conclude that the interest in fetal life outweighs the brutal effect of the Hyde Amendment on indigent women."

The opinion's second theme was precisely how "brutal" the consequences would be. He criticized the Court, not only for its doctrinal approach but also for "blinding itself" to the existence of the real world in which poor women lived. The Court distinguished between the limitation on government power that its basic abortion decision articulated and "an affirmative funding obligation," but, Marshall's opinion said, "For a poor woman attempting to exercise her 'right' to freedom of choice, the difference is imperceptible."

As his opinion in the Hyde Amendment case shows, Marshall's most impassioned statements came in cases dealing with the government's role in regulating the lives of poor people. He wrote the Court's opinion invalidating a Wisconsin statute effectively limiting the right of some impoverished men to marry.[22] The statute said that men under court orders to support their children could not marry unless they showed that they had paid the outstanding support awards and that their children were not likely to become public charges. The statute might seem a reasonable way to deal with the problem of "deadbeat dads" by giving them incentives to pay what they were supposed to. It had a substantial effect on fathers who were not really deadbeats, because they had been unable to pay the support through no fault of their own. Marshall treated the right to marry as "of fundamental importance," although not explicitly guaranteed by the Constitution (another indication of the erosion of the majority's approach in *Rodriguez*). The government, Marshall said, could not serve as a "collection device" for support payments from people who could not make the payments under any circumstances.

Some of the fundamental-interest cases placed pressure on the majority's rigid approach to equal protection doctrine. The approach crumbled in cases involving gender discrimination. The Court's majority found itself unable to fit those cases into the two-tier framework. To justices facing the question in the 1970s, discrimination against women was enough like race discrimination to make them suspicious. Those same justices, however, were men who had grown up in a world where women, it was widely believed, had "proper" roles that governments could recognize. The Court's majority never fully abandoned that belief. It therefore could not treat discrimination against women as completely unjustified. Genderdiscrimination cases did not demand the highest level of scrutiny, but they did require something more than the lowest level. Marshall's sliding-scale approach made it easy for him to deal with these cases. The majority, as in other areas, struggled to work out an approach.

In 1971 the Court entered the area in a seemingly innocuous case, invalidating an Idaho statute specifying that, within the groups entitled to administer estates (parents, children, brothers, and sisters), men would be preferred to women.[23] Burger wrote a short opinion applying low-level review and concluding that the preference for men was not rational.

A year later the Court faced a harder problem. *Frontiero v. Richardson* involved a federal statute that allowed male members of the armed forces automatically to claim their spouses as dependents and thereby get higher benefits but required female members of the armed forces to demonstrate that their spouses were dependent before they could get the increased benefits.[24] The statute gave men in the armed forces a larger package of pay and benefits than it gave women, and most of the justices thought it was clearly unconstitutional. Burger thought the estate case "has nothing to do with this," but most of his colleagues seemed to agree that they could rely on Burger's earlier opinion, apply low-level review, and say the discrimination was irrational.[25]

Douglas assigned the opinion to Brennan, who turned out a draft rather quickly. He was not happy with it, however. The problem, as he saw it, was that the estate case really did not involve a completely irrational judgment: Idaho's legislators would not be irrational in thinking that more men than women had business experiences that would help in administering estates. Even worse, it did not seem completely irrational for Congress to think that additional benefits should be given for truly dependent spouses, that wives were much more likely than husbands to be truly dependent, and that the costs of identifying which wives were not dependent would be so great that it made sense to give additional benefits to all wives and only some husbands. Low-level review did not explain the estate case, and could not easily be used in *Frontiero*.

Brennan's cover note with his draft said that he was ready to work on an alternative opinion treating gender as a "suspect classification" like race and therefore subject to high-level review in the Court's two-tier approach. Marshall indicated that he "share[d]" the view "that this case would provide an appropriate vehicle for recognizing sex as a suspect cr[i]terion." White immediately weighed in with a note saying that Marshall was "right" in asserting that the estate case "applied more than a rational basis test." He also suggested that sex should be treated as a suspect classification, "if for no other reason than the fact that Congress has submitted a constitutional amendment making sex discrimination unconstitutional." But, he said, it might not follow that the right standard was the stringent requirement that classifications serve a "compelling interest." "I agree with Thurgood that we actually have a spectrum of interests." What the Court should do, White said, was say explicitly that sometimes "we will balance or weigh competing interests." White clearly had accepted Marshall's sliding-scale approach. Stewart, in contrast, found "no need to decide in this case whether sex is a 'suspect' classification."[26]

Brennan knew that Douglas would agree with the "suspect classification" approach. With four votes in hand, Brennan's clerks began to work on the alternative opinion, circulated two weeks later. Saying that sex discrimination was "[t]raditionally . . . rationalized by an attitude of 'romantic paternalism' which, in practical effect, put women, not on a pedestal, but in a cage," the new draft also incorporated White's suggestion that the opinion should rely on the "conclusion of a coequal branch of Government" in submitting the Equal Rights Amendment to the states for ratification.

What Burger called a "'shuttlecock' [of] memos" went around the chambers over the next week. Powell's was the most important. His "principal concern," Powell wrote, was that the Court would be "preempting the amendatory process initiated by the Congress." The Equal Rights Amendment would "represent the will of the people" on the question, whereas Brennan's proposed opinion "assumed a decisional responsibility (not within the democratic process) unnecessary to the decision of this case, and at the very time that legislatures around the country are debating the genuine pros and cons of how far it is wise, fair and prudent to subject both sexes to identical responsibilities as well as rights." It was odd, Powell clearly thought, for the draft opinion to rely on an unratified constitutional amendment to accomplish what the amendment would do if it were ratified. Powell found the underlying question difficult. "Women certainly have not been treated as being fungible with men (thank God!). Yet, the reasons for different treatment have in no way resembled the purposeful and invidious discrimination directed against blacks and aliens." And, Powell observed, women were no longer "a discrete minority barred from effective participation in the political process." Burger pointed out that "[t]he author of [the estate case] never contemplated such a broad concept but then a lot of people sire off-spring unintended!"[27]

Douglas found Powell's position "understandable" but disagreed: In employment cases, "the discrimination is as invidious and purposeful as that directed against blacks and aliens." He hoped that Brennan could "sail between *Scylla* and *Charybdis*." Brennan tried, with a letter to Powell, diplomatically saying that after "much thought" he continued to believe that "now is the time, and this is the case" to hold sex a suspect classification. Relying on Marshall's analysis of the estate case, he said that "the only rational explication" of that case was "that it rests on the 'suspect' approach." Nor could the Court "count on the Equal Rights Amendment to make the Equal Protection issue go away." Eleven states had voted against it, and more seemed likely: The Amendment, Brennan wrote, "looks like a lost cause." As a result, he did not see that "we gain anything by awaiting what is at best an uncertain outcome." This view, of course, only heightened the anomaly of relying on the submission of the amendment for ratification as part of the justification for Brennan's proposal.[28]

In the end, Brennan could not find the fifth vote. Stewart suggested that Brennan return to his first draft. Then, in a later case, Stewart stated he "would probably go along with" the suspect-classification approach.[29] Brennan decided against that course, and *Frontiero* ended up only with a plurality adopting that approach. Eight justices, however, did vote to invalidate the statute. Explaining why it was irrational was quite difficult, and *Frontiero* joined the estate case as an example of a decision purporting to invoke the two-tier approach while actually doing something else.

The Court finally reached agreement on gender-discrimination cases in 1976, when it invalidated an Oklahoma statute that allowed sales of 3.2 percent beer to young women but not to young men. Brennan relied on the estate case for the rule that gender discriminations were constitutionally tolerable if they "serve important governmental objectives and . . . [are] substantially related to achievement of those objectives." Although Burger initially told Brennan that he was "'available,' . . . particularly if we do not expand the 'equal advantage' clause or 'suspect' classifications," he ended up dissenting, along with Rehnquist, because Brennan's analysis "read into [the estate case] what was not there." That case, Burger believed, was "innocuous," whereas Brennan's approach "goes beyond what I could accept."[30]

Powell also had "some reservations as to the breadth" of Brennan's analysis, but he said he was "in substantial agreement" with Brennan. He wrote a short opinion noting the Court's "difficulty in agreeing upon a standard . . . that can be applied consistently to the wide variety of legislative classifications." The author of *Rodriguez* now thought there were "valid reasons for dissatisfaction with the 'two-tier' approach." He was unwilling, however, to endorse Marshall's sliding-scale analysis or, it appeared, anything else, saying that he did not "welcome a further subdividing of equal protection analysis."[31]

Powell called the near-beer case "relatively easy." The Court's next gender-discrimination case, in contrast, was plainly an important one. In response to what he believed were renewed military threats from the Soviet Union and concerned about the fact that his political standing was being hurt by the image that he was a weak president, President Jimmy Carter decided to resume draft registration in 1980. Although Carter urged Congress to permit registration and conscription of women, Congress refused. A lower court held that it was unconstitutional to require men but not women to register for the draft.

Dissatisfaction with the framework within which they had to decide the case pervaded the justices' discussion of the case. Burger opened by saying that "[t]his action right or wrong satisfies" the standard in the near-beer case. But, he said, he was willing to go further and say that "this is [the] business of Congress" alone because it involved the power to regulate the military. Stewart immediately disagreed, because he believed "all powers are alike in [being] subject to limitations." He did not agree, he said, "with tier tests." For him, the question was whether the discrimination "invidious[ly]" treated men and women differently. A navy veteran proud of his service and the combat awards he received, Stewart thought the discrimination constitutionally permissible because women were ineligible for combat service. Blackmun thought there was some "danger of stereotyping," but he would uphold the statute under the near-beer case. Powell had been an important figure in U.S. Army Intelligence during World War II. Like Burger, Powell thought the "defense of our country should of all cases require deference to Congressional findings," particularly because Carter's rejected request to Congress was based on "equity" rather than "military need."[32]

Burger assigned the opinion to Rehnquist. Relying on Congress's power to raise and support armies, Rehnquist's opinion argued that the Court should give particularly great deference to the legislative judgment in military matters and expressed discomfort with the use of "tests" like "strict scrutiny," which, he said, could "all too readily become facile abstractions used to justify a result." His opinion also pointed out that the question of including women in the registration process and the constitutionality of excluding them had been discussed extensively in the legislative process. Then, turning to the justification for the exclusion of women from registration, Rehnquist said that the purpose of registration was to ensure the availability of personnel for the military in crisis times. The central fact of military crisis was the use of soldiers in combat, and, Rehnquist noted, a statute not challenged in *Rostker v. Goldberg* barred women from combat roles. Because women could not be used in combat, "Congress concluded that they would not be needed in the event of a draft, and therefore decided not to register them." The combat exclusion meant that "men and women . . . are simply not similarly situated," and registering only men was therefore "closely related to Congress' purpose in authorizing registration." Congress, Rehnquist said, simply did not think that the added burden of registering all women was justified in light of the relatively few who could be used in a draft for noncombat positions.

White wrote a brief dissent and Marshall a much more extensive one.[33] White also took the combat exclusion as a given but argued that it did not make sense to exclude women from registration when they would be available to be drafted for noncombat roles. As he summarized his position, in a crisis the armed forces would need to draft people for combat and noncombat positions; he found "no adequate justification" for registering and drafting only men for the noncombat positions.

Marshall's dissent was more indignant. He chastised the Court for "plac[ing] its imprimatur" on the exclusion of women "from a fundamental civic obligation." For him, the question was whether the discrimination against women substantially served the important end of military preparedness. The combat exclusion in itself could not justify the exclusion of women from registration, because women could be drafted to perform noncombat duties. He argued that Rehnquist had it backward. Rehnquist's opinion asked whether treating women the same as men was necessary to achieve the purpose of registration and concluded that, because the purpose of registration was to prepare for a draft of combat troops, treating women the same as men was not necessary. Marshall said that the question should have been the reverse. The question was, Does treating women *differently from* men promote the purposes of registration? More precisely, does excluding women from registration substantially further the goal of preparing for a combat draft, or would including them interfere with the effort to set up a combat draft? For Marshall, the only barrier to registering both men and women but drafting only men for combat needs was some additional cost in administering the registration system. But, he said, the Court had routinely rejected claims that additional administrative costs justified discrimination against women. Marshall then provided an extensive review of the testimony that members of the armed forces gave to Congress, which showed that there would inevitably be a substantial need to draft people for noncombat positions, for which a registration list that included women would be entirely appropriate.*

---

*In the background of the case but unmentioned by any of the opinions was the fact that the military testimony supporting registration of women occurred primarily because the Carter administration insisted on equal registration over the initial objection of the armed forces. For the preliminary views of some military leaders, see *New York Times*, Feb. 6, 1980, § II, p. 4, col. 5. When Congress rejected the administration's position, it also rejected the articulated stance of the armed forces but not their fundamental views.

The conclusion of Marshall's opinion took direct aim at the language of "deference" to Congress that pervaded the majority opinion, calling that language "hollow shibboleths" that substitute for "constitutional analysis." The tone of the opinion was heightened when it said that "congressional enactments in the area of military affairs must, like all other laws, be *judged* by the standards of the Constitution."

Marshall's opinion as a whole was curiously similar to the majority's. Both had a peculiarly abstracted air. Both tried to explain in rational terms why exclusion of women from draft registration was or was not justified. Those terms, however, were quite unsuitable for the purely political reality: Congress in 1980 simply did not regard women as quite right for the armed forces even if, somehow, the nation had gotten used to the idea that there could actually be women soldiers. That, of course, is what "mere prejudice" is, and Marshall's opinion would have been stronger had it brought into the open and criticized directly the underlying prejudicial judgments.

The gender-discrimination cases reflected the Court's dissatisfaction with the rigidity associated with the high end of its two-tier doctrine. Probably more important in reshaping equal protection law, however, was an obscure case in which the justices struggled over the low end. As the Court prepared to issue its opinion in the near-beer case, Powell sent Brennan a personal note saying that the difficulties in defining the standard were "*Murgia* revisited!"[34] *Murgia* occupies only ten pages in the *United States Reports,* but it resulted from an extended controversy within the Court that affected Powell's understanding of his place within the Court's political and jurisprudential spectrum and, through Powell, pushed equal protection law in the direction of Marshall's sliding-scale approach.

Massachusetts Board of Retirement v. Murgia rejected an equal protection challenge to a state statute requiring all state police officers to retire at the age of fifty.[35] Only Marshall voted to invalidate the Massachusetts statute,* and Burger, assigning the opinion to Brennan, probably believed that nothing Brennan could do would advance the liberal cause. The majority agreed that the statute should be subject only to low-level review. Brennan circulated a draft in January 1976 that immediately set Rehnquist on edge. Brennan used the occasion to rerationalize the Court's recent cases. Commentators had pointed out that the statutes invalidated in some of those cases could readily be justified by some imaginable state purposes and that, as law professor Gerald Gunther put it, the "rationality review" test the Court seemed to be applying actually had some "bite."[36] Brennan's reformulation attempted to incorporate those cases in a new, more flexible standard.

Rehnquist tried a preemptive strike: Saying that he would not get a separate opinion out for "a couple of weeks," Rehnquist sent Brennan a letter "for [his] benefit (?)" expressing concern about the way in which Brennan stated the standard of review, which would, in Rehnquist's view, "give the courts more leeway in striking down state legislation." Although Brennan's standard was drawn from

---

* In 1995 a justice of the Russian Constitutional Court said that, in studying U.S. Supreme Court opinion, he found Marshall's opinion more persuasive than the majority's and relied on it in voting, with a majority of the constitutional court, to strike down a mandatory retirement statute. Brett Gerry to Randall Kennedy, July 26, 1995 (in author's possession).

prior cases, Rehnquist thought Brennan had transformed its meaning. For Rehnquist, the standard "ought to be simply stated and ought to virtually foreclose judicial invalidation except in the rare, rare case where the legislature has all but run amok and acted in a patently arbitrary manner."[37]

Brennan replied on February 9, agreeing that his draft did indeed offer "a more flexible view" of the "minimum scrutiny" standard than Rehnquist supported, though Brennan argued that the Court's cases had "evolved" to the point his draft described. Brennan pointed out that several recent cases could not readily be explained as relying on as loose a standard as Rehnquist suggested. The "fair and substantial relation" standard Brennan proposed, he wrote, came from another half-dozen cases, which, although "fall[ing] into the twilight zone of equal protection," were "part of the warp and woof of equal protection law."[38]

Brennan circulated his correspondence to the other justices on February 12, with a cover letter saying that in his view Rehnquist's position was "at odds with statements in a number of equal protection cases . . . over the past half century." The case made "little progress" toward disposition for a month, perhaps because the correspondence made it clear that Brennan and Rehnquist disagreed about how much flexibility there was in the "minimum rationality" standard.[39]

A side issue began to distract some justices. In explaining why the mandatory retirement statute did not have to satisfy any strict standard of review, Brennan referred to "the political clout of the aged." Blackmun thought that *lack* of "political clout" might justify more stringent review but was "hesitant to go beyond that." And, although he agreed with "much" of Brennan's reasoning, Powell, too, rejected what he called Brennan's "central position that a high degree of political participation in itself is sufficient to support the conclusion that those of middle age do not form a suspect class."[40]

By the beginning of April, it seemed that Brennan's opinion might not get a single additional vote. Powell circulated an opinion attempting to flesh out in some detail an analysis of political power that might be adequate to the case. Anticipating what he wrote in the near-beer case, Powell agreed with Brennan that the Court's application of "minimum rationality" review had become more flexible, citing Gunther's article. Powell discussed the ways in which courts might identify "legitimate" state purposes and cautioned against "imagin[ing] policy where none has been indicated by the legislature." Brennan conferred with Powell and "adopted" Powell's opinion as his own. Even then, "no Court developed," and Brennan basically turned the opinion over to Powell. Powell revised his draft "to attain as much unanimity as possible on a general formulation of the rational basis equal protection test."[41]

Rehnquist continued to find the Powell-Brennan position unsatisfactory. Powell's test, he wrote, "is really a very significant departure from constitutional adjudication as developed in the decisions of this Court." In a memorandum conveying in firm tones the depth of his disagreement with the position Powell and Brennan had worked out, Rehnquist wrote that an extensive discussion of whether the statute affected a suspect classification was unnecessary and particularly objected to Powell's extensive treatment of "the relative success of the aged in obtaining their wishes legislatively." He understood, though, that this discussion was not central to the outcome and focused more on what he called the "expansion" of the rational-basis test.[42]

Rehnquist had two main concerns. Although he agreed that legislation had to pursue "legitimate" purposes, he was unconvinced that much need be said about that. Rehnquist's tone was stern: One implication of a phrase in a footnote was "difficult to support in law or logic"; the basis for another suggestion "escapes me entirely." Second, Rehnquist had "the most serious reservations about that portion of your memorandum which seems to contemplate the bodily assumption into the Equal Protection Clause of Professor Gunther's article." That article, Rehnquist wrote, "seems to me to be in the area of political science, rather than of constitutional law." Rehnquist concluded with a "peroration" because he had "gotten [him]self sufficiently worked up." The "basic shortcoming" of Powell's analysis was that "it sets up this Court . . . to evaluate a legislative decision to implement a particular purpose by enacting some provision of a given statute. It seems to me almost inconceivable that we could correctly conclude that a group of legislators, all devoting a good part of their time to the art of legislation, chose a means which was not 'genuinely' related to their purpose."

Needing to get votes from justices who had not yet responded, Powell tried again. Powell's revisions did not make Rehnquist comfortable, because they did not go to the second problem Rehnquist had. But, Rehnquist wrote, he would "try to do some accommodating of [his] own," and agreed to "swallow [his] objections . . . if the resolution of this battle is by agreement to be left for another day." He was willing to let Powell's discussion of purpose stand, but only if the opinion also included "both sides of the doctrinal dispute" by including a quotation of Rehnquist's preferred standard. "Admittedly," Rehnquist wrote, "this is inconsistent with your analysis, but it will not be the first time that an Equal Protection opinion has contained verbal inconsistencies."[43]

By this point it was clear that the Court was hopelessly divided on equal protection theory or at least on the verbal formulations the justices used to describe standards of review. Powell apparently was uncomfortable with writing an opinion that, in both his and Rehnquist's eyes, was internally inconsistent, and he recirculated a final draft "about as blandly written as one can write." The draft, he told his colleagues, left each of them "free to 'fight again another day.'"[44]

Although the published opinion in *Murgia* reflects nothing of Powell's struggle with the case, the Court's deliberations helped shape its jurisprudence. When he circulated his final draft, which became the Court's opinion, Powell told his colleagues that "my zeal for writing has been so thoroughly dampened by this spring's experience, that it may be sometime before I venture forth again." For the next few years he regularly referred to the "struggle" in *Murgia*.[45]

As Powell understood what had happened, he saw Rehnquist on his right, refusing to adopt what Powell understood to be an entirely reasonable position and fighting for a purely theoretical point, and he saw Brennan on his left, being as reasonable as one could ask. Powell came to see Brennan as closer to him than his more conservative colleagues were. Brennan's liberalism, in short, was more reasonable than Rehnquist's conservatism. *Murgia* contributed to what Powell's biographer John Jeffries describes as Powell's increasing willingness to set aside legislative judgments, even though in that case Powell, Brennan, and Rehnquist all agreed that the Massachusetts statute was constitutional.[46]

Marshall's dissent, addressing only the published opinion and not what lay behind it, "object[ed] to [the] perpetuation" of the majority's "rigid two-tier model" because the two tiers "simply do not describe the inquiry the Court has undertaken—or should undertake—in equal protection cases." He expressed dismay that the Court "has apparently lost interest in recognizing further 'fundamental' rights and 'suspect' classes" but regarded that course as "the natural consequence" of the two-tier analysis because "strict scrutiny" almost always led to invalidating the statute in question. Thus, "the critical decision is whether strict scrutiny should be invoked at all." A Court committed to a two-tier analysis, and committed to the near-automatic invalidation of statutes falling in the upper tier of strict scrutiny, naturally was "hesitant to expand the number of categories of rights and classes subject to strict scrutiny." Yet, Marshall argued, the proper response to that dilemma was not to "drop" all other laws into the lower tier, because there "the challenged legislation is always upheld." Rather, the Court should adopt his sliding-scale approach.

The difficulty that the Court's analysis failed to confront, for Marshall, was that "there remain rights, not now classified as 'fundamental,' that remain vital to the flourishing of a free society, and classes, not now classified as 'suspect,' that are unfairly burdened by invidious discrimination unrelated to the individual worth of their members." He noted, in addition, a large number of cases in which "the Court's deeds have not matched its words" because, "met with cases touching upon the prized rights and burdened classes of our society, the Court has acted only after a reasonably probing look at the legislative goals and means, and at the significance of the personal rights and interests invaded." Though the outcomes of these cases might be satisfactory, the Court's insistence that it really was using the two-tier approach meant that the actual process of decision was "rudderless" and "unpredictable," producing results "on an *ad hoc* basis." He urged the Court to "drop the pretense" that "all interests not 'fundamental' and all classes not 'suspect' are . . . the same."

Murgia itself was, as Marshall saw it, a good example of "the danger of the Court's verbal adherence to the rigid two-tier test." Mandatory retirement of able-bodied police officers simply should not have been "judged by the same minimal standards of rationality that we use to test economic legislation that discriminates against business interests." For Marshall, the case involved a right to work, and it should not matter whether the Court decided to call that right fundamental or not. Taking away anyone's job was "a significant deprivation," but, according to Marshall, it was "particularly burdensome" to older citizens because they "cannot readily find alternative employment": "Deprived of his status in the community and of the opportunity for meaningful activity, fearful of becoming dependent on others for his support, and lonely in his new-found isolation, the involuntarily retired person is susceptible to physical and emotional ailments as a direct consequence of his enforced idleness." And, the opinion continued, "[W]hether older workers constitute a 'suspect' class or not, it cannot be disputed that they constitute a class subject to repeated and arbitrary discrimination in employment."

Marshall noted that "the advantage of a flexible equal protection standard" was precisely "that it can readily accommodate such variables."

The justices regularly referred to *Murgia,* and none found it satisfactory. During the same Court Term, Rehnquist cheerfully referred to the reservations he had expressed *"ad nauseam"* in the discussions of *Murgia;* Burger referred to "the hassle we're now in as to what is proper equal protection analysis"; Powell joined, "unhappily," what he referred to as "the 'neutered' version of Murgia's twin." At the same time, despite Burger's occasional urgings, they were unwilling to abandon the attempt to develop an appropriate language of "tiers and levels of judicial scrutiny."[47]

The Court eventually came to understand that Marshall was right, although a majority never clearly said that the Court abandoned the two-tier analysis. Marshall's argument about equal protection doctrine in *Murgia* was almost openly vindicated by the Court's action nearly a decade later in *Cleburne v. Cleburne Living Center,* and Marshall's separate opinion was almost gleeful, as Supreme Court opinions go, in pointing that out.[48]

The case, decided in 1985, involved a decision by the city of Cleburne to use its zoning powers to prevent the establishment of a group home for the mentally retarded. The home's supporters argued that mental retardation was a "quasi-suspect" classification, akin to gender, and that discrimination against the mentally retarded had to be justified by more substantial reasons than were usually enough to satisfy low-level scrutiny. The court of appeals applied a high level of review.

The persistent confusion about the right approach was reflected in the justices' conference, when Burger said the retarded were not a "discrete [and] insular minority" but thought they were "entitled to special attention but not heightened." White, too, did not want to create a new "category [receiving] heightened" scrutiny. Rehnquist thought the justices should "rein in" the trend to create new categories. Along with O'Connor, they voted to send the case back to the lower court for it to apply low-level review. Brennan, Marshall, and Blackmun disagreed. Blackmun said he could "go along" with treating the retarded, who were "politically weak," as a "quasi-suspect" class. Stevens, applying low-level review, thought there was "no rational basis" for the regulation and voted with them to affirm the lower court. The Court was evenly divided about the outcome because Powell had been ill when the case was argued. Five justices thought that low-level review was appropriate, but Stevens wanted to affirm the lower court instead of sending the case back to it.[49]

The justices ordered reargument. Powell and now O'Connor thought they "could go along" with Stevens's approach. Powell "hesitate[d] to go to" high-level review "which I've never favored." Indeed, he said, he was "not sure even race or gender needs more than rational" basis review. A majority wanted to reject the court of appeals position that treated the retarded as a suspect classification, and White willingly took on the job of writing an opinion that did so even at the cost of invalidating the regulation as failing low-level scrutiny. Powell thought that was a curious way to deal with the case. Because the majority was going to hold the ordinance unconstitutional on the narrow ground that the city "has failed to show any legitimate interest for the curious classifications" it used, there was no reason, he thought, "to consider the quasi-suspect class question." Rehnquist immediately endorsed White's approach. Invalidating the ordinance as irrational "would not bother me greatly," he wrote, but "[t]o simply 'punt' and turn this case into one of five or six hundred decisions . . . applying rational basis equal protection analysis . . . would, to my mind, rob the decision of any importance which it would otherwise have."[50]

White replied to Powell the next day, saying that his draft opinion reflected the discussion among the justices and, he thought, Powell's own views. In a modest reminder to Powell that the Court might end up completely splintered, White said that he would "much prefer" to remand the case to the lower court instead of finding the ordinance unconstitutional. If he did not get a majority for the rejection of heightened scrutiny, he said, the case should be reassigned. Powell apologized for the confusion about his position and ended up "willing to join an opinion holding that only the rational basis standard is applicable." After some additional conversations among Powell, White, and Brennan, White's draft then became the Court's opinion.[51]

Did it apply ordinary rational-basis review, however? Mental retardation did not elicit special scrutiny for several reasons, according to White. First, the mentally retarded were "different, immutably so," from others, and governments properly had an interest in "dealing with and providing for them." The group was "large and diversified," and their proper treatment "[was] a difficult and often a technical matter" best left to "legislators guided by qualified professionals and not by the perhaps ill-informed opinions of the judiciary." Second, statutes providing assistance to the mentally retarded demonstrated that legislatures had acted "in a manner that belies a continuing antipathy or prejudice and a corresponding need for more intrusive oversight by the judiciary." These laws "reflect[ed] the real and undeniable differences between the retarded and others." The laws also showed that the mentally retarded were not "politically powerless." Finally, White was concerned that if the Court held that "the large and amorphous class of the mentally retarded were deemed quasi-suspect," so would many other groups "who have perhaps immutable disabilities setting them off from others . . . and who can claim some degree of prejudice from at least part of the public at large," such as "the aging, the disabled, the mentally ill, and the infirm."

Having concluded that the city's action did not trigger high-level review, White then found that the city's justifications did not satisfy even the Court's weakest standard. He went through the city's reasons for denying the requested permit. The city council "was concerned with the negative attitude" of people in the neighborhood. But, White wrote, "mere negative attitudes, or fear," are not permissible bases for treating a group home for the mentally retarded different from apartment houses. The council also purported to be protecting the potential residents of the home from harassment by students from a nearby school. White pointed out that mentally retarded students actually attended the school and said that the city could not rely on "such vague, undifferentiated fears." The city also expressed concern that the home would be located on a floodplain and that evacuating the residents in an emergency might prove difficult. White responded that the problem of evacuation was no different for the mentally retarded than for residents of nursing homes, which the city permitted in the area. Finally, to the city's objection to the size of the home, Justice White replied that the city had no objection to nursing homes or fraternity houses of the same size. "The short of it is," White concluded, that the city's action "appears to us to rest on an irrational prejudice against the mentally retarded."

Marshall's separate opinion found the Court's holding consistent with his understanding of the equal protection clause, which "requires attention to the capacities and needs of retarded people as individuals." He objected, though, to the Court's disclaimer that it was doing "anything special, in the form of heightened scrutiny," for, the opinion said, the city's action "surely would be valid under the traditional rational-basis test applicable to economic and commercial regulation." For example, in the commercial context it would not have mattered that the city invoked concerns about evacuation for one type of group residence but not for other types, because the Court had repeatedly said that cities could "take one step at a time." He found it "puzzling," therefore, that the Court unnecessarily examined in detail the arguments for treating the mentally retarded as a quasi-suspect classification and was concerned as well that "the Court provides no principled foundation for determining when more searching inquiry is to be invoked." The opinion concluded by criticizing the Court's "obsessive" focus on "the appropriate label to give its standard of review." For him, "the formal label . . . is less important than careful identification of the interest at stake and the extent to which society recognizes the classification as an invidious one."

The opinion applied Marshall's sliding-scale approach. "Excluding group homes deprives the retarded of much of what makes for human freedom and fulfillment—the ability to form bonds and take part in the life of a community." Further, the mentally retarded had been the subjects of a "grotesque" history of segregation and discrimination that "in its virulence and bigotry rivaled, and indeed paralleled, the worst excesses of Jim Crow." As a result, "lengthy and continuing isolation of the retarded has perpetuated the ignorance, irrational fears, and stereotyping that long have plagued them." The city's action indicated that it regarded the retarded as "pariahs who do not belong in the community."

The opinion also addressed White's arguments against giving special attention to discrimination against the mentally retarded. To the argument that legislative action aiding the mentally retarded showed that they were no longer the object of general prejudice, Marshall responded by saying that there should be an interaction between the legislative and the judicial recognition of past prejudice and its continuing effects. Cultural and social patterns shift, and "it is natural that evolving standards of equality come to be embodied in legislation." The courts should take such laws "as a source of guidance on evolving principles" rather than as an obstacle to further advance; otherwise, "the only discrimination courts may remedy is the discrimination they alone are perspicacious enough to see." In Marshall's opinion, "For the retarded, just as for Negroes and women, much has changed in recent years, but much remains the same," requiring heightened judicial attention to "outmoded statutes" that "continue to stymie recognition of the dignity and individuality of retarded people." More generally, the opinion cautioned against reducing the reasons for invoking heightened scrutiny to "a single talisman" or to a checklist. Rather, the courts should act when the group has been "the target of the sort of prejudiced, thoughtless, or stereotyped action that offends principles of equality" and the threat of similar action remains active.

For Marshall, the sliding-scale approach in *Dandridge* and *Rodriguez* had obvious advantages over the majority's two-tier approach. As would become increasingly apparent, the sliding-scale approach simply made more sense of the Court's actions than the two-tier approach. Powell's difficulties with *Skinner* are suggestive, as is the obvious circularity of his treatment of the voting cases: Under the equal protection clause, strict scrutiny is required of classifications treating people unequally with respect to voting because there is an implicit constitutional right to equal treatment with respect to voting. One can fairly ask what the equal protection clause contributes to the analysis if there is such a right.

The doctrinal anomalies, which multiplied over the next decades, resulted from the perception by shifting majorities on the Court that some problems just were not well handled within the rigid two-tier framework. Committed to that framework, majorities continued to squeeze cases into the upper tier when it was obvious to disinterested observers that the language of the two-tier analysis was incompatible with the results the Court was generating. Marshall's approach allowed him to be open about the flexibility he and apparently a fair number of his colleagues thought appropriate to handle the difficult problems of social life that litigation under the equal protection clause brought to the Court.

This analysis provides an indirect answer to the concerns expressed by Stewart and Powell that anything other than the two-tier approach would let judges implement their policy preferences under the guise of enforcing constitutional rights. Enough justices found some cases so troubling that they would find constitutional violations no matter what.[52] Using the two-tier approach, they disguised their reliance on their policy preferences; under the sliding-scale approach, the policy questions would be discussed openly and candidly. In short, Stewart and Powell attempted to construct a doctrine that would avoid what turned out to be unavoidable; Marshall offered an alternative that made it possible to talk about what the justices actually wanted to do.

The Court's discussions of equal protection analysis were, from an outside point of view, highly technical. The cases did not invite jockeying among the justices to attract votes for any reason other than the persuasiveness of the analysis. Personalities did matter, however. Rehnquist's refusal to yield much ground in *Murgia* permanently affected Powell's willingness to loosen up the standard of review that he himself had articulated in *Rodriguez*. The Court's difficulties were important, too, because of the implications of having a rigid doctrine or a more flexible one like Marshall's for the far more contentious issue of affirmative action. There, too, however, the doctrinal difficulties prevented the Court from reaching a consensus on affirmative action during Marshall's tenure.

6

"Now, When a State Acts to Remedy . . . Discrimination"
Affirmative Action

Affirmative action programs increased the controversy over the jurisprudence of equality that arose after *Brown v. Board of Education*. As school desegregation cases shifted focus from desegregation to integration, they also changed from cases dealing with violations of the rights of particular individual students to cases dealing with claimed violations of the rights of African-Americans as a group. Conservatives asserting sympathy with the aims of the civil rights movement criticized affirmative action programs, which they saw as aimed at protecting group rights. Such programs, these critics charged, were inconsistent with the fundamental commitments to individual rights that Marshall made during the segregation litigation.[1]

Marshall was fundamentally nonracialist and constantly aware of race's importance in the United States. At the news conference held on his retirement, Marshall referred to what a Pullman porter told him as a young boy. The porter, Marshall said, "told me that he had been in every city in this country, he was sure, and he had never been in any city in the United States where he had to put his hand up in front of his face to find out he was a Negro." Marshall thought the porter's observation was true even in 1991. At the same time, Marshall led a multiracial personal life. His second wife, Cecilia (Cissy), was of Philippine origin, and both his sons married white women. His 1955 marriage to Cissy occasioned some office gossip, in part because some of Marshall's colleagues at the NAACP thought it somehow inappropriate for a professional to marry a secretary and in part because some thought he should marry an African-American again. As Marshall's former law clerk Cass Sunstein observed, Marshall was committed to equality of opportunity, but his vision of what that commitment entailed, and of its implications for judicial review, was more complex than Marshall's critics understood.[2]

Marshall was familiar with questions of affirmative action long before they became prominent in national politics. During the 1930s and 1940s, African-Americans occasionally campaigned against employment discrimination at stores in African-American communities, using the slogan, "Don't Buy Where You Can't Work." Starting out as straightforward antidiscrimination programs, sometimes these campaigns put pressure on grocery stores and retailers to engage in more aggressive outreach efforts. In 1961 such programs got the label "affirmative action" when President John F. Kennedy issued an executive order requiring employers with federal contracts to "take affirmative action to ensure" that they did not discriminate, an obligation later strengthened by President Lyndon Johnson.[3] And, as *Green* and its successors showed, proponents of aggressive outreach programs could easily come to use numerical measures—which their opponents pejoratively called quotas—to determine whether the employers had in fact stopped discriminating.

In 1947 a group of African-American and white residents of Richmond, California, associated with both the NAACP and the Progressive party, began to picket a Lucky's grocery store in a predominantly African-American neighborhood of Richmond, near San Francisco.[4] They carried signs saying "Lucky Won't Hire Negro Clerks in Proportion to Negro Trade—Don't Patronize" and demanded that African-American clerks be hired as white clerks were transferred or promoted, until the proportion of African-American clerks approximated the proportion of African-American patronage of the store, roughly 50 percent. Lucky got a state court to enjoin the picketing. When it continued, the picketers were held in contempt of court.[5] The picketers argued that their actions were protected by the First Amendment's free-speech clause.

Within the NAACP the Richmond case, *Hughes v. Superior Court,* was controversial. The NAACP's Richmond branch, which sponsored the picketing and the litigation, was one of the organization's more radical branches; in the year before the picketing, NAACP executive Walter White said, "Communists ha[d] achieved virtually complete dominance" of the NAACP branches in the San Francisco Bay area. The branch endorsed the picketing and the ensuing litigation without informing the national legal staff about its details. After receiving some clippings about the picketing, Marshall told the branch that the national office was "vitally interested in this problem" and that there was a good chance that the litigation would succeed.[6]

As the case proceeded through the courts, the national staff became more concerned. Marian Wynn Perry, for example, was "very disturbed" about the branch's attempt to obtain hiring in proportion to patronage, "since it appears to condone a quota system . . . and would be, of course, disastrous" if invoked outside predominantly African-American communities. Cecil Poole, an African-American attorney in San Francisco, also opposed the litigation. Proportional hiring was "unsound," he said. Rather, the NAACP must "base our demands . . . upon the democratic principle that we are entitled to equal opportunity based upon merit and ability to compete in the labor market without being prejudged on account of race or color." Seeking proportional hiring, he continued, "is at variance with this great sustaining principle and in place of the criterion of equality and merit substitutes artificial critera [sic] measured by the amount of business the particular employer may derive in the particular community." Like Perry, Poole objected to the advocacy of proportional hiring on grounds of prudence as well as ethics: Hiring in proportion to patronage could lead to exclusions from jobs in other communities. Jack Greenberg, a member of the national staff, suggested that the NAACP could diffuse the controversy by interpreting the proportional hiring demand as a simple antidiscrimination claim. Ultimately, Marshall decided to disconnect the question of proportional hiring from the free-speech question presented by the case. The NAACP's amicus brief in the case stated the organization's opposition to "proportional or quota hiring of Negroes" and argued only that if quota hiring was permitted by state law, picketing to secure it was protected by the First Amendment.[7]

By the time the Supreme Court considered *Hughes* in 1950, it had developed a law of picketing as free speech in some important labor cases. The labor law background affected the structure of free-speech law, because judges became concerned with both union goals and union methods. Judges thought that labor picketing inevitably involved coercion, either through the numbers of picketers, their behavior on the picket line, or the social pressure they could exert against those who crossed picket lines. The Supreme Court's free-speech doctrine accommodated these concerns. Picketing was protected as speech, according to the Court, if it had a lawful purpose and was conducted in a peaceful manner.[8] Because the picketing at Lucky's had been entirely peaceful, the only issue in *Hughes* was whether the goal of obtaining hiring in proportion to patronage was lawful.

The California Supreme Court held that such a policy would violate the state's common law. The court's majority relied on the NAACP's earlier successful challenge to the legality of a closed-shop collective bargaining agreement requiring the employer to hire only members of a white union.[9] For the majority, "if Lucky had yielded to the demands of [the picketers], its resultant hiring policy would have constituted, as to a proportion of its employees, the equivalent of both a closed shop and a closed union in favor of the Negro race." The positions reserved for African-Americans would have been a "closed shop," and the fact that "race and color are inherent qualities which no degree of striving or of other qualifications for a particular job could meet" meant that those who had such qualifications constituted a "closed union." If the picketers prevailed, "other races, white, yellow, brown and red, would have equal rights to demand discriminatory hiring on a racial basis."[10]

State supreme court justices Jesse Carter and Roger Traynor dissented. For Justice Carter, the picketers were seeking to implement a policy of nondiscrimination. In an African-American neighborhood, equity—the source of the law of injunctions—and fairness justified the attempt to use economic pressure to gain "equality in the labor field" from an employer who the picketers reasonably took to be engaged in discrimination. As Justice Carter saw it, the demand for proportional hiring was a demand for a remedy for discrimination:

> [I]f an employer who employs only one or two of a certain race in 10,000 employees, when hundreds of qualified members of such race are seeking employment, and he can be picketed by the members of such race to induce the employment of an increased number of such members, then it must follow that such employer may be picketed for

the purpose of inducing him to employ a sufficient number of such race to indicate an intention not to discriminate against the members of such race in the selection of his employees.

Justice Traynor's dissent focused on a different point. In his view, "[T]here is no reality in the reasoning that those who seek to secure jobs where they have an opportunity to enlist public support on their behalf are thereby seeking illegal discrimination in their favor, for the fact remains that everywhere they turn for jobs they are likely to encounter the barrier of discrimination." For him, it was dispositive that Lucky could lawfully adopt a policy of proportional hiring "on its own initiative." "The picketing confronts Lucky with the choice of adopting a policy that is not illegal in itself or risking the loss of patronage that may result from the picketing."

The United States Supreme Court upheld the injunction against the picketing. Justice Felix Frankfurter's opinion reiterated some of the California majority's themes, but because the Court was making law for the entire country, Frankfurter added some important qualifications. Frankfurter stressed the diversity of the nation's population:

> To deny California the right to ban picketing [here] . . . would mean that there could be no prohibition of the pressure of picketing to secure proportional employment on ancestral grounds of Hungarians in Cleveland, of Poles in Buffalo, of Germans in Milwaukee, of Portuguese in New Bedford, of Mexicans in San Antonio, of the numerous minority groups in New York, and so on through the whole gamut of racial and religious concentrations in various cities. States may well believe that such constitutional sheltering would inevitably encourage use of picketing to compel employment on the basis of racial discrimination.[11]

Frankfurter embedded his disapproval of proportional hiring in a more general constitutional framework that stressed the options available to states. "The policy of a State may rely for the common good on the free play of conflicting interests and leave conduct unregulated. Contrariwise, a State may deem it wiser to regulate." Regulation could take various forms, and "the form the regulation should take and its scope are surely matters of policy and, as such, within a State's choice."[12] The decision to allow or prohibit proportional hiring was a matter of state discretion.

The tension between individualist themes and group-oriented ones pervaded Marshall's rhetoric about segregation. In 1951 Marshall told the National Dental Association that once segregation was eliminated, "a dentist, or lawyer or a doctor [who] becomes a great man in his field . . . will no longer be considered as a great Negro dentist, a great Negro lawyer, or a great Negro doctor but rather as a great dentist, lawyer or doctor." In a February 1956 interview, Marshall responded to a white Southerner's claim that African-American children were inferior scholastically by saying that "at the very core of his concern was not the Negro but the individual human being." Improving the status of African-Americans "was a worthy cause," he said, but "it wasn't his cause," which was to make a reality of the ideal of "a society whose law and government were based on a fundamental belief in individual worth, individual opportunity, and individual responsibility." Individual problems should be dealt with, but "if ninety-nine Negro children out of a hundred should be found to be stupid, that hundredth one still has a right to equal educational opportunities."[13]

The question of affirmative action emerged almost naturally from the Court's confrontation with desegregation remedies. In *Swann,* Justice Stewart's first response to the Chief Justice's initial draft was to express dismay that the draft "purport[s] not to decide the constitutionality of 'a school authority decision that as a matter of sound educational policy schools should be racially balanced. . . .' I think it important to state that such a school board decision would be wholly constitutional."[14] The Court's final opinion adopted Stewart's position, saying that "[s]chool authorities . . . might well conclude, for example, that in order to prepare students to live in a pluralistic society each school should have a prescribed ratio of Negro to white students."[15]

In the terms used in current law, this ruling implied that public agencies could make race-conscious decisions, for how else could a school board ensure that the prescribed ratio would be met at each school? There is an instructive contrast here with the Court's rejection of the proposition that the Constitution mandates only desegregation, not integration. To its proponents, that proposition meant that governments could *not* take race into account in their decisions, in any way. *Brown* gained its force, in their view, from the moral proposition that race was totally irrelevant to any decisions governments make.

When the Court rejected that view, however, it did not mean that the Constitution required integration. Advocates offered the Court two positions in the years immediately following *Brown v. Board of Education:* Either the Constitution required only desegregation or it required integration. By 1971 *Swann* demonstrated that there was an intermediate position: The Constitution might bar race-conscious decisions that disadvantaged African-Americans, and it might not require governments to make such decisions to overcome prior discrimination, but it certainly allowed them to do so.

The Court's ready acceptance of affirmative action in *Swann* rapidly disappeared. The school context misled some justices about the costs of affirmative action. When affirmative action issues arose in contexts in which the resources to be distributed were obviously limited—in higher education and employment— these justices began to worry that affirmative action programs unfairly distributed those resources on a racial basis. Similar distributional questions lurked in elementary and secondary school cases, but somehow the allocation of children to schools did not seem quite the same, perhaps because, no matter *where* the children were sent, each ended up in a school operated by the school board. Affirmative action programs in higher education excluded some whites from a university, forcing them to give up their aspirations or at least seek education elsewhere, whereas affirmative action programs in employment meant that some whites ended up with less-attractive jobs. These distinctions affected those justices who became increasingly troubled by affirmative action programs, though they may not have made much analytic sense.

According to a Carnegie Foundation study in 1978, these costs led many whites to conclude that "the nation's debt to black people has been so fully paid that whites themselves are becoming victims of reverse discrimination." Workers faced economic stagnation and the disappearance of many traditional jobs as the nation's economy underwent dramatic transformations in the 1970s and 1980s. The costs of this transition were high, and many whites looked for someone to blame. Affirmative action programs provided a convenient focus for their anger. At the same time, however, many whites recognized the social importance of some forms of affirmative action. Polls showed increasing support for the view that without affirmative action programs women and minorities would "continue to fail to get their share of jobs and higher education, thereby continuing past discrimination in the future." By the mid-1980s, polls found more than two-thirds favoring federal affirmative action programs "provided there are no rigid quotas." Even some businesses, *Fortune* magazine reported, "like to hire by [the] numbers." Under these circumstances, it is not surprising that, as law professor Neal Devins put it, from 1980 to 1992 "the Department of Justice fought and lost a holy war over affirmative action." Although, as Devins acknowledged, the campaign against affirmative action "made some inroads," there was more support for affirmative action in Congress, in state and local governments, and among the public than its most fervent opponents believed. The Supreme Court's decisions, in the end, expressed the ambivalence about affirmative action that the public itself felt.[16]

Agreement about affirmative action disappeared for another reason. Everyone on the Court, including those who found affirmative action permissible, agreed that race-conscious decisions were problematic. And, given the nation's history, how could they not be? Virtually every form of race discrimination, including segregated education itself, had been defended in part on the ground that it was the best program to advance African-American interests. That history suggested some degree of skepticism about claims that new programs like affirmative action actually did do so, in contrast to the programs in the past, when the claims about advancing African-American interests were, it now appeared, simply false.

Not all programs that could be described as affirmative action were clearly good public policy. For most justices, however, some were. That determination, in turn, created a doctrinal problem for the Court. The justices' internal discussions focused on the question of the appropriate standard of review to apply in affirmative action cases. Should the Court apply strict scrutiny, rational-basis review, or something else? Marshall's sliding-scale approach was well suited to dealing with the complex issues the justices saw in affirmative action cases, and he had no analytic problems with them. The rest of the Court, committed to the more rigid two- or three-tier approach, found affirmative actions cases analytically quite difficult.

Affirmative action programs caused several problems within the majority's rigid framework. The cases before the era of affirmative action seemed to say that government decisions based on race ought to receive the highest degree of scrutiny, which would imply that affirmative action programs were almost inevitably unconstitutional. Some justices were not bothered by that conclusion, but others were.

One natural analytic move was to refine the prior cases. Instead of saying that race-conscious decisions triggered strict scrutiny, the Court could say that its prior cases involved race-conscious decisions that subordinated African-Americans and that only such decisions should trigger strict scrutiny. Some other standard should be applied to race-conscious decisions that did not subordinate African-Americans.

Within the two-tier system that analytic move implied that affirmative action programs should be upheld if they were rational. And, given the Court's statements about what *rationality* meant, that conclusion then implied that all affirmative action programs were constitutional, which not even Marshall believed. Rather, the justices who approved affirmative action programs agreed that some but not all such programs were constitutional. That meant, however, that they could do what they wanted only by abandoning the two-tier system in favor of a three-tier system in which affirmative action programs received intermediate scrutiny. The difficulty was that some who endorsed some affirmative action programs—Justice Powell and Chief Justice Burger in particular—had forcefully rejected the three-tier approach in other equal protection cases. Their struggle to work out an analysis they found satisfactory dominated the Court's first extended confrontations with affirmative action.

Allan Bakke's 1972 application to the medical school at the Davis campus of the University of California produced the Court's first set of opinions on affirmative action. The medical school had opened only four years earlier. In 1972 it operated a two-track admissions system. White applicants were rejected if their grade-point averages fell below 2.5; those with better grades were rated on a 500-point scale. Applications from members of minority groups, in contrast, were considered by a separate student-faculty committee that used no automatic cutoff. The medical school committed itself to admitting sixteen minority applicants in each class of one hundred. The California Supreme Court found the Davis program unconstitutional because "it denies admission to some white applicants solely because of their race." Race-conscious decisions might be constitutional but only if they survived "rigid scrutiny." Because the program was inflexible and unnecessary, the state supreme court said, it was not justified.[17]

The university appealed to the United States Supreme Court. Justice Brennan thought the case a bad vehicle for deciding whether affirmative action was unconstitutional.[18] That the school set aside sixteen seats for minorities showed that it used the sort of "rigid mathematical quota" that nearly all the justices in *Swann* found problematic. Brennan, Marshall, and Blackmun voted against granting review, but they were joined only by Burger, who was as usual unenthusiastic about getting the Court involved in contentious public issues before it had to.

Brennan focused on two issues in preparing for the *Bakke* argument: Was it constitutionally permissible for a university to take race into account at all in its admission decisions? and "[S]hould heightened standard or rationality be applied?" Brennan noted that he "lean[ed] to the rationality standard." As he saw it, affirmative action programs should be upheld because they met a "need for effective social policies promoting racial justice in a society beset by deep-rooted racial inequities"—to overcome what came to be called societal discrimination.[19]

The justices never had a full-scale, face-to-face discussion of the constitutional issues in *Bakke* before they began to draft their opinions. The conference discussion immediately after the oral argument focused on an issue that arose late in the case: whether the affirmative action program was inconsistent with a federal civil rights statute, Title VI of the 1964 Civil Rights Act. Although some justices expressed their views on that question, most of the discussion dealt with whether the Court should schedule a new argument, or at least ask for additional briefs, dealing solely with the statutory question. In the end, a majority voted to request more briefs.*

Before the briefs were received, Burger and Rehnquist circulated memoranda indicating their "tentative" views. Burger wanted to affirm the state supreme court's decision but "without putting the states . . . in a straitjacket."[20] The university was trying "to accomplish a number of commendable, long-range objectives" but had used "one of the more extreme methods of securing those objectives." Burger was concerned, though, with the "tactical consideration of how best to structure and shape a result so as to confine its impact and yet make it clear that the Court intends to leave states free to serve as 'laboratories' for experimenting with less rigidly exclusionary methods." He said that he was "uneasy with the 'slogans' that have evolved in equal protection analysis" but was inclined to "give the very closest look possible—essentially 'strict scrutiny'—to any state action based on race." Burger thought it was "superficial and problematic" to assert that merely claiming a benign purpose should lower the level of scrutiny. Doing so, he wrote, "proceeds on the dubious assumption that minorities are readily indentifiable [*sic*] 'blocs' which in some way function as units."

Burger did not think the university's "sound and desirable objectives" justified its "rigid" program, and he wanted the Court to "encourage efforts and experimental programs to redefine admissions criteria . . . keeping in mind only the limited constraint imposed by a narrow affirmance here—that race *alone* can never be a permissible basis for excluding an applicant." Nonetheless, Burger's insistence on "strict scrutiny" might have made it difficult to preserve the flexibility he wanted the states to have. He suggested that some alternatives would "account fully for the individual capabilities of each minority applicant," but he did not explain why a system taking race into account would survive strict scrutiny. White had already circulated a memorandum, which he hand-delivered to Marshall, saying that race-sensitive programs "in the end would often make race the determinative factor in administering a seemingly neutral set of qualifications."[21] Burger agreed that this was a serious concern but was "optimistic" that it could be handled. He wanted to defer the Court's consideration of that question until it had some alternative before it. "If it is to take years to work out a rational solution of the current problem," Burger concluded, "so be it. That is what we are paid for."

The tension here indicated that Burger had not figured out how to work his

---

* The decision annoyed Marshall. A month later he dissented when the Court ordered reargument rather than additional briefing in a relatively minor criminal case, sending his colleagues a note saying, "I cannot believe that the Court views the . . . case as raising more momentous issues" than *Bakke*. TM to conference, Nov. 22, 1977, Brennan Papers, box 472, file 2.

views into an opinion. The same tension persisted throughout the Court's deliberations and cropped up most notably in Powell's opinion. The justices were ambivalent about either endorsing affirmative action completely or placing severe
limits on it, but they were committed to an analytic framework, the two-tier
system, that made intermediate positions difficult to develop.

Two weeks later, Rehnquist circulated a "stream of consciousness" memorandum.[22] He began by saying that the Davis policy was "as difficult to sustain" as any
affirmative action program could be, because the university "ma[d]e no bones"
about relying solely on race. And, he said, "difference in treatment of individuals
based on their race or ethnic origin is at the bull's eye of the target at which" the
equal protection clause "was aimed." The Davis program "clearly" satisfied the
rational-basis standard, he thought, but he believed that such a standard could be
applied only if "whites who are in the majority may not assert a claim for denial of
equal protection," a position he found "quite unsatisfying." That argument "con-
fuse[d] the substance of the prohibition with the reason for placing the prohibition
in the Constitution." The equal protection clause may have been included because
of its drafters' concern about discrimination against African-Americans, but "the
language they chose is a good deal more general."

To satisfy the strict scrutiny requirement, "most of the proffered non-race
goals, such as more doctors in the ghetto," were insufficient. And other goals,
"although phrased in non-racial terms, are, at heart, very clearly predicated at
least in part on the idea that racial characteristics are, in and of themselves,
socially significant and permissible bases for governmental action." But, Rehnquist
wrote, the Constitution means that "for governmental purposes nobody 'has'
anything simply by virtue of their race." Finally, he found "unacceptable" the idea
that "past societal discrimination justifies these affirmative action programs." That
was because "the right not to be discriminated against is personal to the individual,
and in this case Bakke's right to equal protection of the laws cannot be denied him
simply because at some other place or at some other time minority group members
have been discriminated against." The broad racial category did not "fit" the
subcategory of those who had been discriminated against on account of race.
"[J]ust because it is easier to identify blacks than people who have suffered discrimination on account of race, the state should not be excused from making a
more individualized determination."

Rehnquist had "no doubt" that programs seeking out "culturally deprived [or]
disadvantaged" people would be valid, and universities could "recruit heavily
among minority students." On the issue White raised, Rehnquist did not think the
Court had to decide whether race could be "used as one of a number of factors,"
but he noted that his analysis would make it "difficult . . . to allow express
consideration of race as a substantial factor at all." Burger's letter indicated a
desire to allow some affirmative action programs, even as it said that strict scrutiny
had to be applied. Rehnquist's memorandum expressed no such desire and showed
that it would be difficult for Burger to invoke the two-tier analysis while allowing
some forms of affirmative action.

With Brennan, White, and Marshall firmly committed to upholding the Davis
program, the votes of Powell and Blackmun were to be crucial. In an earlier

affirmative action case, which the Court eventually dismissed without reaching the merits, Powell told his colleagues that he "strongly believe[d] that courts have no business in limiting admissions policies so long as [there is] no clear racial discrimination." He did not think that "race per se [was an] impermissible consideration."[23]

The California program in *Bakke* seemed different to Powell. He opposed "any quota," because the "symbolic effect of [the] 14th [Amendment] is completely lost." Yet, although "admission policy should be left to [the] university," it had made a "colossal blunder" in "pick[ing] a number." According to Powell, "Each applicant should be able to compete with others." The university could take race into account, but it could "never set[] aside [a] fixed number of places." Justice Stevens echoed Powell's concerns. If this program was upheld, he said, "we'd have a permanent conclusion that blacks can never reach [the] point where they'd not be discriminated against." Stevens thought that affirmative action programs "have performed a fine service but they ought to be temporary." He said that he "can't ever believe [the] day won't come where [a] two track system will be unnecessary." Like Powell, he thought that the Davis program was not the "product of careful thought."[24]

Shortly after the Court received the additional briefs on Title VI, Powell circulated a memorandum dealing only with the constitutional question.[25] According to Powell's law clerk, who drafted the memorandum, Powell thought it was "too late in the day" to eliminate all affirmative action programs, but they had to be limited somehow.[26] The "crucial battle," Powell wrote, is "over the proper scope of judicial review." Because the Davis program used "a line drawn on the basis of race," strict scrutiny had to be applied because "racial and ethnic classifications . . . are odious." Reviewing the nation's racial and ethnic history, Powell argued that many minority groups had "to overcome the prejudices not of a monolithic minority, but of a 'majority' composed of various minority groups." Indeed, "[t]he concepts of 'majority' and 'minority' necessarily reflect temporary judgments and political arrangements. . . . [T]he white 'majority' itself is composed of various minority groups, each of which can lay claim to a history of prior discrimination at the hands of the state and private individuals." Marshall reacted strongly to this thought, scrawling "Kennedy was President" on his copy of a later draft making the same point.[27] But, according to Powell, the Court could not use a standard that would make its analysis "vary with the ebb and flow of political forces." Constitutional principles could not be consistently applied if they depended on "shifting political and social judgments."

For Powell, this meant that "[t]here is no principled basis for deciding which groups will merit 'heightened judicial scrutiny' and which will not." Further, "it may not always be clear that a so-called preference is in fact benign." Some members of a group might be harmed "in order to advance the group's general interest." Again, Marshall disagreed, writing "What about veterans preferences" on his copy. In any event, "there is no warrant in the Constitution for forcing innocent persons" like Bakke "to bear the burden of redressing grievances not of their making."

With strict scrutiny as the standard, the question then was whether the Davis program was justified. Governments could try to "ameliorat[e] . . . the disabling effects of past discrimination," but they could not rely on "societal discrimination," which according to Powell was "a concept of injury that may be ageless in its reach into the past." Only if specific findings of past discrimination were made could the university attempt to overcome its effects.

Powell did find "the attainment of a diverse student body" to be a permissible goal, because students with particular backgrounds may bring "experiences, outlooks and ideas that enrich the training of its student body." Focusing solely on race, however, did not serve that goal. Here Powell quoted a Harvard admissions policy, in which race was one of many factors that added a "'plus' in a particular applicant's file."

By asserting that only good-faith administration of the plan would be required, Powell tried to address White's observation that treating race as a "plus" inevitably meant that race would sometimes be dispositive. As Powell's admiring biographer puts it, "This was pure sophistry."[28] White did not mean that universities would use Harvard-type systems as a disguise for *policies* that were based solely on race. Rather, White meant that when race was a "plus" in one person's file, the next person in line who did not have that "plus" would be denied admission solely because of race. And, given Powell's emphasis on individual rights, it was hard to see why a Harvard-type system really overcame Powell's objections to the Davis program.

According to Bernard Schwartz, Brennan worked up a memorandum attempting "to persuade Powell" to uphold the Davis program.[29] If that was Brennan's aim, it failed, for Powell's final opinion differed only in structure, not in content, from his initial draft. Brennan probably had a different concern. The Court was to discuss *Bakke* again on December 9. By late November all the drafts circulating among the justices came out *against* the Davis program. Brennan circulated his own views to ensure that the December discussion would have some paper laying out the argument *in favor of* the program.

Brennan's memorandum opened with a statement addressing what had emerged as the central issue, whether an affirmative action program simply taking race into account was constitutional.[30] For him, "We long ago crossed that bridge in cases that approved race-sensitive policies." Further, the NAACP Legal Defense Fund brief showed, according to Brennan, that "to read the Fourteenth Amendment to state an abstract principle of color-blindness," as Rehnquist and Powell asserted, "is itself to be blind to history." Rather, states could "pursue the goal of racial pluralism . . . in order to afford minorities full participation in the broader society." The fact that so few minority physicians had been admitted to Davis before it began its program showed that it was entitled to adopt the program "to achieve the participation of minorities in the profession as an end in itself."

Brennan then turned to the means Davis chose to pursue that goal. Its program was clearly not "a governmental slur of whites." Brennan invoked his "21 years here" to point out "the element that is missing from this case"—stigma or invidiousness. The principle that emerged from the cases, Brennan said, was that "government may not on account of race, insult or demean a human being by stereotyping his or her capacities, integrity, or worth as an individual." And, although "Bakke, like thousands of other applicants who fail of admission, was not admitted to medical school . . . he was never stereotyped as an incompetent, or pinned with a badge of inferiority because he is white."

With this background, Brennan asserted that "under any standard of . . . review other than one requiring absolute color-blindness," Davis's program was constitutional. Any alternatives to achieve greater integration of the medical school were, Brennan said, "fanciful." A pure merit-based system, he assumed, "would achieve significant integration," but medical schools had not yet devised such a system; for example, social scientific evidence showed that "formal, cognitive predictors of academic success understate minority applicants' ability to perform well vis-a-vis white applicants." Picking up Burger's theme, Brennan wrote that he "would not abort . . . experiments and hamstring the efforts of educators to develop sound admissions programs." The Court should ask only whether Davis's policy was a "reasonable and considered one in light of the alternatives available and the opportunities that it leaves open for whites."

Finally, Brennan agreed with White that "we are just deluding ourselves if we think that there is a meaningful, judicially enforceable distinction" between programs that set aside a specific number of places "and a process that accomplishes the same end by taking race into account." Admissions decisions were inevitably subjective, and "[h]ow much weight a faculty admissions committee decides to allow the factor of race will almost certainly depend on how many minority applicants should be admitted."

With these memoranda in hand, the Court took up *Bakke* on December 9.[31] Blackmun's position remained unclear; he could not attend the conference because he was recovering from surgery and had not devoted much attention to the additional briefs or the memoranda he had received. Two developments occurred during the discussion. Stewart asserted that because "no state agency can take race into account," the Davis program was unconstitutional. For the first time, it was clear that a majority existed to order Davis to abandon its program. The second development was the confirmation that four votes existed for the proposition that affirmative action programs that "took race into account" were constitutional. Brennan convinced Powell that the state supreme court's opinion held that race could never be taken into account. As a result, Powell agreed that the case should be affirmed in part, holding the Davis program unconstitutional, and reversed in part, allowing Davis to develop an alternative Harvard-type program. By ensuring that the disposition would include a partial reversal, Brennan was able to assert some control over the "spin" the decision would receive when announced. He could stress in his opinion that a majority actually approved some affirmative action programs, and he could take some satisfaction in believing, with White, that programs taking race into account were functionally identical to apparently more rigid programs like Davis's.

When Stevens reiterated his earlier point that affirmative action programs had to be temporary, and might be done away with in a few years, Marshall interjected that "it would be another hundred years." One of Powell's clerks later suggested that Powell might have moved toward the liberals had Marshall said that affirmative action programs would indeed be temporary, perhaps for another ten years.

Brennan's law clerks asserted that Marshall was "livid" over Powell's opinion, "which he regarded as racist." According to them, Marshall was particularly offended by Powell's statement that "it is far too late to argue that the guarantee of equal protection to *all* persons permits the recognition of special wards entitled to a degree of protection greater than that accorded others." This, Marshall thought, echoed the "insensitivity, if not racism," of the Supreme Court's 1883 decision invalidating the 1875 Civil Rights Act. There the Court had said, "When a man has emerged from slavery, . . . there must be some stage in the progress of his elevation when he takes the rank of a mere citizen, and ceases to be a special favorite of the law."[32]

After the conference, Stevens provoked a flurry of memoranda by arguing that Brennan and Powell had misinterpreted the state supreme court's judgment. Although that court's opinion spoke more broadly, the judgment itself only barred Davis from "considering [Bakke's] race or the race of any other applicant in passing upon his application for admission." As Stevens accurately said, this judgment rather clearly did not bar Davis from taking race into account in some redesigned affirmative action program. Brennan and White wanted to guarantee that the Court's judgment was not a flat affirmance of the state supreme court's decision, and they sent around elaborate memoranda trying to explain why that court's judgment really did require some form of reversal. The technical points they made—in response to Stevens's technical point—carried little weight. What mattered was Powell's desire to obtain approval of Harvard-type programs "in the unlikely but welcome event that a consensus develops for allowing the competitive consideration of race as an element."[33] The only question that remained was exactly how to do that. The easiest way was to ignore Stevens's technical point, which is what the majority did. Otherwise, as Justice Powell stated a few weeks later, the Court "would merely perpetuate the confusion and doubt that now exists."[34]

By the end of December it was clear that there were at least five votes to strike down Davis's program and four to state expressly that programs taking race into account were constitutional. Whether there would be five votes for the latter proposition depended on what Blackmun did. He gave no signals about his views for several months. The Court's senior justices, concerned in large part with moving the Court's work along, tried to get Blackmun off the dime, but still nothing happened. Burger proposed to Powell that the Court simply invalidate the Davis program, but Powell thought the Court had to "speak out clearly and unambiguously" to tell universities that they could take race into account. Blackmun blew up a few times at what he regarded as unjustified criticism for holding up the Court's work, but his reactions had no effect on the outcome; Brennan and perhaps other justices came to appreciate more clearly "the enormous strain" Blackmun was under as a result of his surgery and his efforts to carry a full load of Court work.[35]

Marshall rarely took part in any personal efforts to affect outcomes. He, too, became impatient, though. In late March he started to work on a separate opinion in *Bakke*. Ordinarily, Marshall told his law clerks the points he wanted to make and let them draft an opinion. Marshall cared so much about *Bakke* that he blocked out the opinion himself. His handwritten draft expressed his impatience, perhaps less at Blackmun than at all his colleagues for their obtuseness. "I repeat, for next to the last time," Marshall wrote, "the decision in this case depends on whether you consider the action . . . as 'admitting' certain students or as 'excluding' certain other students." "Toward one end we see 'complete equality,'" Marshall wrote, and "[t]oward the other end we see 'quotas' 'constitution is color blind' etc. Take your choice. We should have known we would get to this point. We are up to it. Do we really mean it[?]" Marshall's impatience came through again when he wrote, "You remember so many real good Americans often say: 'Segregation and racial discrimination are bad, should be condemned and must stop—but—move a Negro in a house next to mine—well, that is something different!'"[36] For Marshall, the analogy seemed so clear that he did not need to spell it out, nor could he have done so: His colleagues were willing to endorse desegregation when it did not affect them, but they balked when it came closer to home, to the universities that they and their children attended.

Marshall thought the Court had to decide a case "with a lousy record and [a] poorly reasoned lower court opinion." In deciding, Marshall "address[ed] the question of whether Negroes have 'arrived' or other variation of 'the Constitution is color-blind.'" Here he was acerbic: "Remember, that statement was in the dissenting opinion in *Plessy*. Had it been in the majority we would not be faced with this problem in 1977. We are not yet all equals. As to this country being a melting pot—either the Negro did not get in the pot or he did not get melted down." He pointed out that the Court itself was part of the problem: It had never had an African-American "Officer of the Court" and had had "only three Negro law clerks."

Marshall's clerks reshaped the notes, retaining many of Marshall's comments. The point about *Plessy* was sharpened: "We are not yet all equals, in large part because of the refusal of the *Plessy* Court to adopt the principle of color-blindness. It would be [the] cruelest irony for this Court to adopt the dissent in *Plessy* now."[37]

According to Bernard Schwartz, Brennan was concerned that "Marshall's underlying theory was 'Goddamn it, you owe us'; and he feared that that would not be persuasive to Justice Blackmun."[38] For all of Brennan's efforts and concerns, it appears to have been Marshall's opinion that most affected Blackmun. Three weeks after Marshall's opinion was circulated, Blackmun sent his colleagues his own memorandum.[39] In typical Blackmun fashion, it had numbered paragraphs, the last of which was, "There is much to be said for Thurgood's 'cruelest irony' approach." His memorandum began with some "[g]eneral [c]onsiderations," which, like Marshall's, were some diffuse observations indicating Blackmun's mood as he approached the case. Citing statistics about minority group professionals, Blackmun said, "If ways are not found to remedy this situation, the Country can *never* achieve its professed goal of a society that is not race conscious." He "hope[d] that the time soon will come when an 'affirmative action' program is unecessary. . . . [W]e must reach a stage of maturity, beyond any transitional inequality, where action along this line is no longer necessary. Then persons may be regarded as persons, and past discrimination will be an ugly feature of history that has been overcome." Blackmun thought it "somewhat ironic" to be "so con-

vulsed and deeply disturbed over a program where race is an element of consciousness, and yet to be aware of the fact that institutions of higher learning for many
years have given conceded preferences up to a point to the skilled athlete
. . . and to those having connections with celebrities and the famous."

Blackmun insisted that the justices understand that "[t]his is not an ideal
world. . . . [W]e live in a real world," and the decision must reflect reality.
Rehnquist's position, in contrast, sought "idealistic equality." Alexander Bickel's
criticisms of affirmative action

> speak of the idealistic and have great appeal. But I say, once more, that this is not an
> ideal world, yet. And, of course, his position is—and I hope I offend no one, for I do not
> mean to do so—the 'accepted' Jewish approach. . . . They understandably want 'pure'
> equality and are willing to take their chances with it, knowing that they have the
> inherent abiilty to excel and live with it successfully.

For Blackmun, "[a]n admissions policy that has an awareness of race as an
element seems to me to be the only possible and realistic means of achieving the
societal goal" mentioned earlier. Taking a modest position, Blackmun wrote that
the state supreme court's judgment "does not prevent us" from "decid[ing]
whether race can ever be a permissible consideration." Powell's attack on Davis's
"blatant quota system" was "effective[]," but Blackmun believed that "the line
between a Harvard program and the Davis program is a thin one. . . . At worst,
one could say that under the Harvard program one may accomplish covertly what
Davis does openly." In the end, he believed that "the Davis program is within
constitutional bounds, though perhaps barely so."

With Blackmun's vote, the case was essentially over. Burger and Brennan
worked out a formal assignment of the case to Powell, to announce the Court's
judgment and provide what Powell called a "roadmap" to what the different majorities held. Brennan drafted the opinion that later appeared as his partial dissent.
White was "cool" about the draft and offered a number of suggestions. He told
Brennan he was "inclined to keep the decibel level as low as possible. We won't
accomplish much by beating a white majority over past ills or by describing what
has gone by as a system of apartheid." Some minor revisions satisfied White, and
he joined the opinion, as did Blackmun and Marshall.[40]

Powell added a response to Brennan's opinion, arguing that Brennan's approach, focusing on whether a program rested on judgments about a group's inferiority, would justify programs limiting enrollment of Jews. Such programs, Powell
said, were based on a belief in the "superior ability" of that group. Brennan told
Powell that he found this argument "personally offensive," and Powell took the
comment out of his opinion.[41]

Powell took modest exception to a statement in Brennan's opinion describing
what Brennan called the "central meaning" of the judgment, that "[g]overnment
may take race into account when it acts not to demean or insult any racial group,
but to remedy disadvantages cast on minorities by past racial prejudice." This
statement, Powell thought, went "somewhat beyond" the actual holding, although
it might be a fair statement of the holding's implications. At the end, Powell sent a
note to his colleagues with the draft of the statement he proposed to use in

announcing the Court's judgment, "As I am a 'chief' with no 'indians,' I should be in the rear rank, not up front!" After the opinions were announced, White wrote Brennan a note saying, "You were great."[42]

Marshall's separate opinion began with two sentences defining the structure of his analysis in all later affirmative action cases:

> [I]t must be remembered that, during most of the past 200 years, the Constitution as interpreted by this Court did not prohibit the most ingenious and pervasive forms of discrimination against the Negro. Now, when a State acts to remedy the effects of that legacy of discrimination, I cannot believe that this same Constitution stands as a barrier.

The themes in these sentences are history, the continuing consequences of discrimination, and state choice.

The opinion's first section examined the history of the "denial of human rights" to African-Americans in the nation's history. It noted that the "self-evident truths and the unalienable rights" stated in the Declaration of Independence "were intended . . . to apply only to white men." The compromises over slavery in the Constitution showed that "'we the people,' for whose protection the Constitution was designed, did not include those whose skins were the wrong color." The opinion then turned to the effects of slavery's abolition, describing the Southern black codes adopted immediately after the Civil War as "the first steps to re-enslave the Negroes." Congress's response promised, "for a time, [that] the Negro might be protected from the continued denial of his civil rights" but "that time . . . was short-lived." Marshall's opinion criticized the Supreme Court itself for "assist[ing]" in stripping African-Americans of their civil rights. The opinion described Supreme Court decisions narrowly construing the Civil War amendments, culminating in the "bankrupt[ ]" decision in *Plessy v. Ferguson*. It described the rapid spread of segregation laws after *Plessy* and emphasized that segregation was a national and not merely a regional policy. A brief section followed on the "position of the Negro today in America," in which Marshall offered summaries of the health and employment conditions of the African-American community.

Having set the stage with this survey of history and current conditions, the opinion turned to the Fourteenth Amendment. The argument started with the observation that the amendment plainly "was not intended to prohibit measures designed to remedy the effects of the Nation's past treatment of Negroes"; otherwise, the same Congress that proposed the Fourteenth Amendment could not have allowed the Freedman's Bureau to assist newly freed African-Americans. Supporters and opponents alike described the Freedmen's Bureau bill as "special treatment," and its enactment over President Andrew Johnson's veto demonstrated that it was "inconceivable that the Fourteenth Amendment was intended to prohibit all race-conscious relief measures." The Court's more recent decisions, Marshall continued, also approved such measures.

The opinion concluded by finding it "more than a little ironic that, after several hundred years of class-based discrimination against Negroes, the Court is unwilling to hold that a class-based remedy for that discrimination is permissible." For Marshall, the "mark" of inferiority that racism had placed on African-American people "has endured. The dream of America as the great melting pot has not been realized for the Negro; because of his skin color he never even made it into the pot." Marshall continued:

> It is because of a legacy of unequal treatment that we now must permit the institutions of this society to give consideration to race in making decisions about who will hold the positions of influence, affluence, and prestige in America. . . . If we are ever to become a fully integrated society, one in which the color of a person's skin will not determine the opportunities available to him or her, we must be willing to take steps to open those doors.

The opinion ended by chastising the Court for "com[ing] full circle": After the Civil War, the Freedmen's Bureau was an affirmative action program, but the Court in *Plessy* "destroyed the movement toward complete equality"; then came *Brown* and congressional civil rights statutes, "followed by numerous affirmative-action programs. *Now,* we have this Court again stepping in, this time to stop affirmative-action programs."

Whether it kept the decibel level low enough for White, Marshall's separate opinion eloquently laid out the case for upholding affirmative action programs. It stressed the legacy of discrimination and treated affirmative action programs as remedies for the continuing effects of discrimination on the African-American community as a whole. Further, Marshall treated affirmative action programs as an appropriate *choice* for state institutions to make rather than as a step the Constitution required them to take.

For all its emphasis on the weight of the past upon the present, however, the opinion did not abandon the aspiration for a fully integrated society; rather, it considered affirmative action programs an appropriate step in the direction of such a society, given the conditions of the African-American community in the United States at the present. As Marshall told the judges of the Second Circuit in 1987, "[A]ll of the participants in the current debate . . . agree that the ultimate goal is the creation of a colorblind society." But, he said, "the vestiges of racial bias in America are so pernicious, and so difficult to remove, that we must take advantage of all the remedial measures at our disposal." For him, "given the position from which American began, we still have a very long way to go."[43]

Powell's opinion in *Bakke* applied strict scrutiny to affirmative action programs. Brennan waffled over the right doctrinal formulation. He toyed with the idea of accepting strict scrutiny as the standard but watering it down so that it would not be "'strict' in theory and fatal in fact," in Gerald Gunther's famous phrase. Brennan also tried out alternative doctrinal statements, referring to a requirement that affirmative action programs have "an important and articulated purpose."[44] The question of doctrinal formulations preoccupied the justices as they considered, in *Fullilove v. Klutznick* in 1979 and 1980, the Court's next major confrontation with affirmative action.

According to one of Marshall's law clerks, *Fullilove* was "more important than *Bakke,* since [it] involves an affirmative action plan adopted by Congress."[45] In *Fullilove* the Court upheld the constitutionality of a program in which 10 percent of the federal funds for public works projects had to be used for services supplied by businesses owned by members of minority groups.[46]

Throughout the Court's deliberations, Burger restated the view he expressed in *Bakke,* that "slogans" were unhelpful in resolving the case. His statement to the conference emphasized the fact that Congress was the decision maker here. The Court had to show "deference to Congress." Although Burger was troubled by some aspects of Congress's list of minority groups, he did not think that Congress had to make "explicit finding[s]" about discrimination against "Indians and blacks." He also emphasized that "this is a temp[orary] experimental program" dealing with the contruction industry, which had a "clear . . . history of exclusion of Negroes." Stewart took the lead in opposition, saying that the Constitution he "understood is being replaced by [a] new Const[itution]." No matter how "loftily motivated," Congress could not "predicate exclusions on race."[47]

Powell said that he would have agreed with Stewart "20 years ago," but now he thought that a "substantial or compelling state interest" allowed "classification on race." And, he said, the interest in *Fullilove* was "very substantial." He would have preferred "definitive findings," but he thought that the "record" in *Fullilove* was "adequate": Although Congress held no hearings on the particular bill at issue in *Fullilove,* the need for a set-aside program had been ventilated repeatedly in other congressional proceedings. Stevens found himself in the middle. "Racial groups may in some instances be made beneficiaries of special legis[lation]." He was reluctant to uphold the program as a way of remedying past discrimination, because the "benefits go to only a few Negroes." Perhaps, he thought, the program might be justified on the ground that it "does better to spread this business around," but he was unsure about that conclusion.[48]

Because the case was so important, the Chief Justice took the opinion on himself. Although the Court heard argument in late November 1979, Burger's draft opinion was not circulated until late May. Its basic structure survived in the published opinion, but it did not end up as an opinion for the Court. Burger's draft can best be understood as an extended description of the federal statute, presented so as to show that Congress's decision made sense but without containing much conventional legal analysis. Prior cases were described, parallels were pointed out, and readers were left to make the necessary connections.

On June 4, 1980, Brennan and Marshall sent White and Blackmun a draft letter they proposed to send to Burger. The letter expressed concern that the diffuse legal analysis in Burger's draft did not define the constitutional limits on Congress's spending power. In their view, the opinion should say that when Congress employed racial categories "to accomplish the important objective of remedying past discrimination," its methods must be "narrowly tailored to the achievement of that goal."[49] In light of *Bakke,* this was a statement that the test was intermediate scrutiny.

After the letter was sent and circulated to the other justices, Powell countered by insisting that the test should be strict scrutiny. Blackmun indicated that he, too, was "somewhat troubled" by Burger's failure to specify a well-defined standard of review. The Chief Justice replied to his critics on both sides, "I do not share the passion expressed by some for stating 'tests.' The test is the Constitution." Citing an earlier comment by Blackmun, Burger continued, "[T]ests are often announced by us to fit the result reached in a given case!" Nonetheless, on June 16 he circulated a revision, incorporating some of the suggestions Brennan and Marshall had made but also including a disclaimer: "Any preference based on racial or ethnic criteria must necessarily receive a most searching examination to make sure that it does not conflict with constitutional guarantees. This case . . . has received [] that kind of examination. This opinion does not adopt, either expressly or implicitly, the formulas of analysis articulated in" *Bakke*.[50]

Brennan and Marshall said that they appreciated Burger's revisions, but they objected to the disclaimer. They told their colleagues that they planned to circulate a concurring opinion "that articulates our view of the correct standard and explains how that standard is implicit in the analysis you apply to this case." At this point Burger lost patience. "[I]t seems to me that there is a 'tempest in a saucer' aspect as to terms," he wrote his colleagues. "I frankly believe that adopting a magic 'word-test' is a serious error and I will neither write nor join in these 'litmus' approaches." He also insisted that his opinion speak for itself: "I am not prepared to subscribe to a Court opinion that is undermined by concurring opinions which undertake to say that the author of the Court opinion adopts a particular test."[51]

Marshall got the point and immediately circulated an opinion concurring in the result, which Brennan and Blackmun joined. Marshall found that Congress "had a sound basis for concluding that minority-owned construction enterprises, though capable, qualified, and ready and willing to work, have received a disproportionately small amount of public contracting business because of the continuing effects of past discrimination" and that the program setting aside 10 percent of federal contracts for such businesses did not stigmatize white owners or "penaliz[e] those least able to protect themselves in the political process." His opinion concluded by praising Congress for "recogniz[ing] the . . . realities" of the history of racial discrimination in the country by adopting the set-aside provision: "Today, by upholding this race-conscious remedy, the Court accords Congress the authority necessary to undertake the task of moving our society toward a state of meaningful equality of opportunity, not an abstract version of equality in which the effects of past discrimination would be forever frozen into our social fabric. I applaud this result."[52] Powell, in contrast, wrote separately but concurred in Burger's opinion. Powell began by saying that he would have preferred the lead opinion to "articulate judicial standards of review in conventional terms," but he joined it because he viewed it "as substantially in accord" with his own views.[53]

For lawyers, *Fullilove* was important because it was more generous about set-asides adopted by Congress than *Bakke* had been about set-asides adopted by states. What is most striking about the Court's internal discussions, though, is different. A solid majority of six quickly agreed on the result, and no one wavered. Further, no one expressed suspicion that the Chief Justice had taken the opinion to write in a way that would cast doubt on the majority's commitment to its result. Brennan and Marshall would have reached that result by applying intermediate scrutiny, while Powell did so by applying a stricter standard. Under the circumstances, Burger's inclination to paper over the disagreement by refusing to be explicit about stating a standard of review would seem to have offered a perfect solution. Why did it matter so much to some justices that the Court opinion articulate a specific standard of review?

Marshall, Brennan, and Powell were primarily concerned, not about legal doctrine, but about the signals the Court sent lower courts and the public about what it believed was constitutionally permissible.[54] Invoking a strict standard preserved the two-tier structure that promised to limit the judicial role in evaluating legislation. Using such a standard, even in the course of upholding a racial categorization as Powell would have, would signal that the result was extraordinary. From Powell's point of view, Burger's diffuse opinion threatened to undermine the clarity of the two-tier structure. In contrast, Brennan and Marshall were committed to a more flexible analysis and did whatever they could to advance that cause. They cared about the issue because the intermediate tier gave courts more latitude to overturn legislation. As they saw it, the two-tier structure made it too easy for judges to say that, although they believed that a statute was seriously unwise, it was not irrational. The structure they preferred gave such judges a chance to find such a statute unconstitutional and deprived them of the easy rhetorical "out" of deference to legislative judgment.

When *Bakke* arrived at the Court, the justices knew that it was only their first confrontation with the issue of affirmative action. The fact that Justice Powell spoke only for himself and nonetheless defined "the law" that emerged from *Bakke* is symptomatic of the Court's groping for a position on affirmative action. From 1972 to the late 1980s, the justices gradually worked out a set of distinctions— between court-ordered and voluntary affirmative action programs and among programs with effects on hiring, promotion, and discharge—that made sense to them. Here, too, the Court was divided but largely harmonious.

One dimension of disagreement surfaced first in *Franks v. Bowman Transportation Co.* in 1976.[55] The Court held that district courts ordinarily should award seniority retroactive to the date of an individual's job application, once they found that an employer had violated the federal statutory ban on employment discrimination. Doing so would usually place the plaintiffs higher up on the seniority list than some other employees, who therefore might be laid off earlier than they would have been if the plaintiffs did not get seniority relief. Powell was concerned about the inequity of that result. As he saw it, seniority relief affected the rights of "innocent employees," who might not have had anything to do with the employer's discriminatory policies.[56]

In response, Brennan pointed out that the plaintiffs, who had been discriminated against, were surely equally innocent. As Stevens put it in a similar case, "[I]nnocent people always get hurt in situations like this." At one point Brennan said that Powell appeared "to have made a full scale retreat." As Powell put it, "This case is rapidly becoming a bit like a 'shuttlecock,' but I certainly don't want Bill Brennan to have the last 'hit.'" Marshall tried to calm the waters, pointing out that the case was narrower than many: "In this case we deal only with identifiable individuals who actually applied for jobs and were discriminated against . . . and leave for another day the knotty problems of quotas, non-identifiable discriminatees, and discrimination claimed by those who were deterred from ever applying for jobs." After the relatively heated exchanges over the case, Powell sent a gracious note to Brennan when the opinion was announced: "This was renewed evidence of your superb craftsmanship in the law—as clearly (at least to me) you were on the *wrong* side!"[57]

Powell eventually gained a majority for his view that the effect of affirmative action on layoffs was a central concern. In the 1986 decision in *Wygant v. Jackson Board of Education,* a majority of the Court invalidated a program providing for layoffs of teachers by seniority within white and minority groups separately.[58] The Jackson school board and its teachers union negotiated a collective bargaining agreement specifying that layoffs would occur by seniority, restricted by a rule that the percentage of minority employees laid off could not exceed the existing percentage of minority employees in the system. The rule ensured that whites and African-Americans would be laid off only in proportion to their current employment, and *that* meant that some white teachers would be laid off even if they had greater seniority than some African-American teachers.

The issue of the appropriate standard of review, so important in *Fullilove,* resurfaced in *Wygant.* The conference discussion showed a majority to strike the affirmative action program down but division among the majority on the standard of review. Burger wanted "close scrutiny" and a "searching examination" of the government's interests; Powell thought there had to be a "compelling state interest" promoted by the "least restrictive means"; O'Connor wanted strict scrutiny but thought that the means used in Jackson might be justified. Stevens said he "disagree[d] with everyone," because he did not "like separate levels of equal protection." The school board had a "legitimate" interest in trying "to teach kids that black or white everyone has [a] chance to be a teacher."[59]

Powell's first draft obscured the standard of review because of the division among the majority. Marshall circulated a proposed dissent, sharply criticizing Powell for "paying no heed to the significant division on the Court with respect to a standard of review." In a personal note, Justice Brennan told Marshall that his "superb dissent . . . ought to change some votes."[60]

In one sense, it did. Powell could not gain five votes for his opinion, and he circulated a revision more than two months later including an extended discussion of the standard of review. That was enough to persuade O'Connor to join most of the opinion, but White still refused. Powell's final opinion said that affirmative action programs must be "supported by a compelling state purpose" and must use "narrowly tailored" means to accomplish that purpose.[61] It rejected the argument that the board's desire to provide minority students with a sufficient number of role models justified the agreement, because that was in effect to allow the board to remedy the general effects of past societal discrimination, a purpose, Powell said, that "has no logical stopping point." Even if the purposes the board was attempting to promote were important, though, according to the Court the remedy was not narrowly tailored, because there was no particularly strong relation between preserving the proportion of African-American teachers in the system and remedying past discrimination.[62]

Much of Marshall's dissent was devoted to showing that the Jackson school board may well have discriminated against African-Americans in the past and argued that the case should be sent back to the lower courts for a more complete examination of the factual setting, for "no race-conscious provision that purports to serve a remedial purpose can be fairly assessed in a vacuum." Turning to the merits of the layoff protection, Marshall criticized the court for "nullify[ing] years of negotiation and compromise designed to solve serious educational problems in the public schools" and said that "a public employer, with the full agreement of its employees, should be permitted to preserve the benefits of a legitimate and constitutional affirmative-action hiring plan even while reducing its work force."

An important portion of Marshall's opinion dealt with the suggestion, implicit in Powell's plurality opinion but rejected by O'Connor, that formal findings of prior discrimination were an essential predicate for the adoption of affirmative action programs. Such a requirement, he said, would interfere with the "long-standing goal of civil rights reform, that of integrating schools without taking every school system to court. . . . It would defy equity to penalize those who achieve harmony from discord" by reaching negotiated agreements. This harmony, in turn, affected Marshall's analysis of how the board chose to deal with the problem of preserving gains in African-American employment during times of economic hardship. As he saw it, the layoff protection was a sufficiently narrow method of "allocat[ing] the impact of an unavoidable burden proportionately between two racial groups." At this point Marshall returned to his emphasis on the agreement that produced the provision at issue. For him, the provision "was forged in the crucible of clashing economic interest" in a process that "yielded consensus." He saw the collective bargaining process as "a legitimate and powerful vehicle for the resolution of thorny problems," which could "naturally avert[]" the "perceived dangers of affirmative action" through "the bilateral process of negotiation, agreement, and ratification."

The tone of Marshall's dissent in *Wygant* differed from that of his separate opinion in *Bakke*. The complexity of the case and the limited scope of the question presented to the Court called for

> calm, dispassionate reflection upon exactly what has been done, to whom, and why. . . . When an elected school board and a teachers' union collectively bargain a layoff provision designed to preserve the effects of a valid minority recruitment plan by apportioning layoffs between two racial groups, as a result of a settlement achieved under the auspices of a supervisory state agency charged with protecting the civil rights of all citizens, that provision should not be upset by this Court on constitutional grounds.

Wygant left the law uncertain. As one of Marshall's clerks put it a few years later, in a memorandum on *City of Richmond v. J. A. Croson Co.*,[63] "it is hard to tell whether the [court of appeals] has 'misread' *Wygant*, since nobody knows what that opinion stands for now that Justice Powell has retired."[64] What it stood for, though, was that the Constitution placed limits on the effects affirmative action could have on what Powell called "innocent parties."[65] Powell made that clear when, with the opinions in *Wygant* still circulating, he voted to uphold an affirmative action plan in *Local 28, Sheet Metal Workers v. EEOC*.[66] In that case a district court found that the union had discriminated against African-Americans in admissions to the union and imposed a quite rigid numerical membership "goal" as a remedy. Marshall called the Sheet Metal Workers the "most racially biased union today." Initially uncertain about what to do, Powell ultimately agreed that the record reflected "gross discrimination . . . and, importantly for me, unlike *Wygant*, there is nothing before us to suggest that individual members will have to be laid off." Brennan nursed Powell along, sending him drafts of opinions before they were circulated to the rest of the Court. Powell found the case "troublesome" and eventually wrote a short opinion concurring in the result, which again left the Court without a majority statement of the controlling legal standard.[67]

Local 28 was different from *Wygant* along another dimension that the justices regarded as significant. *Local 28* involved a court-ordered affirmative action program. The distinction between court-ordered plans and voluntary ones first surfaced in 1976, in *McDonald v. Santa Fe Trail Transportation Co.*[68] Two white employees who were fired for stealing alleged that they had been discriminated against because an African-American coemployee charged with the same offense had not been fired. The lower courts dismissed their claim, saying that whites could not invoke the civil rights laws against racial discrimination. The Supreme Court unanimously disagreed, in an opinion by Marshall.

The implications of the case for challenges to affirmative action programs were clear; had *McDonald* come out differently, whites would have no vehicle by which to challenge such programs. Marshall's opinion contained a footnote "emphasiz[ing] that we do not consider here the permissibility of [affirmative action] program[s], whether judicially required or otherwise prompted."[69] Stevens thought "we are kidding ourselves . . . to the e[x]tent that you disavow consideration of a voluntary affirmative action program. I agree that a judicially required program would not be covered, but the reasoning in the text will surely support the typical reverse discrimination claim, which any quota system will stimulate." Marshall disagreed, denying that "a program which a judge can lawfully require is necessarily illegal without a judge's order."[70]

The distinction became crucial in *Local 93 v. Cleveland,*[71] decided on the same day as *Local 28* in 1986. *Local 93* involved an affirmative action program dealing with promotions, adopted as part of a consent decree. Because it involved promotions, it fell between the hiring preferences in *Local 28*, which Powell believed would not "burden[]" whites "directly, if at all,"[72] and the layoff preferences in *Wygant;* some whites might be adversely affected by affirmative action in promotions.

Here the key votes were from Powell and O'Connor. At the conference the outcome was not entirely clear, and Burger retained some hope that he would get a majority to hold the promotion preferences unconstitutional. O'Connor and Powell, though, found it crucial that the program in *Local 93* involved a court order, even a consent decree: "There is a difference," Powell wrote, "between the approval by a court of an agreement between the parties, and an order of a court that is contested by the employer." As Powell understood the record, this case did not involve a sweetheart deal in which the employer simply rolled over and accepted the employees' challenges. He remained uncertain about the proper result, however, because he found the record unclear on whether "non-minority members of the union will be discriminated against in promotions."[73]

Brennan took on the opinion himself because Burger initially passed and then voted to invalidate the program. Powell was uncomfortable with Brennan's draft and urged Brennan to make extensive revisions. He wanted Brennan to emphasize that the case involved only the interpretation of federal statutes, not the Constitution. He also found inadequate Brennan's treatment of precedents about a court's ability to order relief beyond what a statute required in the absence of a court order. Brennan accepted the first set of suggestions but resisted the second. When, however, it appeared that he could not get the crucial votes he needed from Powell and O'Connor, he modified his opinion again, and Powell and O'Connor immediately joined it.[74]

Brennan again wrote the lead opinion when the Court upheld a judicial order requiring one-for-one promotions of whites and African-Americans in the Alabama state police.[75] To secure Powell's vote, Brennan relied heavily on Powell's opinions in *Wygant* and *Local 28*. The effect, as Stevens put it, was to suggest that *Wygant's* strict approach "should be applied in reviewing a judicial decree entered in response to proven violations of law." Stevens thought, in contrast, that "[v]oluntary race-conscious decisions by employers . . . are presumptively unlawful." Relying on *Swann,* Stevens said that "the burden of demonstrating that the relief granted by the district court is excessive rests squarely on the law violator—not on the victim of the wrongdoing."[76]

As the law of affirmative action worked itself out, the inside story was that there is no real inside story. The discussions within the Court simply identify the lines the justices wrote into the law in their published opinions. Of course there were disagreements, both between majority and dissenters, and within majorities themselves. And of course there were disputes over how much one or another aspect of a particular case ought to be emphasized. And finally, of course, there were occasional "strategic" votes and draft opinions, as in the Alabama police case, in which a justice may have shaped an opinion to obtain votes rather than to express his or her most deeply held views. But, in the end, there was nothing that went on inside the Court that the published opinions do not fairly reflect. What drove the Court was its difficulty in developing a standard of review that allowed justices to appear to approve affirmative action in principle while invalidating most affirmative action programs and upholding a few.

In 1989 the Court seemed to settle the analytical problem that dogged it throughout its dealings with affirmative action. In *City of Richmond v. J. A. Croson Co.,* the Court invalidated a city policy designed to direct 30 percent of the city's contracts to minority-owned construction companies.[77] Marshall's dissent returned to the passionate tone of his opinion in *Bakke,* but here there were no internal manueverings of any moment.

For Marshall, if Congress recognized reality in enacting the set-aside program at issue in *Fullilove,* the Court closed its eyes to reality in invalidating Richmond's set-aside program. The city's plan set aside 30 percent of its construction contracts in a five-year period for minority-owned firms. Its definition of "minority" tracked the federal definition and so included African-Americans, Spanish-speaking individuals, and Aleuts. The city adopted the plan after a hearing at which there was testimony that only two-thirds of 1 percent of the city's construction contracts had been awarded to minority businesses even though 50 percent of the city's population was African-American and that the contractors' associations in the city had virtually no minority members.

The Supreme Court held that such a plan had to be "strictly scrutinized" to ensure that "the legislative body is pursuing a goal important enough to warrant use of a highly suspect tool" with methods that "'fit' this compelling goal so closely that there is little or no possibility that the motive for the classification was illegitimate racial prejudice or stereotype." This standard had to be used in cases in which legislatures claimed to be serving remedial goals because the judgment that the goal was in fact remedial implicated precisely the same concerns about prejudice that justify the standard in the first place. O'Connor's majority opinion noted that the circumstances under which the Richmond plan was adopted were suspicious anyway: One purpose of the strict standard was to protect political minorities, and in Richmond the city council was controlled by African Americans. "The concern that a political majority will more easily act to the disadvantage of a minority based on unwarranted assumptions or incomplete facts would seem to militate for, not against, the application of heightened judicial scrutiny in this case."[78]

Applying this standard to the Richmond case, the Court found the set-aside plan wanting. Richmond attempted to justify its plan by saying that it was designed to remedy past discrimination in the construction industry. O'Connor responded that "a generalized assertion that there has been past discrimination in an entire industry provides no guidance for a legislative body to determine the precise scope of the injury it seeks to remedy." In short, this purported justification went too far because it would allow essentially any program to be justified as a remedy. Although O'Connor agreed with the city that the "sorry history of both private and public discrimination in this country has contributed to a lack of opportunities for black entrepreneurs," she said that "this observation, standing alone, cannot justify a rigid racial quota." She thought it "sheer speculation" to believe, as the Richmond plan assumed, that in the absence of discrimination the number of African-American entrepreneurs would have matched their proportion in the city's population. Further, she said, the 30 percent set aside could not "be tied to any injury suffered by anyone." The evidence of discrimination in the Richmond construction industry was too thin to justify a remedial plan of this scope. The statistical disparity between contracts awarded and minority population was meaningless, she said, in the absence of evidence about the numbers of minority contractors qualified on nonracial grounds for city contracts. Finally, the city could not rely on Congress's determination, upheld in *Fullilove,* that there was discrimination in the construction industry nationwide. She concluded that Richmond had failed to justify its program as a remedy for identified discrimination.

Turning to the question of the plan's scope, O'Connor made two observations. The city apparently had not even considered using race-neutral criteria, such as relaxing requirements for performance bonds, to increase minority participation.

In addition, there was no connection between the 30 percent quota and any goal other than "outright racial balancing." For O'Connor, the figure rested on the "'completely unrealistic' assumption that minorities will choose a particular trade in lockstep proportion to their representation in the local population." In a portion of her opinion that did not receive the agreement of Scalia and Stevens and that was therefore not part of the opinion of the Court, O'Connor suggested that cities could take steps to remedy identified discrimination within their boundaries, including "in the extreme case some form of narrowly tailored racial preference." Before doing so, however, the city would have to explore nonracial methods of responding to evidence suggesting discrimination and compile a more substantial factual basis on which it could rest a conclusion that discrimination had in fact occurred.

In words evocative of Frankfurter's in *Hughes v. Superior Court,* O'Connor wrote:

> To accept Richmond's claim that past societal discrimination alone can serve as the basis for rigid racial preferences would be to open the door to competing claims for 'remedial relief' for every disadvantaged group. The dream of a Nation of equal citizens in a society where race is irrelevant to personal opportunity and achievement would be lost in a mosaic of shifting preferences based on inherently unmeasurable claims of past wrongs.

Marshall began his dissenting opinion strongly: "It is a welcome sign of racial progress when the former capital of the Confederacy acts forthrightly to confront the effects of racial discrimination in its midst." He found "deep irony" in "second-guessing Richmond's judgment" that past discrimination had limited minority participation in the city's construction industry. "As much as any municipality in the United States, Richmond knows what racial discrimination is; a century of decisions by this and other federal courts has richly documented the city's disgraceful history of public and private racial discrimination." He continued:

> Cynical of one municipality's attempt to redress the effects of past racial discrimination in a particular industry, the majority launches a grapeshot attack on race-conscious remedies in general. The majority's unnecessary pronouncements will inevitably discourage or prevent governmental entities . . . from acting to rectify the scourge of past discrimination. This is the harsh reality of the majority's decision, but it is not the Constitution's command.

From this beginning, Marshall proceeded to defend the constitutionality of Richmond's action. He severely criticized the Court's "exceedingly myopic view of the factual predicate on which the Richmond City Council relied." Reviewing the history of discrimination in the nation's construction industry and noting that the city council had been made aware of that history, Marshall concluded that local industry practices in Richmond could be understood only against that broader background. "The majority's refusal to recognize that Richmond has proven itself no exception to the dismaying pattern of national exclusion . . . infects its entire analysis of this case." As Marshall saw it, the evidence about the limited participation of African-American contractors in the Richmond industry was sufficient to establish that the national pattern held for Richmond as well. The statistical evidence showed such a gross difference between population and receipt of contracts that the city properly inferred that there had been racial discrimination in the industry in the past. For Marshall, the testimony of local officials familiar with the local scene also deserved more weight than the Court gave it: "Local officials, by virtue of their proximity to, and their expertise with, local affairs, are exceptionally well-qualified to make determinations of public good" within their cities. Marshall described a series of court cases holding that the city itself had discriminated on the basis of race. "When the . . . leaders of cities with histories of pervasive discrimination testify that past discrimination has infected one of their industries, armchair cynicism like that exercised by the majority has no place."

Marshall's opinion argued that the Constitution required that programs serving remedial goals further important governmental aims and be substantially related to achieving those goals. The verbal formulation of this standard differed from the Court's more stringent standard, but the differences in wording might have been inconsequential in application. They were not, however, because Marshall believed that the city's goals were indeed important and that its plan was closely enough related to achieving those goals to satisfy the Constitution. In addition to the goal of remedying past discrimination, which Marshall found to have occurred, the city could properly try to prevent its money from being used for "reinforcing and perpetuating the exclusionary effects of past discrimination."

On these matters Marshall disagreed with the Court primarily in his vision of what contemporary society was really like. The majority did not see the residual effects of past discrimination to be as pervasive as Marshall did and therefore believed that the city's interest in directing its money elsewhere was relatively slight. For Marshall,

> when government channels all its contracting funds to a white-dominated community of established contractors whose racial homogeneity is the product of private discrimination, it does more than place its imprimatur on the practices which forged and which continue to define that community. It also provides a measurable boost to those economic entities that have thrived within it, while denying important economic benefits to those entities which, but for prior discrimination, might well be better qualified to receive valuable government contracts.

The city's system also satisfied the requirement that remedial plans be substantially related to the city's goals. Marshall found most important the fact that the city's plan essentially tracked the one upheld in *Fullilove*. It was limited to five years, it did not encompass enormous amounts of the contracting business, and it affected only contracts to be written in the future. The Court's desire for nonracial methods, Marshall said, was misplaced. The city already prohibited racial discrimination by its contractors and yet had been unable to overcome the effects of past discrimination. Even Congress had concluded that such methods were likely to be ineffective; that, after all, was why it adopted the program in *Fullilove*.[79]

The final section of Marshall's opinion addressed the broader questions raised by the majority's rejection of his approach. He found the Court's reliance on "strict scrutiny" "an unfortunate development. A profound difference separates governmental actions that themselves are racist, and governmental actions that seek to remedy the effects of prior racism." The former rely on irrelevant considerations, whereas the latter "have a highly pertinent basis: the tragic and indelible fact that discrimination against blacks and other racial minorities in this Nation has pervaded our Nation's history and continues to scar our society." To adopt a single standard for remedial classifications and "the most brute and repugnant forms of state-sponsored racism," Marshall said, signaled that the Court "regards racial discrimination as largely a phenomenon of the past." Marshall, in contrast, "d[id] not believe that this Nation is anywhere close to eradicating racial discrimination or its vestiges."

He also resented the majority's stress on the fact that African-Americans, finally in control of the city government, had adopted a program favoring African-Americans. Their numerical predominance in Richmond, which gave rise to the Court's fear of racial politics, was checked by the "numerical and political predominance" of whites in Virginia and the nation as a whole. Cities where African-Americans had recently taken over the reins of political power were, to Marshall, precisely those "with the most in the way of prior discrimination to rectify." Undoubtedly recalling that his classmate Oliver Hill had been Richmond's first African-American city council member and that Henry Marsh, the city's first African-American mayor, was a member of Hill's law firm, Marshall said that the Court's assessment of racial politics in Richmond "implies a lack of political maturity on the part of this Nation's elected minority officials that is totally unwarranted. Such insulting judgments have no place in constitutional jurisprudence."

Marshall's opinion concluded with a paragraph restating his deep dismay at the Court's action, calling the decision "a full-scale retreat" and saying that it embraced a "cramped vision" of the Constitution. He dissented, the opinion ended, because "the battle against pernicious racial discrimination or its effects is nowhere near won." He referred as much to the Court's decision as to Richmond's.

J. A. Croson Co. appeared to end the Court's divisions over the standard of review to apply to affirmative action. Five justices agreed that affirmative action programs had to meet the stringent standards of strict scrutiny.[80] Or so it seemed in 1989.

A year later the Court decided *Metro Broadcasting Inc. v. Federal Communication Commission.*[81] The conference discussion revealed a narrow majority to uphold a congressionally mandated program giving preference to minority firms in awarding broadcast licenses. White voted to uphold the program even though he had joined the plurality opinion in *J. A. Croson Co.*, because in his constitutional vision the national government had broad powers. Brennan took the opinion for himself. In light of *J. A. Croson Co.*, he believed it necessary to write an opinion applying strict scrutiny to the program. After receiving the draft opinion, White told Brennan that strict scrutiny was inappropriate in evaluating *federal* affirmative action programs. As he saw it, *Fullilove* rather than *J. A. Croson Co.* was the key case.

Surprised but pleased by White's position, Brennan immediately set about rewriting the draft opinion. The revisions were, as O'Connor put it, "surprisingly extensive." Instead of strict scrutiny, the test was to be a version of intermediate scrutiny drawn from the *Fullilove* opinions of Burger and Marshall.[82] The law of affirmative action remained as unsettled at the end of Marshall's tenure as it had been when the question first arose.

Marshall's affirmative action opinions may seem in tension with the positions he took in *Hughes* and *Brown*. As a litigator and strategist, Marshall supported a meritocratic approach to the remedy in *Brown* and opposed a quotalike remedy in *Hughes*, yet, as a judge, Marshall regularly voted in favor of allowing affirmative action programs. There is, nonetheless, a deep continuity in Marshall's jurisprudence of affirmative action. Although resentment—the sense that "they owe us"—may have played some part, Marshall's positions were driven more strongly by his understanding of the way the Court treated race discrimination cases. For Marshall, the Court owed African-Americans precisely the same deference when they managed to eke out legislative victories as it gave whites when they controlled the political process. The Court had tolerated gradual rectification of school segregation, deferring to the political process. As Marshall saw it, the Court owed the same deference as politicians worked out a method of addressing other forms of discrimination.

A change in role might explain changes in position. As a strategist, Marshall had to select a program he thought both legally correct and likely to succeed. The range of issues he could consider in coming to that judgment was wide indeed. As a judge, Marshall was in a different position. Liberated from the constraint of representing a particular client, he did not have to worry about deciding which position would persuade the judges. More important, the issue for Marshall the judge was not whether *he* believed that affirmative action programs were good. It was, instead, whether the authority that had adopted the program—Richmond's city council or Jackson's school board—was within its rights in doing so. Marshall could uphold programs that, all things considered, he personally might oppose.

The role differences, however, plainly cannot account for much of the rhetoric in Marshall's opinions, which typically describe the programs at issue approvingly. Marshall's judgments as a strategist included a significant strain of pragmatism. He opposed the quota-oriented picketing in *Hughes* in part because hiring in proportion to patronage was unlikely to benefit the wider interests of the African-American community. Pragmatic judgments like that, however, are necessarily sensitive to changes in circumstances. In particular, Marshall may have made a pragmatic judgment in the 1950s that the substitution of meritocratic standards for racial ones would be sufficient to place African-Americans in the position in the nation's society and economy to which, on Marshall's view, they were entitled. By the 1980s he may have concluded that such a substitution had not worked—a term used in the argument in *Brown*—and that new programs, such as affirmative action plans, had to be adopted to reach the goal Marshall had been seeking from the beginning. The rhetorical structure of Marshall's opinions, which typically opened with a discussion of the history of discrimination and its continuing legacy to the nation, suggests that this pragmatic orientation was uppermost in Marshall's approach.

Finally, Marshall's approach to affirmative action cases simply asked the Court to respect legislative choices. His opinions stressed the importance of the fact that government decision makers have *chosen* to adopt the challenged affirmative action programs. The opening lines in Marshall's separate opinion in *Bakke* juxtaposed the historical toleration of discrimination with the fact that "now . . . a State acts to remedy the effects of that legacy of discrimination." His dissent in *Wygant* made much of the fact that the layoff policy there had been freely negotiated and chosen by the school board and the union. His dissent in the Richmond case opened by praising "the former capital of the Confederacy" for "act[ing] forthrightly." This emphasis on choice is consistent, of course, with the argument that the judge's role is to decide whether a government's policies are permissible. As he put it in a 1989 interview, "[E]verybody agrees to do it and the court moves in and says no. . . . I don't see why it's the business of the court to come in over the top of all that and say because of our majesty . . . 'No!'"[83]

The rhetoric of choice had deeper roots. The Supreme Court's cautious approach to the question of remedy in *Brown* left it to local school boards and governments to select methods to accomplish desegregation. They could choose the policy that would best advance desegregation. Marshall's position on affirmative action was a straightforward application of the remedial principle adopted by the Court in *Brown*: Governments should have substantial discretion to choose among possible remedies for constitutional violations. Marshall sought a different, more aggressive set of remedies when he argued the desegregation cases. The Court never went along with him. His affirmative action opinions may be seen as his acceptance of the Court's principles in *Brown II*.

7

"Compassion in Time of Crisis"
The Death Penalty

As a law student, Marshall worked with his mentor Charles Hamilton Houston to defend George Crawford in a celebrated case in Virginia's "hunt country." Crawford was charged with murder and faced a death sentence. Supported by some legal research Marshall did, Houston succeeded in securing only a life sentence for Crawford, and Houston regarded the outcome as quite favorable because he had concluded Crawford was indeed guilty. Marshall himself defended W. D. Lyons in an Oklahoma murder case that reached the Supreme Court. Marshall's experiences in these and other death penalty cases made him a committed opponent of capital punishment. As he saw it, death sentences were imposed arbitrarily; the risk of mistake, both factual and legal, was great enough that the government should never take the irreversible step of executing a defendant even when guilt seemed clearly established; and the risks and arbitrariness were enhanced by the fact that defense counsel in capital cases were rarely up to the difficult task of providing a vigorous defense. During most of his career on the Supreme Court, Marshall was the only justice who had substantial experience in trying criminal cases, and that experience worked its way into his opinions articulating legal doctrines against the death penalty.[1]

The death penalty issue divided the Court more severely, and more personally, than any other during Marshall's tenure. In other areas the liberal and conservative justices won some decisions and lost others. The pattern in affirmative action cases was typical: The losers accepted the outcome in each case and used later cases to do what they could to erode the decisions they disliked. Even when the losers remained fundamentally opposed to the decision, as in the abortion cases, they acknowledged they could do little until the Court's composition changed.

Death penalty cases were different. The Court invalidated existing death penalty statutes in 1972 by a narrow majority. Four years later a new majority found that states had revised their statutes in a way that satisfied the Constitution. The Court's conservatives thought they had won in 1976. As they saw it, the Court said that capital punishment was constitutionally permissible, and, they believed, states would soon set about executing people. As the years passed, however, the conservatives discovered that they were facing a protracted guerilla war.[2] The basic challenges to capital punishment occurred in cases that the Court heard and decided. The key battles in the guerilla war, in contrast, occurred behind the scenes.

The Eighth Amendment says that governments cannot use "cruel and unusual punishments." Capital punishment was part of the U.S. punishment system since it began, but by the 1960s many people believed it served no useful purpose. In 1966 a public opinion survey showed that only 42 percent of the people supported capital punishment. In 1910 and again in 1958 the Supreme Court said that the constitutional ban on cruel and unusual punishments had to be interpreted according to what "public opinion . . . enlightened by a humane justice" would say about "the evolving standards of decency that mark the progress of a maturing society." Marshall's opposition to capital punishment seemed consistent with the enlightened public opinion that constitutional law would support.[3]

The death penalty was bound up with issues of race as well. In 1963 Justice Arthur Goldberg wrote a "highly unusual" memorandum to his colleagues asking them to consider the constitutionality of the death sentence for rape, because of "the well-recognized disparity in the imposition of the death penalty for sexual crimes committed by whites and nonwhites." As scholars observed, "From the 1880s onward, almost all executions for rape . . . took place in the South, and . . . 85 percent [of those executed] were black."[4]

Goldberg's memorandum crystallized thinking among Marshall's former colleagues at the NAACP Legal Defense and Education Fund. Anthony Amsterdam, an energetic and brilliant young law professor, pushed the NAACP Inc. Fund lawyers to develop a large-scale attack on the death penalty. They managed to get a moratorium on executions by raising constitutional challenges to every aspect of the death penalty: racial discrimination in its administration, unfair methods of choosing jurors, unfair procedures for deciding who should get a death sentence. When Marshall arrived at the Court, the justices were ready to work through the challenges to reach a final decision on the constitutionality of capital punishment.[5]

The Court took the first step in 1968, dealing with "death-qualified" juries. An Illinois statute allowed prosecutors to remove jurors with "conscientious scruples against capital punishment," without showing that those jurors might not be able to set aside their scruples in any particular case. When William Witherspoon was tried for murdering a police officer in 1959, his jury was death-qualified: The prosecutor said, "Let's get these conscientious objectors out of the way, without wasting any time on them" and removed forty-seven jurors. Witherspoon's lawyers asked the Court to set aside his conviction because the jurors who remained were more likely to lean to the prosecution's side. Amsterdam filed a friend-of-the-Court brief offering a more limited ground: The death sentence, not the conviction, should be set aside because the death-qualified jury was not a fair cross section of the community. Justice Potter Stewart persuaded his colleagues to change their initial vote to deny review. As he saw it, because "half the country opposed capital punishment," disqualifying the jurors who shared those views would "deny [a] proper jury trial." After hearing the case, the Court, in an opinion by Stewart, agreed with the main lines of Amsterdam's argument. Stewart called the jury a "hanging jury" and the procedure one that "stacked the deck" against Wither-spoon.[6]

Justice Black dissented, saying that if the Court "is to hold capital punishment unconstitutional, . . . it should do so forthrightly, not by making it impossible for States to get juries that will enforce the death penalty." Although Stewart's opinion did not directly cast doubt on capital punishment, its tone was sharply critical, calling its supporters a "dwindling" minority and quoting death penalty abolitionist Arthur Koestler's description of the "division" between abolitionists and supporters of capital punishment as a divide "between those who have charity and those who have not."

Amsterdam hoped the next step in the litigation campaign would be the in-validation of capital punishment for rape. He and his colleagues developed an extensive factual record in the case of Willie Maxwell, showing that only race could explain a pattern in which, with few exceptions, only African-Americans were sentenced to die for raping white women. The federal court of appeals, in an opinion written by then-Judge Harry Blackmun, rejected the statistical argument.

When the case got to the Supreme Court in 1969, the focus on race discrimina-tion disappeared. The justices were more concerned with two other issues: Should the Court impose standards to identify more precisely the cases in which a death sentence should be imposed? Should it require that juries first decide guilt and only then consider the penalty? After the argument, eight justices voted to vacate Maxwell's death sentence, but they were quite divided on why. Warren said that the "jury cannot be given [the] absolute right to say death without standards to guide the choice." He also noted that the death penalty "seems to be reserved usually for [the] poor [and] underprivileged." Harlan said that he could not "go along" with requiring standards, which might preclude "compassion of [the] jury." But he did "have trouble" with the one-stage trial, because it put the defendant to a hard choice: If the defendant testified to try to get juror sympathy on the question of sentence, he would have to answer questions about the crime itself. Fortas, too, thought the one-stage trial a "denial of due process in a rudimentary sense," because defendants could not "get facts before [the] jury relevant to a judgment of life or death."[7]

Warren assigned the opinion to Douglas, who wanted two-stage trials. Work-ing quickly, Douglas turned out a draft that Brennan found entirely unsatisfac-tory. The opinion dealt with the issue of standards as well as the two-stage trial because, as Douglas told his colleagues, "[a]s I got deeper into the two problems they became inseparable to me" even though there had never been a majority on the question of standards. The discussion of standards was quite disjointed, par-ticularly on the crucial question of what exactly the standards should be. Harlan thought it impossible to require standards for death sentences without reworking criminal procedure entirely: "Where do we stop?" he asked.[8]

Black replied to Douglas with a dissent restating his point in *Witherspoon:* "If this Court is determined to abolish the death penalty, I think it should do so forthrightly, not by nibbles." Stewart relied on *Witherspoon* to vacate the death sentence. The majority began to unravel when Fortas decided he had been wrong on the question of standards. He ended up thinking that legislatures could not "prescribe different punishments for the kaleidoscope of crime and the infinite variety of persons who commit them." He also worried that "if standards are to be legislated, the result will be substantially to increase the number of cases of imposition of [the] death penalty." Two weeks later, Marshall agreed with Fortas, saying that "in this area, we do not yet have the skills to produce words which would fit the punishment to the crime." Without Fortas's vote, there was no majority on the issue of standards, and Douglas withdrew that part of his proposed opinion.[9]

Warren and Brennan agreed with Douglas's view that the Court could not decide whether two-stage trials were necessary without discussing the issue of standards. As they saw it, the second stage would be pointless unless it was focused on the standards for imposing a death sentence. Brennan prepared a response to Fortas, but the crucial vote came from Harlan when Fortas resigned. Harlan drafted an opinion saying that a defendant had a constitutional right to present personal testimony to persuade a jury not to sentence him to death, which moved in the direction of requiring a two-stage trial. After thinking about the problem more, however, Harlan decided that he needed more time to work on his opinion. Without a majority for any position, the Court asked for reargument.

By the time of reargument, Warren and Fortas were gone. The new Chief Justice, Warren Burger, saw no way to define standards, because jury decisions rested on "the sum total of the life experience of the jurors." Harlan finally seemed to come down in favor of a two-stage trial, but now his vote did not matter; the Court was evenly divided on the question because Blackmun, having heard the case earlier, could not vote now. Burger told his colleagues that he was "not sure" that the two-stage trial was "a useful device or even helpful" to defendants. Black again said that this case was "only a fight to abolish capital punishment," which should be left to legislatures. Harlan was now certain that a one-stage trial was "one of [the] clearest cases of denial of fundamental fairness," because "if the sentence is committed to [the] unrestricted judgment of [the] jury," the trial could not restrict what the defendant wanted the jury to consider, which might include evidence diminishing the defendant's responsibility while acknowledging his guilt. But he did not think that standards were required. Stewart responded that, in his view, the Constitution did not require either standards or a two-stage trial, but, he said, if the majority found that two stages were required, he thought standards were then necessary.[10]

As Brennan counted the votes, six justices would have reversed because of an improper exclusion of jurors under *Witherspoon*. But only four justices appeared to want a two-stage trial, and only three thought the Constitution required standards. In the end, the Court went along with Stewart's view that Maxwell's jury might have been selected in violation of *Witherspoon,* but the Court immediately took two new cases raising the issues of standards and the two-stage trial.[11]

The struggle over those issues in *Maxwell* did not occur again. Blackmun could vote on these cases, and there was finally a clear majority to reject the attacks. Surprisingly, Harlan himself ended up rejecting even the argument for a two-stage trial, which he had been attracted to before. His opinions seemed to signal that the litigation campaign against the death penalty had failed: Only Douglas, Brennan, and Marshall voted in favor of standards and a two-stage trial.[12]

The justices then met to decide what to do next. Law clerks for Brennan, White, and Blackmun worked through the pending cases to select ones in which the Court could consider the basic question of capital punishment's constitutionality. Oddly, Douglas balked. "[F]or the life of me," he wrote his colleagues, "I do not see from listening to any member of the Court, how anyone would entertain the thought that as a matter of constitutional law the death penalty was prohibited in a straight, clear-cut first degree murder case." To grant review in such cases would "merely clog the dockets of lower courts" and delay legislative reconsideration of capital punishment. Indeed, after he had been outvoted, Douglas drafted a dissent saying that "the ostensible purpose in granting [review] . . . is not to explore the problem of capital punishment in all of its constitutional, sociological, and penological aspects, but to announce in Draconian fashion that capital punishment passes muster."[13]

The justices picked two murder cases and two rape cases for review.[14] Douglas's perception of the likely outcome was shared by Brennan's law clerks, who prepared a long memorandum in the form of a draft dissent to a majority opinion upholding the death penalty. By the time the cases were argued in January 1972, Brennan said he believed the death penalty to be unconstitutional, and Marshall had drafted an opinion finding that the death penalty "served no legitimate purpose and was repugnant to contemporary standards of decency." The results of the votes were a surprise: Five justices agreed that the death penalty was unconstitutional. Each had a different theory, however, and each justice's chambers went to work on individual opinions.[15]

The lead case was *Furman v. Georgia*. Brennan's draft concluded that the death penalty violated the Eighth Amendment, which "prohibits the infliction of uncivilized and inhuman punishments." Punishment could not be excessive, and "[i]f there is a significantly less severe punishment adequate to achieve the purposes for which punishment is inflicted," the punishment would be unconstitutional. The death penalty "has been almost totally rejected by contemporary society." Because it was imposed so rarely, "it smacks of little more than a lottery system." Douglas thought that without standards, death sentences were "imposed under a procedure that gives room for the play of . . . prejudices."

Stewart hoped to fashion an opinion for all five justices in the majority. His law clerks drafted a memorandum criticizing Brennan's draft opinion for failing to "have any single, coherent theory" and for relying on "an *ipse dixit* based as much on the values of this court as on the values uncovered in contemporary or enlightened morality." Douglas's opinion, according to the memorandum, rested on an underdeveloped theory that the death penalty was handed down in a discriminatory way. Finally, Marshall's opinion was "vulnerable" because it "proceeds as if he were a legislator, weighing the evidence and concluding that there is little deterrent effect" and because, by relying "heavily on the 'enlightened morality' approach," he left himself "wide open to the charge of arrogance." The memorandum outlined an alternative that would be "more intuitively plausible" and "less vulnerable to attack by the vociferous minority of critics, both lay and academic, who will disapprove the result." It melded four approaches: A punishment could not "degrad[e] the dignity of man"; it could not "offend contemporary morality"; it could "not be imposed arbitrarily or discriminatorily"; and it could not be "excessive in the sense of unnecessary." These approaches were not all that different from Brennan's approach, and Stewart passed the memorandum on to Brennan.[16]

Nothing came of this attempt to forge a single opinion for the Court. In the end, Stewart took a narrower path. He was concerned that complete abolition would "sow[] the seeds of anarchy—of self-help, vigilante justice, and lynch law." But, Stewart wrote, "[D]eath sentences are cruel and unusual in the same way that being struck by lightning is cruel and unusual." For him, the Constitution could not "tolerate the infliction of a sentence of death under legal systems that permit this unique penalty to be so wantonly and freakishly imposed." White, too, emphasized how infrequently death sentences were imposed. During the justices' discussions, White had said that "we shouldn't validate [the] death penalty at this stage of our history." He noted that "steadily the jury has rejected the death penalty" and that the "community has accepted [abolition] whether . . . by judges or juries." Under those conditions, capital punishment could not serve an "existing general need for retribution," and it could not deter when it was "so seldom invoked that it ceases to be a credible threat."[17]

Marshall's opinion was the longest. It began by acknowledging the brutality of murders for which death sentences were often imposed but pointed out that the issue for the Court was whether the penalty was unconstitutional, not whether the murders were "ugly, vicious, [and] reprehensible." For Marshall, "candor is critical," and "candor compels me to confess that I am not oblivious to the fact that this is truly a matter of life and death," meaning that "the decision [must] be free from any possibility of error."[18]

The opinion reviewed the Eighth Amendment's history and the Court's decisions interpreting it. The fact that capital punishment was permitted earlier, even by the framers of the Constitution themselves, did not dispose of the claim that by the late twentieth century it had become cruel and unusual. For Marshall, "evolving standards" invalidated punishments that were either excessive or unnecessary, or were "abhorrent to currently existing moral values."

The opinion's core examined the standard reasons for criminal penalties, including retribution and deterrence. It argued that "retaliation, vengeance, and retribution have been roundly condemned as intolerable aspirations for a government in a free society." Otherwise, the ban on cruel and unusual punishments would be drained of any meaning, for any punishment whatever could be justified as a form of retribution for the criminal's offense. The opinion acknowledged the evident fact that "there is a demand for vengeance on the part of many persons in a community against one who is convicted of a particularly offensive act," but "the Eighth Amendment is our insulation from our baser selves." It was how the citizens of a free society "recognize their inherent weaknesses and seek to compensate for them" by using a Constitution to impose restraints on themselves. Examining the evidence regarding the deterrent effect of capital punishment, the opinion concluded that, despite the problems with statistical studies, the studies did provide "clear and convincing evidence that capital punishment is not necessary as a deterrent to crime in our society" even if they did not prove that proposition "beyond a reasonable doubt." And, for Marshall, that was enough.

Having found the death penalty excessive because it was unnecessary, the opinion then found that it was also "morally unacceptable to the people of the United States at this time in their history." This conclusion, of course, flew in the face of the fact that legislatures in many states, apparently representing their constituents' views, found the death penalty morally acceptable. The opinion discounted both legislation itself and opinion polls as measures of the public's moral views, because the issue was whether "people who were fully informed as to the purposes of the penalty and its liabilities" would find it "shocking, unjust, and unacceptable." For Marshall, this approach did not require that the public be "rational" but only that its "subjective, emotional reactions" be informed. The opinion then argued that most people "know almost nothing about capital punishment," reviewed the discussion of deterrence, and concluded that "this information would almost surely convince the average citizen that the death penalty was unwise." What was left was the possibility that citizens would find the penalty acceptable as retribution. But, the opinion said, "no one has ever seriously advanced retribution as a legitimate goal of our society."

"I cannot believe," the opinion continued, "that at this stage in our history, the American people would ever knowingly support purposeless vengeance." But, if more was needed, it could be found in evidence about the discriminatory use of the death penalty, about the execution of innocent people, and about the "havoc" the administration of the death penalty wrought on the criminal justice system. Marshall recited evidence that the death penalty "falls upon the poor, the ignorant, and the underprivileged members of society," because "it is the poor, and the members of minority groups who are least able to voice their complaints against capital punishment. . . . So long as the capital sanction is used only against the forlorn, easily forgotten members of society, legislators are content to maintain the status quo." Further, "no matter how careful courts are, the possibility of perjured testimony, mistaken honest testimony, and human error remain all too real." Inevitably, some innocent people will be executed.

The opinion concluded by saying that

> the measure of a country's greatness is its ability to retain compassion in time of crisis. . . . This is a country which stands tallest in troubled times, a country that clings to fundamental principles, cherishes its constitutional heritage, and rejects simple solutions that compromise the values that lie at the roots of our democratic system. . . . Only in a free society could right triumph in difficult times.

As in virtually all of his decisions, Marshall here offered what he presented as the simple common sense of the situation. The opinion does not convey a sense that Marshall was struggling to overcome uncomfortable facts, such as the approval of the death penalty throughout the history of the United States and its widespread support even in 1972. Perhaps the opinion presented the case for the death penalty in too simple terms, and it certainly underestimated the appeal of two propositions: that a person who is executed will commit no further crimes and that most people, and probably most potential murderers, want to live. The unabashed patriotism of the concluding passage expresses Marshall's deepest views. For him, the Constitution embodied all that is good about the United States; all we needed to do is understand it properly.

Burger's dissent in the 1972 death penalty cases provided states with a guide to enacting death penalty statutes that would satisfy a Supreme Court majority. He pointed to passages in the opinions of Stewart and White indicating that states could define capital offenses narrowly or could use mandatory death sentences. Although Burger may have believed that "[t]here will never be another execution in this country," the pressure for capital punishment was so strong that many states quickly followed his guide and adopted new death penalty statutes.[19]

Cases under these new statutes got to the Court in 1976. The justices surveyed the candidates and picked five. Two involved mandatory death penalty statutes. North Carolina required death sentences for all premeditated murders, and Louisiana required the death penalty for first-degree murder, allowing juries to impose a life sentence by convicting a defendant of second-degree murder. The other statutes, from Georgia, Texas, and Florida, tried in varying ways to eliminate the "freakishness" that led Stewart and White to vote against the death penalty in 1972. Each statute listed "aggravating circumstances" that a jury had to find before it could impose a death sentence; this provision limited the class of murders for which the death penalty was available. Each statute also identified the "mitigating circumstances" a jury could take into account in deciding whether to impose a death sentence, although Texas's statute simply asked the jury to consider here whether the defendant might commit future violent crimes.

Although Powell thought the Court would invalidate these new statutes, Brennan more accurately predicted that White would uphold mandatory death penalty statutes and that Justice John Paul Stevens, who had replaced Douglas a year before, would find all the new statutes constitutional. When the vote was taken, only Brennan and Marshall voted against all the new statutes. Burger reiterated his view that "this is primarily a legislative prerogative." Stewart emphasized that the new statutes showed what "evolving standards of decency are in 1976." The Louisiana and North Carolina statutes kept the "jury irrationality" that he found unconstitutional in 1972, but the Georgia and Florida statutes, he said, were "constitutionally tolerable systems." White said that by providing juries with standards, the states had increased the number of death sentences, which eliminated his concern with the "infrequency of [the] imposition" of capital punishment. Powell thought that the 1972 cases had "served a salutary role" by providing "safeguards against systems that operated like bolts of lightning." Stevens thought that the abolitionist views of Brennan and Marshall would "inevitably become law but not yet." The North Carolina statute, Stevens said, "produced more [death] penalties that [it] should, rather than cutting down numbers of executions." It was "a monster" that was "abhorrent" to him. Both North Carolina and Louisiana had "escape hatch[es]," which were "a lawless use of legal systems."[20]

Brennan's clerks wrote short memoranda after the arguments indicating why none of the statutes really addressed the problems the majority had identified in

1972. Texas's statute, for example, asked the jury to speculate about future dangers and nothing else; Louisiana's introduced discretion by allowing the jury to convict a defendant of second-degree murder.[21]

Burger, White, and Rehnquist voted to uphold all the statutes. White found mandatory death penalty statutes the easiest to defend; they showed, he believed, that society really was willing to follow through on its commitment to capital punishment. Stewart and Powell, in contrast, found such statutes too bloodthirsty, but they were willing to uphold the statutes giving juries guidelines to identify the limited class of cases in which the death penalty was appropriate. Blackmun and Powell initially voted to uphold Louisiana's mandatory statute but were bothered by North Carolina's, which had yielded a fivefold increase in the number of death sentences handed down. Stevens thought that mandatory death sentences were "monstr[ous]."[22]

Burger asked White to write in all five cases, in part because White had been with the majority in 1972. Stewart, Powell, and Stevens were puzzled, because, as they counted the votes, a majority had voted to strike down North Carolina's statute. As White worked on his opinion, Powell, Stevens, and Stewart—who have come to be known as "the troika"—met to work an approach they could agree on. By early May, White knew that his drafts would "no longer command a majority," and Burger asked Stewart to work on "a 'joint opinion'" for the Court. The opinion, Burger hoped, would make it clear that the Eighth Amendment did not foreclose capital punishment. Individual justices could then explain what, in their views, the amendment did permit. "After considerable thought and discussion" with Powell and Stevens, however, Stewart rebuffed Burger's attempt to salvage a clear majority holding, telling Burger that he could not write a separate opinion dealing only with the Eighth Amendment.[23]

The troika still had problems to work out. Mandatory death sentences certainly eliminated the freakishness that bothered Stewart before, but Stevens and Powell ended up thinking that such statutes went too far. Stewart worked out a theory for them: Because some murders were not as heinous as others, not all murderers deserved death sentences, but mandatory statutes treated them identically. To be constitutional, a death penalty statute had to allow juries to consider the "particularized circumstances" of each murder and each defendant. That, however, introduced a new problem. The more that juries could consider, the easier it would be for juries to bring back the arbitrary decision making that produced the problems the majority addressed in 1972. The troika concluded, somewhat uneasily, that the "guided discretion" statutes did enough to constrain juries. The lists of aggravating circumstances "reduce[d] the likelihood that [the jury] will impose a sentence that can fairly be called capricious or arbitrary."[24]

Marshall dissented from the Court's approval of these systems of "guided discretion." His opinion started by noting that thirty-five states and Congress adopted statutes approving capital punishment even after the Court's decision in *Furman*. "I would be less than candid," Marshall wrote, "if I did not acknowledge that these developments have a significant bearing on a realistic assessment of the moral acceptability of the death penalty to the American people." He reiterated his position that his standard required consideration only of "informed" views and also asserted that the reenactment of death penalty statutes after *Furman* had no bearing on the separate question of whether the death penalty was excessive. Here the opinion discussed a then-recent economic study of the death penalty, which purported to find a significant deterrent effect. Relying on critics of that study, Marshall recited flaws in its methods and concluded that it did not undermine his earlier conclusion that the opponents of the death penalty had provided enough evidence to show that it was not a distinctively effective deterrent.

In some ways, the weakest part of Marshall's earlier position was his dismissal of retribution as a permissible purpose for the death penalty. The new majority relied in part on retribution as a justification, which Marshall found "to be the most disturbing aspect" of the 1976 decisions. One of the opinions for the justices in the majority argued that "the instinct for retribution is part of the nature of man, and channeling that instinct . . . serves an important interest in promoting the stability of a society governed by law." Marshall called this "wholly inadequate to justify the death penalty," whatever its merits as an argument for the existence of some system of criminal punishment, because "it simply defies belief to suggest that the death penalty is necessary to prevent the American people from taking the law into their own hands." Nor was it necessary to impose the death penalty to signal society's retributive disapproval of the underlying crimes. Finally, there was the purely retributive argument, that "the death penalty is appropriate, not because of its beneficial effect on society, but because the taking of the murderer's life is itself morally good." Marshall's opinion pointed to language in his colleagues' opinion suggesting that argument without quite making it. A purely retributive argument was "fundamentally at odds with the Eighth Amendment. . . . [T]he taking of life 'because the wrongdoer deserves it' surely must fail, for such a punishment has as its very basis the total denial of the wrongdoer's dignity and worth." The opinion hinted at another argument as well: The very fact that none of the justices upholding the death penalty openly offered the purely retributive argument suggested that no one actually believed it.

Marshall's opposition to capital punishment placed him on the Court's fringe. He spoke for the Court in death penalty cases only four times from 1976 to his retirement. In 1985 he wrote an important opinion for the Court insisting that juries could not be misled about their responsibility in sentencing a defendant to death. Responding to defense efforts to impress the jury with the gravity of its decision, the prosecutor in *Caldwell v. Mississippi* told the jury that its decision was not final, because it was going to be reviewed.[25] Marshall's opinion said that "it is constitutionally impermissible to rest a death sentence on a determination made by a sentencer who has been led to believe that the responsibility for determining the appropriateness of the defendant's death rests elsewhere." Telling the jury that its decision would be reviewed would lead to unreliable and possibly biased decisions "in favor of death sentences," because jurors might not understand the limits that appellate courts imposed on themselves in reviewing death sentences and because they might want to use the sentence to "send a message" without feeling responsible for the ultimate outcome. By passing responsibility elsewhere, the prosecutor's argument "offers jurors a view of their role which might frequently be highly attractive" to people "called on to make a very difficult and uncomfortable choice." As the opinion noted, "[O]ne can easily imagine that in a case in which the jury is divided on the proper sentence, the presence of appellate review could effectively be used as an argument for why those jurors who are reluctant to invoke the death sentence should nevertheless give in."[26]

The Court at first voted to deny review in *Ford v. Wainwright,* in which the defendant claimed it was unconstitutional to execute him as long as he was insane. Marshall circulated a dissent from the denial of review, which persuaded the Court to hear the case in 1986. The argument showed that the case involved two issues: Could a state execute someone who was insane? If not, what procedures did a state have to use to determine whether the prisoner was insane? A majority voted for the defendant on the first issue. The ban on executing the insane went back centuries; as Stevens said, "Shouldn't one have [the] opportunity to make peace with his maker?" The resolution of the second was unclear. Because of Marshall's earlier influence on the case, he was assigned the opinion. His draft relied in part on "international opinion" and "our own best judgment" to show that executing the insane was unconstitutional. Powell had a "negative reaction to relying on [these] speculative 'sources'." The Court, Powell said, "is often criticized by those who say that we base our decisions on such factors rather than on the Constitution and the law itself." He also objected to Marshall's citation of a United Nations study. "Capital punishment is still extensively carried out in many sections of the world, and I doubt that the suspect's sanity receives much attention in a number of countries." Powell mentioned the Soviet Union, saying that "few people doubt that in effect the sending of offenders to Siberia may result in their death."[27]

Powell objected to Marshall's treatment of the procedural question as well. As Powell saw it, Marshall had unnecessarily required states to have full hearings on the convict's sanity. Instead, Powell believed, states should have "flexibility in designing appropriate procedures for conducting psychiatric examinations" and should be able "to structure fair procedures where the decision-maker determines sanity based on written reports." Marshall eliminated the references to international practices in his next draft but told Powell that he "must stand firm" on the procedural issue: The prisoner's interest was simply too strong to permit "a paper hearing."[28]

Powell then joined the part of Marshall's opinion discussing executing the insane, giving Marshall a majority, and wrote separately on the procedural one, leaving Marshall with only a plurality supporting him there. Marshall relied on the nation's "common law heritage" as the basis for constitutional protection against execution.[29] The framers' generation, Marshall wrote, believed that executing the insane was "savage and inhumane." The opinion argued that "we may seriously question the retributive value of executing a person who has no comprehension of why he has been singled out and stripped of his fundamental right to life" and that "the intuition that such an execution simply offends humanity is evidently shared across this Nation."

Ake v. Oklahoma, another 1985 decision, also involved a death sentence, but Marshall's opinion had a broader reach, which led to a minor confrontation with

Burger.[30] Glen Ake was charged with murdering a father and mother and attempting to murder their two children. After Ake behaved bizarrely in jail, the trial judge ordered a psychiatric examination. The psychiatrist reported that Ake was probably schizophrenic at that time, and he was sent for treatment so that he could be tried. Ake went to trial a few months later, after receiving antipsychotic drugs. His lawyer asked the state to pay for a psychiatrist who would examine Ake's sanity at the time he committed the murders, which no prior examination had gone into. The trial judge denied the request, so there was no testimony about Ake's mental condition at the time of the murders. The jury rejected Ake's insanity defense and sentenced him to death.

As in *Ford,* the Court decided to hear Ake's case after Marshall circulated a dissent from an initial decision to deny review. All but Rehnquist ultimately agreed that Ake was entitled to the psychiatric witness he asked for. Marshall circulated a draft that bothered Burger. He sent Marshall a letter listing the "problems." Burger objected to Marshall's discussion of psychiatric testimony during the sentencing phase, saying that the Court's decision that Ake's case had to be retried made moot "any errors in the sentencing phase." More broadly, Burger was concerned that "[t]he fact that this is a capital case is barely mentioned." For Burger, "the prospect of a capital *sentence* is critical to this case." He doubted that the Constitution required states "to provide expert witnesses generally to all criminal defendants." Burger wanted a more extensive discussion of "the costs to the State," because he did not want defendants to "use this as a 'gimmick' to delay a trial." A week and a half later, Burger reiterated that he could join Marshall's opinion if it were restricted to capital cases.[31]

Burger's insistence on limiting the reach of the decision bothered Marshall. He went through a copy of his opinion, underlining for himself every point that mentioned the capital sentence. Other justices indicated some sympathy with some of Burger's concerns. Powell, for example, said that the decision could be limited to capital cases, but he "would not insist on this. As a practical matter, the due process reasoning of your opinion will apply equally in noncapital cases when the defendant is charged with a serious crime." Powell did think that the opinion should discuss the sentencing stage. In contrast, O'Connor agreed with Burger on the sentencing question. Stevens, though joining Marshall's opinion, said there was "a good deal of merit" in Burger's suggestions, but he, too, wanted to keep the discussion of sentencing.[32]

Marshall modified his opinion slightly to deal with some of Burger's concerns, but he did not limit the opinion to capital cases and retained the discussion of expert witnesses at the sentencing stage. In a note to those who had joined his opinion, Marshall wrote, "Since seven of us agree, my current plan is not to make the change suggested in the Chief's ultimatum." Burger sent Marshall a personal note saying that he "did not know I sent you an 'ultimatum.' I rarely start the new year with such!" Stevens said that it was up to Marshall to decide what to do. Restating one of Powell's earlier points, Stevens wrote that "the logic of your excellent opinion will carry the day in all events, and it would be more advantageous to have [Burger's] name on the opinion than to have him write separately." In the end, Marshall decided to stick with his revised opinion, and Burger did write a separate opinion saying that "[n]othing in the Court's opinion reaches noncapital cases."[33]

Marshall's opinion in *Furman* is significantly less powerful than the accumulation of his opinions in later cases. *Furman* involved the general and relatively abstract question of the constitutionality of the death penalty itself. The later cases involved what might seem details about how the penalty was administered. Marshall understood from his days as a litigator, however, that the abstract question about the death penalty was only a generalization from all the cases in which the death penalty was sought and imposed. The details, in short, were what mattered, and Marshall brought his sensibility as a litigator to his discussion of those details. His experience made it possible for him to display a more acute sense of the reality of the death penalty when he discussed particular cases than when he dealt with the general question of capital punishment.

During most of his time on the Court, Marshall was the only justice with substantial experience in trying criminal cases and the only one who had ever represented a defendant in a capital case. He brought his experience to bear in his dissents when the Court upheld death sentences. When a majority found that some procedure limited sentencing discretion, Marshall devoted his efforts to demonstrating that the procedure was bound to fail; when a majority found that some challenged action did not lead to the arbitrary imposition of a death sentence, Marshall set out to show how it did.

For example, *Lowenfield v. Phelps,* decided in 1989, involved a defendant who killed five people.[34] The jury spent thirteen hours considering the question of guilt; when the jurors told the judge that they were having "much distress" after eleven hours, the judge directed them to arrive at a verdict, a very strong instruction. The jury came back with a verdict, and the judge allowed the jurors a one-hour break before they began considering the sentence. The jury was told that if it did not agree unanimously to a death sentence, the defendant would receive a life sentence. Just before midnight the jury requested permission to retire for the night. Late the next afternoon, the jurors told the judge they could not reach a decision. The judge asked each juror to sign a note indicating whether he or she believed "further deliberations would be helpful." After some confusion, eleven jurors said they thought they could arrive at a verdict with more time. The judge then instructed the jurors to "consider each other's views" and to reach a verdict "if you can do so without violence to [your] individual judgment." In contrast to the instruction at the guilt stage, this instruction was relatively mild. The jury came back with a death sentence a half-hour later.

A majority of the Supreme Court held that the judge's actions did not coerce the jury into returning a death sentence. For Marshall, the procedure, considered in the entire context of the trial, was impermissible. He emphasized a number of facts that went into the "totality" of circumstances: The judge suggested that the jury might return a verdict near midnight, asked the jurors to identify themselves by name in indicating whether they believed further discussion would help—in a context in which the jurors knew that stopping the process would lead to a life sentence—and reinstructed the jury when accepting their inability to decide would have produced a life sentence. Marshall's opinion pointed out that one juror who indicated that additional discussion would not help "could not help feeling that the verdict-urging charge was directed at him and him alone." As in *Caldwell*, Marshall noted that jurors in capital cases are asked to make a difficult moral decision and that "given the amorphous and volatile nature of their inquiry, capital sentencing juries that have reached an impasse in their deliberations may be particularly prone to coercion from the court." Lowenfield was executed on April 13, 1988.

Lowenfield is characteristic of Marshall's attempt to assess capital cases as they would feel in the courtroom itself. Bringing his experience as a litigator to bear on the cases, Marshall put himself in the position of ordinary jurors and offered his colleagues analyses grounded in the common sense of the courtroom situation. His analyses were usually much more realistic than the majority's: It is hard to escape the feeling that Marshall better understood what was happening in *Lowenfield* than the majority.

One of Marshall's most striking dissents came in *Gray v. Lucas,* in which the defendant mounted a constitutional challenge to the use of the gas chamber as a *method* of execution.[35] The opinion included substantial excerpts from affidavits describing "in graphic and horrifying detail" what actually happens in a gas chamber. Marshall found the method "cruel" because it involved "extreme pain" over a ten-minute period and because lethal injections were equally effective and "though equally barbaric in [their effects], involve[] far less physical pain." Marshall's opinion surely was directed at more than the legal point he made, because the gas chamber had been widely used as a method of execution and indeed was probably the central image along with the electric chair in the popular understanding of the death penalty. He found in the case an opportunity to place on the pages of the *United States Reports* a vivid description of what capital punishment really was. His opinion was a form of public education, aimed at disabusing people of any illusions they might have had about a death sentence. In this way Marshall returned to the theme he articulated in *Furman:* that a fully informed public would not approve of the death penalty as it was actually administered. Gray was executed on September 2, 1983.

Having lost their major battle against capital punishment, death penalty litigators continued their campaign in a series of smaller but still significant battles and a skirmish whenever a defendant faced execution. The Court's majority rejected the main challenges, but the attacks on particular death sentences continued to plague the Court.[36]

The NAACP Inc. Fund's interest in death penalty litigation was fueled by concerns about race discrimination, and such concerns clearly affected some justices' votes against the constitutionality of the death sentence. The Court rarely was faced with direct evidence that prosecutors sought the death penalty, or jurors imposed it, because of the defendant's race. In 1988, when it did see such a case, the Court denied review, and Marshall dissented. A lower court refused to give a hearing to a defendant who claimed that a juror had given a court official a napkin with a gallows and "Hang the Niggers" drawn on it. The case involved "gruesome" murders, though the defendant himself played what Marshall called "only a secondary role"; the case also had attracted a great deal of attention and elicited racial hostility in the community. Marshall wrote that the allegations described "a vulgar incident of lynch-mob racism reminiscent of Reconstruction days" and found it "conscience-shocking" that no federal court was willing to investigate the allegations. Andrews was executed on July 30, 1992.[37]

Death penalty litigators relied on statistical studies because Andrews's case was unusual; ordinarily direct evidence of discrimination was difficult to discover. The Court had to decide whether the statistics cast doubt on the death penalty in the 1987 case of *McCleskey v. Kemp*.[38] Warren McCleskey, an African-American, and three accomplices robbed a furniture store in Fulton County, Georgia. The four men tied up the store's employees, but someone sounded a silent alarm, and a police officer came in the door. As he entered, he was killed by two shots from a revolver. Inconclusive ballistics evidence suggested that McCleskey had fired the fatal shots, and two prisoners who had been in jail with McCleskey testified that he told them he shot the officer.

McCleskey's lawyers introduced a large-scale statistical study directed by law professor David Baldus. Baldus and his colleagues studied more than two thousand Georgia murder cases, identifying 230 variables that might explain disparity in sentencing on nonracial grounds. The study yielded results that have since been repeatedly confirmed. It disclosed that there were basically three kinds of capital cases. In some, the particularly awful cases, juries would always impose the death penalty. In others, as when a woman deliberately stabbed her abusive husband, juries would almost never impose it. McCleskey's case fell in the middle category, cases in which killings were not particularly vicious and in which the evidence against the defendant, though enough to convict, was not overwhelming. Baldus found race discrimination in this middle category. It was, however, a surprising kind of discrimination. The study did not find that African-Americans who committed murders in this category were more likely to receive a death sentence than whites in the same category. Instead, the study found discrimination based on the victim's race: People who killed whites were far more likely to be sentenced to death than people who killed African-Americans. Even though McCleskey was charged with killing a police officer, he was the only defendant who received a death sentence for doing so in Fulton County between 1973 and 1979, out of seventeen charged with such murders.

The lower courts found Baldus's study incomplete, but McCleskey faced more serious problems at the Supreme Court. McCleskey raised a number of challenges to his death sentence, and the Court held off on deciding whether to hear the race-discrimination claim until it decided a case dealing with one of the other issues. After that decision, the justices voted to hear McCleskey's case. Powell wrote a memorandum to his colleagues explaining that he would vote to deny McCleskey's application for review. As he saw it, "No study can take all . . . individual circumstances into account. . . . [T]he aggravating and mitigating factors in each case differ in ways that are real but difficult to calibrate." If race discrimination did affect capital punishment, Powell said, he would expect it to show up in discrimination against defendants, rather than in the form that Baldus discovered, discrimination based on the victim's race.[39]

When the justices took up McCleskey's case after argument, there were five votes against him. Rehnquist correctly observed that accepting McCleskey's claim "would dismantle Georgia's whole system." He would invalidate a death sentence only if a defendant showed intentional discrimination in his individual case. Powell said that he "couldn't decide criminal cases on statistics alone," and O'Connor observed that the remedy, if the Court found for McCleskey, would have to reduce jury discretion, "and that bothers me." Scalia initially thought that the Court could not rely on what he called "statistics of this kind." Later, however, his position appeared to shift subtly. After Powell circulated a proposed majority opinion, Scalia noted his disagreement with the emphasis the opinion placed on the inadequacies of the Baldus study. "I disagree with the argument that the inferences that can be drawn from the Baldus study are weakened by the fact that each jury and each trial is unique, or by the large number of variables," he wrote. He rejected "the view . . . that an effect of social factors upon sentencing, if it could only be shown by sufficiently strong statistical evidence, would require reversal." As he saw it, "[T]he unconscious operation of irrational sympathies and antipathies, including racial, upon jury decisions and (hence) prosecutorial decisions is real, acknowledged in the decisions of this court, and ineradicable." So, he concluded, "I cannot honestly say that all I need is more proof." In the end, however, Scalia joined Powell's opinion without expressing his views on the "ineradicable" nature of racial "antipathies."[40]

Powell's opinion accepted the statistical validity of Baldus's study but found it insufficient to establish a constitutional violation. McCleskey had to show that "decisionmakers in his case acted with discriminatory purpose." Accepting McCleskey's claim, Powell wrote, would "throw[] into serious question the principles that underlie our entire criminal justice system," because similar statistical cases could be made about every stage of the process.

Brennan's eloquent dissenting opinion opened, "At some point in this case, Warren McCleskey doubtless asked his lawyer whether a jury was likely to sentence him to die. A candid reply to this question would have been disturbing." As Brennan put it, "The story could be told in a variety of ways, but McCleskey could not fail to grasp its essential narrative line: there was a significant chance that race would play a prominent role in determining if he lived or died." Responding sharply to Powell's concerns about the implications of accepting McCleskey's claim, Brennan said, "[S]uch a statement seems to suggest a fear of too much justice."

Brennan, sometimes viewed by Marshall's law clerks as an "opinion hog" with the "interesting habit . . . [of] assign[ing] a greatly disproportionate share of the best . . . opinions to himself," wrote the other dissenters that he expected "considerable writing" in *McCleskey* and invited them to decide for themselves whether to write separately. As Randall Kennedy, law professor and Marshall's former law clerk, put it, Marshall maintained a "stony silence," perhaps, Kennedy suggested, "to convey the extremity of his sense of alienation from the Court," whose opinion might have been "beneath discussion."[41]

Marshall did write when McCleskey's case came back to the Supreme Court. After the Court's decision, McCleskey's lawyers managed to obtain the government's files on his case. They discovered evidence suggesting to them that one of the jail witnesses had been planted in the cell next to McCleskey and instructed to get a confession from him. A 1964 Supreme Court decision indicated that the prosecution could not use a statement obtained under such circumstances. The lawyers went back to federal court and asked for relief. The federal trial judge agreed, finding that their failure to raise this claim earlier was excusable because they had not had the prosecution's files. The appeals court reversed, saying that McCleskey's lawyers made a similar claim about the jail informant earlier (although without as much factual information to back it up) and then decided to abandon it.[42]

The Supreme Court agreed, rejecting the trial judge's findings about how the government had concealed information about the jail informant. Marshall was reminded of the conservative view that courts should not exclude evidence seized in unlawful searches merely because of what Marshall called "the stumble of the constable"; if prosecutors should not suffer because of police errors, why should defendants suffer because of their lawyers' mistakes? Marshall thought the opinion went so far beyond the facts and so sharply curtailed the availability of review that he called Kennedy's opinion "lawless." Stevens wrote Marshall a note saying, "[E]ven though I agree that the majority's holding is outrageous, I wonder if the word 'lawless' is not too strong. . . . After all, when five members of the Court agree on a proposition, it does become the law." Marshall immediately replied that he excised the word "within a minute after I received your note," but his opinion retained its sharp tone.[43]

McCleskey came back to the Court a third time after Marshall announced his retirement but before he left the Court. This time McCleskey argued that the Georgia clemency board was biased against him because the state's attorney general had vowed to "wage a full scale campaign" against the board if it voted in favor of clemency. The Supreme Court denied a stay of execution. Marshall issued a strong dissent. He said that the Court had "somehow rejected" McCleskey's claim of race discrimination in 1987, "unconscionably denied" him relief in 1991, and, in denying the stay of execution, "values expediency over human life." Marshall concluded, "Repeatedly denying Warren McCleskey his constitutional rights is unacceptable. Executing him is inexcusable." McCleskey was executed the next morning.[44]

8

"We Are Dealing with a Man's Life"
Administering the Death Penalty

The big stories about the death penalty were major cases like *McCleskey v. Kemp*.[1] Inside the Court, however, the smaller details proved to be more irritating. The guerilla campaign against the death penalty was conducted in the theater of procedure. Litigators did all they could to keep their clients alive. They appealed convictions to state supreme courts and then sought Supreme Court review. After that they went back to state court, using state postconviction procedures to raise new challenges. Again, they tried to get Supreme Court review, and then they shifted to the lower federal courts. Federal law allows people convicted in state courts to get federal courts to consider constitutional challenges to their convictions through the procedure known as habeas corpus. During Marshall's tenure there were no formal limits on the number of times a state defendant could bring a habeas corpus action. So, after losing in the state courts, death penalty litigators took their cases to federal court, all the way through the Supreme Court. Then they could try again if they could come up with a new constitutional theory. McCleskey's second trip to the Supreme Court and similar cases led the Court to tighten the rules on bringing these successive habeas corpus actions, but the Court's new approach did not have much effect on the pace of litigation before Marshall's retirement.

The Court's majority beat back broad-based attacks on capital punishment in cases like *McCleskey*. But death penalty litigators had other weapons. In every capital case, they could raise a host of issues about the fairness of each particular trial. The justices who found the death penalty constitutional in principle sometimes fractured over these individual challenges.

The overall picture is clear: Death penalty litigators devised a number of broad-based attacks on capital punishment even after 1976. These attacks covered a large number of cases. Until the Court resolved them, it would be unfair to execute someone who might benefit from a ruling against the death penalty. Even after the Court ruled against one broad-based challenge, another slightly less broad one could still be mounted. It would be unfair to execute anyone in the slightly smaller group covered by that challenge. And the individual claims of each defendant still remained.

The slow pace of execution may have accurately reflected divisions in the country. Some observers suggested that a large majority of Americans approved of the death penalty in the abstract but were much more divided over how frequently it should be administered and in which cases. Personal relations became strained when that ambivalence was reflected inside the Court. Two justices, Marshall and Brennan, always voted against capital punishment. In nearly every case, the Court's rules made it possible for them to delay executions if they found one or two allies. The Court's conservatives only gradually discovered that the rules contributed to the guerilla war against capital punishment.

The conservatives' problems arose from the "rule of four." Before 1925 the Supreme Court had to hear argument in almost every case brought to it. The justices found the burden of deciding all those cases nearly impossible and persuaded Congress to give the justices discretion to hear only the cases they wanted to. Some members of Congress were concerned that this might close the Court's doors too tightly. To allay those fears, the justices promised Congress that a minority on the Court would always have the power to force the majority to hear a case. The "rule of four" means that it takes only four justices to get a case heard, even though it takes five votes to get a decision.[2]

The rule of four itself contributed to delay. After the Court announces its decision to hear a case, lawyers have several months to write their briefs. Then the case has to fit into the Court's schedule. The hearing could be delayed for a few more months if the Court's calendar was already full, as sometimes happened during Marshall's tenure. After the case is heard, the justices have to decide it and write opinions and dissents. In all, the rule of four allowed four justices to put off an execution date by nearly a year without much effort.

But the rule of four had other consequences. Suppose a capital defendant applies for review after the state has set a date for the execution. Four justices can get the Court to grant review. But the execution date might fall before briefs are due, before argument is scheduled, or before a Court decision could be expected. Ordinarily, the state could go ahead with the execution. Letting a state execute someone whose case was being considered by the Supreme Court struck many justices as peculiarly unfair. They had a procedural device to prevent that. The state would have to wait if the Supreme Court itself issued a stay of execution. But, under the Court's rules, it takes *five* justices to issue a stay.

The position taken by Marshall and Brennan made the question of when to issue stays of execution particularly difficult for justices who did not think capital punishment was unconstitutional. Perhaps two other justices thought a capital defendant presented a serious claim about an individual case, whose merits the Court should consider, but, the conservatives thought, Marshall and Brennan voted to grant review because they opposed capital punishment completely. Often, then, the four votes to grant review seemed almost insincere. Should a justice in the majority join the four others to issue a stay of execution?

There was an even more arcane issue that caused problems. In many areas not limited to death penalty cases, several cases arrive at the Court presenting similar though not quite identical issues. Sometimes the Court decides to hear a group of related cases. Sometimes, however, it decides to "hold" the related cases until it decides the lead case. Then the justices take a look at the cases they have held in light of the decision they have made. The decision might have nothing to say about the issues in the related cases, and the Court will deny review. Or the decision might have some bearing on the related cases. The Court could decide to hear argument in one of them. More commonly, the Court remands the case, sending it back to the lower courts for them to consider how the new case affects the one that was held.

How many votes should it take to hold a case pending a decision in the related one? For most of Marshall's tenure, the Court's rules said that a case would be held if three justices thought it related to one in which the Court was hearing argument. The argument for that rule was simple: No one could tell whether the decision in the primary case would affect the related ones until the justices wrote opinions in the primary case. If three justices thought a case was related to the primary one, they might be able to persuade a fourth to grant review in light of the decision, once it was handed down. Until then, it was prudent to let three justices hold a case, almost as insurance against the possibility that something surprising might happen in the primary case.

Holding cases was not a real problem when the primary case raised a broad-based challenge to the death penalty. If the Court was considering whether the Constitution allowed states to execute people who were minors when they committed their crimes, the Court would hold all cases involving such minors. Once those broad-based challenges were disposed of, the question of which cases to hold became more difficult inside the Court. For, by that time, Marshall and Brennan had been joined by Justices Blackmun and Stevens as reasonably consistent opponents of capital punishment. Too frequently, the conservatives thought, either Blackmun or Stevens became the third vote to hold a case as related when it really had little to do with the primary case.

The problem was exacerbated after the justices heard argument and voted on the principal case. They knew, although the public did not, what the result was going to be. But the justices felt they had to follow what Marshall once called "the fiction that a case is not 'decided' until it is officially announced."[3] If the Court was going to uphold the death penalty in the principal case, the conservatives found it particularly galling that three justices could nonetheless delay executions in cases only tangentially implicating an issue that they knew was about to be rejected.

In the long run, the conservatives believed themselves most disadvantaged by what they saw as the liberals' manipulation of the Court's rules. But the conservatives themselves took the first steps that divided the Court.

In 1981, five years after the Court again authorized capital punishment, Justice Rehnquist became impatient. He used two cases involving murders committed in 1973 and 1976 as vehicles for a proposal he believed would break the "stalemate" he saw in administering the death penalty. The Court, Rehnquist proposed, should grant review in *every* capital case, even if the claims presented would not ordinarily be treated as worth the Court's time. In one of the cases, for example, the defendant argued that a state procedural rule made it difficult for him to show in the state postconviction proceeding that jurors at his trial were affected by adverse pretrial publicity. Marshall wrote an opinion showing that the defendant's argument was not frivolous, but it was unlikely to win because the procedural limits in state postconviction proceedings would not affect the defendant's ability to get a federal court to decide whether the pretrial publicity made his trial unconstitutional.[4]

Stevens called Rehnquist's bluff. With Marshall and Brennan voting to grant review, Rehnquist's vote in the two cases left the petitioners only one vote short of getting Supreme Court review. Stevens looked at the cases and chose to vote to grant review—satisfying the rule of four—in the case in which the defendant made the stronger constitutional claim. Rehnquist was now faced with the prospect of having the Court hear a case showing that careful examination of constitutional claims in death penalty cases was desirable. To avoid that, he withdrew his vote to grant review in that case. He did publish a dissent from the denial of review in the other case. Stevens responded with an opinion explaining that Rehnquist's proposal was "an improper allocation of the Court's limited resources" because hearing all death penalty cases "would consume over half of [the] Court's argument calendar" on issues of no national significance. He tweaked Rehnquist in observing that death penalty issues "have not been difficult for three Members of the Court"—Marshall and Brennan, of course, but also Rehnquist: Stevens wrote, "[I]f my memory serves me correctly, Justice Rehnquist has invariably voted to uphold the death penalty."[5]

Three years later, tensions within the Court increased as the possibility of more executions grew. The problems seemed minor at first. Early in 1984 Justice Powell noted that defendants' efforts to stay their executions disrupted the Court. He pointed out that the Court's staff had to stay in the building through the night because they could not be sure whether a stay would be sought. Soon after that, the Court accepted Powell's suggestion that it establish procedures to keep the justices informed of the status of death penalty cases.[6]

The justices were notified when a court of appeals was considering a stay of execution, then after it decided whether to issue or deny the stay, and then about counsel's plans to seek review and a stay from the Supreme Court. Sometimes, of course, the cases never reached the Court—a lower court, sometimes a state court, would delay the execution. The overall effect was to increase the flow of paper inside the Court and to heighten the justices' awareness of the details of death penalty cases. The justices became almost micromanagers in death penalty cases. Memoranda like one from Justice White saying "The state is apparently making some noises about trying to do something about the stay" in one case became almost routine. It became more difficult to see the Court's role as resolving large questions of constitutional law when the justices had to think about what to do in every case in which a murderer faced execution.[7]

Again, the conservatives made an already difficult situation worse. In May 1984 James Adams faced execution in Florida. On May 8 he persuaded the federal court of appeals to stay his execution, arguing that his federal habeas corpus petition presented issues that the appeals court was already considering in two other cases. Florida's attorney general immediately went to the Supreme Court and argued that Adams was barred from presenting his claim at such a late date because he failed to present it in an earlier federal proceeding. On May 9 the justices agreed, voting 5–4, to vacate the stay. Marshall was outraged. In a memorandum to his files, he noted that the discussion of the case had taken only eighteen minutes and that his motion to be given twenty-four hours to write a dissent had been denied. In a published dissent, Marshall chastised the majority for its "indecent desire to rush to judgment in capital cases," which was "especially egregious" when the Court overrode a lower court's decision to issue a stay: "Caution has been thrown to the winds with an impetuousness that is truly astonishing." The Court "appears to have . . . forgotten here . . . that we are not dealing with mere legal semantics; we are dealing with a man's life."* Adams was executed on May 10.[8]

The next year Willie Darden's case produced "real bitterness."[9] Darden was convicted of murdering the owner of a furniture store. Darden was on a furlough from prison at the time of the murder. Shortly after it occurred, his speeding car slid off a wet road and crashed, a few miles from the furniture store. The car matched the description the police had of a car that had been at the store, and the police searched the crash area, discovering a gun that turned out to be of the type used in the murder (although it was never identified as the murder weapon). The store owner's wife identified Darden as the killer when she saw him at the preliminary hearing at which he was charged with murder.

Darden's main claim was that his trial was unfair because the prosecutor engaged in serious misconduct. As Powell wrote, the prosecutor's closing argument to the jury "deserves the condemnation it has received from every court to review it." Violating well-established standards, the prosecutor called Darden "an animal," said that he should not "be out of his cell unless he has a leash on him," said that "I wish that I could see him sitting here with no face," criticized the prison authorities for giving Darden a furlough, and stated his personal belief that Darden was guilty. Darden claimed he was innocent; as his lawyer put it, "They took a coincidence and magnified that into a capital case."[10]

The Supreme Court considered Darden's claims serious enough to justify review. In its first consideration of the case in 1977, however, the Court decided it had made a mistake in attempting to review what was so clearly a fact-bound decision with few implications for national law and dismissed the case "as improvidently granted." After eight years of habeas corpus proceedings, in which the appeals court was severely divided, the case came back to the Supreme Court.[11]

Darden's lawyers had to stay his execution if they were to get the Supreme Court to consider his claims. On September 3, 1985, the Court received an application for a stay. The Court voted to deny the application by a 5–4 vote, and notified the lawyers. Around 9:00 P.M., the Court received a letter from Darden's

---

* Carol Steiker, one of Marshall's law clerks in 1987–88, recalls Marshall writing "in his big blue marking pen" in another case, "A man's life is at stake. We should not be playing games." "'Did You Hear What Thurgood Marshall Did for Us?'—A Tribute," *American Journal of Criminal Law* 20 (Winter 1993): vii, ix.

lawyers asking that the application for a stay be treated as a request for review of the lower courts' decision that Darden's trial had not been unfair. Without further discussion, the four justices who voted to grant the stay—Brennan, Marshall, Blackmun, and Stevens—voted to grant review. Powell then joined them to stay Darden's execution, despite his evident belief that Darden's case did not deserve any further consideration. Burger was so upset at what happened that he published an unprecedented dissent from a *grant* of review. Noting that Darden's claims "have been passed upon no fewer than 95 times by federal and state court judges," Burger said that the Court was wrong to "accept meritless petitions presenting claims that we rejected only hours ago."[12]

The justices discussed what to do over the next few weeks. Powell wrote that the "experience" with granting review in *Darden* "disturbs me." He called what Brennan and the other justices in the minority had done "more than a little unusual" and was "not at all sure it was done in accordance either with our Rules or precedent." As he saw it, they had "exploited" the rule of four. But he had broader concerns as well. The case, he said, "illustrates how easily the system is manipulated in capital cases." Perhaps writing too hastily under time pressure, Powell mistakenly said that "[n]o one suggests that [Darden] is innocent—a fact that all too often under our law is irrelevant." He continued, "Unless the habeas corpus statute is substantially changed, . . . the states should rescind their capital punishment laws."[13]

Brennan replied, agreeing that the Court's procedures should be reexamined because they "exposed the Court to criticism that its own decisions are arbitrary." The real problem, he suggested, was the tension between the rule of four and the requirement of five votes to stay an execution. "We are all endebted to Lewis," he wrote, "for twice sparing the Court and the petitioner" the fate of being executed even though four justices thought he presented serious claims. He proposed that the rule of four be extended to applications for stays, at least in cases like Darden's, in which the defendant was trying to get review of his first habeas corpus action. Blackmun agreed: "The Court as an institution would surely appear intellectually and morally bankrupt if we were to announce that a petitioner's claims are worthy of review but that we would abandon our responsibility to perform such review if the state chooses to execute in the meantime."[14]

Justice Rehnquist equably said that "we have been living in reasonable peace and harmony for several years" requiring five votes for a stay, although he thought it might make sense to have a rule of four for stays if there was a "reasonable prospect of success on the merits." Burger set Stevens on edge with his observation that the Court's dismissal of Darden's case in 1977 "should have removed any doubt . . . as to our view of the merits"; as Stevens correctly said, the Court's dismissal was the equivalent of a denial of review, which ought to suggest nothing about the Court's view of the merits.[15]

The Court considered changing its rules at the end of September. It had one suggestion (Powell's) to require five votes to grant review and one formal proposal (Brennan's) to allow a stay with four votes. Brennan wrote a long memorandum supporting his proposal. Because the "use of capital punishment by the states is only beginning to hit full stride," the Court could expect "the difficulties we experienced" in *Darden* "to recur." And, because "the law in this area continues to develop and as the views of each of us continue to evolve"—perhaps here alluding to the positions Blackmun and Stevens were taking—"we must expect more close cases in which at least four Justices are not prepared to make a final decision based only on the papers accompanying a stay application under the staggering time pressures we have experienced." As Brennan saw it, the issue was whether the Court or the states determined when the Court decided to hear cases. He agreed with Blackmun that "this Court should refuse to be pushed into premature review . . . by the states' scheduling of execution dates."[16]

Brennan was clearly concerned that Powell's memorandum expressed a troubling attitude about divisions within the Court. He tried to allay concern that some justices were using the rule of four "in bad faith" by noting that four justices might vote to grant review if "forced to make a last minute decision under great time pressure" but that "with a little more time, there might have been fewer votes." He rejected Powell's claim that anyone had "'exploit[ed]' anything," saying that "four members of the Court honestly felt that an issue warranting plenary review was presented, and they voted accordingly." After that, Brennan believed, the law and even more strongly the Court's traditions meant that a stay should "automatically" be granted, to avoid the "unpalatable" result that the state could moot the case by executing the defendant.

Brennan continued to defend his proposal, but nothing came of it. Indeed, it seems likely that he offered his proposal at least as much to forestall action on Powell's suggestion—to show that changing the rules would divide the Court once again—as to accomplish a change in the rules.

Frustration over the rules continued. Just before the formal discussion of Brennan's proposal, for example, Burger objected to a request from Brennan. Sometimes, after the justices make their initial decision to deny review in a case, one justice will request that the case be "relisted" to give time to prepare a memorandum that might change a vote or two. When Brennan requested relisting a capital case, Burger saw the request as merely another tactic to delay execution because the relisting would extend the Court's consideration of the case beyond the scheduled execution date. Brennan replied that he was "entitled" to relist a case. A few months later, Marshall wrote his colleagues about a petition for rehearing. He pointed out that the petition showed that the case was related to one on which review had already been granted, and he hoped that someone who had voted to deny the original request for review would at least request a response from the state to the petition for rehearing.[17]

Procedural irritants continued to disturb relations among the justices. Aubrey Adams was convicted of murdering an eight-year-old girl in 1978. Florida scheduled his execution for early March 1986. By that time, death penalty litigators had managed to persuade some courts that it was unconstitutional to try defendants with "death-qualified" juries, whose members said they had no objections in principle to imposing a death sentence. Other courts disagreed, and the Supreme Court had already agreed to decide the question when Adams's application for a stay of his execution arrived at the Court. It had also already voted to reject the challenge, but the decision had not been announced.

Four justices voted to hold the case until the "death-qualification" decision was announced. A majority thought, however, that Adams's case was different, because no potential juror had actually been removed from the jury in the process of death qualification. What should be done about Adams's application for a stay of execution? Powell made it a practice "solely for institutional reasons" to provide the fifth vote for a stay when four justices voted to grant review. Burger occasionally did so as well.[18]

Powell was confused about the state of the votes in Adams's case. At first he thought that four justices had voted to grant review, and therefore he voted for the stay even though he believed that "Adams and his counsel are 'playing games with us.' " When he realized that the four justices had voted only to hold the case until the death-qualification decision was announced, he told his colleagues that he felt "differently about votes to hold" and now voted to deny the stay.

Marshall told his colleagues that the issues needed a full discussion "because these unresolved disputes invite confusion, changes of mind, and strategic behavior when a person's life is at stake." He believed that "whether the vote is a grant or a hold, the power given to four or three by our rules is nugatory if an execution is permitted to moot the case." He said that "the power to issue a stay under these circumstances simply should not depend on an *ad hoc* act of generosity by some fifth Justice." As Marshall saw it, "the fate of each prisoner . . . seems to depend primarily upon whim and accident." Marshall called the Court's own "contribution to the arbitrariness of the death penalty" itself "alarming."[19]

Brennan may have illustrated the problem of strategic behavior when he responded to Powell's vote change by asserting that his first choice was to grant review and that his alternative vote was to hold the case,[20] which meant that there might be four votes to grant review and would trigger Powell's policy. Although Powell continued to believe that the Court was "simply being exploited," he grudgingly voted to grant the stay. But, he wrote, "[t]he effect of the Court's action will not be misunderstood" by antideath penalty litigators. Pointing to the fact that Adams's lawyers had filed three petitions for review and four applications for stays of execution within the prior week, Powell told his colleagues that "there has been a gross abuse of the processes of our Court." He would not "criticize counsel for taking advantage of us if we permit it," but he thought that the Court should change its rules to avoid "indefinite delay in enforcing the law of the law."[21]

Burger backed Powell up. He said he was "not prepared to adopt the novel proposition that 'four to hold' should automatically constitute a stay in a capital case." He, too, derided some "counsel's protestations" that their cases were related to the death-qualification case; the "mere ritualistic invocation" of that case "cannot be enough to justify a stay of a lawfully imposed death sentence."[22]

Marshall replied to Burger's concerns about death penalty lawyers by saying that if "lawyers are routinely able to hoodwink three Justices into voting to hold a case that is actually unrelated" to a pending case, "the Court's problems . . . far exceed" the procedural matters the justices were considering. As he saw it, "when this Court has chosen to give some number of Justices less than a majority certain powers," such as to grant review or hold a case, "the majority may not take action to void the exercise of such powers," as denying stays of execution would.[23]

In the end, Adams could not get four votes to grant review. Brennan drafted a dissent from the denial of review describing the Court's processes, including a statement that the justices "internally agreed" that once four justices voted to grant review, a fifth would join them to stay an execution. That statement set Burger off. That decision, he said, "must have taken place when I was in Moscow or Peking." He and Powell gave "a 'comity' vote twice," but that did not "establish an 'agreement.'" He also criticized Brennan for proposing to publicize internal discussions. Burger was annoyed at Brennan's assertion that "the only reason that Adams' petition has not been granted is that [the lawyer in the pending death-qualification case] beat him in the race to the Clerk's office." The issues in the cases were different, Burger said; "Adams' lawyer 'raced' to raise the claims only at the eleventh hour." He suggested that Brennan "may well want to alter his draft in light of the facts . . . I have pointed out."[24]

Brennan took out the draft's statement about an "agreement" to provide a fifth vote for a stay, but he continued to describe the Court's practices as a "rule that the five [voting against review] will give the four an opportunity to change at least one mind." One justice who voted against review "will nonetheless vote to stay." Burger replied that he had "never heard of such a 'rule.'" He again mentioned his "practice," but, he wrote, "If that 'practice' does not make an 'agreement,' it certainly does not make a 'rule.'" Brennan had had enough. Mildly tweaking Burger for misunderstanding the difference between using "three periods rather than four" when quoting from a text, Brennan told Burger that "if you read again" the draft dissent, he would find that the word "rule" referred to the "Rule of Four," rather than the practice of voting to stay an execution. After further delays, Adams was executed on May 4, 1989.[25]

Burger repeatedly fulminated against what he called "the 'phoniness' of this eleventh hour business" and "spurious claims of 'rush to judgment.'" Those on the other side, however, hardly thought the claims spurious. As they saw it, the Court itself was rushing to judgment. In a memorandum he never sent to his colleagues, for example, Brennan replied to Burger's observation about the rush to judgment by noting that "at the time the Chief voted in this case, no papers had been filed by counsel, and therefore the Chief voted on the merits . . . without having had the opportunity to read the papers. Spurious indeed!"[26]

Marshall's concern about the Court's desire to expedite executions was the focus of his 1983 dissent in *Barefoot v. Estelle*.[27] After his case had proceeded through the state court system, Thomas Barefoot asked the federal district court to overturn his conviction and sentence. The district judge directed the state not to execute Barefoot while the judge was considering the case. When the judge rejected Barefoot's claims on November 9, 1982, he also vacated this stay of execution but authorized Barefoot to appeal to the court of appeals. Barefoot filed his appeal on November 24. The state then set an execution date of January 25, 1983. On January 14, after failing to get a stay from the state courts, Barefoot asked the court of appeals for one. Three days later, the court of appeals told the parties to present briefs and oral argument on January 19. On the day after that argument, the court of appeals denied the stay, with an opinion rejecting Barefoot's claims on the merits. Barefoot asked the Supreme Court to hold that the appeals court's expedited consideration of his claims violated the statutes regulating federal court consideration of challenges to state convictions and sentences.

A majority of the Supreme Court found that the court of appeals had acted properly: The procedure it followed had given Barefoot a fair opportunity to present the merits of his case. The Court did suggest that lower courts might want to "adopt expedited procedures" for death penalty cases, after considering "whether the delay that is avoided by summary procedures warrants departing from the normal, untruncated processes of appellate review."

Marshall vigorously disagreed with the Court's "perverse suggestion" that expedited procedures were appropriate in capital cases. Because the death penalty was "irreversible," it was "hard to think of any class of cases for which summary procedures would be less appropriate." Marshall found nothing in the Court's opinion to justify its suggestion, except for a passage hinting that appeals in capital cases were "generally frivolous." That, however, he believed was "contrary to both law and fact." As a matter of law, the only cases to which the expedited procedures would apply would be ones in which the trial judge authorized an appeal, as had happened in *Barefoot*. On the factual issue, Marshall said that "experience shows that prisoners on death row have succeeded in an extraordinary number of their appeals"—even in cases in which the state courts and a federal trial court had rejected the claim. Barefoot was executed on October 30, 1984.[28]

In *Dobbert v. Florida,* crucial evidence at trial came from Ernest Dobbert's son.[29] Shortly before the scheduled time of Dobbert's execution in 1984, Dobbert presented an affidavit from his son that Dobbert had not committed the murder for which he was convicted. Marshall joined Brennan's dissent from the Court's refusal to stay Dobbert's execution and also wrote separately. His opinion opened by saying that "the 'right' of the State to a speedy execution has now clearly eclipsed the right of an individual to considered treatment" of his claims. "Here is the entire history of the deliberate speed with which the claim was considered": Dobbert filed his petition for relief on August 30. It was denied on September 3. Three days later, the court of appeals, using the expedited procedures approved in *Barefoot,* affirmed the decision. That afternoon Dobbert asked the Supreme Court to stay his execution, scheduled for the next day. "A scant 19 hours after Dobbert asked this Court to consider his claim . . . Dobbert is to be executed. This is swift, but is it justice?" Marshall asked. Dobbert was executed on September 7.

By the late 1980s, the majority's impatience led to occasional sloppiness of the sort Marshall worried about in *Barefoot*. Once in 1987 the conservatives voted to grant a state's petition for review of a state court decision vacating a death sentence before the prisoner's response was even due. Marshall drafted what Blackmun called a "devastating dissent" criticizing the Court's action. Referring to comments of some of his colleagues that they would vote to review the case "even though the opposition material had not yet been seen," Blackmun observed that "the Spring rush to judgment is really bad this year." Marshall's dissent led the Court to wait, and in the fall the Court denied the state's application for review.[30]

During 1986 the Court was prepared to deny review, but a proposed dissent led the justices to hold the case until another one was decided. After that decision was handed down, the Court vacated the death sentence without hearing argument. In the same year, four justices voted to grant review in *Turner v. Murray*. The Court stayed an execution and then, over the dissent of four justices, denied the state's motion to vacate the stay. After the case was argued, O'Connor and White, who had initially voted to deny review, voted to overturn Turner's death sentence because the trial judge had barred his lawyer from questioning jurors about racial prejudice. White was influenced by the fact that this was a capital case involving a white victim and an African-American defendant. Powell responded that "Virginia is not Texas or Florida," because Virginia was more restrained in administering death sentences. The prosecutor, Powell said, had "never hinted at" the racial questions, and the trial, he pointed out, had been "changed from [a] racial bias county to [Virginia's] eastern shore." O'Connor decided not to dissent from the reversal. Turner was sentenced to death once again and was executed on May 25, 1995.[31]

Cases like these were too rare to overcome the conservatives' view that the Court was interfering with the fair administration of justice. Under Chief Justice Rehnquist, the Court adopted the practice of scheduling arguments in capital cases as soon as possible "where it appears that there will be a fair number of 'holds' for the case, because of the desirability of getting the 'lead' case decided and disposing of the 'holds.'" Marshall objected in vain, saying that he saw "no reason to *rush* in death cases unless it is to save a life."[32]

The practice of granting stays when four justices wanted to grant review eroded as well. In June 1990 four members of the Court indicated they would grant certiorari in *Hamilton v. Texas* to consider Hamilton's claim that her son James Smith was mentally incompetent and should not be allowed to withdraw his appeal from his death sentence.[33] Smith's execution date had already been set. Only the four justices who voted to grant review voted for a stay. As a result, Smith was executed in late June. Hamilton's petition for certiorari came up in the normal course in October, and, unsurprisingly, the Court denied review because the case was mooted by Smith's death. Marshall expressed his "frustration" at this outcome, saying that "the Court's willingness . . . in this case to dispense with the procedures that it ordinarily employs to preserve its jurisdiction only continues the distressing rollback of the legal safeguards traditionally afforded." Ironically, Marshall's efforts to delay executions may only have fueled public dismay at the slow pace of executions, enhancing public support for capital punishment in the abstract and denying the public the opportunity to learn the lessons Marshall hoped it would learn, as he had, from actual experience with capital punishment.

After Brennan retired, the conservatives had the votes not only to deal with cases on the merits but also to change the Court's rules. On May 23, 1991, a month before Marshall himself retired, the justices voted to require four votes to hold cases. It was a fitting conclusion to the Court's internal battles, an unpublicized change in procedures designed to restore what Rehnquist had almost a decade earlier called "reasonable peace and harmony." For Marshall, however, it was purchased at the cost of the decent consideration that people sentenced to death ought to receive from the nation's highest court.[34]

On the morning of June 27, 1991, the Supreme Court issued its opinion in *Payne v. Tennessee*, another death penalty case.[35] That afternoon, Marshall announced his retirement.[36] Marshall's dissent in *Payne* was his final word as a justice on the Constitution's meaning.

In 1987 the Court decided *Booth v. Maryland* by a 5–4 vote. *Booth* held that juries in capital cases should not be told about the impact of a murder on the crime's victims and their survivors. Such evidence, Powell's majority opinion said, was often highly inflammatory. Further, victim-impact evidence threatened to return to a system in which the death sentence was imposed unequally, because evidence about sympathetic victims—those with "eloquent" surviving members or with high status in the community—would be presented, but not evidence about less-articulate victims, even though the defendant's guilt was the same.[37]

Marshall had been surprised to find a majority for the result in *Booth*. The Court revisited the question two years later. Powell had been replaced by Anthony Kennedy. The conference discussion ended with a number of justices saying they wanted to overrule *Booth*. It seemed that a majority preferred to distinguish it instead. O'Connor circulated an opinion doing so. White, a dissenter in *Booth*, decided that he could not go along with distinguishing the case, although he might have been willing to overrule it. Scalia then circulated an opinion overruling *Booth*. Kennedy agreed that *Booth* should be "overruled now rather than chipping at it bit by bit." O'Connor told Scalia, "If you can persuade three other members . . . to overrule" *Booth*, she would change her opinion. At that point there seemed to be a majority to overrule *Booth*. White, however, thought it was too late: O'Connor's opinion distinguishing *Booth* ended up as the Court's opinion even though White's would have been the fifth vote to overrule it.[38]

Two years later the majority was ready. In *Payne*, Rehnquist rejected the arguments the earlier majority found persuasive. Even so, he had to deal with the question of whether it should overrule cases decided so recently. Although, Rehnquist said, stare decisis was an important policy, it was not an "inexorable command." The earlier cases, he continued, "were decided by the narrowest of margins, over spirited dissents challenging the[ir] basic underpinnings." The dissenters continued to disagree with the decisions, and the cases "have defied consistent application by the lower courts." That was enough, for the majority, to overcome the policy of stare decisis.

Marshall's dissent focused on this question. As he put it, "neither the law nor the facts" supporting the earlier decisions "underwent any change in the last four years. Only the personnel of this Court did." Powell and Brennan had retired, replaced by Anthony Kennedy and David Souter. Marshall found it "ominous" and "radical" to alter constitutional law only because the Court's membership had changed. That threatened the Court's "historical commitment to a conception of the 'judiciary as a source of impersonal and reasoned judgments.'"

Marshall acknowledged that the Court had the power to overrule its decisions, but, he argued, the power should be exercised only when there was some reason, beyond mere disagreement with the earlier decision, for overruling. For him, "the striking feature" of Rehnquist's opinion was that it did not "even try" to show why overruling the earlier cases was imperative. Marshall, of course, was an enthusiastic supporter of the Warren Court's criminal procedure decisions, which involved many overrulings. But, Marshall explained, those decisions were different. Sometimes the Warren Court overruled decisions that had been given a long time to work and had failed. For example, *Gideon v. Wainwright* overruled a 1942 decision saying that lawyers had to be provided to criminal defendants in exceptional cases only; the Court struggled to define those cases for twenty years and found the task impossible.[39] Sometimes the Court overruled decisions resting on a constitutional theory it had gradually abandoned. That explained Marshall's opinion in *Benton v. Maryland,* overruling a 1937 decision refusing to invoke the double jeopardy clause against the states; during the decade before *Benton,* the Court had moved away from the theory the 1937 decision rested on. Neither reason, though, was present in *Payne.* Two years was surely too short for experience to undermine the theory of the earlier decisions, and the majority cited only one case to show that lower courts had trouble with the victim-impact cases.

What was left, then, was the majority's assertion that it could overrule cases that were decided by a narrow margin "over spirited dissents." For Marshall, this "impoverished conception of *stare decisis* cannot possibly be reconciled with the values that inform the proper judicial function." Judicial review required the Court "to rein in the forces of democratic politics." The Court could exercise that power and could demand compliance with its decisions "only if the public understands the Court to be implementing 'principles . . . founded in the law rather than in the proclivities of individuals.'" But, if the Court's decisions changed dramatically simply because its membership changed, it could "hardly expect" the public to respect them. Marshall pointed out that the Tennessee court in *Payne* provided a clear example of this threat, because it "did nothing to disguise its contempt for" the Court's earlier victim impact decisions. The lower court's contempt showed why allowing the Supreme Court to overrule its decisions freely would "squander the authority and the legitimacy of this Court as a protector of the powerless."

Tellingly, Marshall cited *Cooper v. Aaron,* the Little Rock school decision in which the Court chastised Arkansas governor Orval Faubus for refusing to accept the Court's desegregation decisions as the law of the law, to show that the majority's action in *Payne* threatened the fundamental values of the rule of law. His dissent's first sentence described his view of the majority and, implicitly, of the importance of the rule of law: "Power, not reason, is the new currency of this Court's decisionmaking." Marshall's last words as a justice were spoken in the same voice he used throughout his career as a lawyer, standing up for reason against mere power.

Marshall's dissent in *Payne* raises broader questions about his practice in death penalty cases. After the Court upheld the death penalty, Brennan and Marshall dissented whenever the Court denied review in a death penalty case. In more than fourteen hundred cases, they entered a dissent stating, "Adhering to our views that the death penalty is in all circumstances cruel and unusual punishment prohibited by the Eighth and Fourteenth Amendments, we would grant certiorari and vacate the death sentence in this case," and Marshall continued the practice after Brennan retired.[40] Some critics called this practice "lawless" and inconsistent with *Cooper v. Aaron.*[41]

Marshall's critics pointed out that a majority of the Court decided that the death penalty is not cruel and unusual punishment. The Court in *Cooper* asserted that all officials had a duty to follow the Constitution as interpreted by the Court. Brennan and Marshall, the critics argued, should have faithfully applied the Eighth Amendment doctrine that the Court developed, including its holding that the death penalty was not cruel and unusual punishment. To the critics, the Brennan-Marshall position resembled the position taken by then Attorney General Edwin Meese, that the Constitution, rather than what the Supreme Court says about it, is the law of the land to which officials must adhere.[42] Like Meese, Brennan and Marshall appeared to be asserting that they could act on their own constitutional views notwithstanding the Court's interpretation of the document.[43]

Jordan Steiker, law professor and Marshall's former law clerk, defended Marshall's practice. Pointing to the many cases in which Marshall wrote opinions dissenting from the denial of review, Steiker argued that Marshall regularly documented how the lower courts failed to avoid the arbitrary imposition of capital punishment. Those dissents, Steiker argued, operated within the Court's Eighth Amendment framework.[44]

Steiker's argument did not meet all of Marshall's critics, however, because it did not deal with the many cases in which Marshall and Brennan simply dissented without further elaboration. Indeed, the dissents that Steiker discussed may help Marshall's critics. If he so often found reasons within the Court's framework for criticizing the lower courts, perhaps the fact that he did not write a dissent in many cases shows that he could *not* criticize the courts on those terms. In one case, for example, Marshall initially "thought it was outrageous that . . . an inexperienced attorney would be handling a capital case." His law clerk's research into the record showed, however, that the lawyer was not as inexperienced as it seemed from the petition for review. Marshall told his law clerk to "let [the dissent] go," and Marshall simply noted his dissent without opinion. Here Marshall could not use the Court's Eighth Amendment jurisprudence to argue against a death sentence; he simply had to disagree with it.[45]

Was Marshall's position in death penalty cases consistent with *Cooper* and his dissent in *Payne*? The most obvious answer is that Marshall dissented in capital cases because he believed that the Court's decisions allowing capital punishment were egregiously wrong. That, however, is too simple: Orval Faubus undoubtedly believed that *Brown v. Board of Education* was egregiously wrong. If *Cooper* is to mean anything, something more than error, even gross error, must occur to justify a judge's refusal to follow the Supreme Court's declarations of constitutional law.

Often, of course, officials can act on their own constitutional interpretations even if those interpretations differ from the Court's. A legislator can refuse to vote for a statute that, as he or she sees it, would violate the Constitution even if the legislator is certain that the Court would uphold the statute. In 1832 President Andrew Jackson vetoed the rechartering of the Bank of the United States in part because he believed that the Constitution did not give Congress the power to create a national bank, even though the Supreme Court had held in 1819 that Congress did indeed have that power. President Thomas Jefferson pardoned people convicted of violating the Alien and Sedition Acts because he believed that the acts violated the First Amendment, even though the courts had rejected the defendants' constitutional claims.

If Jackson and Jefferson acted properly, what did Governor Faubus do wrong? Jackson and Jefferson acted when there was no possible lawsuit that could force them to sign the recharter or send the defendants to jail. In contrast, in *Cooper,* Governor Faubus could have been enjoined from interfering with desegregation in Little Rock. He would have defended his actions with legal arguments, but any qualified lawyer would have told Faubus that the courts would reject his defense.[46] So, in *Cooper,* Faubus was engaging in an essentially futile act of resistance, which itself interfered with the orderly administration of justice. The mere fact that he was willing to submit to an order directed at him should not outweigh the trouble he caused. In short, Faubus acted in a politically imprudent way, given the large social costs and small benefits of his conduct. Faubus's actions were improper, not because of some fundamental principle that officials must adhere to the Constitution as interpreted by the Court, but because in the circumstances his actions were unlikely to yield any social good and were highly likely to produce substantial social turmoil, as indeed they did.

Justices of the Supreme Court are in a different position from other officials. They, too, are limited by prudence, but the consequences of their actions differ from those of the actions of governors or legislators. For a justice to take a principled stand in dissenting from a denial of review in a death penalty case is, from that justice's point of view, to adhere to the Constitution as supreme law, with essentially no consequences that a prudent official ought to worry about.

Two facts about Marshall's actions in death penalty cases show that they rest on a judgment about prudence. As Steiker's argument suggests, Marshall never refused to address the merits of claims raised in death penalty cases after the Court granted review. Black's position in obscenity cases provides a useful contrast. The Court's majority believed that some but not all sexually explicit material could be suppressed, and the majority therefore had to examine the material to decide whether it was obscene. Black disagreed with that approach. He believed that the First Amendment barred government regulation entirely, and he reportedly took the position that he did not have to examine any obscene material to determine whether it could be suppressed. Marshall might have acted similarly in death penalty cases. He might have said that, because imposing the death penalty was always unconstitutional, he had no need to examine the procedures used in any particular case. Instead, taking the majority's position as providing the governing standards, Marshall addressed the merits. In cases decided on the merits, each justice was to apply the law, and Marshall did. The decision to grant review is a matter of discretion and prudence, not guided by strictly legal standards. Marshall's dissents without opinion in such cases, guided as they were by his discretionary judgments, were not inconsistent with any law—at least as long as Marshall remained willing to apply the law on the merits.

A second practice is more subtle but quite revealing. Although Brennan and Marshall routinely dissented from denials of review, they almost never noted their dissent from denials of rehearings sought by capital defendants.[47] When a defendant sought a rehearing, the relevant law was not the Constitution but the internal operating procedures of the Supreme Court, which stated that a rehearing could be granted only if a member of the prior majority voted for it. Marshall insisted on following those rules. As he told a law clerk, "If you read our rules you will discover that unless you vote *for* you can't vote to rehear!" A dissent from denying review was a statement that the majority misinterpreted the Constitution. A dissent from denying rehearing would imply that the majority was misinterpreting its own rules. Although there was some connection between the Court's internal rules and the constitutional principles Marshall honored in his death penalty dissents, the connection was weak. As he saw things, his dissents vindicated the rule of law. Dissenting from a denial of rehearing would not.[48]

Justice Sandra Day O'Connor's tribute to Marshall after he retired focused on how much she had been "personally affected by Justice Marshall as raconteur." Many of his stories involved capital punishment. He told Justice O'Connor that he had "mixed feelings" about the *Crawford* case, because he did not think Crawford "got a fair shake." He later came to believe that he had an innocent client, Marshall said, "when the jury returned a sentence of life imprisonment, rather than execution." He told of waiting for the verdict after a trial in the South: The jury retired to deliberate; the sheriff smoked a cigar and immediately told the lawyers to get back to the courtroom for the verdict. When Marshall asked how he knew the jury was ready, the sheriff pointed out that he had just finished his cigar, and the jury's members would just have finished theirs. He told of a judge instructing the jury that it could find a defendant not guilty, guilty, or guilty with mercy. Then the judge cautioned the spectators "not to move before the bailiff took the defendant away." The comment assumed the defendant would be convicted, and Marshall asked, "What happened to 'not guilty'?" The judge, Marshall said, just looked at him and said, "Are you kidding?"[49]

As O'Connor knew, Marshall's stories always had a point. He was the only person on the Supreme Court who ever represented defendants facing death sentences. He knew from the experiences he used for his stories that in the trenches the law was not administered with the antiseptic precision that the Supreme Court's decisions sometimes suggested. The messiness of the way the law operated in action, more than an abstract abhorrence at the state's taking a life, lay beneath Marshall's opposition to capital punishment. As Marshall stated, "If you put a man in jail wrongfully, you can let him out. But death is rather permanent. And what do you do if you convict a man illegally and unconstitutionally—and find it out later? What do you say? 'Oops'?" For him, "That's the trouble with death. Death is so lasting."[50]

9

"Some Clear Promise of a Better World"
The Jurisprudence of Thurgood Marshall

Responding in 1973 to columnist Dorothy Gilliam, who had written requesting permission to do an article on his "life style" as a Supreme Court justice, Thurgood Marshall wrote, "Believe it or not, there is nothing in my life that will be of interest to anyone. My life style consists of leaving home, coming to the Court, returning home and waiting to return to the Court the next day."[1] Marshall accurately described the life of a Supreme Court justice. His modest description of his daily life also suggests the kind of lawyer and family man he was. Although he had been involved in some of the nation's most important legal issues, Marshall was not an introspective person. After starting a diary of the events during a 1951 trip he took to investigate the treatment of African-American soldiers in Korea, Marshall quickly converted it into a shorthand summary of the day's visits and then stopped making entries, even though the trip became the source of several of Marshall's favorite stories.[2]

In many ways Marshall was firmly embedded in the middle-class culture common to many American lawyers. He bought a house in an expensive suburb of Washington and then faced some financial strain when residents had to pay to refill the neighborhood's lake after it had been drained in a storm. He took his sons to early-morning athletic practices and weathered a period of adolescent rebellion by one of them. He and Mrs. Marshall were proud parents who enjoyed their children's ultimate success: In 1996 Thurgood Jr. was director of legislative affairs for Vice President Al Gore, and John was the head United States marshal in northern Virginia, after spending more than a decade with the Virginia State Police. The boys' careers produced a permanent family joke after Goody spent some time as a criminal defense lawyer: "John locks them up," Mrs. Marshall said, "Goody defends them, and Thurgood lets them off."[3]

Marshall cut himself off from many of his former associates when he became a judge and felt the loss of a congenial circle of friends. He did continue two activities that were important to him. Indeed, one mattered so much that Marshall complained when his official portrait initially failed to reflect it. The portrait, he believed, failed to show him as the "curmudgeon" he was, and it did not show his ring. Simmie Knox, the African-American artist who painted the portrait, could not do anything to make Marshall into a curmudgeon, because, Knox said, Marshall had never acted curmudgeonly during his sittings. But Knox could add a ring to the portrait, and he painted in Marshall's wedding ring. Marshall, however, thought the portrait deficient because it did not show his Masons' ring as well. In 1965 Marshall held one of the main offices with the Prince Hall Masons, the "Grand Minister of State." He reveled in the Masonic rituals and the meetings he attended. His Masonic affiliation is another indication of Marshall's social location.[4]

Marshall was also active in the Episcopal Church. After his appointment to the Second Circuit, Marshall declined most speaking invitations, but he made the time to read the Second Lesson at a Tuesday afternoon church service and to give a talk at the Brooklyn Heights parish dinner.[5] Marshall's church work was of a piece with his legal work. His parish dinner talk offered "a no-holds-barred message based upon *Christian* responsibility" for civil rights. In 1964 Marshall was a lay delegate from the New York diocese to the Episcopal Church's triennial convention in St. Louis. Marshall walked out when the convention defeated a resolution recognizing the right to disobey segregation laws in "basic conflict with the concept of human dignity under God." Reportedly, he was disappointed not only with the resolution's defeat but also with the fact that the primary opponents were the lay delegates, not the clergy. Four delegates sent a telegram to Marshall urging him to return. They pointed out that the convention had condemned racial discrimination in other resolutions, including one that was understood to mean that "persons of different racial backgrounds may marry and receive the church's blessing." Marshall criticized the "reasonably small group of well-heeled lawyers and businessmen" who, he believed, controlled the convention. "This same group," he wrote a correspondent, "reject our women, reject anything pointing toward real desegregation and so far as I am concerned cannot wait for the return of the horse and buggy."[6]

Marshall's walkout was highly publicized. The *St. Louis Globe-Democrat* editorialized, "Here is a federal judge, the very embodiment of our law, acting as though he had turned in his judicial robes for a pair of sneakers and a CORE sweater. . . . The terrible danger of such an official endorsement of civil disobedience is that it leaves to the individual to judge what laws to violate." The bishop of Missouri apologized to Marshall for what he called "an unfair editorial attack" and noted that the convention had endorsed the "classical doctrine of obedience to God's law and its corollary, the right of conscience under extreme circumstances to reject unjust laws which deny human dignity," and he called Marshall's walkout "a judgment on us all."[7]

A lawyer and member of the solid middle class, active in the Masons and his church, but an African-American lawyer as well, insisting that his church take a stand on civil rights, Marshall saw his job as ensuring that society's commitment to social improvement through law would be honored.

Marshall's principal contribution to constitutional law may have been the substantive vision of justice his work embodied. Marshall was a New Deal liberal particularly devoted to advancing the interests of African-Americans. But Marshall's approach to law went deeper than the specific substantive values he sought to advance. His career, both with the NAACP Legal Defense Fund and as a judge, embodied the tradition of the lawyer-statesman, "devoted," in law school dean Anthony Kronman's words, "to the public good but keenly aware of the limitations of human beings and their political arrangements." For Kronman, the lawyer-statesman must simultaneously be sympathetic to all concerned and detached enough to avoid being "swept along by the tide of feeling [of] any sympathetic identification with a particular way of life," allowing the lawyer-statesman to "withdraw to the standpoint of decision." As his Supreme Court colleagues said, the stories Marshall told combined his understanding of how whites and African-Americans lived together with a passionate devotion to improving the nation.[8]

Marshall's experiences shaped his jurisprudence. Kronman believes that lawyer-statesmen are people of "practical wisdom." Marshall's mentor, Dean Charles Hamilton Houston of Howard Law School, taught Marshall that lawyers should be "social engineers." As engineers, they were engaged in an intensely practical activity. They had to use the legal materials available to them to shape a working solution to the pressing problems of social life that lawyers confronted. When Marshall was a law student, it was almost unimaginable that an African-American lawyer would become a federal judge, much less a Supreme Court justice. Houston's teachings were directed at students who would become practicing lawyers, but they were adaptable for judges as well.[9]

Marshall's vision of law as social engineering came out early in his Supreme Court work. In 1962 the Court held that California violated the Constitution's ban on cruel and unusual punishments in making it a crime for a person to be a drug addict.[10] The Court's theory was that a person who was a drug addict had no control over the addiction and that the nation's theory of criminal liability rested on the premise that people could be made criminals only for doing things over which they had some control. That analysis threatened to rework the country's system of criminal law: All aspects of criminal liability—the insanity defense, for example—would have to be examined to see if they comported with the theory of criminal responsibility the Court found in the Constitution. Drunkenness came closest to drug addiction, both in terms of the Court's theory and in terms of public importance. If alcoholism was a disease, as many doctors were coming to believe in the 1960s, it was just as unfair to punish someone for being an alcoholic as for being a drug addict: Neither addicts nor alcoholics could control the behavior that made them criminals.

In a case that the Supreme Court decided in 1968, during Marshall's first term, Leroy Powell was convicted of public drunkenness.[11] His attorney saw the case as an opportunity to extend the drug addiction case. He had a doctor testify as an expert that alcoholics like Powell could not control their dependency on alcohol and therefore could not refrain from being drunk in public. Powell was convicted and fined $50. His attorney brought the case directly to the Supreme Court. After the Court heard Powell's argument, it voted 5–4 to overturn his conviction. The dissenters were Chief Justice Warren and Justices Black, Harlan, and Marshall.

This unusual coalition of two Warren Court liberals, the conservative Harlan, and Black, who had come to apply his idiosyncratic combination of judicial activism and restraint in an increasingly conservative way in the 1960s, eventually took control of the case.

Justice Abe Fortas circulated a proposed majority opinion saying that being drunk in public was, according to the expert testimony at trial and other reputable medical sources, "a characteristic part of the pattern of [Powell's] disease." Given this medical evidence, Fortas argued, the drug addiction case required the Court to accept Powell's claim. That case stood "upon a principle which . . . is the foundation of individual liberty and the cornerstone of the relations between a civilized state and its citizens: Criminal penalties may not be inflicted upon a person for being in a condition he is powerless to change." Powell's condition fit that principle perfectly.

Warren and Black circulated proposed dissents, and it soon appeared that the majority in favor of Fortas's opinion was extremely shaky. Two weeks after Fortas's opinion went to his colleagues, Justice Byron White sent around a separate opinion, telling Fortas that White had gone "back and forth" on the question before arriving at the position he proposed. That position, as one of Warren's law clerks noted, was "puzzling." As White saw it, Powell was not being punished simply for being drunk; he was being punished for being drunk in public. And that, for White, was something Powell could control; he disagreed with the trial judge's finding that Powell was compelled to go out in public when drunk.[12]

With White's change in vote, Fortas lost his majority. It was not clear, however, that Warren had a new majority, for, according to a law clerk, Marshall appeared to be waffling. Warren talked with Marshall and reassigned the majority opinion to him, in an effort to solidify Marshall's vote against Powell. Marshall circulated an opinion adopting essentially all of Warren's earlier draft dissent. The Marshall-Warren opinion was highly critical of the "expert" testimony on which Fortas relied: "[I]t goes much too far on the basis of too little knowledge." The record, the opinion said, was "utterly inadequate to permit the sort of informed and responsible adjudication which alone can support the announcement of an important and wide-ranging new constitutional principle." The opinion emphasized divisions within the medical community over the status of alcoholism. It devoted substantial attention to the linked propositions that public drunkenness was a serious problem in the country and that as yet the nation had been unable to devise acceptable methods to handle the problem, other than the criminal process. "It would be tragic to return large numbers of helpless, sometimes dangerous and frequently unsanitary inebriates to the streets of our cities without even the opportunity to sober up adequately which a brief jail term provides." The picture of society's treatment of alcoholics was "not a pretty one," but, the opinion said, "[B]efore we condemn the present practice . . . perhaps we ought to be able to point to some clear promise of a better world for these unfortunate people." The opinion turned, finally, to the drug addiction case, which it said should be narrowly confined to avoid creating a comprehensive "constitutional doctrine of criminal responsibility."[13]

Powell shows Marshall as social engineer and demonstrates that social engineering did not necessarily lead to conventionally liberal positions. Perhaps Marshall was troubled by the fact that Powell's supporters had failed to make the sort of comprehensive presentation of sociological and psychological evidence that Marshall assembled in the segregation litigation. Marshall and Warren saw public drunkenness as a practical problem of government, and it certainly mattered that no one had any better ideas to deal with the problem. Similarly, in an early death penalty case, Marshall agreed with an opinion drafted by Fortas arguing that the Constitution did not require that judges instruct juries on the standards they should use to decide whether to impose a death sentence. "In this area," Marshall said, "we do not yet have the skills to produce words which would fit the punishment to the crime."[14]

Marshall's approach to law was often described as pragmatic, reflecting the understanding his wide experience gave him "of the way in which law worked in practice as well as on the books, of the way in which law acted on people's lives." A student of Marshall's antitrust decisions summarized them as having "a practical, commonsense approach, relatively uncomplicated by academic distinctions and elaborate doctrinal analysis." When the Court voted to uphold a procedure allowing someone storing a person's goods to sell them without notifying the owner, Marshall told his colleagues, "This result is the opposite of what common sense would dictate." The opinion he published criticized the majority for its "callous indifference to the realities of life for the poor" and said, "[W]e cannot close our eyes to the realities that led to this litigation." His law clerks reported the ease with which Marshall assimilated complex records in criminal cases. Having represented defendants in criminal cases, Marshall had a feel for the record: He understood what was going on in the courtroom even when it was not reflected in the cold words of a transcript.[15]

Marshall's feel for the courtroom made him less concerned than some of his Supreme Court colleagues with the precise way in which an opinion stated the law.* A fair amount of the justices' correspondence involves one justice's suggestion that another modify slightly some words or phrases in a draft opinion. In one case, for example, Rehnquist asked Marshall to change the word *duty* in a footnote because Rehnquist believed it to be a term of art from tort law with more expansive implications than Rehnquist was comfortable with; Marshall changed the word to *responsibility*.[16]

Those who make such suggestions, and those who take them seriously, have a jurisprudence in which the precise formulations in Supreme Court opinions have

---

* Marshall did pay attention, though. Marshall's former law clerk Stephen Carter reviewed a draft opinion in a death penalty case by Justice Harry Blackmun, who was less adamant than Marshall in his opposition to capital punishment. Carter informed Marshall that "[i]t does not expressly approve any of this Court's precedents holding that the death penalty may constitutionally be imposed." Marshall read the opinion and noticed a footnote that seemed to accept the death penalty's constitutionality and joined Blackmun's opinion only after Blackmun eliminated the footnote. SLC [Stephen Carter] to TM, March 24, 1981, Marshall Papers, box 280, file 2 (Bullington v. Missouri); TM to Blackmun, April 1, 1981, Marshall Papers. Marshall's copy of Carter's memo has "See fn 17 of HAB's opinion" in Marshall's hand on it.

significant effect on the arguments lawyers can make and the ones lower court judges can accept. As Powell stated in making some suggestions that he called "flyspecks," "[W]e know that lawyers, as well as the courts below, scrutinize every word we write." Justices with this philosophy were concerned about sentences that, as Rehnquist put it, "seem[] fine at the time, but could come back to haunt us" or, in Brennan's terms, "might lay a hidden trap for later cases."[17]

Marshall was almost completely indifferent to these suggestions, because he thought they overestimated the effect of precise wording on lawyers and lower courts. In one opinion, Marshall's draft referred to the "reliability" of certain procedures. Scalia "worr[ied] about somebody taking literally (and therefore litigating)" the question of reliability. Marshall responded that Scalia's concern was misplaced, because neither "future litigants [n]or the lower courts will read our decision to require perfection."[18]

Marshall's approach to drafting opinions reflects his pragmatic jurisprudence. As Stevens put it to Marshall in another case, "[T]he logic of [an] opinion will carry the day in all events." Only in exceptional circumstances would particular language constrain courts from developing what they believed to be sensible solutions to practical problems. For example, White once asked Marshall to change a reference from the "right to travel" to the "right to interstate travel." The former reference might imply something about international travel, while the latter would not. Yet, lawyers and judges in later cases could easily take the right to interstate travel as an example of a broader right reaching international travel as well. Had Marshall's original words prevailed, lawyers and judges could limit the case to the interstate context in which it arose. Marshall could go along with the suggested changes because saying things either way would have much the same effect in the real world of litigation and adjudication.[19]

Sometimes Marshall got his back up. Brennan asked Marshall to tone down a separate opinion in *Batson v. Kentucky,* in which the majority held unconstitutional prosecutors' decisions to eliminate jurors because of their race. Marshall's opinion, Brennan said, "might inadvertently help an unscrupulous prosecutor . . . to convince [lower courts] to read this Court's opinion as embracing [a] narrow standard." Marshall responded, "I see no reason to be gentle in pointing out" that the majority's approach was bound to be ineffective, and "I doubt that pulling my punches would make the situation any better." An experienced trial lawyer and appellate advocate, Marshall understood that the Supreme Court could define in broad terms what the Constitution required but that the precise meaning of the Court's decisions would be worked out, not among the justices, but in the lower courts by litigants and judges not always sympathetic to the Court's broad conclusions. Unlike Scalia, Marshall thought it unproductive to worry about what a sentence "might be read to suggest." How the sentence would be read depended far more on the circumstances of the cases the lower courts would face than it did on the linguistic meaning of the words the Supreme Court wrote.[20]

If Marshall's social engineering made him a liberal, he nonetheless had a conservative streak. Sometimes he would take positions in discussions with his law clerks that they regarded as inconsistent with Marshall's liberal views. Regularly, a law clerk would say, "Judge, you can't do that." And regularly, Marshall would reply, "There are only two things I *have to* do—stay black and die." Marshall took these positions in part because he knew they elicited outrage from his law clerks, and he delighted in tweaking them. He knew, as well, that he could prod them to develop the strongest arguments for the liberal position by pretending to be on the other side. That was one of the ways in which he demonstrated the detachment and sympathy characteristic of the lawyer-statesman.[21]

This side of Marshall was not entirely feigned, however, because it sometimes shaped his votes at conference and even his ultimate position. His conservative streak came out in one of only two Marshall opinions Chief Justice Rehnquist referred to in his eulogy for Marshall. In *Loretto v. Teleprompter Manhattan CATV Corp.*, New York required apartment-building owners to allow operators of cable television systems to install receivers on their buildings, so that tenants could get cable service.[22] Blackmun's dissent called Marshall's majority opinion "curiously anachronistic" and "formalistic." Marshall had reacted to the initial civil rights sit-ins by "storm[ing] around the room proclaiming . . . [that] he was not going to represent a bunch of crazy colored students who violated the sacred property rights of white folks."[23] For Marshall, "sacred property rights" were involved here too. The New York statute authorized "a permanent physical occupation of an owner's property," for which the government had to pay. The physical occupation of property was "perhaps the most serious form of invasion of an owner's property interests"; the owner could not use the occupied space, nor could it exclude the cable operator from it. As Marshall saw it, the statute said that someone else could put something on the apartment owners' property, which was incompatible with the idea that it was *their* property in the first place.

Marshall was not a strong traditionalist, though he felt traditionalism's pull. In *Loretto* a New York agency had already found that a one-time fee of $1 per receiver was reasonable, and Marshall may have thought that such a small fee would indeed be sufficient compensation. Marshall's traditionalism might be understood, then, as the result of a judgment that, in the circumstances, the traditionalist approach offered a sensible solution to the problem at hand.

Another dimension of Marshall's traditionalism was his respect for legal rules. Marshall's law clerks were familiar with what they called his "'rules is rules' theory": Lawyers were supposed to follow the rules. *Torres v. Oakland Scavenger Co.* invoked those rules in an extremely rigid way.[24] A litigant must file a notice of appeal after losing in the trial court. The rules of appellate procedure state that the notice "shall specify the party or parties taking the appeal." Jose Torres was one of a group of sixteen plaintiffs who claimed that Oakland Scavenger had discriminated against them. The trial court dismissed their complaint. The plaintiffs filed a notice of appeal in the name of the fifteen other plaintiffs *"et al."* Torres's name did not appear on the notice of appeal because of a clerical error by his lawyer's secretary. Marshall's law clerks "pleaded with [him] to vote" with Brennan to allow the appeal. Marshall refused: As he told his colleagues in another procedural case, "Rules mean what they say."[25]

Marshall was unwilling to allow attorneys to get away with sloppy practices. At one conference, he grumbled, "Don't bail this stupid guy out." Marshall's background as a litigator for African Americans was part of the reason for his insistence on procedures. When his law clerks argued for "liberal" interpretations of procedural rules, Marshall replied that as a litigator, he had to follow the rules carefully and was never allowed to get away with sloppiness simply because he was on the right side of the case, as he saw it. "All you could hope for," he said, "was that a court didn't rule against you for illegitimate reasons; you couldn't hope, and you had no right to expect, that a court would bend the rules in your favor." He told an audience of African-American law students and lawyers that Dean Houston "taught us that you will get no favors, and I emphasize that." Today's litigants, in his view, should be held to the same standards of meticulous preparation that he imposed on himself and his staff.[26]

This interpretation is not entirely satisfactory, however, because it overlooks the difference between a litigator and a judge. As a litigator, Marshall had to accept the rules as they were interpreted and applied by judges often hostile to his substantive views; as a judge, he was in a position to interpret the rules and thereby make the life of litigators easier than it had been for him.

His former law clerks Martha Minow and Randall Kennedy suggested a deeper explanation for Marshall's proceduralism. They argued that "respect for procedural rules . . . can guard against abuses committed by officials in the name of the law" by allowing advocates to invoke basic norms of fair play. Procedural rules can also promote substantive goals when the advocate is better at maneuvering within the rules than his or her opponent. Here procedural rigor is a positive virtue, for the looser the interpretation of the rules, the more difficult it is for an advocate to trap an opponent in a procedural error. Finally, they said, "[R]espect for procedural rules is perhaps the purest form of respect for the Rule of Law."[27]

There is undoubtedly something to this explanation of Marshall's views. In particular, Marshall's basic position throughout his career with the NAACP was that once the same rules were applied to African-Americans and whites, African-Americans would show they could accomplish anything whites could. In that sense, his advocacy was procedural, too: Make sure the rules were followed and fairly applied, and African-Americans would achieve all they sought.

This explanation, too, misses the difference between a litigator's position and a judge's. The litigator attempts to invoke existing procedural rules against his or her opponents and can properly say, "Here are the rules; just apply them fairly—that is, as I suggest they should be interpreted." The judge, however, actually must choose which of competing interpretations of the rules is the one that is then to be applied evenhandedly. Minow and Kennedy invoked an image of the procedural rules as already in place and ready to be applied for their arguments to be persuasive; yet, for Marshall as a judge, the point of the enterprise was to determine what the procedural rules were.

In the end, therefore, Marshall's proceduralism can be understood only by referring to his traditionalist streak: Lawyers, he thought, should continue to do things as he learned to do them. Here, too, he was the lawyer-statesman, insisting that lawyers always behave as true professionals.

Marshall's concern for professionalism pervaded his thinking about capital punishment. In speeches to the judges of the Second Circuit, Marshall said that "capital defendants do not have a fair opportunity to defend their lives in the courtroom." Their lawyers were "ill-equipped to handle capital cases," because "death penalty litigation has become a specialized field of practice" in which even well-trained lawyers unfamiliar with the field "inevitably make very serious mistakes." As a result, Marshall argued, the federal courts should be more receptive to claims that capital defendants had not received *effective* assistance from their lawyers:

> I can remember way back in the good old days when people used to say that every man is entitled to his day in court, and they left off the rest of that sentence—if he had the money. We have come a long way from that. But I still don't feel we have come far enough.

Not just counsel, but effective counsel, was needed, he argued, particularly in capital cases:

> Many of these lawyers—and bless them for taking the cases for nothing—but many of them just do not know their way around the courtroom. And it seems to me that before we take a man's life, we should be sure that he has a lawyer who is at least as capable as the prosecution—and this just is not true.

When the Court allowed a defendant to represent himself without a lawyer, Marshall wanted to "make sure he understands [the] consequences of not having a lawyer" and would have required "a lawyer there to be consulted." For Marshall, the documents that lawyers produced were "sacrosanct."[28]

Marshall's impatience with sloppy lawyering led him to develop a careful theory of ineffective assistance of counsel. He articulated that theory in *Strickland v. Washington,* the only death penalty case after 1972 in which he and Brennan disagreed. Brennan wanted an opinion that "set the right tone—one that will sensitize the lower courts to the question of fairness to the defendant but not one that will allow defendants to retry every aspect of their cases." Marshall was less compromising.[29]

The Sixth Amendment requires that defendants have the assistance of counsel, and the Court has held that this means that they must have "effective assistance." Determining what constitutes effective assistance has been difficult, however. Lawyers have to make many decisions in the heat of a trial, some of which will in hindsight appear to have been quite bad. A defendant is entitled to a lawyer with some grasp of the law applicable to the case and some insight into possible defense strategies. The Supreme Court did not want to develop a doctrine of ineffective assistance of counsel that routinely allowed courts to second-guess the strategic decisions defense lawyers made, but it could not develop a doctrine leaving defendants with no more than a warm body next to them—no more than a "potted plant," as Oliver North's lawyer put it.

The facts of *Strickland* suggest some of the difficulties faced by defendants and their attorneys in capital cases. David LeRoy Washington committed an extended series of crimes in September 1976, including three murders, kidnapping, attempted murder, and assaults. He eventually surrendered and gave the police a lengthy confession. An experienced criminal lawyer was appointed to defend him. The lawyer was active in the early stages of the defense but lost hope when he discovered that Washington had confessed to all three murders. Against the lawyer's advice, Washington pleaded guilty and waived his right to a jury determination of sentence. To prepare for the sentencing hearing, the lawyer spoke with Washington and telephoned his wife and mother but did not meet them or seek any other character witnesses. At the hearing, the lawyer urged that Washington did not deserve a death sentence, because the very fact that he confessed showed his remorse. After being sentenced to death, Washington argued that his lawyer had not given him effective assistance of counsel: The lawyer, Washington said, did not try to get a psychiatric evaluation or to present character witnesses and did not offer the judge a meaningful argument against a death sentence.

The Supreme Court rejected Washington's claim, in the Court's first extended consideration of the requirement of effective assistance. The Court adopted a general standard instead of providing detailed guidelines for acceptable behavior of an attorney. The Constitution was violated, according to the Court, when defense attorneys "made errors so serious that counsel was not functioning as the 'counsel'" required by the Constitution, if those errors deprived the defendant of "a fair trial, a trial whose result is reliable." The Court said that "the proper measure of attorney performance remains simply reasonableness under prevailing professional norms." It emphasized that courts should be "highly deferential" to the attorneys themselves and "must indulge a strong presumption that counsel's conduct falls within the wide range of reasonable professional assistance."

Only Marshall dissented from this approach. His copy of the draft of the majority opinion is covered with his underlinings indicating the places he disagreed. His opinion opened by pointing to the "unfortunate but undeniable fact that a person of means . . . usually can obtain better representation" than poor people, who have to rely on appointed counsel with "limited time and resources to devote to a given case." Then it asked, "Is a 'reasonably competent attorney' a reasonably competent adequately paid retained lawyer or a reasonably competent appointed attorney?" Marshall found the Court's approach "unhelpful" because it rested on numerous "unacceptable" generalizations about what defense attorneys could reasonably be expected to do. For Marshall, some aspects of criminal defense were clear enough that the courts could develop appropriate guidelines: At least the lawyer should confer with the client and object to "significant, arguably erroneous rulings."

Marshall also objected to the Court's requirement that a defendant, even one whose attorney acted unreasonably and incompetently, show "prejudice." Commenting on this in a speech later, Marshall asked, "Well, how under the sun can a deficient performance not register in the defense?"[30] He knew that "it is often very difficult to tell whether a defendant convicted after a trial in which he was ineffectively represented would have fared better if his lawyer had been competent"; enough of his NAACP cases ended with retrials in which defendants had both better lawyers and better results. A "cold record" could not show, for example, how "a shrewd, well-prepared lawyer" might have devastated a "seemingly impregnable case." He also thought that the Court's focus on the "reliability" of the outcome treated results as the only concern in a criminal proceeding, whereas, for Marshall, under the Constitution "every defendant is entitled to a trial in which his interests are vigorously and conscientiously advocated by an able lawyer," even if the defendant is "manifestly guilty." Washington's lawyer had been deficient, in Marshall's eyes, because, immobilized by his reaction to Washington's behavior, he failed to locate character witnesses who, by testifying that Washington was "a responsible, nonviolent man, devoted to his family, and active in the affairs of his church," would have "humanized" Washington "to counter the impression conveyed by the trial that he was little more than a cold-blooded killer."

In another case, *Alvord v. Florida,* the defense attorney completely failed to investigate the "only plausible line of defense" that Alvord, who had been found insane at an earlier criminal trial, was still insane.[31] The lower courts accepted the argument that the attorney acted reasonably because Alvord himself did not want to rely on an insanity defense. Marshall thought that "this result renders meaningless defense counsel's vital functions as an adviser." Perhaps, Marshall said, Alvord could forgo the insanity defense, but he could do so only after his lawyer advised him fully about its prospects and possible consequences. Yet, having done no investigation whatever of the insanity issue, the attorney was in no position to provide such advice. Marshall's opinion offered a dramatic summary of the facts: The lawyer met with Alvord for only fifteen minutes, when Alvord was

> in jail, under suicide watch, with no lights in his cell, no furniture except a mattress, no blanket, and no clothing. . . . Alvord refused to talk with psychiatrists unless his lawyer was present, yet his lawyer never visited him in jail, nor attended the interview sessions. It is difficult to imagine how the trial would have differed had Alvord had no counsel at all.

Lawyers can be ineffective, too, when they fail to make valid objections. In *Jacobs v. Wainwright,* the trial judge refused to allow the defendant to testify about mitigating factors that, the judge erroneously believed, the jury should not consider.[32] His counsel did not object to the ruling, nor did he raise the issue on appeal. Eventually, a new lawyer for Jacobs argued that the failure to object amounted to ineffective assistance of counsel. The state courts held that the first lawyer's failure to tell the trial judge what the defendant would have said barred a later challenge to the erroneous exclusion. Marshall thought the Constitution could not "countenance . . . [the] inhumane result" that "the shortcomings of an attorney . . . will be permitted to take their toll on the life of a defendant."

Lankford v. Idaho, decided during Marshall's last term on the Court, was probably the most dramatic example of Marshall's impatience with sloppy lawyering.[33] Bryan Lankford distracted two campers, allowing his older brother, Mark, to beat them to death. Both brothers were sentenced to death. Bryan Lankford's case came to the Supreme Court twice. In the first appeal, one justice of the Idaho Supreme Court voted to overturn Bryan's death sentence because he had not been deeply enough involved in the murders. The justices were troubled by the case and sent it back to the Idaho Supreme Court to consider whether the trial judge had improperly considered testimony that Bryan had given against Mark. One additional justice of the Idaho court was persuaded, but Bryan's death sentence was again affirmed by a vote of 3–2.

Justice Stevens was determined to overturn Bryan's death sentence. Under the Court's rules, it takes six justices to decide a case without hearing oral argument. Stevens got four other justices to join a draft opinion reversing the sentence, and Sandra Day O'Connor orally agreed as well. When Scalia circulated a dissent, however, O'Connor changed her mind and voted to hear the case.[34] The Court limited its review to a question about the process by which the death sentence was imposed. After the jury found Bryan guilty, the judge asked the prosecutor whether he would seek a death sentence. The prosecutor said no, believing that Mark was responsible for the murders and that Bryan was under Mark's influence. The prosecution and defense at the sentencing hearing concentrated on whether Bryan should receive consecutive sentences and what term of years he should serve. The judge then sentenced Bryan to death despite the prosecutor's position.

As Stevens posed the question, the issue for the Court was whether it was fair to impose a death sentence when the prosecutor had not sought it and no one had specifically alerted the defense that the judge might sentence Bryan to death. He thought the judge's behavior outrageous; as Stevens saw it, the defense had been lured into thinking there was no risk of a death sentence and then had been blindsided with one. There was, he said, "a grossly deficient lack of fair notice." The trial judge's behavior, the Court held, "had the practical effect of concealing from the parties the principal issue." White and Scalia responded that the defense lawyer should have known better: The case was a capital one from the outset; under Idaho law, judges impose sentences and can ignore a prosecutor's recommendation. Indeed, early in the proceedings the trial judge expressly refused to rule out a death sentence.[35]

When the justices discussed the case, Marshall voted to affirm the Idaho Supreme Court. He did not want to bail the defense lawyer out of a bad situation. As he initially saw it, the legal issue was whether the defense had enough notice that a death sentence was possible. The question of notice arose from the Sixth Amendment's requirement that defendants have lawyers and the Fourteenth Amendment's requirement of fair notice. The Idaho statutes should have alerted any decent lawyer that a death sentence was possible. If Lankford's lawyer was worried about avoiding a death sentence for Bryan, Marshall thought, she should have tried to pin the trial judge down. Neither the Sixth nor the Fourteenth Amendment was violated.

Marshall's vote placed Rehnquist in an awkward position. With Marshall's vote, there were five to affirm the Idaho court. But the case involved a death sentence, and Marshall never voted to uphold death sentences. Who could Rehnquist ask to write the majority opinion? If he asked White or Scalia, Marshall might well change his position, converting the majority into a minority and wasting the work the drafter would have done. Rehnquist did the best he could by assigning the opinion to Marshall.* Marshall did indeed change his vote. His law clerks

---

* Jeffrey Rosen, "Court Marshall," *The New Republic*, June 21, 1993, p. 14, provides a more critical assessment, describing Rehnquist as "delighted" and saying that Marshall "does not appear to have grappled with the constitutional issues the case present[ed]."

persuaded him that the case also involved the Eighth Amendment's ban on cruel and unusual punishments, and Marshall said to Rehnquist, "I cannot bring myself to endorse the death penalty under the Eighth Amendment."[36] The inexcusably unprofessional sloppiness of Bryan Lankford's lawyer did not mean that Bryan should die.

Marshall's concern for professionalism connects his view of lawyers as social engineers—technicians with professional skills—to his role as lawyer-statesman. Marshall's jurisprudence was problematic for a judge making constitutional law. How could he deal with disagreement about what was a sensible solution to the practical problems of social life that law addressed?

As long as his colleagues were acting as lawyer-statesmen, Marshall could fit disagreement within his approach to law. When a law clerk produced a draft that Marshall disagreed with, Marshall would most frequently sit on it until the law clerk realized it was not going anywhere. If the law clerk pressed for an explanation, Marshall would say, "This is pretty good, but it's missing two things." The puzzled law clerk would wonder what legal arguments had been omitted, what cases overlooked. After a pause, Marshall would point to his commission on the wall: "Nomination by the president and confirmation by the Senate."[37]

Although other judges often point out to their law clerks that the judges have commissions and the law clerks do not, Marshall used his commission to show not simply that he had the final authority to make a decision but that his authority was justified. For Marshall, nomination and confirmation expressed public confidence in the quality of his judgment and embodied the hope that he would continue to exercise that judgment as a justice. His experience, in short, justified the exercise of his judgment.

Marshall's comment when President George Bush nominated David Souter to the Supreme Court echoed, albeit in reverse, Marshall's distaste for the Senate's treatment of Robert Bork. As Marshall saw it, Bork had not been treated with the seriousness that a person who had served the nation in high positions deserved. When asked about Souter's nomination, Marshall replied, "Never heard of him. And when his name came down, I was listening to the television. . . . I called my wife and said, 'Have I ever heard of this man?'"[38] Marshall believed that he should have heard of anyone nominated to the Supreme Court, because the very fact that Marshall had heard of a nominee demonstrated that the nominee had shown the public the character necessary in a lawyer-statesman.

Marshall was troubled as well when judges were captured by some theory that diverted them from exercising judgment. He was particularly critical of approaches that focused exclusively on original intent. Concern for original intent was a major stumbling block in writing the NAACP's briefs in *Brown v. Board of Education,* and Marshall ended up hoping that he and his colleagues could persuade the justices that the evidence about original intent was evenly balanced. "Both as a lawyer and as a judge," he later wrote, "I have constantly had to dig into these matters and I am constantly left, on balance, unable to determine exactly what was intended."[39]

During the bicentennial celebrations of the Constitution's adoption, Marshall made a widely publicized speech criticizing original intent approaches to constitutional interpretation. He did not believe, he said, "that the meaning of the Constitution was forever 'fixed'" in 1787. By describing the original Constitution's treatment of slavery and the corrections made as a result of "amendments, a civil war, and momentous social transformation," Marshall criticized the conservative purposes to which the jurisprudence of original intent was being put. Perhaps as important, however, was that the jurisprudence of original intent had a "tendency . . . to oversimplify." Marshall's treatment of constitutional development echoed a famous opinion of Justice Oliver Wendell Holmes, which also mentioned the Civil War, that the Constitution's words "have called into life a being the development of which could not have been foreseen completely by the most gifted of its begetters." The "true miracle," Marshall said, "was not the birth of the Constitution, but its life, a life nurtured through two turbulent centuries of our own making." Precisely because the Constitution was "of our own making," judges went wrong if they refused to exercise their judgment and passed responsibility off onto the framers.[40]

Disagreements between judges and legislators were, of course, the heart of constitutional law. Calling Marshall a pragmatic judge obscures the difficulties with pragmatism in constitutional law. A judge who finds a statute unconstitutional is disagreeing with the judgment of legislators. Some constitutional theorists regard legislators as too implicated in the day-to-day grind of governing to be statesmen. From a pragmatic point of view, however, that immersion might make legislators more sensitive to how their solutions to practical problems would work.

The metaphor of social engineering is illuminating again. Legislators, it might be thought, have designed and built a bridge. The pragmatic judge could ask, "Does this bridge work well enough? Can I design a better one?" Such a judge might also be cautious about attempting to replace the legislators' design with an untested one. Yet Marshall regularly adopted constitutional positions that might lead to large-scale social transformations. *Powell v. Texas* shows that Marshall's jurisprudence did not always lead him to overturn existing arrangements; there his reluctance was based precisely on his concern about what alternatives were available to deal with alcoholism as a social problem. Marshall's positions on the death penalty and on racial equality, however, were hardly those of a cautious reformer.

Marshall had a lot of experience with constitutional reform. *Brown v. Board of Education* appeared to promise a major transformation in Southern education. But, Marshall knew, the words the justices wrote had to be implemented by school boards, legislatures, and lower courts. His experience after *Brown* showed him that a Supreme Court opinion apparently requiring large-scale social change could end up meaning something rather different, and more limited, when it was inserted into the overall political and social system. As a judge, then, Marshall could be bold without betraying his pragmatism, because the ultimate outcome would be unlikely to track precisely what Marshall as a judge dictated. Because Marshall was a pragmatic judge, disdainful of grand theories that obscured the question of judgment, the test of his jurisprudence was how his opinions were assimilated in the nation's political and legal culture.

The Supreme Court's course over the decades of Marshall's service suggests some difficulties with Marshall's jurisprudence of social engineering. The substantive values he articulated were widely admired. But the nation appeared to repudiate his views on the issues he cared most about. If Marshall's pragmatism could be validated only by public acceptance of the outcomes he urged, at the time he retired in 1991, it would be difficult to conclude that he had been successful. From the perspective of this form of pragmatism, Marshall might be seen as a social engineer who built an elegant bridge that seemed to lead nowhere.

Marshall was more than a pragmatist, however. He played a role well established in the tradition of lawyer-statesmen. He was one of the Supreme Court's great dissenters. Even in 1991, when Marshall's seat was taken over by Clarence Thomas, Marshall's admirers continued to hope that his judgments, however out of tune with what much of the nation desired then, would be vindicated in the larger forum of history.

Epilogue
"He Did What He Could with What He Had"

Asked at the press conference held on his retirement in June 1991 how he wanted to be remembered, Marshall replied, "That he did what he could with what he had." Although many comments at Marshall's retirement and on his death in January 1993 suggested that Marshall's work at the NAACP made a greater contribution to constitutional law than his work at the Supreme Court, Marshall himself referred to his career as a whole, not to any one part.[1]

Marshall's modest statement, which did not mention his role in *Brown v. Board of Education* or the fact that he was the first African-American Supreme Court justice, was his effort to spell out for himself and for history what he had done. The division in his career posed a problem. His work at the NAACP helped define an era of Supreme Court jurisprudence, but that era effectively ended a few years after he arrived at the Court. As a justice, Marshall was generally in dissent in the cases he cared most about. At the end of his career, then, Marshall had to make sense of its entire course, the victories as well as the defeats.

Marshall's colleague William Brennan had been on the Court during good times and bad. Brennan could say that he managed to pull out whatever liberal victories there were during the last years of his tenure. To many, the Supreme Court during Marshall's tenure was the Brennan Court. In contrast, Marshall had so rarely experienced victory as a justice that he had to devise some other course. Relatively early in his tenure, and after his retirement, some observers described him as a "Great Dissenter," speaking out for "people neglected, the misunderstood, and the politically underrepresented." Accurate as far as it goes, this characterization understates the significance of Marshall's constitutional vision.[2]

In saying, "He did what he could with what he had," Marshall simultaneously deprecated and praised his talents. He did not expressly claim that what he had was a brilliant legal mind, a sharp tactical sense, or sound legal judgment. But, read against the evident accomplishments of his career, the statement demands that one determine "what he had" with reference to what Marshall did.

A proud man, Marshall was particularly sensitive to what he saw as slights to his reputation. He stalked out of a dinner honoring members of the solicitor general's office who had become judges because he mistakenly believed that he had been overlooked. Marshall's pride was only one dimension of his concern for his reputation. For him, the verdict of history was central to coming to terms with his life, and he would not do anything that might make that verdict a qualified one. For nearly twenty years he refused to sit in any cases in which the NAACP was a party, believing that observers might think him biased. He broke off an arrangement with Carl Rowan for an "as told to" autobiography, returning a $250,000 publisher's advance, when Rowan pressed Marshall to tell inside stories about the Supreme Court. As he told a former law clerk, "I can just see the headlines in the *Washington Post*. The first Negro on the Supreme Court opens up the Conference Room and discloses the confidences of the justices."*[3]

Three days after Marshall's death on January 24, 1993, an extraordinary procession of ordinary citizens circled the Supreme Court Building, waiting hours on a cold and windy day to pass by his coffin. Nearly twenty thousand people went through the building during the twelve hours it was open with Marshall's coffin. Some paid their respects by leaving copies of the Supreme Court's opinion in *Brown* next to the coffin. A retired government clerk recalled living in segregated Washington, D.C., and said that her children and grandchildren "won't see colored fountains, colored restaurants. No, sir. Justice Marshall saw to that." Marshall "stood for justice and equality for all people and especially for African Americans," another said. Yet another echoed Marshall himself: "He stood for so many things he helped me learn to stand for, to do what you can, and that color of skin really should not make any difference, and that you have to fight for what you believe in."[4]

These comments, and the simple fact that so many people felt compelled to pay their respects to Marshall, show that Marshall transcended the category of Supreme Court justice. He was honored because what he had done demonstrated that the Constitution, however imperfectly it was enforced and interpreted, embodied values fundamental to the nation's identity. Marshall symbolized the possibilities of the United States. But, in repeating a Pullman porter's observation that he never "had to put his hand up in front of his face to find out he was a Negro," Marshall also reminded the nation of the ways in which those possibilities had not been realized.[5]

Although he "had a firm rule against speaking extrajudicially on public issues,"

---

* Marshall gave his Supreme Court papers to the Library of Congress, authorizing them to be made available "at the discretion of the Library" to "researchers or scholars engaged in serious research." The library opened the papers to the public, including journalists, on Marshall's death. Marshall's family and many family friends protested the release, reflecting Marshall's concerns and sometimes explicitly referring to the Rowan episode. My personal view is that the library would not have acted responsibly had it interpreted the deed, which was in a rather standard form, to authorize it to limit access to Marshall's papers in any manner different from the way it allows access to other papers. (Marshall's representatives argued that the library abused its discretion in allowing journalists to use the papers.) Whether the library should have accepted the deed in those terms or whether it should have insisted that Marshall have another lawyer look the deed over are, yet again, separate questions. Here my view is that the library probably should have asked Marshall to consult another lawyer but that the failure of the library's employees to do so when they were dealing with a Supreme Court justice is entirely understandable.

Marshall labored hard on the speech he gave during the nation's celebration of the Constitution's bicentennial. For him, celebration of the events of 1787 was "unfortunate," because it "invite[d] a complacent belief that the vision of those who debated and compromised in Philadelphia yielded the 'more perfect Union' it is said we now enjoy." Citing the constitutional compromise counting slaves as three-fifths of a person for purposes of determining representation, Marshall did not "find the vision, foresight, and sense of justice exhibited by the framers particularly profound." The Constitution's treatment of slavery made the national government "defective from the start, requiring several amendments, a civil war, and momentous social transformation to attain the system of constitutional government, and its respect for individual freedoms and human rights, that we hold as fundamental today." The Civil War, Marshall said, destroyed the original Constitution. "In its place arose a new, more promising basis for justice and equality." But, he continued, "almost another century would pass before any significant recognition was obtained of the rights of black Americans to share equally" in education, housing, and voting.[6]

Marshall's speech emphasized that African-Americans "were enslaved by law" and "segregated by law," but, "finally, they have begun to win equality by law." Indeed, it was not the framers but "those who refused to acquiesce in outdated notions of 'liberty,' 'justice,' and 'equality,' and who strived to better them" who most deserved credit. Concluding his speech by referring to "hopes not realized and promises not fulfilled," Marshall expressed his enduring skepticism about the possibility that the nation would live up to its constitutional principles.[7] And yet his references to the struggles to improve the Constitution expressed his equally enduring commitment to those principles.

Marshall had a set of experiences unique on the Supreme Court: The product of segregation, he deployed his legal training, energy, and judgment to seek the fulfillment of the nation's promises, both as a lawyer and a Supreme Court justice.* Ironically, Marshall died when his own constitutional vision had been displaced by another, more skeptical about the power of government to advance the common good. His opinions on equality and fair procedures stand as exemplars of Great Society jurisprudence. In celebrating Marshall, and through him the Constitution, his mourners simultaneously expressed their regretful understanding that the vision Marshall worked to make real no longer animated the Supreme Court.

Visitors at Marshall's gravesite at Arlington National Cemetery who arrive at the right time may be struck by what they find there. Occasionally, scattered on the marker with its simple description "Civil Rights Advocate" may be a few pennies. Evoking the African-American tradition of grave decoration, the pennies have a deeper meaning as well. William T. Coleman's eulogy for Marshall said, "History will ultimately record that Mr. Justice Marshall gave the cloth and linen to the work that Lincoln's untimely death left undone."[8] The pennies reflect the judgment of visitors on what Marshall had done with what he had: For them, Abraham Lincoln, depicted on the pennies, was the first "Great Emancipator"; Thurgood Marshall was the second.

---

* All of Marshall's colleagues, of course, were also products of segregation.

Notes

Prologue

1. William H. Rehnquist, "Tribute to Justice Thurgood Marshall," *Stanford Law Review* 44 (Summer 1992): 1213, 1213; Rehnquist, Eulogy, Jan. 28, 1993, quoted in transcript, *McNeil/Lehrer NewsHour*, Jan. 28, 1993; "Fighter for His People: Thurgood Marshall," *New York Times*, Sept. 8, 1962, p. 11 (describing Marshall's treatment in "Negro press"). For my treatment of Marshall's career as a lawyer, see *Making Civil Rights Law: Thurgood Marshall and the Supreme Court, 1936–1961* (New York: Oxford University Press, 1994).

2. Quoted in Tushnet, *Making Civil Rights Law,* 301.

3. Neil McFeeley, *Appointment of Judges: The Johnson Presidency* (Austin: University of Texas Press, 1987), 112.

4. 502 U.S. vi (1991).

5. Personal recollection (from 1972 to 1973); Mark Stern, *Calculating Visions: Kennedy, Johnson, and Civil Rights* (New Brunswick, N.J.: Rutgers University Press, 1992).

6. Robert Gordon, "The Independence of Lawyers," *Boston University Law Review* 68 (Jan. 1988): 1, 15; Anthony Kronman, *The Lost Lawyer* (Cambridge: Harvard University Press, 1993), 12.

7. Transcript, TM press conference, June 28, 1991, p. 4; Beal v. Doe, 432 U.S. 438, 463 (1977) (Blackmun, J., dissenting); Blackmun to TM, Nov. 12, 1980, Thurgood Marshall Papers, Manuscript Division, Library of Congress, box 279, file 6 (H.L. v. Matheson); Gay Gellhorn, "Justice Thurgood Marshall's Jurisprudence of Equal Protection of the Laws and the Poor," *Arizona State Law Journal* 26 (Summer 1994): 429, 456.

8. Tushnet, *Making Civil Rights Law,* 132, 62, 54–55; Elena Kagan, "For Justice Marshall," *Texas Law Review* 71 (May 1993): 1125, 1127.

9. Kagan, "For Justice Marshall," 1126; Anthony Kennedy, "The Voice of Thurgood Marshall," *Stanford Law Review* 44 (Summer 1992): 1221, 1222.

10. Sandra Day O'Connor, "Thurgood Marshall: The Influence of a Raconteur," *Stanford Law Review* 44 (Summer 1992): 1217–18, 1219; Kennedy, "Voice of Thurgood Marshall," 1222; Byron White, "A Tribute to Justice Thurgood Marshall," *Stanford Law Review* 44 (Summer 1992): 1215, 1216.

11. White, "Tribute," 1216; 1217, 1218.

12. 409 U.S. 434 (1973).

13. Susan Low Bloch, "Thurgood Marshall: Courageous Advocate, Compassionate Judge," *Georgetown Law Journal* 80 (Aug. 1992): 2003, 2004. For additional citations to *Kras* along these lines, see Owen Fiss, "Thurgood Marshall," *Harvard Law Review* 105 (Nov. 1991): 49, 53; Martha Minow, "Thurgood Marshall," *Harvard Law Review* 105 (Nov. 1991): 66, 69.

14. Powell draft, May 4, 1981, Marshall Papers, box 277, file 3 (Rhodes v. Chapman); Marshall draft, May 15, 1981, ibid.

15. David J. Garrow, *Liberty and Sexuality: The Right to Privacy and the Making of* Roe v. Wade (New York: Macmillan, 1994), 580–82; John C. Jeffries, Jr., *Justice Lewis F. Powell, Jr.: A Biography* (New York: Scribner's, 1994), 341–42.

16. Garrow, *Liberty and Sexuality,* 583–84; Jeffries, *Powell,* 343.

17. TM to conference, Nov. 16, 1967, William J. Brennan Papers, Manuscript Division, Library of Congress, box 172, file 3 (Lee v. Washington); TM to conference, Jan. 28, 1982, Marshall Papers, box 283, file 6; TM to conference, July 31, 1980, box 262, file 3, ibid.

18. Conference notes, Brennan Papers, box 453, file 1 (Moore v. East Cleveland); TM to Burger, Nov. 23, 1976, Marshall Papers, box 194, file 2.

19. Jim Mann, "Prepping for the Justices," *American Lawyer,* Nov. 1982, p. 98; Nathan Lewin, "The Justice and the Hairpiece," *Washington Jewish Week,* July 4, 1991, p. 1; Carol Steiker, "'Did You Hear What Thurgood Marshall Did For Us?'—A Tribute," *American Journal of Criminal Law* 20 (Winter 1993): vii, ix; Blackmun to Stevens, July 19, 1988, Marshall Papers, box 436, file 4. For expressions of Marshall's perspective, as it was communicated to Marshall's law clerks, see Virginia Whitner Hoptman to TM (undated, 1987) ("You instilled in me the need to remember that there are living, breathing human beings who are affected by legal decisions; and that, often, the 'cold' record does not do them justice"); Walter Kamiat to TM, Oct. 20, 1987 ("what made it special was a feeling of purpose, a feeling that in your chambers at least the humanity of the cases was not lost"); Richard Revesz to TM, Oct. 19, 1987 ("your deep sense that abstract legal principles matter but that people's lives matter more"); Danny Richman to TM, May 15, 1987 ("what you taught us during our brief tenure: . . . how to remember that people's lives will be affected by decisions"), all in a collection of letters presented to Justice Marshall on his twentieth anniversary on the Court (in author's possession).

20. Bostick v. Florida, 501 U.S. 429 (1991); draft opinions, Marshall Papers, box 532, file 9; conference notes, Brennan Papers, box 432, file 5 (United States v. Chadwick).

21. O'Connor, "Raconteur," 1219.

Chapter 1

1. TM, interview by Ed Erwin, March 11, 1977, Columbia University Library, Oral History Collection, pp. 99–100; Victor Navasky, *Kennedy Justice* (New York: Atheneum, 1971), 243; William T. Coleman to Frank D. Reeves, May 9, 1961, John Fitzgerald Kennedy Library, White House Central Name File, box 1736, Thurgood Marshall, correspondence folder. For an analysis of the political dimensions of Marshall's appointment, see Puzant Merdinian, "The Nomination and Confirmation of Thurgood Marshall as a Judge of the Second Circuit Court of Appeals in 1961–62" (undergraduate thesis, Merton College, Oxford University, 1994).

2. Louis Martin, interview with author (telephone), Nov. 15, 1988; Juan Williams, "Marshall's Law," *Washington Post Magazine,* Jan. 7, 1990, pp. 12, 27. Williams has

Marshall saying that this exchange occurred in a face-to-face meeting with Robert Kennedy. As Richard Revesz points out, there is "an inconsistency" in Marshall's version. "Thurgood Marshall's Struggle," *New York University Law Review* 68 (May 1993): 237, 259 n.136. I believe that my account is the most likely version of the events, although it blends statements made by Martin and Marshall.

3. Martin interview; Deborah Rhode, notes of conversations with TM (in author's possession).

4. Joseph Dolan to author, Oct. 18, 1988; Burke Marshall, interview with author (telephone), May 26, 1988.

5. *New York Times,* Sept. 25, 1961, p. 32, col. 1 (editorial); id., Sept. 24, 1961, p. 54, col. 3; id., Oct. 7, 1961, p. 10, col. 8; id., Oct. 24, 1961, p. 29, col. 1.

6. *New York Times,* April 6, 1962, p. 8, col. 4; id., April 13, 1962, p. 23, col. 2; id., April 30, 1962, p. 6, col. 2; id., May 2, 1962, p. 34, col. 7; Senate Committee on the Judiciary, *Hearings on the Nomination of Thurgood Marshall,* 87th Cong., S. 1532, 4 [hereinafter *Second Circuit Hearings*].

7. *New York Times,* May 5, 1962, p. 26, col. 1 (editorial); id., May 16, 1962, p. 40, col. 8 (letter from Prof. Norman Dorsen); id., July 9, 1962, p. 13, col. 5; *Second Circuit Hearings,* at 14–32. For a discussion of the Texas suit, see Mark Tushnet, *Making Civil Rights Law: Thurgood Marshall and the Supreme Court, 1936–1961* (New York: Oxford University Press, 1994), 272–73.

8. *New York Times,* July 13, 1962, p. 9, col. 1; id. July 14, 1962, p. 8, col. 4 (Frank Lausche (D-Ohio) and Jacob Javits (R-New York)); id., July 18, p. 30, col. 2 (Steven Young (D-Ohio)); id., July 28, p. 7, col. 6 (Clifford Case (R-New Jersey)); id., Aug. 4, 1962, p. 9, col. 5; id., Aug. 7, 1962, p. 18, col. 7; id., Aug. 9, p. 53, col. 3; id., Aug. 14, 1962, p. 36, col. 6; id., Aug. 15, 1962, p. 16, col. 6; id., Aug. 18, 1962, p. 22, col. 3.

9. *Second Circuit Hearings,* at 58, 105–10, 164–84; *New York Times,* Aug. 21, 1962, p. 19, col. 1.

10. CONG. REC. 15,215 (1962) (statement of Sen. Keating); id. at 16,383 (statement of Sen. Javits); id. at 16,075 (statement of Sen. Javits); *New York Times,* Aug. 21, 1962, p. 1, col. 2; id., Aug. 22, 1962, p. 20, col. 1; id., Aug. 23, 1962, p. 30, col. 1; Dolan to author; Nicholas Katzenbach, interview with author (telephone), June 8, 1988.

11. *New York Times,* Aug. 25, 1962, p. 20, col. 5; id., Aug. 28, 1962, p. 16, col. 6; id., Aug. 29, 1962, p. 9, col. 2; id., Aug. 30, 1962, p. 18, col. 6; id., Sept. 8, 1962, p. 1, col. 2; id., Sept. 9, 1962, § IV, p. 12, col. 1; id., Sept. 12, 1962, p. 1, col. 2; Simon Sobeloff to TM, Sept. 12, 1962, Thurgood Marshall Papers, Manuscript Division, Library of Congress, box 6, file 8. On Sobeloff's nomination, see Michael Mayer, "Eisenhower and the Southern Federal Judiciary: The Sobeloff Nomination," in *Reexamining the Eisenhower Presidency,* Shirley Anne Warshaw, ed. (Westport, Conn.: Greenwood Press, 1993).

12. Dolan to author; *New York Times,* Aug. 21, 1962, p. 19, col. 1; Edwin O. Guthman and Jeffrey Shulman, eds. *Robert Kennedy In His Own Words: The Unpublished Recollections of the Kennedy Years* (New York: Bantam Books, 1988), 369; Clarence Mitchell, oral history interview by John Stewart, Feb. 9, 1967, pp. 46–47 (John Fitzgerald Kennedy Library).

13. TM to Edward Lumbard, Jan. 2, 1962, Marshall Papers, box 9, file 5; James O. Freedman, interview with author (telephone), Dec. 16, 1988. Marshall continued his isolation when he became a justice; in Washington, virtually the only old friends he kept up with were Wiley Branton and Spottswood Robinson, who was a judge by that time. William T. Coleman, interview with author, Washington, D.C., Oct. 17, 1989. According to Marshall's son, one reason was that Marshall took very seriously the criticisms lodged against Abe Fortas for continuing to maintain contacts with professional associates. Thurgood Marshall, Jr., interview with author (telephone), April 26, 1991.

14. Ralph K. Winter, interview with author, New Haven, April 20, 1989; Owen Fiss, interview with author, New Haven, April 20, 1989.

15. For a discussion of the business of the Second Circuit a decade before Marshall joined it, see Marvin Schick, *Learned Hand's Court* (Baltimore: Johns Hopkins University Press, 1970), 305–27. The overall shape of the court's business did not seem to have changed by the time Marshall came.

16. Winter interview; Frankfurter to Coleman, Jan. 2, 1962, Felix Frankfurter Papers, Harvard Law School, box 206, folder 10; Winter to Marshall, Dec. 10, 1962, Marshall Papers, box 7, file 6; Winter to Marshall, Nov. 7, 1962, id.; James O. Freedman to author, April 26, 1988 (referring to Brown letter). The tax case was Nassau Lens Co. v. Commissioner, 308 F.2d 39 (2d Cir. 1962).

17. Sidney Zion, "Thurgood Marshall Takes a New 'Tush-Tush' Job," *New York Times Magazine*, Aug. 22, 1965, p. 70; Freedman interview; Fiss interview; Winter interview; Henry Friendly to Frankfurter, Jan. 9, 1962, Felix Frankfurter Papers, Manuscript Division, Library of Congress, reel 34, file: Friendly, Henry; Friendly to Frankfurter, Feb. 2, 1962, id. For Marshall's tribute to Friendly, see Extraordinary Session of the Court of Appeals for the Second Circuit, "In Memoriam: Honorable Henry J. Friendly," 805 F.2d lxxxvii–lxxxviii (1986).

18. Winter interview; Freedman interview; Fiss interview.

19. United States *ex rel.* Angelet v. Fay, 333 F.2d 12 (2d Cir. 1964), *aff'd,* 381 U.S. 654 (1965). The majority ruled against retroactivity even though, according to one judge, "all of us expect" that the Supreme Court would decide the issue the other way. Paul Hays memorandum, June 9, 1964, Marshall Papers, box 15, file 15. The Court in fact ruled against retroactivity. Mapp v. Ohio, 367 U.S. 643 (1961).

20. 348 F.2d 844 (2d Cir. 1965), *cert. denied,* 383 U.S. 913 (1966).

21. Palko v. Connecticut, 302 U.S. 319 (1937). For a survey of the incorporation controversy to the early 1960s, see Geoffrey Stone, L. Michael Seidman, Cass Sunstein, and Mark Tushnet, *Constitutional Law* (Boston: Little, Brown, 1986), 707–17.

22. Cichos v. Indiana, 385 U.S. 76, 81–82 (1966) (Fortas, J., dissenting); Benton v. Maryland, 395 U.S. 784 (1969); Price v. Georgia, 398 U.S. 323 (1970). One of Marshall's law clerks pointed out that the opinion in *Price* "not only comes out the right way, but it cites *Hetenyi* twice." TCG [Thomas Grey] note on draft opinion, Marshall Papers, box 60, file 22. For law review comments favorable to Marshall's opinion in *Hetenyi,* see James H. Griggin, Jr., "Case Comment," *Boston University Law Review* 46 (Spring 1966): 260; "Comment on Recent Case," *Iowa Law Review* 52 (Aug. 1966): 109; Don Le Duc, "Note," *Wayne Law Review* 12 (Spring 1966): 685.

23. 28 U.S.C. § 1443 (1994). For a general discussion of civil rights removal as of the mid-1960s, see Anthony Amsterdam, "Criminal Prosecutions Affecting Federally Guaranteed Civil Rights: Federal Removal and Habeas Corpus Jurisdiction to Abort State Court Trial," *University of Pennsylvania Law Review* 113 (April 1965): 793.

24. New York v. Galamison, 342 F.2d 255 (2d Cir.), *cert. denied,* 380 U.S. 977 (1965).

25. TM memorandum, Dec. 9, 1969, Marshall Papers, box 19, file 7.

26. TM, "Law and the Quest for Equality" (the Tyrell Williams Lecture), delivered at the School of Law, Washington University of St. Louis, March 8, 1967; *New York Times,* June 7, 1967, p. 37, col. 3.

27. 341 F.2d 815 (2d Cir. 1965); Fiss interview; see also "Recent Development," *Michigan Law Review* 63 (Feb. 1965): 720, which discusses the district court decision without treating the racial aspects of the case as introducing a special factor.

28. 341 F.2d at 820–21; Elliott D. Woocher, "Case Comment," *Boston University Law Review* 45 (Spring 1965): 283, 288–89.

29. For an overview of Bruce's travails, see Edward de Grazia, *Girls Lean Back Everywhere: The Law of Obscenity and the Assault on Genius* (New York: Random House, 1992), 447–52; Albert Goldman, from the journalism of Lawrence Schiller, *Ladies and Gentlemen: Lenny Bruce!!* (New York: Random House, 1974), 510–75.

30. de Grazia, *Girls Lean Back*, 451–52; Goldman, *Lenny Bruce*, 573.

31. For memoranda on the case, see Marshall Papers, box 21, file 4.

32. Ralph Spritzer, interview with author, Tempe, Ariz., April 8, 1988; Jerome I. Chapman, interview with author, Washington, D.C., March 7, 1988; *New York Times*, July 14, 1965, p. 1, col. 5, p. 36, col. 1 (editorial); TM, oral history interview by Thomas Baker, July 10, 1969, p. 10, Lyndon Baines Johnson Library.

33. *Hearings on the Nomination of Thurgood Marshall Before the Subcomm. of the Senate Comm. on the Judiciary*, S-1700-2, 89th Cong., 1st Sess. 7 (1965); Zion, "Thurgood Marshall Takes a New 'Tush-Tush' Job," p. 69; TM interview by Ed Erwin, March 11, 1977, pp. 102–04, and June 7, 1977, pp. 159–60; Katzenbach interview; Fiss interview; Freedman interview.

34. Transcript, TM press conference, June 28, 1991, p. 9.

35. The solicitor general also decides whether to authorize appeals by the government or most of its agencies, including appeals from trial courts to the courts of appeals. In making these decisions, the solicitor general sometimes must resolve disputes within the government about the position it should take.

36. For discussions of the solicitor general, see Lincoln Caplan, *The Tenth Justice: The Solicitor General and the Rule of Law* (New York: Alfred Knopf, 1987); Symposium, "The Role and Function of the United States Solicitor General," *Loyola of Los Angeles Law Review* 21 (June 1988): 1047.

37. Nathan Lewin, "The Justice and the Hairpiece," *Washington Jewish Week*, July 4, 1991, p. 9. Except as indicated in the notes, information on Marshall's work as solicitor general is based on interviews with the following attorneys in the office of the solicitor general: Ralph Spritzer, Tempe, Ariz., April 8, 1988; Jerome I. Chapman, Washington, D.C., March 7, 1988; Robert Rifkind, New York, March 30, 1988; Francis X. Beytagh, Columbus, Ohio, May 9, 1988; Nathan Lewin, Washington, D.C., June 1, 1988; J. Nicholas McGrath, Aspen, Colo., June 10, 1988; Louis F. Claiborne, San Francisco, Nov. 17, 1988.

38. For example, Marshall once convened a meeting in which the judgments of Louis Claiborne, who was one of his assistants, and Jerome Chapman, who was on the office's staff, were arrayed against the judgments of the head of the Lands Division of the Department of Justice and Stewart Udall, the secretary of the interior. The issue involved a rather arcane problem, but the case was of special interest to Udall because the case involved people Udall knew. Marshall overrode his staff's recommendations and authorized an appeal of the lower court's decision against Udall. The court of appeals ultimately upheld Udall. Littell v. Udall, 242 F. Supp. 635 (D.C.D.C. 1965), *rev'd*, 366 F.2d 668 (D.C. Cir. 1966), *cert. denied*, 385 U.S. 1007 (1967).

39. Lewin, "The Justice and the Hairpiece."

40. Claiborne interview.

41. Navasky, *Kennedy Justice*, 68–71, 84–95, 451–52.

42. Black v. United States, 384 U.S. 927 (1966) (initially denying Black's request for review of his conviction), 384 U.S. 983 (1966) (requesting memorandum), 385 U.S. 26 (1966), (vacating conviction).

43. For discussions of the negotiations, see Athan Theoharis and John Stuart Cox, *The Boss: J. Edgar Hoover and the Great American Inquisition* (Philadelphia: Temple University Press, 1988), 368–93, especially at 391–92; Laura Kalman, *Abe Fortas: A Biography* (New

Haven: Yale University Press, 1990), 313–16. The conflict between Hoover and Kennedy broke out into the open later in 1966, when Hoover informed Congress that the bureau had never engaged in either wiretapping or bugging without specific authorization from the attorney general. The paper trail on which Hoover relied for this claim was full of ambiguous phrases, and the most that can be said is that Kennedy almost certainly should have known that the FBI was using bugs. By the time the conflict between Hoover and Kennedy came out into the open, Marshall was out of the picture, having handled the problem put to him rather more deftly than Hoover or Kennedy were able to handle their conflict.

44. Spritzer interview; Rebecca Mae Salokar, "The Solicitor General: Balancing the Interests of the Executive and Judicial Branches, 1959–1982," (Ph.D. diss., Syracuse University, 1988), 118–19.

45. Transcript of Oral Argument, Baltimore & O.R.R. v. United States, 386 U.S. 372 (1967) (No. 642) (Penn-Central merger case); Hammond Chaffetz to author, Aug. 30, 1988, regarding oral argument in FTC v. Dean Foods Co., 384 U.S. 597 (1966); Howard C. Equitz to author, Aug. 30, 1988, regarding oral argument in NLRB v. Allis-Chalmers Mfg. Co., 388 U.S. 175 (1967). Catha DeLoach, an assistant to J. Edgar Hoover, reported in a memorandum to Hoover that Justice Fortas said that Marshall made "inept and stupid" presentations to the Court. Tony Mauro, "Files Shed Unflattering Light on Fortas," *Legal Times*, Feb. 5, 1990, p. 17. I suspect that Fortas may well have said that Marshall made a "stupid"argument in a particular case and that the government's presentation was "inept," but I doubt that Fortas meant to make an overall judgment on Marshall's performance as solicitor general.

46. *See, e.g.,* Transcript of Oral Argument, FTC v. Procter & Gamble Co., 386 U.S. 568 (1967) (No. 342).

47. For the political background, see Joseph A. Califano, Jr., *The Triumph and Tragedy of Lyndon Johnson: The White House Years* (New York: Simon & Schuster, 1991), 159–63.

48. Id. at 162. Califano says that the revised draft was "a far cry" from the one he had first reviewed. Id. at 163. Califano appears to have reviewed the Justice Department's draft first, then the solicitor general's draft; he refers to Claiborne's position as involving "certain procedural technicalities." (Califano reports that Johnson had conversations with Abe Fortas, who participated in the decision of the case by the Court, about the government's position as it developed. Id. at 162–63.)

49. Transcript of Oral Argument, Baltimore & O.R.R. v. United States, 386 U.S. 372 (1967) (No. 642); Claiborne interview.

50. Transcript of Oral Argument, Linn v. United Plant Guard Workers, 383 U.S. 53 (1966) (No. 45).

51. Harper v. Virginia Board of Elections, 383 U.S. 663 (1966); Philip Kurland and Gerhard Casper, eds. *Landmark Briefs and Arguments of the Supreme Court of the United States: Constitutional Law,* vol. 62 (Arlington, Va.: University Publications of America, 1975), especially at 1034–37.

52. TM note, Marshall Papers, box 26, file 6 ("If we appoint counsel he will have to be efficient [*sic;* probably meaning 'effective']").

53. TM to Clinton Riggs, March 4, 1966, Marshall Papers, box 26, file 5.

54. Miranda v. Arizona, 384 U.S. 436 (1966); Kurland and Gerhard, eds., *Landmark Briefs,* vol. 63; Liva Baker, *Miranda: Crime, Law and Politics* (New York: Atheneum, 1983), especially at 46–47; conference notes, William J. Brennan Papers, Manuscript Division, Library of Congress, box 427, file 2 (Michigan v. Mosley).

55. According to Ramsey Clark, Johnson initially told him he would not appoint him attorney general, because it would not be fair to force his father to resign. Ramsey Clark,

oral history interview by Harri Baker, Oct. 30, 1968, pp. 24–25, LBJ Library. Johnson had received an opinion that appointing Ramsey Clark would *not* create a conflict of interest. Liz Carpenter to Johnson, March 1, 1967, Ex FG 535, White House Central Files, box 359, LBJ Library. Edwin Weisl told an interviewer that, in his view, the major reason for appointing Ramsey Clark was to get his father to resign. Edwin Weisl, oral history interview by Joe B. Frantz, May 23, 1969, p. 21, LBJ Library.

56. Califano, *Triumph and Tragedy,* 208; Katzenbach interview; Neil McFeeley, *Appointment of Judges: The Johnson Presidency* (Austin: University of Texas Press, 1987), 112. As the possibility of Justice Clark's resignation became apparent, Norman Dorsen, a liberal academic, wrote Joseph Califano and also suggested Hastie and Clyde Ferguson as potential nominees "better qualified" than Marshall. Dorsen to Califano, April 3, 1967, Ex FG 535, White House Central Files, box 359, LBJ Library.

57. *New York Times,* June 14, 1967, p. 1, col. 7, and p. 46, col. 1; Roscoe Drummond, "The Race Revolution: Marshall—A Symbol of Change," *Washington Post,* June 17, 1967, p. A13; Joseph Kraft, "Hung Court," *Washington Post,* June 15, 1967, p. 21; "LBJ Packs the Court," *Human Events,* June 24, 1967, p. 4; James J. Kilpatrick, "Term's End," *National Review,* July 25, 1967, p. 805.

58. Beytagh interview; McGrath interview.

59. *Hearings on the Nomination of Thurgood Marshall Before the Senate Comm. on the Judiciary,* 5-1826-3, 90th Cong., 1st Sess. 3–13 (July 13, 1967).

60. Id. at 49–60 (July 14, 1967).

61. Id. at 67–100 (July 18, 1967).

62. Id. at 162–72 (July 19, 1967).

63. For an analysis concluding that "state racial composition seems to have had a large and negative impact on senators' voting," see L. Marvin Overby et al., "African-American Constituents and Supreme Court Nominees: An Examination of the Senate Confirmation of Thurgood Marshall," *Political Science Research Quarterly* 47 (Dec. 1994): 839.

64. *New York Times,* Aug. 31, 1967, p. 1, col. 2; "Justice Marshall," *Washington Post,* Sept. 1, 1967 (editorial) p. A20.

Chapter 2

1. William C. Berman, *America's Right Turn: From Nixon to Bush* (Baltimore: Johns Hopkins University Press, 1994), 40, 43, 58–59; Thomas Ferguson and Joel Rogers, *Right Turn: The Decline of the Democrats and the Future of American Politics* (New York: Hill & Wang, 1986), 103.

2. Thomas Byrne Edsall, with Mary D. Edsall, *Chain Reaction: The Impact of Race, Rights, and Taxes on American Politics* (New York: W. W. Norton, 1991), 9.

3. Ferguson and Rogers, *Right Turn.*

4. Board of Regents v. Roth, 408 U.S. 564 (1972).

5. See chapter 5.

6. Edsall, *Chain Reaction,* 8.

7. Jonathan Reider, "The Rise of the 'Silent Majority,'" in *The Rise and Fall of the New Deal Order, 1930–1980,* Steve Fraser and Gary Gerstle, eds., (Princeton: Princeton University Press, 1989), 254–55.

8. Edsall, *Chain Reaction,* 8.

9. Vincent Blasi, ed., *The Burger Court: The Counter-Revolution That Wasn't* (New Haven: Yale University Press, 1983); James F. Simon, *The Center Holds: The Power Struggle Inside the Rehnquist Court* (New York: Simon & Schuster, 1995).

10. Exceptions are cases involving discrimination based on gender, discussed in chapter 5.

11. G. Edward White, *Earl Warren: A Public Life* (New York: Oxford University Press, 1982), 228.

12. James J. Kilpatrick, "Marshall's Appointment Upsets Court Balance," *Washington Sunday Star,* June 18, 1967 (clipping in TM file at Moorland-Spingarn Research Center, Howard University).

13. Mempa v. Rhay, 389 U.S. 128 (1967); Certiorari memorandum and conference notes, William O. Douglas Papers, Manuscript Division, Library of Congress, box 1399, file: Argued Cases, O.T. 1967, No. 16; Black to TM, Nov. 9, 1967, Earl Warren Papers, Manuscript Division, Library of Congress, box 553, file: Mempa v. Rhay.

14. 395 U.S. 147 (1969).

15. TM to White, June 10, 1968, Douglas Papers, box 1399, file: Memoranda by the Court O.T. 1967; Fortas to White, Jan. 23, 1969, Douglas Papers, box 1431, file: Argued Cases, No. 200; TM to conference, Feb. 25, 1969, Hugo Black Papers, Manuscript Division, Library of Congress, box 405, file: No. 200 O.T. 1968, Frank v. United States.

16. Benton v. Maryland, 395 U.S. 784 (1968) (Harlan & Stewart, JJ., dissenting).

17. Stanley v. Georgia, 394 U.S. 557 (1969); conference notes, Douglas Papers, box 1432, file: Argued Cases, O.T. 1968, No. 293.

18. Amalgamated Food Employees v. Logan Valley Plaza, 391 U.S. 308 (1968) (Black, Harlan & White, JJ., dissenting).

19. *In re* Whittington, 391 U.S. 341 (1968).

20. Memorandum to files and conference notes, Douglas Papers, box 1402, file: Argued Cases, No. 701.

21. For details of the Fortas affair, see Robert Shogan, *A Question of Judgment: The Fortas Case and the Struggle for the Supreme Court* (Indianapolis: Bobbs-Merrill, 1972), and Bruce Alan Murphy, *Fortas: The Rise and Ruin of a Supreme Court Justice* (New York: William Morrow, 1988). A general study of the Fortas affair and the later nominations of Haynsworth and Carswell is John Massaro, *Supremely Political: The Role of Ideology and Presidential Management in Unsuccessful Supreme Court Nominations* (Buffalo: State University of New York Press, 1990).

22. *See* Shogan, *A Question of Judgment;* Murphy, *Fortas.*

23. *See* Richard Harris, *Justice: The Crisis of Law, Order, and Freedom in America* (New York: E. P. Dutton, 1970), 252; Louis Kohlmeier, *"God Save This Honorable Court!"* (New York: Scribner's, 1972), 130–32. A full study of the nomination is John P. Frank, *Clement Haynsworth, the Senate, and the Supreme Court* (Charlottesville: University Press of Virginia, 1991).

24. *See* Harris, *Justice.* Hruska is quoted in Murphy, *Fortas,* 279.

25. Black resigned on September 17, 1971, Harlan on September 23. Black died on September 25, Harlan on December 29. Bob Woodward and Scott Armstrong, *The Brethren: Inside the Supreme Court* (New York: Simon & Schuster, 1979), 258–59; 404 U.S. iv (1972).

26. SAS [Stephen Saltzburg] certiorari memorandum, Thurgood Marshall Papers, Manuscript Division, Library of Congress box 75, file 4 (Tillmon v. Wheaton-Haven); Black to Harlan, Oct. 26, 1970, box 63, file 8, ibid.; White to Burger, Dec. 21, 1972, William J. Brennan Papers, Manuscript Division, Library of Congress, box 287, file 3 (Illinois v. Somerville).

27. Douglas to Brennan, White, and TM, Feb. 4, 1973, Marshall Papers, box 104, file 10 (Otter Tail Power Co. v. United States) (case in which two justices were disqualified); David J. Garrow, *Liberty and Sexuality: The Right to Privacy and the Making of* Roe v. Wade (New York: Macmillan, 1994), 556; Douglas to Stewart, May 31, 1972, Marshall Papers,

box 92, file 5 (Fuentes v. Shevin); Burger to Douglas, May 31, 1972, ibid.; Douglas to Burger, May 31, 1972, ibid.; Burger to Douglas, May 31, 1972 (second note), ibid.

28. TM note on Burger to White, Dec. 27, 1977, Marshall Papers, box 201, file 4 (Procunier v. Navarette); John C. Jeffries, Jr., *Justice Lewis F. Powell, Jr.: A Biography* (New York: Scribner's, 1994), 248, 249, 432; Stephen L. Wasby, "Justice Harry A. Blackmun: Transformation from 'Minnesota Twin' to Independent Voice," in *The Burger Court: Political and Judicial Profiles,* Charles M. Lamb and Stephen C. Halpern, eds. (Urbana: University of Illinois Press, 1991), 70; Blackmun to Brennan, undated, Brennan Papers, box 498, file 8 (Michigan v. Doran); Rehnquist to Burger, May 19, 1976, Marshall Papers, box 158, file 5 (Connor v. Coleman); Stevens draft concurrence, June 1, 1982, box 594, file 2 (School Board of Island Trees v. Pico), Brennan Papers.

29. TM to Burger, April 7, 1972, Marshall Papers, box 78, file 6; Burger to conference, April 10, 1972, ibid.; Woodward and Armstrong, *Brethren,* 178.

30. The details of the Court's discussions are in Garrow, *Liberty and Sexuality,* 528–34.

31. Id. at 548–55.

32. Burger to conference, Jan. 17, 1972, Brennan Papers, box 256, file 1 (Gooding v. Wilson); Brennan to Burger, Jan. 17, 1972, ibid.; Burger to Brennan, Jan. 17, 1972, ibid.; Brennan to Burger, March 6, 1973, box 297, file 1 (Brown v. Chote), ibid.; Stevens to Burger, Oct. 11, 1984, box 354, file 7, Marshall Papers; Burger to conference, Oct. 3, 1975, box 155, file 8, ibid.

33. Note attached to Black to Brennan, Feb. 25, 1970, Brennan Papers, box 216, file 3 (United States v. Seckinger). For other nonideological cases, see Burger to conference, Nov. 14, 1984, Marshall Papers, box 364, file 3 (Metropolitan Life Co. v. Ward); Burger to Powell, Feb. 15, 1978, box 201, file 5 (Raymond Motor Transp. v. Rice), ibid.

34. Burger to Douglas, April 24, 1972, Brennan Papers, box 268, file 8 (Lloyd Corp. v. Tanner); Douglas to Brennan, April 24, 1972, ibid.; Blackmun to Marshall, April 24, 1972, Marshall Papers, box 89, file 7; Blackmun to Burger, May 8, 1972, ibid.; Burger to conference, May 8, 1972, ibid.

35. Brennan to Burger, Dec. 13, 1985, Marshall Papers, box 397, file 2 (Lee v. Illinois); Burger to Blackmun, Oct. 17, 1983, Marshall Papers, box 339, file 1 (Migra v. Warren County School Dist.), ibid.; Blackmun to Burger, Oct. 18, 1983, ibid.

36. For a discussion of Burger's role in *Swann v. Charlotte-Mecklenburg Board of Education,* see chapter 4.

37. The most detailed account of the opinion-drafting process in the Watergate tapes case is Woodward and Armstrong, *Brethren,* 308–47. Other accounts, less overdramatized, are Howard Ball, *"We Have a Duty": The Supreme Court and the Watergate Tapes Litigation* (New York: Greenwood Press, 1990), 112–30; Jeffries, *Powell,* 382–97. Jeffries states that Woodward and Armstrong's account "is largely confirmed by the records." Id. at 395.

38. 472 U.S. 703 (1985).

39. Powell to Burger, May 23, 1985, Marshall Papers, box 363, file 10; Burger to Powell, May 23, 1985, ibid.; Burger to conference, June 12, 1985, ibid.; Brennan to Burger, June 12, 1985, ibid.

40. Draft opinions, Brennan Papers, box 716, file 3 (Arcara v. Cloud Books); draft opinions, box 649, file 8 (Hishon v. King & Spalding), ibid.; Brennan to Burger, May 29, 1985, box 686, file 4 (*In re* Snyder), ibid.; Jim Feldman to Brennan, Dec. 6, 1984, box 606, file 4, ibid.; Powell to Burger, March 10, 1979, box 492, file 8 (Parham v. J.L.), ibid.

41. Burger to O'Connor, Jan. 29, 1985, Marshall Papers, box 365, file 9 (Marrese v. American Academy of Orthopedic Surgeons); draft opinions, Brennan Papers, box 626, file 2 (Illinois v. Andreas); draft opinions, May 23 and June 12, 1986, Marshall Papers, box 390, file 3 (Bethel School Dist. v. Fraser); O'Connor to Burger, June 2, 1986, box 396, file 2

(Bowsher v. Synar), ibid.; Burger to conference, June 3, 1986, ibid.; Burger to conference, June 4, 1986, ibid.

42. Marshall Papers, box 237, file 4.

43. 441 U.S. 786 (1977).

44. Burger to conference, March 9, 1977, Marshall Papers, box 190, file 3; Burger to Blackmun, April 18, 1977, ibid.

45. Scalia to Brennan, May 4, 1990, Marshall Papers, box 497, file 7 (McKesson Corp. v. Division of Alcohol); Powell to conference, June 3, 1987, box 420, file 1 (Welch v. Texas Dep't of Highways), ibid. For an analysis of Brennan's contributions, stressing the merits of his views rather than his personality, see Robert Post, "William J. Brennan and the Warren Court," in *The Warren Court in Historical and Political Perspective*, Mark Tushnet, ed. (Charlottesville: University Press of Virginia, 1993), 123.

46. Stevens to Brennan, Jan. 9, 1978, Brennan Papers, box 468, file 4 (City of Lafayette v. Louisiana Power & Light); Brennan to Douglas, May 11, 1973, box 301, file 1 (U.S. Department of Agriculture v. Moreno), ibid.; Brennan to Rehnquist, Feb. 14, 1986, box 704, file 9 (Goldman v. Weinberger), ibid.; Rehnquist to Brennan, Feb. 18, 1986, ibid.

47. Brennan to O'Connor, May 18, 1984, Brennan Papers, box 660, file 4 (Brock v. Community Nutrition Inst.). For sharing advance copies, see O'Connor to Brennan, Nov. 12, 1981, box 582, file 6 (Fair Assessment in Real Estate v. McNary), ibid.; for Brennan's accommodations, see, e.g., Marshall Papers, box 417, file 4 (School Board v. Arline).

48. Powell to Brennan, June 14, 1984, Brennan Papers, box 661, file 4 (Roberts v. United States Jaycees); Powell to Brennan, June 4, 1982, box 589, file 3 (Youngberg v. Romeo), ibid.; Powell to Brennan, undated, box 535, file 5 (Richmond Newspapers v. Virginia), ibid.; Brennan to Powell, June 21, 1972, box 268, file 7 (Healy v. James), ibid.; Powell to Brennan, June 8, 1976, box 401, file 4 (Doyle v. Ohio), ibid.; Powell to Brennan, Jan. 20, 1987, Marshall Papers, box 417, file 8 (Lukhard v. Reed).

49. Brennan to TM, May 4, 1987, Marshall Papers, box 423, file 12 (Crawford Fitting Co. v. Gibbons); Brennan to TM, Dec. 12, 1986, box 389, file 8 (Morris v. Mathews), ibid.

50. Pennsylvania v. Muniz, 496 U.S. 582 (1990).

51. O'Connor to Brennan, June 4, 1990, Marshall Papers, box 507, file 4; O'Connor to Brennan, June 6, 1990, ibid.; Brennan to TM, June 7, 1990, ibid.; Brennan to TM, June 13, 1990, ibid.

52. Jeffries, *Powell*, 562.

53. Powell to Brennan, Stewart, and Marshall, June 16, 1975, Brennan Papers, box 353, file 2 (United States v. Brignoni-Ponce); United States v. Brignoni-Ponce, 422 U.S. 873 (1975); United States v. Ortiz, 422 U.S. 880 (1975).

54. Jeffries, *Powell*, 260, 261; author's recollection.

55. Powell to Marshall, June 25, 1985, Marshall Papers, box 373, file 1 (Sedima v. Imrex); Nixon v. Fitzgerald, 457 U.S. 731 (1982).

56. SLC [Stephen Carter] memorandum to 1981–82 law clerks, undated, Marshall Papers, box 269, file 2 (Kissinger v. Halperin); Powell to TM, Dec. 10, 1980, box 279, file 10 (Wood v. Georgia), ibid.; Powell to TM, May 20, 1981, box 273, file 3 (Hodel v. Virginia Surface Mining Ass'n), ibid.

57. Jeffries, *Powell*, 334; Powell to conference, Dec. 12, 1972, Brennan Papers, box 305, file 1 (Braden v. 30th Judicial Cir. C.); Black to Blackmun, Jan. 11, 1971, box 230, file 3, ibid.; Blackmun to Black, Jan. 11, 1971, ibid.

58. Bradley C. Canon, "Justice John Paul Stevens: The Lone Ranger in a Black Robe," in *The Burger Court: Political and Judicial Profiles*, Charles M. Lamb and Stephen C. Halpern, eds. (Urbana: University of Illinois Press, 1991), 343.

59. Canon, "Stevens," 373, 346; Consolidated Edison Co. v. Public Serv. Comm'n, 447

U.S. 530, 544–45 (1980) (Stevens, J., concurring in judgment); TM note on draft opinion, Marshall Papers, box 254, file 10 (Consolidated Edison Co. v. Public Service Comm'n); TM note on draft opinion, box 265, file 4 (Coleman v. Balkcom), ibid.; TM note on draft opinion, box 304, file 3 (Mills v. Hableutzel), ibid.; Stevens to Brennan, May 4, 1987, box 419, file 6 (Hewitt v. Helms), ibid.; Brennan to Stevens, May 5, 1987, ibid.; Stevens to TM, June 16, 1987, ibid.

60. Beverly B. Cook, "Justice Sandra Day O'Connor: Transition to a Republican Court Agenda," in *Burger Court,* Lamb and Halpern, eds., 239–40; Brennan to Blackmun, Jan. 5, 1982, Brennan Papers, box 583, file 9 (Rose v. Lundy); O'Connor to White, Jan. 27, 1988, Marshall Papers, box 443, file 3 (ETSI Pipeline v. Missouri); Stuart Taylor, Jr., "Glimpses of Thurgood Marshall," *The American Lawyer,* March 1993, p. 36. For an interchange between O'Connor and Marshall on federalism issues, see O'Connor to TM, May 22, 1985, Marshall Papers, box 372, file 5 (Johnson v. Mayor of Baltimore); TM to O'Connor, May 23, 1985, ibid.; Powell to TM, May 28, 1985, ibid.; O'Connor to TM, June 7, 1985, ibid.

61. Jeffries, *Powell,* 533; Rehnquist to conference, Nov. 24, 1989, Marshall Papers, box 492, file 7.

62. Stevens to Rehnquist, Dec. 19, 1989, Marshall Papers, box 492, file 7; Brennan to Scalia, May 27, 1987, box 424, file 4 (United States v. Stanley), ibid.; Scalia to Rehnquist, April 5, 1989, box 483, file 3, ibid.

63. Taylor, "Glimpses," 36; Sue Davis, "Justice William H. Rehnquist: Right-Wing Ideologue or Majoritarian Democrat?" in *Burger Court,* Halpern and Lamb, eds., 319; Rehnquist to TM, June 7, 1982, Brennan Papers, box 600, file 8 (Blum v. Bacon); Rehnquist to TM, March 25, 1989, Marshall Papers, box 476, file 9 (Neitzke v. Williams); Rehnquist to TM, Dec. 23, 1985, box 388, file 7 (Fisher v. City of Berkeley), ibid.; Rehnquist to TM, Jan. 31, 1989, box 469, file 2 (Hernandez v. Commissioner), ibid.; Rehnquist to conference, June 10, 1981, Brennan Papers, box 560, file 6 (Federated Dep't Stores v. Moitie); Rehnquist to Brennan, March 8, 1977, box 442, file 6 (Kremens v. Bartley), ibid.

64. Rehnquist draft opinion, May 17, 1983, Marshall Papers, box 322, file 10 (Morrison-Knudsen Constr. Co. v. Director); Rehnquist to TM, May 18, 1983, ibid.; notes on Rehnquist draft opinion, May 17, 1983, Brennan Papers, box 626, file 7.

65. Davis, "Rehnquist," 318 (quoting Warren Weaver); Blackmun to Rehnquist, May 14, 1980, Brennan Papers, box 536, file 3 (PruneYard Shopping Center v. Robins); Rehnquist to Stevens, Feb. 8, 1982, box 582, file 1 (Herweg v. Ray), ibid.; Brennan to conference, Dec. 13, 1978, Marshall Papers, box 226, file 3 (Quern v. Jordan); TM to conference, Dec. 13, 1978, ibid.; Rehnquist to conference, Dec. 14, 1978, ibid. For an analysis of Rehnquist's positions, see Sue Davis, *Justice Rehnquist and the Constitution* (Princeton: Princeton University Press, 1989).

66. 501 U.S. 560 (1991).

67. Rehnquist to conference, Feb. 27, 1991, Marshall Papers, box 534, file 9; Scott [Brewer] to TM, April 11, 1991, ibid.; Rehnquist draft, April 12, 1991, ibid.

68. Jeffries, *Powell,* 534; Kennedy to Scalia, April 4, 1989, Marshall Papers, box 472, file 5 (Pennsylvania v. Union Gas); draft opinions, id.; White to Brennan, June 6, 1988, box 448, file 4 (Riley v. National Fed'n of the Blind), ibid.; Scalia to Brennan, June 17, 1988, id.; Scalia to Brennan, May 4, 1988, box 445, file 10 (Pierce v. Underwood), id.

69. Scalia to Brennan and TM, March 15, 1989, Marshall Papers box 466, file 12 (NTEU v. Von Raab); Scalia to White, Feb. 14, 1990, box 503, file 7 (United States Dep't of Labor v. Triplett), ibid.

70. Stevens to Scalia, March 28, 1988, Marshall Papers, box 451, file 3 (McCoy v. Court of Appeals); Stevens to Scalia, March 28, 1991, box 535, file 5 (Kay v. Ehrler), ibid.;

Stevens to Scalia, April 30, 1990, box 506, file 7 (Burnham v. Superior Court), ibid.; O'Connor to Scalia, Nov. 29, 1989, box 510, file 6 (Holland v. Illinois), ibid.; O'Connor v. Ortega, 480 U.S. 709 (1987).

71. White to Scalia, June 2, 1989, Marshall Papers, box 482, file 8 (Carella v. California); Scalia to White, May 19, 1987, box 420, file 8 (California v. Rooney), ibid.; White to Scalia, May 19, 1987, ibid.

72. Scalia to Blackmun, June 9, 1988, Marshall Papers, box 446, file 4 (Doe v. United States); Blackmun to Scalia, June 15, 1988, ibid.; Blackmun to Rehnquist, Scalia, and Kennedy, May 31, 1988, box 446, file 7 (Michigan v. Chesternut), ibid.; Scalia to Blackmun, June 14, 1989, box 478, file 3 (United States v. Zolin), ibid.; Blackmun to Scalia, June 9, 1988, box 446, file 13 (INS v. Pangilinan), ibid.; Scalia to Blackmun, June 9, 1988, ibid. (There are two letters from Blackmun and two from Scalia, each with the same date.)

73. Stevens to Scalia, Jan. 13, 1989, Marshall Papers, box 470, file 6 (Chan v. Korean Air Lines); Scalia to Stevens, Jan. 13, 1989, ibid.; O'Connor to Scalia, Jan. 17, 1989, ibid.; Blackmun to Scalia, Feb. 2, 1989, ibid.; Scalia to O'Connor, Feb. 2, 1989, ibid.; Stevens to Scalia, May 10, 1989, ibid.; Blackmun to Brennan and Scalia, June 5, 1989, box 472, file 8 (H.J. v. Northwestern Bell), ibid.

74. Scalia to Stevens, April 20, 1990, Marshall Papers, box 507, file 7 (California v. American Stores); Scalia to Brennan, Jan. 18, 1990, box 501, file 9 (Dole v. United Steelworkers), ibid.; Stevens to Brennan, Jan. 18, 1990, ibid.; Scalia to Stevens, Jan. 22, 1990, ibid.; Brennan to TM, April 26, 1987, box 423, file 13 (Burlington N.R.R. v. Oklahoma Tax Comm'n), ibid.

75. Scalia draft concurrence, Nov. 9, 1987, Marshall Papers, box 440, file 4 (Gwaltney of Smithfield v. Chesapeake Bay Found'n); TM to conference, Nov. 10, 1987, ibid.; Scalia draft concurrence, Nov. 11, 1987, ibid.; Scalia to TM, June 12, 1989, box 481, file 2 (Department of Justice v. Tax Analysts), ibid.; TM to Scalia, June 13, 1989, ibid.; Scalia draft concurrence, June 18, 1989, ibid.; TM to Scalia, June 21, 1989, ibid.; Scalia to TM, June 21, 1989, ibid.; TM to Scalia, Feb. 16, 1990, box 505, file 9 (Adams Fruit Co. v. Barrett), ibid.; Blackmun to TM, March 5, 1990, ibid.

76. 500 U.S. 44 (1991).

77. TM to Scalia, Jan. 29, 1991, Marshall Papers, box 533, file 4; Scalia draft dissent, March 6, 1991, ibid.

78. Kennedy to O'Connor and Scalia, March 13, 1991, Marshall Papers, box 533, file 4; Scalia to Kennedy, March 15, 1991, ibid.; Kennedy to Scalia, March 16, 1991, ibid.; Kennedy to O'Connor, March 20, 1991, ibid.

79. Scalia to O'Connor, April 1, 1991, Marshall Papers, box 533, file 4; Stevens to Scalia, April 3, 1991, ibid.; Blackmun to O'Connor and Scalia, April 3, 1991, ibid.; Scalia to conference, April 3, 1991, ibid.; Scalia draft dissent, May 10, 1991, ibid.; Stevens draft dissent, May 6, 1991, ibid.

80. Blackmun to Scalia, June 6, 1990, Marshall Papers, box 508, file 5 (PBGC v. LTV); Scalia to Blackmun, June 6, 1990, ibid.

81. David O'Brien, *Storm Center: The Supreme Court in American Politics,* 3d ed. (New York: W. W. Norton, 1993), 111–16; Taylor, "Glimpses," 36.

82. Simon, *Center Holds,* 27–28, 67–71.

83. For an overview of the case, see id. at 19–27.

84. Patterson v. McLean Credit Union, 485 U.S. 617 (1988); Kennedy to Rehnquist, April 8, 1988, Marshall Papers, box 437, file 8 (Patterson v. McLean Credit Union); Taylor, "Glimpses," 36.

85. Simon, *Center Holds,* 43–81; Patterson v. McLean Credit Union, 491 U.S. 164 (1989).

86. Transcript, TM press conference, June 28, 1991, pp. 1, 3.

87. Proposed dissent, Marshall Papers, box 92, file 12 (Kirby v. Illinois).

88. White to TM, March 18, 1982, Marshall Papers, box 291, file 6 (Jacksonville Bulk Terminals v. ILA).

89. Transcript, TM press conference, June 28, 1991, pp. 8, 3.

Chapter 3

1. Rehnquist to conference, Nov. 10, 1981, William J. Brennan Papers, Manuscript Division, Library of Congress, box 579, file 2; David O'Brien, *Storm Center: The Supreme Court in American Politics,* 3d ed. (New York: W. W. Norton, 1993), 164; *see also* Douglas to Brennan, Stewart, Marshall, and Powell, Nov. 21, 1973 (Smith v. Goguen), Brennan Papers, box 317, file 12 (suggesting that "the five of us should have a brief conference").

2. For Burger, see Burger to Brennan, March 24, 1983, Brennan Papers, box 608, file 1 (referring to "my longhand 'talking papers'"); for Marshall, see SB [Scott Brewer] to TM, Docket #89-1217, Thurgood Marshall Papers, Manuscript Division, Library of Congress, box 513, file 8 ("I attach a proposed statement for use in Conference tomorrow").

3. Conference notes, Brennan Papers, box 695, file 9 (Goldman v. Weinberger); conference notes, box 667, file 2 (Bell v. New Jersey), ibid.; conference notes, box 638, file 1 (Selective Serv. Sys. v. Minnesota PIRG), ibid.; conference notes, box 604, file 4 (Kolender v. Lawson), ibid.

4. Many of Marshall's law clerks went on to teach at some of the nation's most prominent law schools. A list compiled in 1994 shows Marshall's former law clerks teaching at that time: Janet Cooper Alexander (Stanford); Susan Law Bloch (Georgetown); Scott Bewer (Harvard); Rebecca Brown (Vanderbilt); Stephen Carter (Yale); William W. Fisher III (Harvard); Philip Frickey (Minnesota); Elizabeth Garrett (Chicago); Gay Gellhorn (District of Columbia); Paul Gewirtz (Yale); Bruce Green (Fordham); Thomas Grey (Stanford); Howell Jackson (Harvard); Vicki Jackson (Georgetown); Elena Kagan (Chicago); Dan Kahan (Chicago); Randall Kennedy (Harvard); Martha Minow (Harvard); Eben Moglen (Columbia); Richard Pildes (Michigan); Richard Revesz (New York University); Deborah Rhode (Stanford); Stephen Saltzburg (George Washington); Lewis Sargentich (Harvard); L. Michael Seidman (Georgetown); John Siliciano (Cornell); Kenneth Simons (Boston University); Carol Steiker (Harvard); Jordan Steiker (Texas); Cass Sunstein (Chicago); Mark Tushnet (Georgetown); Jonathan Weinberg (Wayne State); Virginia Whitner-Hoptman (George Washington); David Wilkins (Harvard). The information is taken from William T. D'Zurilla, ed., "Directory of Law Clerks of the Justices of the United States Supreme Court" (mimeographed, Sept. 19, 1994), and augmented in a few instances by personal knowledge. In addition, the four clerks who worked with Marshall at the court of appeals became academics: Ralph Winter (Yale; United States Court of Appeals for the Second Circuit); James O. Freedman (University of Pennsylvania; president, Dartmouth College); Owen Fiss (Yale); Norman Lane (Southern California). Two other former law clerks to Marshall are federal judges as well: Douglas Ginsburg (United States Court of Appeals for the District of Columbia Circuit) and William Bryson (United States Court of Appeals for the Federal Circuit).

5. It seems appropriate for me to note that my examination of the files containing information on Marshall's law clerks indicates that my law school record was among the weakest of those whom Marshall chose to work with him. He relied heavily on the recommendation of George Edwards, the appeals court judge for whom I worked. Judge Edwards's father assisted Marshall in defending the NAACP against Texas's effort to stop the organization's work there. Mark Tushnet, *Making Civil Rights Law: Thurgood*

Marshall and the Supreme Court, 1936–1961, (New York: Oxford University Press, 1994), 272–73.

6. Powell to Brennan, Feb. 3, 1984, Brennan Papers, box 654, file 3 (Hoover v. Ronwin); notes on draft opinion, April 7, 1982, Marshall Papers, box 295, file 2 (Plyler v. Doe); EM [Eben Moglen] bench memo, box 403, file 5 (Ross v. Oklahoma), ibid.

7. O'Brien, *Storm Center,* 174 (describing use of bench memos in other chambers).

8. Id. at 212–14 (quoting Brandeis), 127.

9. TCG [Thomas Grey] to TM, note on draft, Marshall Papers, box 59, file 4 (Ashe v. Swenson); Herbert Buchsbaum, "The Kids on the Court," *Scholastic Update,* Sept. 17, 1993, p. 9 (quoting Caroline Brown). For an example of a Brennan draft, see Jennings v. Mahoney, Brennan Papers, box 276, file 4.

10. O'Brien, *Storm Center,* 127–29 (describing practices of Chief Justice Warren and Justices Reed, Butler, Byrnes, Murphy, and Rehnquist); Andrea Sachs, "Laurence Tribe," *Constitution* 3 (Spring–Summer 1991): 24, 28; John C. Jeffries, Jr., *Justice Lewis F. Powell, Jr.: A Biography* (New York: Scribners, 1994), 532, 295; Brennan to Mike [Becker], Brennan Papers, box 238, file 9 (International Bhd. of Teamsters v. Hardeman); Steve to Brennan, Nov. 26, 1982, box 616, file 4 (Pillsbury Co. v. Conboy); Bernard Schwartz, *The Unpublished Opinions of the Burger Court* (New York: Oxford University Press, 1988), 18–19; Bernard Schwartz, *The Ascent of Pragmatism: The Burger Court in Action* (Reading, Mass.: Addison-Wesley, 1990), 38. See also William Domnarski, *In the Opinion of the Court* (Urbana: University of Illinois Press, 1996), 30–31.

11. PM [Paul Mahoney] memorandum, Marshall Papers, box 317, file 10 (United States v. Rylander); HJ [Howell Jackson] to TM, Dec. 22, 1983, box 338, file 3 (Southland Corp. v. Keating), ibid.

12. Tony Mauro, "Preserving Marshall's Greatness," *Legal Times,* Feb. 8, 1993, p. 18 (I believe that Mauro is quoting from an interview with me, but my recollection is unclear and Mauro does not name his source); Elena Kagan, "For Justice Marshall," *Texas Law Review* 71 (May 1993): 1125, 1129.

13. Powell to Marshall, March 17, 1977, Brennan Papers, box 444, file 9 (Casteneda v. Partida); draft opinion, Marshall Papers, box 482, file 4 (Perry v. Leake). The clerk's draft of *Kras* does not survive in Marshall's papers, because his office discarded most preliminary drafts, and I rely on my recollection of the draft as I wrote it.

14. Bench memo, Marshall Papers, box 261, file 1 (Pennhurst State School v. Halderman); TM to conference, March 11, 1981, box 272, file 6, ibid.

15. Meg [Margaret Tahyar] to TM, March 20, 1989, Marshall Papers, box 476, file 10 (Midland Asphalt v. United States).

16. Uncirculated draft, box 113, file 2 (Committee for Pub. Educ. v. Nyquist), ibid.; James [Costello] to TM, June 11, 1991, box 532, file 7 (Pauley v. Bethenergy Mines), ibid.; TM to Rehnquist, June 11, 1991, ibid.

17. SLC [Stephen Carter] to law clerks, undated, Marshall Papers, box 269, file 2 (Kissinger v. Halperin).

18. Geoffrey Stone, "Marshall: He's the Frustrated Conscience of the High Court," *National Law Journal,* Feb. 18, 1980, p. 24.

19. Brennan to TM, March 4, 1985, Marshall Papers, box 369, file 1 (Oregon Dep't of Fish & Wildlife v. Klamath Indian Tribe) (in which Brennan and Marshall were the only dissenters); Brennan to Douglas, Dec. 12, 1974, Brennan Papers, box 334, file 3. For withdrawals from assignments, see TM to Burger, May 3, 1972, box 78, file 3 (Kleindienst v. Mandel), ibid. ("I am convinced that my vote was in error"); TM to Burger, June 1, 1974, box 117, file 2 (Warden v. Marrero), ibid.; TM to Burger, Dec. 13, 1976, box 194, file 3 (Fiallo v. Bell), ibid.; TM to conference, Dec. 20, 1985, box 383, file 4 (South Carolina v.

Catawba Indian Tribe), ibid. For the statistics, see "The Supreme Court, 1967 Term," *Harvard Law Review* 82 (Nov. 1968): 93, 306; "The Supreme Court, 1968 Term," id. 83 (Nov. 1969): 60, 278; "The Supreme Court, 1969 Term," id. 84 (Nov. 1970): 30, 251; "The Supreme Court, 1970 Term," id. 85 (Nov. 1971): 38, 350; "The Supreme Court, 1971 Term," id. 86 (Nov. 1972): 50, 300; "The Supreme Court, 1972 Term," id. 87 (Nov. 1973): 55, 303; "The Supreme Court, 1973 Term," id. 88 (Nov. 1974): 41, 274; "The Supreme Court, 1974 Term," id. 89 (Nov. 1975): 49, 275–81; "The Supreme Court, 1975 Term," id. 90 (Nov. 1976): 56, 276; "The Supreme Court, 1976 Term," id. 91 (Nov. 1977): 70, 295.

20. For the term "least persuaded," see Burger to Blackmun, Oct. 17, 1983, Marshall Papers, box 339, file 1 (Migra v. Warren County School Dist.).

21. Draft opinion, Dec. 9, 1982, box 317, file 5 (U.S. Postal Serv. v. Aikens), ibid.; TM draft dissent, Jan. 11, 1983, ibid.; Rehnquist "alternate draft," Feb. 13, 1983, ibid.; Stevens to Rehnquist, Jan. 4, 1984, box 340, file 13 (McDonough Power Equip. v. Greenwood); Brennan to conference, Jan. 1, 1979, box 231, file 4 (County of Los Angeles v. Davis), ibid.

22. Burger to conference, Feb. 8, 1971, Marshall Papers, box 70, file 4 (Coates v. Cincinnati); draft opinions, March 10 and March 22, 1977, Brennan Papers, box 444, file 5 (Wooley v. Maynard); Powell to Brennan, TM, Blackmun, and Stevens, June 28, 1984, Marshall Papers, box 347, file 14 (Wasman v. United States).

23. Rehnquist to Scalia, Dec. 4, 1990, Marshall Papers, box 528, file 10 (Owen v. Owen); Rehnquist to TM, May 4, 1974, box 130, file 3 (Bellis v. United States), ibid.; Powell to TM, May 7, 1974, ibid.; Stewart to TM, May 8, 1975, ibid.; White and Powell to TM, May 31, 1977, Brennan Papers, box 447, file 9 (Shaffer v. Heitner); draft opinions, Marshall Papers, box 298, file 6 (Ralston v. Robinson); draft opinions, box 350, file 5 (Berkemer v. McCarty), ibid.

24. Meg [Margaret Tahyar] to TM, undated, Marshall Papers, box 469, file 1 (Goldberg v. Sweet); TM note on Stevens draft, Nov. 29, 1988, ibid.; TM to O'Connor, May 22, 1984, box 348, file 13 (California v. Trombetta), ibid.; O'Connor to TM, Nov. 16, 1987, box 443, file 8 (Thompson v. Thompson), ibid.; Scalia to TM, Nov. 17, 1988, id.; Scalia to TM, Nov. 18, 1988, id.; Rehnquist to TM, Dec. 3, 1988, id.; Scalia to TM, Nov. 4, 1986, box 412, file 3 (CalFed v. Guerra), ibid.; TM to Scalia, Dec. 5, 1986, id.; Kennedy to TM, Feb. 21, 1989, box 474, file 3 (Blanton v. Las Vegas), ibid.; TM to Rehnquist, White, and Kennedy, Feb. 28, 1989, id.; Kennedy to TM, March 1, 1989, id.

25. TM to conference, Oct. 26, 1976, Marshall Papers, box 184, file 7 (Estelle v. Gamble); Powell to TM, Dec. 3, 1985, box 384, file 8 (Witters v. Washington Dep't of Serv. for the Blind), ibid.; TM to Powell, Jan. 3, 1986, ibid.; Rehnquist to TM, Jan. 9, 1986, ibid.

26. Terry Eastland, "While Justice Sleeps," *National Review,* April 21, 1989, pp. 24, 26; *see also* Bob Woodward and Scott Armstrong, *The Brethren: Inside the Supreme Court* (New York: Simon & Schuster, 1979), 270 ("Stewart wasn't working too hard. The joke around the Court was that he and Marshall passed each other in the corridor most days just before noon—Stewart on his way to work, Marshall on his way home.").

27. Woodward and Armstrong, *Brethren,* 258–59; Jeffries, *Powell,* 260 (relying on interview with Blackmun).

28. Note on draft opinion, Marshall Papers, box 393, file 9 (ILA v. Davis); note on draft opinion, box 495, file 6 (Smith v. Ohio), ibid.; note on draft dissent, box 342, file 6 (TWA v. Franklin Mint), ibid.; notes on draft dissents, box 362, file 2 (Wallace v. Jaffree), ibid.; notes on draft opinion, box 89, file 4 (Colten v. Kentucky), ibid.; notes on draft opinion, box 387, file 9 (Moran v. Burbine), ibid.; notes on draft opinion, box 322, file 8 (United States v. Grace), ibid.; notes on draft opinion, box 327, file 1 (Solem v. Helm), ibid.; notes on draft

opinion, box 316, file 1 (Larkin v. Grendel's Den), ibid.; notes on submission, box 363, file 1 (Ohio v. Kovacs), ibid.; notes on Rehnquist to conference, Feb. 18, 1987, box 407, file 8, ibid.; conference notes, Brennan Papers, box 668, file 1 (Thomas v. Union Carbide); TM note on draft opinion, Marshall Papers, box 372, file 2 (Thomas v. Union Carbide Agric. Prod. Co.); TM to Brennan, June 24, 1985, ibid, box 372, file 2.

29. Jeffries, *Powell,* 260; Juan Williams, "Marshall's Law," *The Washington Post Magazine,* Jan. 7, 1990, p. 12; Woodward and Armstrong, *Brethren,* 59.

30. Swain v. Alabama, 380 U.S. 202 (1965); Randall Kennedy, "Doing What You Can with What You Have: The Greatness of Justice Marshall," *Georgetown Law Journal* 80 (Aug. 1992): 2081.

31. Kennedy, "Doing What You Can," 2085; McCray v. New York, 461 U.S. 961 (1983).

32. Gilliard v. Mississippi, 464 U.S. 867 (1983).

33. Williams v. Illinois, 466 U.S. 981 (1984); McCray v. Abrams, 576 F. Supp. 1244 (E.D.N.Y. 1983), *aff'd,* 750 F.2d 1113 (2d Cir. 1984).

34. Brennan notes for conference discussion, Brennan Papers, box 718, file 2, (Batson v. Kentucky).

35. Conference notes, box 698, file 5, id.

36. 476 U.S. 79 (1986).

37. Brennan to TM, Feb. 24, 1986, Marshall Papers, box 396, file 8.

38. TM to Brennan, Feb. 28, 1986, ibid.; Tony Mauro, "Marshall Nugget," *Legal Times,* April 25, 1994, p. 11; Kennedy, "Doing What You Can," 2091.

39. Sandra Day O'Connor, "Thurgood Marshall: The Influence of a Raconteur," *Stanford Law Review* 44 (Summer 1992): 1217, 1220, 1218, 1217.

Chapter 4

1. TM, "Law and the Quest for Equality" (the Tyrell Williams Lecture), delivered at the School of Law, Washington University of St. Louis, March 8, 1967; *New York Times,* May 2, 1967, p. 23, col. 5; id., June 7, 1967, p. 37, col. 3.

2. 391 U.S. 430 (1968).

3. Conference notes, William J. Brennan Papers, Manuscript Division, Library of Congress, box 415, file 3 (Green v. New Kent County); Warren to Brennan, May 22, 1968, box 177, file 2, ibid.; Bernard Schwartz, *Swann's Way: The School Busing Case and the Supreme Court* (New York: Oxford University Press, 1986), 59.

4. Briggs v. Elliott, 132 F. Supp. 776 (E.D.S.C. 1955).

5. For a discussion of this strategy, see Mark Tushnet, *Making Civil Rights Law: Thurgood Marshall and the Supreme Court, 1936–1961* (New York: Oxford University Press, 1994), 242–55.

6. 391 U.S. at 437–38.

7. *See* Tushnet, *Making Civil Rights Law,* 192. For a discussion of Black's misgivings in United States v. Montgomery County Board of Educ., 395 U.S. 225 (1969), a year later, see Mark Tushnet, "The Supreme Court and Race Discrimination, 1967–1991: The View from the Marshall Papers," *William & Mary Law Review* 36 (Jan. 1995): 473, 480–81.

8. 386 U.S. 19 (1969).

9. 386 U.S. 1218, 1222 (1969) (Black, Cir. J.).

10. Schwartz, *Swann's Way,* 69–70.

11. Bob Woodward and Scott Armstrong, *The Brethren: Inside the Supreme Court* (New York, Simon & Schuster, 1979), 49–50. Schwartz, *Swann's Way,* 70–86, recounts the

Court's deliberations in detail. For the drafts and memoranda, see box 62, file 1, Thurgood Marshall Papers, Manuscript Division, Library of Congress; Brennan Papers, box 218, file 10.

12. Roger K. Newman, *Hugo Black: A Biography* (New York: Pantheon, 1994), 601.

13. *See* Tushnet, *Making Civil Rights Law,* 264.

14. I believe that Bernard Schwartz misunderstands the Harlan-Marshall position as one that would have given school boards *more* time to desegregate than the Brennan position. Rather, Harlan and Marshall understood desegregation to be more limited than the more expansive interpretations of *Green* might suggest, and they believed that desegregation *as they understood it* could be completed rather quickly.

15. 402 U.S. 1 (1971).

16. History of Memphis school case, Brennan Papers, box 222, file 5; Schwartz, *Swann's Way,* 89–91.

17. Justice Marshall was disqualified because he had been involved in the case as solicitor general, and there was one vacancy on the Court because of Justice Abe Fortas's recent resignation.

18. Burger to conference, March 9, 1970, Marshall Papers, box 57, file 6; history of Memphis school case, Brennan Papers, box 222, file 5; Schwartz, *Swann's Way,* 91.

19. For the background and aftermath of *Swann,* see Davison M. Douglas, *Reading, Writing, and Race: The Desegregation of the Charlotte Schools* (Chapel Hill: University of North Carolina Press, 1995).

20. Swann v. Charlotte-Mecklenburg Bd. of Educ., 243 F. Supp. 667, 670 W.D.N.C. 1965).

21. For a detailed account of the Court's internal deliberations, see Schwartz, *Swann,* 100–184.

22. Conference notes, Brennan Papers, box 419, file 4 (Swann v. Charlotte-Mecklenburg School Dist.).

23. Id.

24. Draft opinion, Brennan Papers, box 241, file 5; Brennan to Burger, March 8, 1971, Marshall Papers, box 71, file 6 (Parker's statement "raised so much trouble for so long a time").

25. Schwartz, *Swann's Way,* 131–32; Burger to Brennan, March 19, 1971, Brennan Papers, box 241, file 6.

26. TM to Burger, March 23, 1971, Marshall Papers, box 71, file 6.

27. Black circulated a proposed dissent, which sharply criticized busing and endorsed neighborhood schools. Schwartz plausibly interprets this dissent as "a bargaining ploy," Schwartz, *Swann's Way,* 179, designed to keep Burger from modifying his opinion even further in the direction Brennan continued to press.

28. 433 U.S. 451 (1972).

29. Burger draft, March 16, 1972, Brennan Papers, box 264, file 6; Stewart draft, May 22, 1972, id.; conference notes, Brennan Papers, box 420, file 5, (Wright v. City of Emporia).

30. Keyes v. School Dist. No. 1, 413 U.S. 189 (1973).

31. Douglas to Brennan, undated, Brennan Papers, box 202, file 3; Black to conference, April 17, 1971, box 227, file 2, ibid.

32. Conference notes, Brennan Papers, box 420B, file 1, (Keyes v. School Dist.).

33. Id.

34. Brennan to conference, April 3, 1973, Brennan Papers, box 285, file 5; John C. Jeffries, Jr., *Justice Lewis F. Powell. Jr.: A Biography* (New York: Scribner's, 1994), 290–98.

35. Brennan to conference, April 3, 1973, Marshall Papers, box 100, file 9; Blackmun to Brennan, May 30, 1973, ibid.

36. Powell proposed dissent from denial of certiorari, Jan. 11, 1979, Marshall Papers, box 245, file 7; Jeffries, *Powell,* 318–30.

37. Docket book, October 1979 Term, Brennan Papers, box 513, file 2.

38. Stevens to conference, Oct. 31, 1979, Marshall Papers, box 245, file 7.

39. Burger to conference, Nov. 2, 1979, ibid.

40. For background on these developments, see J. Harvie Wilkinson, *From* Brown *to* Bakke: *The Supreme Court and School Integration, 1954–1978* (New York: Oxford University Press, 1979).

41. Stewart to conference, Dec. 1, 1972, Jan. 2 and 16, 1973, Brennan Papers, box 279, file 6; Burger to Brennan, May 30, 1973, box 285, file 5, ibid.; Brennan to Burger, May 30, 1973, ibid.

42. Woodward and Armstrong, *Brethren,* 267; conference notes, Brennan Papers, box 420B, file 1 (Richmond School Board v. Bradley).

43. Blackmun to Burger, April 25, 1973, Marshall Papers, box 112, file 3; White memorandum opinion, April 30, 1973, ibid.; White to Brennan, [April 30, 1973], Brennan Papers, box 301, file 3 (attached to typescript of draft).

44. Rehnquist to conference, May 3, 1973, Brennan Papers, box 301, file 3; Burger to conference, May 10, 1973, ibid.; White to Brennan, [April 30, 1973], Brennan Papers, box 301, file 3 (attached to typescript of draft); Blackmun to Rehnquist, May 11, 1973, ibid.

45. Conference notes, Brennan Papers, box 420B, file 1 (Richmond School Board v. Bradley); TM to White, May 10, 1973, Marshall Papers, box 112, file 3.

46. Jeffries, *Powell,* 313–14.

47. 418 U.S. 717 (1974).

48. TM to conference, June 13, 1974, Marshall Papers, box 115, file 15.

49. Milliken v. Bradley, 433 U.S. 267 (1977).

50. Powell to conference, June 18, 1977, Marshall Papers, box 192, file 8.

51. 433 U.S. 406 (1977).

52. Conference notes, Brennan Papers, box 433, file 3 (Dayton Board of Educ. v. Brinkman).

53. Brennan to Rehnquist, June 1, 1977, Marshall Papers, box 193, file 1; Rehnquist to Brennan, June 2, 1977, ibid.; Brennan to Rehnquist, June 3, 1977, ibid.

54. Rehnquist to conference, June 6, 1977, ibid.

55. 433 U.S. at 414, 417, 418.

56. Conference notes, Brennan Papers, box 487, file 3 (Columbus Board of Educ. v. Penick); Dayton Board of Educ. v. Brinkman, 443 U.S. 529 (1979). (*Penick* was a companion case to *Brinkman.*)

57. 498 U.S. 237 (1991).

58. Rehnquist to conference, Nov. 16, 1990, Marshall Papers, box 529, file 4; White to Rehnquist, Dec. 4, 1990, ibid.; O'Connor to Rehnquist, Dec. 4, 1990, ibid.; Rehnquist to White, Dec. 13, 1990, ibid.

59. Justice David Souter did not participate in the decision, because the case had been argued a week before he took his seat.

60. 451 U.S. 100 (1981).

61. SLC [Stephen Carter], bench memo, Marshall Papers, box 261, file 1 (Memphis v. Greene).

62. The dissent was joined by Brennan and Blackmun.

63. Jeffries, *Powell,* 331.

Chapter 5

1. The Slaughterhouse Cases, 83 U.S. (16 Wall.) 36, 81 (1873); Buck v. Bell, 274 U.S. 200, 208 (1927).

2. "Marshall: He's the Frustrated Conscience of the High Court," *National Law Journal*, Feb. 18, 1980, p. 24.

3. Fifth Ave. Coach Co. v. New York, 221 U.S. 467 (1911).

4. Lochner v. New York, 198 U.S. 45 (1905); Adkins v. Children's Hosp., 261 U.S. 525 (1923).

5. Railway Express Agency v. New York, 336 U.S. 106 (1949); Williamson v. Lee Optical, 348 U.S. 483 (1955).

6. United States v. Carolene Prods., 304 U.S. 144, 153 n.4 (1938).

7. 316 U.S. 535 (1942).

8. *See* Susan Lawrence, *The Poor in Court: The Legal Services Program and Supreme Court Decision Making* (Princeton: Princeton University Press, 1990); Martha Davis, *Brutal Need: Lawyers and the Welfare Rights Movement, 1960–1973* (New Haven: Yale University Press, 1993).

9. John C. Jeffries, Jr., *Justice Lewis F. Powell, Jr.: A Biography* (New York: Scribner's, 1994), 347.

10. 408 U.S. 92 (1972).

11. 405 U.S. 330 (1972).

12. Powell and Rehnquist, who had been recently appointed to the Court, did not participate.

13. For a general discussion, see Frances Piven and Richard Cloward, *Poor Peoples' Movements: Why They Succeed, How They Fail* (New York: Pantheon, 1977), 271–95.

14. 397 U.S. 471 (1970).

15. Conference notes, William J. Brennan Papers, Manuscript Division, Library of Congress, box 420B, file 1 (San Antonio School Dist. v. Rodriguez).

16. 411 U.S. 1 (1973).

17. "On Marshall's Conception of Equality," *Stanford Law Review* 44 (Summer 1992): 1267, 1269, 1268, 1270.

18. "For Justice Marshall," *Texas Law Review* 71 (May 1993): 1125, 1129; 487 U.S. 450 (1988).

19. Marshall's dissent was joined by Brennan. Stevens and Blackmun also dissented.

20. Harris v. McRae, 448 U.S. 297 (1980).

21. Conference notes, Brennan Papers, box 515, file 5 (Harris v. McRae).

22. Zablocki v. Redhail, 434 U.S. 374 (1978). Only Rehnquist dissented, although Stewart, Powell, and Stevens wrote opinions concurring only in the result.

23. Reed v. Reed, 404 U.S. 71 (1971).

24. 411 U.S. 677 (1973).

25. Conference notes, Brennan Papers, box 420B, file 3 (Frontiero v. Laird); Bob Woodward and Scott Armstrong, *The Brethren: Inside the Supreme Court* (New York: Simon & Schuster, 1979), 254. Woodward and Armstrong erroneously state that Burger was in the majority and that he assigned the opinion to Brennan.

26. Brennan to conference, Feb. 14, 1973, Thurgood Marshall Papers, Manuscript Division, Library of Congress, box 109, file 8; TM note on draft, undated, ibid.; White to Brennan, Feb. 15, 1973, ibid.; Stewart to Brennan, Feb. 16, 1973, ibid.

27. Burger to Brennan, March 7, 1973, Brennan Papers, box 298, file 1; Powell to Brennan, March 2, 1973, box 297, file 1, ibid.

28. Douglas to Brennan, March 3, 1973, Brennan Papers, box 298, file 1; Brennan to Powell, March 6, 1973, ibid.

29. Woodward and Armstrong, *Brethren*, 255.

30. Craig v. Boren, 429 U.S. 190 (1976); Burger to Brennan, Oct. 18, 1976, Marshall Papers, box 182, file 7; Burger to Brennan, Nov. 11, 1976, ibid.; Burger to Brennan, Oct. 15, 1976, ibid.

31. Powell to Brennan, Dec. 6, 1976, Brennan Papers, box 439, file 5.

32. Conference notes, box 545, file 4 (Rostker v. Goldberg), ibid.

33. Rostker v. Goldberg, 453 U.S. 57 (1981). Brennan joined both dissents.

34. Powell to Brennan, Dec. 6, 1976, Brennan Papers, box 439, file 5.

35. 427 U.S. 307 (1976).

36. "The Supreme Court, 1971 Term—Foreword: In Search of Evolving Doctrine on a Changing Court: A Model for a Newer Equal Protection," *Harvard Law Review* 86 (Nov. 1972): 1, 18–20.

37. Rehnquist to Brennan, Jan. 30, 1976, Marshall Papers, box 165, file 8.

38. Brennan to Rehnquist, Feb. 9, 1976, ibid.

39. Brennan to conference, Feb. 12, 1976, ibid.; Blackmun to Brennan, March 11, 1976, ibid.

40. Brennan to Rehnquist, Feb. 9, 1976, ibid.; Blackmun to Brennan, March 11, 1976, ibid.; Powell draft opinion, April 7, 1976, ibid.

41. Powell draft opinion, April 7, 1976, ibid.; Powell to conference, May 19, 1976, id.

42. Rehnquist to Powell, May 25, 1976, ibid.

43. Powell to conference, May 19, 1976, ibid.; Powell to conference, June 7, 1976, ibid.; Rehnquist to Powell, June 9, 1976, ibid.

44. Powell to conference, June 15, 1976, ibid.

45. *See, e.g.,* Powell to Rehnquist, Nov. 10, 1980, Brennan Papers, box 555, file 2 (United States Railroad Retirement Board v. Fritz) (mentioning "getting caught in a 'cross-fire'" in *Murgia*); Powell to Brennan, Dec. 14, 1979, box 523, file 6 (United States v. Crews), ibid. ("This case reminds me a little bit of *Murgia*"); Powell to Stevens, April 12, 1978, box 474, file 7 (McAdams v. McSurely), ibid. ("I have already spent as much time on this 'loser' as Bill Brennan and I did a couple of years ago in *Murgia*"); *see also* Stevens to Rehnquist, Jan. 4, 1977, Marshall Papers, box 183, file 12 ("Possible we have another *Murgia*").

46. Powell to conference, June 15, 1976, Marshall Papers, box 183, file 12; Jeffries, *Powell*, 425.

47. Rehnquist to Blackmun, June 7, 1976, Brennan Papers, box 391, file 8; Burger to Powell, April 1, 1976, box 390, file 4, ibid.; Powell to Brennan, June 17, 1976, box 376, file 1, ibid.; Burger draft opinion, Nov. 19, 1981, Marshall Papers, box 289, file 7 (Citizens Against Rent Control v. Berkeley); O'Connor to Burger, Nov. 19, 1981, ibid.

48. 473 U.S. 432 (1985).

49. Conference notes, Brennan Papers, box 668, file 1 (City of Cleburne v. Cleburne Living Center).

50. Id.; Powell to White, June 5, 1985, Marshall Papers, box 371, file 11; Rehnquist to White, June 5, 1985, ibid.

51. White to Powell, June 6, 1985, ibid.; Powell to White, June 7, 1985, ibid.; Powell to Brennan, June 10, 1985, ibid.

52. In *Rodriguez*, White wrote a dissenting opinion joined by Douglas and Brennan. White argued that the school-finance system in Texas did not satisfy the "rational basis" test, primarily because state law placed a cap on local property tax rates; as a result, people

in some property-poor districts could not fund their schools at a level equal to that in other districts. Marshall's opinion contained a footnote agreeing with the substance of White's analysis but suggesting that "the care with which he scrutinizes the practical effectiveness" of the system "reflects the application of a more stringent standard of review" than the "rational basis" test.

Chapter 6

1. William Bradford Reynolds, "In Honor of *Brown v. Board of Education:* Individualism v. Group Rights: The Legacy of *Brown,*" *Yale Law Journal* 93 (May 1984): 995.

2. Transcript, TM press conference, June 28, 1991; Gloria Branker, interview with author, Washington, D.C., Jan. 30, 1991 (describing reactions in NAACP office to Marshall's second marriage); Cass Sunstein, "On Marshall's Conception of Equality," *Stanford Law Review* 44 (Summer 1992): 1267, 1270–74.

3. Exec. Order No. 10,925, 26 Fed. Reg. 1977 (1961); id. No. 11,246, 30 Fed. Reg. 12,327 (1965). For the background of these orders, see Hugh Davis Graham, *The Civil Rights Era: Origins and Development of National Policy, 1960–1972* (New York: Oxford University Press, 1990), 27–43, 186–89.

4. The affiliation with the Progressive Party is stated in the opinion of the Court in Hughes v. Superior Court, 339 U.S. 460 (1950); on the affiliation with the NAACP, see TM to C. Brown, Oct. 25, 1949, NAACP Papers, Manuscript Division, Library of Congress, box II-B-87, file: Labor, California, Hughes v. Superior Court, 1947–50. For a study of the *Hughes* case, see Paul Moreno, "Direct Action and Fair Employment: The *Hughes* Case," *Western Legal History* (forthcoming).

5. Hughes v. Superior Court, 32 Cal. 2d 850, 198 P.2d 885 (1948).

6. White to Committee on Administration, Nov. 16, 1946, NAACP Papers, box II-A-201, file: Communism, General, 1940–April 1947; Noah Griffin to TM, June 3, 1947, box II-B-87, file: Labor, California, Hughes v. Superior Court, 1947–50, ibid.; TM to Griffin, June 13, 1947, id.

7. Perry to Clarence Mitchell, Feb. 18, 1948, NAACP Papers, box II-B-87, file: Labor, California, Hughes v. Superior Court, 1947–50; Poole to TM, Jan. 10, 1949, id.; Greenberg to Legal Department, Nov. 3, 1949, id.; Loren Miller to TM, Oct. 27, 1949, id.

8. Thornhill v. Alabama, 310 U.S. 88 (1940); Giboney v. Empire Storage & Ice Co., 336 U.S. 490 (1949).

9. James v. Marinship Corp., 25 Cal. 2d 721, 155 P.2d 329 (1944).

10. Hughes, 198 P.2d at 889, Carter, dissenting, 198 P. 2d at 895, Traynor, dissenting at 896.

11. 339 U.S. at 464. As one of Justice Clark's law clerks noted, Frankfurter's description of California's policy made it clear that he, and the Court, disapproved of proportional hiring. The clerk prepared a dissent, which Clark decided not to file, saying that Frankfurter was suggesting that California had "establish[ed] an F.E.P.C. under the aegis of the judiciary" and "doubt[ing] that the N.A.A.C.P. would urge reversal if this were true." Larry Tolan to Clark, April 13, 1950, Tom C. Clark Papers, Tarlton Library, University of Texas Law School, box A-3, folder 1; draft dissent (Hughes v. Superior Court), ibid. Three justices concurred in the result, disagreeing with Frankfurter's general statements about picketing as free speech. 399 U.S. at 469 (Black & Minton, JJ., concurring in judgment; Reed, J., concurring). A law clerk to Chief Justice Vinson also drafted a dissent, which went unused, on the free-speech question.

12. 339 U.S. at 468.

13. TM, Speech to National Dental Association Convention, Aug. 8, 1951, NAACP Papers, box II-A-535, file: Speakers, Thurgood Marshall, General, May–Sept. 1950; Bernard Taper, "A Reporter at Large: A Meeting in Atlanta," *The New Yorker,* March 17, 1956, pp. 93–95.

14. Bernard Schwartz, *Swann's Way: The School Busing Case and the Supreme Court* (New York: Oxford University Press, 1986), 124.

15. 401 U.S. at 16.

16. Carnegie Foundation report quoted in Stephen C. Halpern, *On the Limits of the Law: The Ironic Legacy of Title VI of the 1964 Civil Rights Act* (Baltimore: Johns Hopkins University Press, 1995), 183; polling data cited in Thomas Ferguson and Joel Rogers, *Right Turn: The Decline of the Democrats and the Future of American Politics* (New York: Hill & Wang, 1986), 17; Anne Fisher, "Businessmen Like to Hire by Numbers," *Fortune,* Sept. 16, 1985, p. 26; Neal Devins, *"Adarand Constructors, Inc. v. Pena* and the Continuing Irrelevance of Supreme Court Affirmative Action Decisions," *William & Mary L. Rev.* 37 (Winter 1996): 673.

17. 533 P.2d. 1152 (Cal. 1976).

18. The Court's internal processes are detailed in Bernard Schwartz, *Behind* Bakke: *Affirmative Action and the Supreme Court* (New York: New York University Press, 1988).

19. Id. at 44.

20. *See* Schwartz, *Behind* Bakke, 167–72.

21. White to conference, Oct. 13, 1977, Marshall Papers, box 204, file 3.

22. *See* Schwartz, *Behind* Bakke, 175–94.

23. Conference notes, Brennan Papers, box 421, file 6 (DeFunis v. Odegaard).

24. Conference notes, ibid. box 456, file 1 (University of Cal. v. Bakke).

25. Bernard Schwartz notes that Powell's memorandum "was virtually identical" with the opinion he published. Schwartz, *Behind* Bakke, 81.

26. John C. Jeffries, Jr., *Justice Lewis F. Powell, Jr.: A Biography* (New York: Scribner's, 1994), 469, 478.

27. Marshall's copy of Powell draft, May 9, 1978, Marshall Papers, box 203, file 7.

28. Jeffries, *Powell,* 484.

29. Schwartz, *Behind* Bakke, 87.

30. Id. at 227–44.

31. Id. at 93–98.

32. Jeffries, *Powell,* 487–88; draft history of *Bakke,* Brennan Papers, box 464, file 5; Civil Rights Cases, 109 U.S. 3 (1883). For an explanation of the history's authorship, see David to Brennan, July 28, 1978, ibid. The history is written in Brennan's voice; it offers Brennan's law clerks' interpretation of the events inside the Court.

33. Schwartz, *Behind* Bakke, 105.

34. Id. at 112.

35. Jeffries, *Powell,* 489; Schwartz, *Behind* Bakke, 127. Schwartz offers various tactical accounts of what happened—for example, that Brennan was reluctant to prod Blackmun too forcefully out of fear that Blackmun would out of irritation vote against allowing race to be taken into account—but in my view the more plausible interpretation of what happened is simply that people got impatient because the Court's work was moving along too slowly. *See* id. at 121–23.

36. Undated draft of memorandum circulated April 13, 1978, Marshall Papers, box 204, file 2.

37. TM draft, April 13, 1978, Marshall Papers, box 204, file 1.

38. Schwartz, *Behind* Bakke, 129. The draft history, box 464, file 4, says that Brennan

asked Marshall, "If —— (TM's son) were a candidate for admission to medical school, he thought it would be proper for school administrators to accord his application special consideration because of his race." Marshall responded, "Damn right, they owe us."

39. Schwartz, *Behind* Bakke, 247–59.

40. Draft history, Brennan Papers, box 464, file 5 (University of California v. Bakke); White to Brennan, June 13, 1978, box 466, file 2, ibid. The draft history of *Bakke* has an elaborate and self-centered account of Brennan's decision to draft the principal dissent himself rather than to rely on White and some overdramatic statements treating minor flaps of a sort not unusual in the Court as major events. The draft history makes it clear that these flaps went away quickly and suggests that, to the extent there are explanations for their disappearance, they lie in Brennan's talents as a peacemaker and opinion writer. In my view, the events were quite ordinary and do not show much about anything other than routine operation inside the Court.

41. Jeffries, *Powell,* 491–92.

42. Id. at 139–41; White to Brennan, undated, Brennan Papers, box 464, file 5.

43. "Address to the Judicial Conference of the Second Circuit," 115 F.R.D. 349, 351–52 (1987).

44. Draft history, Brennan Papers, box 464, file 5; Gerald Gunther, "The Supreme Court, 1971 Term—Foreword: In Search of Evolving Doctrine on a Changing Court: A Model for a Newer Equal Protection," *Harvard Law Review* 86 (Nov. 1972): 1, 8.

45. PPF [Philip Frickey], bench memo, Marshall Papers, box 239, file 9 (Fullilove v. Kreps).

46. 448 U.S. 448 (1980).

47. Conference notes, Brennan Papers, box 513, file 2 (Fullilove v. Kreps).

48. Id.

49. Brennan and Marshall to Burger, June 4, 1980 (draft), Marshall Papers, box 248, file 8.

50. Powell to Burger, June 5, 1980, ibid.; Blackmun to Burger, June 9, 1980, ibid.; Burger to conference, June 9, 1980, ibid.

51. Brennan and Marshall to conference, June 17, 1980, ibid.; Burger to conference, June 18, 1980, ibid.

52. 448 U.S. at 520, 522.

53. Id. at 495–96.

54. One of Brennan's law clerks described some aspects of the daily discussions in the chambers about *Bakke* and referred explicitly to concern about the "signal" the Court's decision would send. Whit Peters to Brennan, Oct. 14, 1977, Brennan Papers, box 465, file 2.

55. 424 U.S. 747 (1976).

56. Id. at 788–89.

57. Conference notes, Brennan Papers, box 605, file 2 (Boston Firefighters v. Castro); Brennan to conference, Feb. 11, 1976, Marshall Papers, box 162, file 5; Powell to conference, Feb. 12, 1976, ibid.; Marshall to conference, Feb. 16, 1976, ibid.; Powell to Brennan, undated, Brennan Papers, box 373, file 1.

58. 476 U.S. 267 (1986).

59. Conference notes, Brennan Papers, box 695, file 10 (Wygant v. Jackson Board of Educ.).

60. Marshall draft, Feb. 5, 1986, Marshall Papers, box 386, file 9; Brennan to Marshall, Feb. 6, 1986, box 387, file 1, ibid.

61. 476 U.S. 267 (1986).

62. The latter point was the burden of O'Connor's opinion concurring only in the result on this question. Id. at 294.

63. 488 U.S. 469 (1991).

64. CS [Carol Steiker], bench memo, no. 87–998, Marshall Papers, box 429, file 4.

65. 476 U.S. at 282.

66. 478 U.S. 421 (1986).

67. Conference notes, Brennan Papers, box 695, file 11 (Local 28 v. EEOC); Powell to Burger, March 6, 1986, box 390, file 1, Marshall Papers; Brennan to Powell, May 25, 1986, Brennan Papers, box 710, file 7; Powell to Brennan, May 30, 1986, ibid.; 478 U.S. at 488 (Powell, J., concurring).

68. 427 U.S. 273 (1976).

69. Id. at 281 n.8.

70. Stevens to Marshall, June 14, 1976, Marshall Papers, box 171, file 13; Marshall to Stevens, June 15, 1976, ibid.

71. 478 U.S. 501 (1986).

72. 478 U.S. at 488.

73. Powell to Burger, March 6, 1986, Marshall Papers, box 392, file 4.

74. Burger to conference, March 10, 1986, ibid.; Powell to Brennan, June 20, 1986, ibid.; Brennan revised drafts, June 22 and 26, 1986, ibid.; Powell to Brennan, June 26, 1986, ibid.; O'Connor to Brennan, June 26, 1986, ibid.

75. United States v. Paradise, 480 U.S. 149 (1987).

76. Stevens to Brennan, Dec. 12, 1986, Marshall Papers, box 415, file 1; *see also* Paradise, 480 U.S. at 193.

77. 488 U.S. 469 (1989).

78. Id. at 495–96.

79. O'Connor's opinion argued that *Fullilove* was inapposite because the Court there found the statute constitutional as an exercise of a particularly important power given to Congress to enforce the antidiscrimination provisions of the Fourteenth Amendment. States, she argued, did not have that particularly important power given to them by the national Constitution and indeed were the targets of the Fourteenth Amendment. Id. at 490–91. Marshall argued in response that it was bizarre to interpret the Fourteenth Amendment as depriving states of a power, derived ultimately from the inherent rights of sovereignty, to take exactly the same action that Congress could under the Fourteenth Amendment. Id. at 546.

80. Scalia refused to join the portions of O'Connor's plurality opinion that suggested some ways to satisfy strict scrutiny that he believed would uphold affirmative action programs too frequently.

81. 497 U.S. 547 (1990).

82. Brennan draft, May 31, 1990, Marshall Papers, box 508, file 8; Brennan revised draft, June 15, 1990, box 508, file 9, ibid.; O'Connor to conference, June 18, 1990, ibid.

83. Juan Williams, "Marshall's Law," *Washington Post Magazine,* Jan. 7, 1990, p. 28.

Chapter 7

1. TM, interview with author, Washington, D.C., May 23, 1989. For a discussion of the *Crawford* case, see Mark Tushnet, *The NAACP's Legal Strategy Against Segregated Education, 1925–1950* (Chapel Hill: University of North Carolina Press, 1987), 39–41; for a discussion of the *Lyons* case, see Mark Tushnet, *Making Civil Rights Law: Thurgood Marshall and the Supreme Court, 1936–1961* (New York: Oxford University Press, 1994), 61–64.

2. David Von Drehle, *Among the Lowest of the Dead: The Culture of Death Row* (New York: Random House, 1995), provides an account of this guerilla war in Florida.

3. James Alan Fox et al., "Death Penalty Opinion in the Post-*Furman* Years," *New York University Review of Law & Social Change* 18 (1990–91): 499, 517; Weems v. United States, 217 U.S. 349 (1910); Trop v. Dulles, 356 U.S. 86 (1958).

4. Rudolph v. Alabama, 375 U.S. 889 (1963); William J. Brennan, "Constitutional Adjudication and the Death Penalty," *Harvard Law Review* 100 (Dec. 1986): 313, 314; Samuel Gross and Robert Mauro, *Death and Discrimination: Racial Disparities in Capital Sentencing* (Boston: Northeastern University Press, 1989), 122.

5. For an overview of the litigation campaign, see Michael Meltsner, *Cruel and Unusual: The Supreme Court and Capital Punishment* (New York: Random House, 1973). My account draws on my book *Constitutional Issues: The Death Penalty* (New York: Facts on File, 1994).

6. Conference notes, William J. Brennan Papers, Manuscript Division, Library of Congress, box 415, file 4 (Witherspoon v. Illinois); Witherspoon v. Illinois, 391 U.S. 510 (1968).

7. Conference notes on first argument, Brennan Papers, box 417, file 5.

8. Tushnet, *Death Penalty*, 37–38; Douglas draft opinion, Brennan Papers, box 197, file 3 (Maxwell v. Bishop) (with extensive markings); Douglas to conference, April 4, 1969, Thurgood Marshall Papers, Manuscript Division, Library of Congress, box 57, file 13.

9. Tushnet, *Death Penalty*, 38–39; Fortas to Douglas, April 7, 1969, Marshall Papers, box 57, file 13; Marshall to Fortas, April 21, 1969, ibid.

10. Conference notes on reargument, Brennan Papers, box 417, file 5.

11. Tushnet, *Death Penalty*, 39–40; Maxwell v. Bishop, 398 U.S. 262 (1970). More detail on the Court's deliberations is in Bernard Schwartz, *The Unpublished Opinions of the Warren Court* (New York: Oxford University Press, 1985), ch. 10.

12. McGautha v. California, 402 U.S. 183 (1971).

13. Douglas to conference, June 3, 1971, Marshall Papers, box 64, file 5; Douglas to conference, June 1971, box 63, file 6, ibid.; Douglas proposed dissent, June 18, 1971, box 65, file 4 (Aikens v. California), ibid.

14. One of the murder cases was dropped after the California Supreme Court held that capital punishment violated the state constitution.

15. Tushnet, *Death Penalty*, 46–47; Mike Becker to Brennan, July 26, 1971, Brennan Papers, box 271, file 5.

16. Memorandum on death cases, April 12, 1972, Brennan Papers, box 271, file 2; Benjamin Heineman, Jr., to author, Aug. 22, 1994.

17. Conference notes, Brennan Papers, box 420A, file 4 (Aikens v. California).

18. Furman v. Georgia, 408 U.S. 238 (1972). Marshall's opinion begins on page 314 and ends on page 371, with three appendices presenting statistics about the imposition of the death penalty.

19. Bob Woodward and Scott Armstrong, *The Brethren: Inside the Supreme Court* (New York: Simon & Schuster, 1979), 219.

20. Conference notes, Brennan Papers, box 429, file 5 (Jurek v. Texas).

21. Tushnet, *Death Penalty*, 56–57.

22. Id. at 57.

23. Id.; John C. Jeffries, *Justice Lewis F. Powell, Jr.: A Biography* (New York: Scribner's, 1994), 426; Burger to conference, May 4, 1976, Brennan Papers, box 363, file 5; Stewart to Burger, May 7, 1976, Marshall Papers, box 156, file 4; Burger to conference, May 5, 1976, Brennan Papers, box 362, file 8.

24. Roberts v. Louisiana, 428 U.S. 325 (1976); Gregg v. Georgia, 428 U.S. 153 (1976).

25. 472 U.S. 320 (1985).

26. Marshall dissented five years later when the Court held that, because *Caldwell* developed a "new rule" of constitutional law, it did not apply to defendants whose con-

victions had become final before 1985. Sawyer v. Smith, 497 U.S. 227 (1990). His dissent argued that misleading comments by the prosecutor made the outcome "fundamentally unfair" and unreliable. His opinion concluded, somewhat bitterly, with the observation that the decision "is yet another indication that this Court is less concerned with safeguarding constitutional rights than with speeding defendants, deserving or not, to the executioner."

27. Conference notes, Brennan Papers, box 698, file 7 (Ford v. Wainwright); Powell to TM, June 5, 1986, Marshall Papers, box 397, file 12.

28. Powell to TM, June 5, 1986, ibid.; TM to Powell, June 16, 1986, ibid.

29. 477 U.S. 399 (1986). Rehnquist, joined by Burger, argued that the common law prohibition against executing the insane did not establish the existence of a similar constitutional right, an argument with which O'Connor, writing separately and joined by White, agreed. Because four justices found no constitutional violation in executing an insane prisoner, Powell's, not Marshall's, description of the required procedures, probably represents the current state of the law on the question.

30. 470 U.S. 68 (1985).

31. Burger to TM, Dec. 18, 1984, Marshall Papers, box 373, file 10; Burger to TM, Dec. 27, 1984, ibid.

32. Powell to TM, Dec. 19, 1984, ibid.; O'Connor to TM, Dec. 18, 1984, ibid.; Stevens to TM, Dec. 19, 1984, ibid.

33. TM to colleagues, Jan. 3, 1985, ibid.; Burger to TM, Jan. 3, 1985, ibid.; Stevens to TM, Jan. 3, 1985, ibid.; TM to Burger, Jan. 8, 1985, ibid.

34. 484 U.S. 231 (1988).

35. 463 U.S. 1237 (1983).

36. The Court revisited one aspect of *Witherspoon* when it rejected the argument that death-qualified juries were biased in favor of conviction. Lockhart v. McCree, 476 U.S. 162 (1986). *Witherspoon* said that the empirical studies supporting that argument were too "tentative and fragmentary." 391 U.S. 510, 517 (1968). Death penalty litigators developed additional studies, but in *McCree* the Court found them insufficient, too. Because the Court had extended *Witherspoon,* which involved a statute disqualifying jurors, to decisions by prosecutors to disqualify jurors for cause, *Lockhart v. McCree* affected a rather large number of cases in which defendants claimed that prosecutors had improperly excluded one or more jurors.

37. Andrews v. Shulsen, 485 U.S. 919 (1988).

38. 481 U.S. 279 (1987).

39. Powell to conference, June 27, 1986, Marshall Papers, box 378, file 4.

40. James F. Simon, *The Center Holds: The Power Struggle Inside the Rehnquist Court* (New York: Simon & Schuster, 1995), 179–80; Scalia to conference, Jan. 6, 1987, Marshall Papers, box 425, file 8.

41. Stephen L. Carter, "Thurgood Marshall," *Valparaiso Law Review* 26 (Fall 1991): xxxv, xxxviii; Brennan to TM, Blackmun, and Stevens, Oct. 17, 1986, Marshall Papers, box 425, file 7; Randall L. Kennedy, *"McCleskey v. Kemp:* Race, Capital Punishment, and the Supreme Court," *Harvard Law Review* 101 (May 1988): 1388, 1418 n.142.

42. Simon, *Center Holds,* 184–86.

43. McCleskey v. Zant, 499 U.S. 467 (1991); bench memo, Marshall Papers, box 514, file 3 (McCleskey v. Zant) (TM note refers to "Holmes [*sic;* actually Cardozo] statement about the stumble of the constable"); Stevens to TM, April 3, 1991, box 538, file 4, ibid.; TM to Stevens, April 3, 1991, ibid.

44. Simon, *Center Holds,* 220–22.

Chapter 8

1. 481 U.S. 279 (1987). The final large-scale challenges to capital punishment sought to invalidate death sentences imposed on people who were minors when they killed their victims and on people who were mentally retarded. The Court held that defendants could point to their age and mental retardation as mitigating circumstances but that there was no absolute constitutional bar to imposing the death sentence on sixteen-year-olds or the mentally retarded. Stanford v. Kentucky, 492 U.S. 361 (1989); Penry v. Lynaugh, 492 U.S. 302 (1989).

2. David O'Brien, *Storm Center: The Supreme Court in American Politics*, 3d ed., (New York: W. W. Norton, 1993), 246–55.

3. TM to conference, probably March 20, 1986, William J. Brennan Papers, Manuscript Division, Library of Congress, box 719, file 16.

4. Coleman v. Balkcom, 451 U.S. 949 (1981).

5. Id. at 950–51. The shifting votes are shown in Brennan Papers, box 549, file 4.

6. Powell to Burger, Jan. 31, 1984, Brennan Papers, box 640, file 4.

7. White to conference, May 19, 1986, Thurgood Marshall Papers, Manuscript Division, Library of Congress, box 378, file 3.

8. Wainwright v. Adams, 466 U.S. 964, 965–66 (1984); TM memorandum to files, May 9, 1984, Marshall Papers, box 330, file 3. Details on Adams's crime are provided in David Von Drehle, *Among the Lowest of the Dead: The Culture of Death Row* (New York: Random House, 1995), 241–51.

9. Tony Mauro, "Courtside: Reading Between Blackmun's Lines," *The Recorder*, March 2, 1994, p. 7 (quoting Blackmun's law clerk Pamela Karlen).

10. Darden v. Wainwright, 477 U.S. 168, 179–80 (1986).

11. Darden v. Florida, 430 U.S. 704 (1977).

12. Powell to colleagues, Sept. 4, 1985, Brennan Papers box 700, file 7; Darden v. Wainwright, 473 U.S. 929 (1985) (Burger, C.J., dissenting). Blackmun wrote that he "knew of no other recent case in which a Justice has dissented [from a grant of review] on the ground that the claims raised by the petitioner—which at least four Justices must have found worthy of full consideration—were meritless." Darden v. Wainwright, 477 U.S. at 205 n.9 (Blackmun, J., dissenting). After hearing argument, the Court rejected Darden's claims by the same 5–4 vote that occurred earlier. Darden was executed on March 15, 1988. Blackmun sent a statement on the execution (published as Darden v. Dugger, 485 U.S. 943 (1988) (Blackmun, J., dissenting)) to Brennan, Marshall, and Stevens with a cover note saying, "For what it is worth (and it will not be worth very much). . . ." Blackmun to Brennan et al., Jan. 21, 1988, Marshall Papers, box 435, file 6.

13. Powell to colleagues, Sept. 4, 1985, Brennan Papers, box 700, file 7.

14. Brennan to conference, Sept. 6, 1985, Marshall Papers, box 355, file 10; Blackmun to conference, Sept. 10, 1984, ibid.

15. Rehnquist to conference, Sept. 9, 1985, ibid.; Burger to conference, Sept. 10, 1985, ibid.; Stevens to conference, Sept. 12, 1985, ibid.

16. Brennan to conference, Sept. 19, 1985, ibid.

17. Burger to Brennan, Sept. 28, 1985, box 354, file 6, ibid.; Brennan to Burger, Sept. 28, 1985, ibid.; TM to conference, Nov. 29, 1985, box 354, file 8, ibid.

18. Powell to conference, March 6, 1986, Brennan Papers, box 719, file 16; Burger to conference, March 4, 1986, ibid. After Burger and Powell retired, Kennedy and White continued the practice. Kennedy to conference, Sept. 14, 1988, Marshall Papers, box 436, file 7; White to conference, Nov. 29, 1989, box 492, file 7, ibid. ("Since there are four votes to grant . . . I shall change my vote and make a fifth to grant a stay").

19. TM to Burger, March 4, 1986, Marshall Papers, box 395, file 4.

20. Powell to conference, March 3, 1986, Brennan Papers, box 719, file 16; Brennan to conference, March 3, 1986, ibid.

21. Powell to conference, March 6, 1986, ibid.

22. Burger to conference, March 20, 1986, ibid.

23. Marshall to conference, probably March 20, 1986, ibid.

24. Burger to conference, March 25, 1986 (two memoranda), ibid.

25. The procedural history is laid out in Dugger v. Adams, 489 U.S. 401 (1989).

26. Burger to Powell, Jan. 13, 1984, Marshall Papers, box 334, file 1; Burger to Powell, March 20, 1986, Brennan Papers, box 700, file 10; Brennan to conference, March 20, 1986, ibid. (marked "not circulated—for histories").

27. 463 U.S. 880 (1983).

28. *Barefoot* raised another issue. To show that Barefoot posed a continuing threat to society, two psychiatrists testified that he would probably commit violent acts in the future. Although the majority appeared to agree that this sort of psychiatric testimony was probably quite unreliable, the majority said that it was "not persuaded . . . that the factfinder and the adversary system will not be competent to uncover, recognize, and take due account of its shortcomings." Marshall joined a dissenting opinion by Blackmun dealing with this issue.

29. 468 U.S. 1231 (1984). For details on Dobbert, see Von Drehle, *Among the Lowest of the Dead,* 251–55.

30. TM dissent, May 11, 1987, Marshall Papers, box 408, file 1 (Texas v. Williams); Blackmun to conference, May 12, 1987, id.; Texas v. Williams, 484 U.S. 816 (1987).

31. Draft dissent, Nov. 7, 1986, Marshall Papers, box 410, file 6; Truesdale v. Aiken, 480 U.S. 527 (1987); conference notes, Brennan Papers, box 698, file 5 (Turner v. Sielaff); Turner v. Murray, 476 U.S. 28 (1986).

32. Rehnquist to conference, Feb. 14, 1990, Marshall Papers, box 493, file 2; TM to conference, Nov. 15, 1990, box 523, file 4, ibid.

33. 498 U.S. 908 (1990).

34. Rehnquist to conference, May 23, 1991, Marshall Papers, box 525, file 1.

35. 501 U.S. 808 (1991).

36. To ensure that the Court would be able to function effectively over the summer— for example, to have a justice available to deal with applications for stays—Marshall said that he would retire when a successor was qualified. He formally retired on October 1, 1991.

37. Booth v. Maryland, 482 U.S. 496 (1987).

38. Bench memo, Marshall Papers, box 399, file 6 (Booth v. Maryland) (TM note: "G[len Darbyshire] said we will win!!!"); South Carolina v. Gathers, 490 U.S. 805 (1989); O'Connor draft, June 3, 1989, Marshall Papers, box 478, file 9; Scalia draft, June 7, 1989, ibid.; Kennedy to Scalia, June 7, 1989, ibid.; O'Connor to Scalia, June 7, 1989, ibid.

39. For a discussion, see Anthony Lewis, *Gideon's Trumpet* (New York: Random House, 1964).

40. *See, e.g.,* Benner v. Ohio, 494 U.S. 1090 (1990).

41. For a version of the criticism, see Leonard Levy, *Original Intent and the Framers' Constitution* (New York: Macmillan, 1988), 372–73: "What makes this humane opinion so arrogant is that Brennan knows that the Fifth Amendment three times assumes the legitimacy of the death penalty. . . . Moreover, he understands that a majority of his countrymen and his fellow Justices disagree with his opinion. . . . No one has a right to veto the Constitution because his moral reasoning leads him to disagree with it in so clear a case. Brennan and Thurgood Marshall corrupt the judicial process and dis-

credit it." *See also* Wallace Mendelson, "Brennan's Revolution," *Commentary* 91 (Feb. 1991): 36.

42. *See* Edwin Meese, "The Law of the Constitution," *Tulane Law Review* 61 (April 1987): 979.

43. Many liberal supporters of Justices Brennan and Marshall severely criticized Meese's position as a license for anarchy. For a sampling of reactions to Meese, see Mark Tushnet, "The Supreme Court, the Supreme Law of the Land, and Attorney General Meese: A Comment," *Tulane Law Review* 61 (April 1987): 1017, 1017 n.1.

44. Jordan Steiker, "The Long Road Up from Barbarism: Thurgood Marshall and the Death Penalty," *Texas Law Review* 71 (May 1993): 1131. A broader view of the relation between Court decisions and the Constitution is offered by Gary Jacobsohn, *The Supreme Court and the Decline of Constitutional Aspiration* (Totowa, N.J.: Rowman & Littlefield, 1986).

45. MD [Michael Doss] to TM, No. 87-5984, Marshall Papers, box 432, file 5 (Noland v. North Carolina).

46. That the end result was certain is important to the analysis. If Faubus could reasonably claim that, because of changes in the composition of the Supreme Court, *Brown* might be reversed, he would not act improperly in attempting to get that question before the Court. The likelihood of overruling had played a part in Abraham Lincoln's position on this question, developed in connection with his opposition to the Court's decision favoring slavery in Dred Scott v. Sandford, 60 U.S. (19 How.) 393 (1857).

47. I located approximately one hundred cases in which rehearings were sought and denied; Justices Marshall and Brennan dissented from the denial of rehearing in only two of them, and in one they were joined by Justices Stevens and Stewart, at least one of whom must have voted to deny review initially. Morgan v. Georgia, 444 U.S. 976 (1979) (rehearing denial). (Morgan's death sentence was ultimately vacated by a federal court on habeas corpus, 743 F.2d 775 (11th Cir. 1984). The most recent report of the case that I have been able to locate is a 1987 decision by the Georgia Supreme Court affirming a decision below to allow certain evidence to be introduced at Morgan's resentencing.)

48. TM note on MT [Margaret Tahyar] memorandum, No. 87-7311, Marshall Papers, box 434, file 4 (Poindexter v. Ohio). In contrast, during the short period between Blackmun's announcement of his conclusion that the death penalty was unconstitutional in all cases and his retirement, Blackmun did vote to rehear cases from which he had dissented. *See, e.g.*, Conklin v. Zant, 114 S. Ct. 1871, 2775 (1994).

49. Sandra Day O'Connor, "Thurgood Marshall: The Influence of a Raconteur," *Stanford Law Review* 44 (Summer 1992): 1217; Elena Kagan, "For Justice Marshall," *Texas Law Review* 71 (May 1993): 1125, 1127.

50. Transcript, "Searching for Justice: Three American Stories," hosted by Carl Rowan, WUSA-TV, Sept. 13, 1988, pp. 9–11; Transcript, TM, interview with Sam Donaldson, ABC News, *Primetime Live*, July 26, 1990, p. 4.

Chapter 9

1. TM to Dorothy Gilliam, Feb. 14, 1973, Thurgood Marshall Papers, Manuscript Division, Library of Congress, box 568, file 17.

2. Marshall Papers, box 579.

3. For the destruction of Lake Barcroft, see Kenneth Biedemeier, "Frustration: Lake Dwellers Who Lost Their Lake," *Washington Post*, May 10, 1971, p. C1. I heard variants on the family joke in several settings.

4. Tony Mauro, "Honoring Thurgood Marshall, the Advocate," *Legal Times,* Nov. 22, 1993, p. 9; list of elective officers, United Supreme Council, Prince Hall Masons, Marshall Papers, box 24, file 7. The Prince Hall Masons, in turn, helped fund two positions at the NAACP Inc. Fund. Mark Tushnet, *Making Civil Rights Law: Thurgood Marshall and the Supreme Court, 1936–1961* (New York: Oxford University Press, 1994), 311.

5. TM to Rev. Bernard C. Newman, June 17, 1963, Marshall Papers, box 6, file 12; Covington Hardee to TM, May 7, 1965, box 3, file 8, ibid.

6. *New York Times,* Oct. 22, 1964, p. 23; id., Oct. 23, 1964, p. 16; TM to Mrs. Edward L. Cushman, Nov. 12, 1964, Marshall Papers, box 2, file 7.

7. *New York Times,* Oct. 24, 1964, p. 34 (quoting editorial).

8. Anthony Kronman, *The Lost Lawyer* (Cambridge: Harvard University Press, 1993), 12, 72.

9. Tushnet, *Making Civil Rights Law,* 6–7.

10. Robinson v. California, 370 U.S. 660 (1962).

11. Powell v. Texas, 392 U.S. 514 (1968).

12. White to Fortas, May 8, 1968, Hugo Black Papers, Manuscript Division, Library of Congress, box 401, file: Case file No. 405 O.T. 1967, Powell v. Texas; ECD [law clerk] to Warren, May 9, 1968, Earl Warren Papers, Manuscript Division, Library of Congress, box 555, file: Powell v. Texas.

13. Powell v. Texas, 392 U.S. 514 (1968) (plurality opinion of Marshall, J.); Bernard Schwartz, *Super Chief* (New York: New York University Press, 1983), 693–94.

14. TM to Fortas, April 21, 1969, Marshall Papers, box 57, file 13 (Maxwell v. Bishop).

15. Victor Kramer, "The Road to *City of Berkeley:* The Antitrust Position of Justice Thurgood Marshall," *Antitrust Bulletin* 32 (Summer 1987): 335, 364; TM to conference, Jan. 23, 1978, Marshall Papers, box 212, file 5 (Flagg Bros. v. Brooks); Flagg Bros. v. Brooks, 436 U.S. 149, 166, 167 (1978); Elena Kagan, "For Justice Marshall," *Texas Law Review* 71 (May 1993): 1127–28; Janet Cooper Alexander, "TM," *Stanford Law Review* 44 (Summer 1992): 1231, 1233.

16. Rehnquist to TM, Feb. 22, 1983, Marshall Papers, box 320, file 8 (Block v. Neal).

17. Powell to Brennan, May 24, 1983, William J. Brennan Papers, Manuscript Division Library of Congress, box 629, file 4 (Del Costello v. Teamsters); Rehnquist to Stevens, Dec. 17, 1982, Marshall Papers, box 312, file 3 (Community Television v. Gottfried); Brennan to Stevens, March 21, 1983, box 317, file 9 (Illinois v. Abbott & Associates), ibid.; Scalia to Blackmun, Feb. 19, 1987, box 412, file 8 (Illinois v. Krull), ibid.

18. Scalia to TM, March 10, 1987, Marshall Papers, box 418, file 10 (Brock v. Roadway Express); TM to Scalia, March 11, 1987, id.

19. Stevens to TM, Jan. 3, 1985, Marshall Papers, box 373, file 10 (Ake v. Oklahoma) (discussed in more detail in chapter 7); White to TM, Jan. 31, 1974, box 122, file 10 (Memorial Hosp. v. Maricopa County), ibid.

20. Brennan to TM, Feb. 24, 1986, Marshall Papers, box 396, file 8 (Batson v. Kentucky); TM to Brennan, Feb. 28, 1986, id.; Scalia to White, Dec. 20, 1990, box 531, file 3 (Mobil Oil v. United Distribution), ibid.

21. Kagan, "For Justice Marshall," 1128; Tushnet, *Making Civil Rights Law,* 39–40. (Kagan has "stay black"; I recall the statement, as of 1972–73, as "stay Negro.")

22. Remarks by Supreme Court Chief Justice William Rehnquist at the Funeral of Supreme Court Justice Thurgood Marshall, Washington, D.C., Jan. 28, 1993 (Federal News Service); 458 U.S. 419 (1982).

23. Quoted and discussed in Tushnet, *Making Civil Rights Law,* 310.

24. 487 U.S. 312 (1988).

25. Kagan, "For Justice Marshall," 1128; TM, "Address," *Texas Southern Law Review* 4 (Special Issue 1977): 171, 193; conference notes, Brennan Papers, box 695, file 12 (Schiavone v. Fortune).

26. Conference notes, Brennan Papers, box 514, file 2 (Walker v. Armco Steel); Kagan, "For Justice Marshall," 1128; TM, "Address," 193; Martha Minow and Randall Kennedy, "Thurgood Marshall and Procedural Law: Lawyer's Lawyer, Judge's Judge," *Harvard Blackletter Journal* 6 (Spring 1989): 95, 98.

27. Minow and Kennedy, "Procedural Law," 99.

28. Transcript, TM, interview with Sam Donaldson, ABC News, *Primetime Live,* July 26, 1990, p. 4; Transcript, "Searching for Justice: Three American Stories," hosted by Carl Rowan, WUSA-TV, Sept. 13, 1988, pp. 9–11; TM, "Remarks on the Death Penalty Made at the Judicial Conference of the Second Circuit," *Columbia Law Review* 86 (Jan. 1986): 1, 1–2; TM, "Remarks at the Judicial Conference of the Second Circuit," 125 F.R.D. 197, 201 (1989); conference notes, Brennan Papers, box 426, file 4 (Faretta v. California); conference notes, box 605, file 3 (FTC v. Grolier), ibid.

29. 466 U.S. 668 (1984); Alan I. Bigel, "Justices William J. Brennan, Jr. and Thurgood Marshall on Capital Punishment: Its Constitutionality, Morality, Deterrent Effect, and Interpretation by the Court," *Notre Dame Journal of Law, Ethics & Public Policy* 8 (Issue 1, 1994): 11, 158; conference memorandum, Brennan Papers, box 654, file 6.

30. "Remarks at the Judicial Conference of the Second Circuit," 125 F.R.D. 197, 201, 202 (1989).

31. 469 U.S. 956 (1984).

32. 469 U.S. 1062 (1984).

33. 500 U.S. 110 (1991).

34. Bench memo, Marshall Papers, box 513, file 7, (Lankford v. Idaho).

35. White to conference, June 8, 1990, box 493, file 8, ibid.; Stevens to conference, June 11, 1990, ibid.

36. TM to conference, March 5, 1991, Marshall Papers, box 537, file 7.

37. For a short version of this story, see Kagan, "For Justice Marshall," 1128 ("As always when he disagreed with us, he pointed to the framed judicial commission hanging on his office wall and asked whose name was on it").

38. "Marshall: Speaking Ill of the Dead," *Newsweek,* Aug. 6, 1990, p. 18.

39. Tushnet, *Making Civil Rights Law,* 196–200; TM to Leland Henry, Aug. 5, 1964, Marshall Papers, box 23, file 7.

40. TM, "Commentary: Reflections on the Bicentennial of the United States Constitution," *Harvard Law Review* 101 (Nov. 1987): 1, 2, 5; Missouri v. Holland, 252 U.S. 416 (1920).

Epilogue

1. Transcript, TM press conference, June 28, 1991, p. 9. Sometimes Marshall gave the answer "He did the best he could with what he had" to the question about how he wanted to be remembered. *See, e.g.,* Transcript, "Thurgood Marshall the Man," WUSA-TV, Dec. 13, 1987.

2. Mark Tushnet, "Mr. Justice Marshall: A Tribute," *Black Law Journal* 6 (Fall 1978): 142; Kathleen M. Sullivan, "Marshall, the Great Dissenter," *New York Times,* June 29, 1991, p. A23; Martha Minow, "Thurgood Marshall," *Harvard Law Review* 105 (Nov. 1991): 66, 67.

3. Mrs. Thurgood Marshall, interview with author, Washington, D.C., April 24,

1991; Carl T. Rowan, "Library of Congress Betrayed Marshall," *Washington Post*, May 26, 1993, p. A19; Susan Low Bloch and Vicki Jackson, "Marshall Papers: The Library (and Our Colleague) Got It Wrong," *Legal Times*, June 14, 1993, p. 28.

4. Elena Kagan, "For Justice Marshall," *Texas Law Review* 71 (May 1993): 1125, 1125; Paul Duggan, "Mourners Reflect Breadth of Marshall Legacy," *Washington Post*, Jan. 28, 1993, p. A1; Transcript, "Remembering Thurgood Marshall," National Public Radio's Weekend Edition, Jan. 30, 1993.

5. Transcript, TM press conference, June 28, 1991, p. 4.

6. Janet Cooper Alexander, "TM," *Stanford Law Review* 44 (Summer 1992): 1231, 1234; TM, "Commentary: Reflections on the Bicentennial of the United States Constitution," *Harvard Law Review* 101 (Nov. 1987): 1.

7. TM, "Reflections," 5.

8. Stephen Labaton, "Thousands Fill Cathedral to Pay Tribute to Marshall," *New York Times*, Jan. 29, 1993, p. A16.

Bibliography

Manuscript Collections

Hugo Black Papers, Manuscript Division, Library of Congress
William J. Brennan Papers, Manuscript Division, Library of Congress
Tom C. Clark Papers, Tarlton Library, University of Texas Law School
William O. Douglas Papers, Manuscript Division, Library of Congress
Felix Frankfurter Papers, Harvard Law School
Felix Frankfurter Papers, Manuscript Division, Library of Congress
John Marshall Harlan Papers, Seeley Mudd Library, Princeton University
Thurgood Marshall Papers, Manuscript Division, Library of Congress
NAACP Papers, Manuscript Division, Library of Congress
Earl Warren Papers, Manuscript Division, Library of Congress
White House Central Name File, John Fitzgerald Kennedy Library
White House Central Files, Lyndon Baines Johnson Library

Interviews

AUTHOR'S INTERVIEWS

Francis X. Beytagh, Columbus, Ohio, May 9, 1988
Gloria Branker, Washington, D.C., Jan. 30, 1991
Jerome I. Chapman, Washington, D.C., March 7, 1988
Louis F. Claiborne, San Francisco, Nov. 17, 1988
William T. Coleman, Washington, D.C., Oct. 17, 1989
Owen Fiss, New Haven, April 20, 1989
James O. Freedman, Dec. 16, 1988 (telephone)
Nicholas Katzenbach, June 8, 1988 (telephone)
Nathan Lewin, Washington, D.C., June 1, 1988
Burke Marshall, May 26, 1988 (telephone)
Mrs. Thurgood Marshall, Washington, D.C., April 24, 1991
Thurgood Marshall, Washington, D.C., May 23, 1989

Thurgood Marshall, Jr., April 26, 1991 (telephone)
Louis Martin, Nov. 15, 1988 (telephone)
J. Nicholas McGrath, Aspen, Colorado, June 10, 1988
Robert Rifkind, New York, March 30, 1988
Ralph Spritzer, Tempe, Arizona, April 8, 1988
Ralph K. Winter, New Haven, April 20, 1989

ORAL HISTORY COLLECTIONS

Ramsey Clark, by Harri Baker, Oct. 30, 1968, Lyndon Baines Johnson Library
Thurgood Marshall, by Thomas Baker, July 10, 1969, Lyndon Baines Johnson Library
Thurgood Marshall, by Ed Erwin, March 11, 1977, Columbia Oral History Collection,
        Columbia University Library
Clarence Mitchell, by John Stewart, Feb. 9, 1967, John Fitzgerald Kennedy Library
Edwin Weisl, by Joe B. Frantz, May 23, 1969, Lyndon Baines Johnson Library

MISCELLANEOUS

Marshall, Thurgood. Interview with Sam Donaldson, ABC News, *Primetime Live,* July 26,
        1990 (transcript).
———. "Law and the Quest for Equality" (the Tyrell Williams Lecture), delivered at the
        School of Law, Washington University of St. Louis, March 8, 1967.
———. Press conference, June 28, 1991 (transcript).
New York Times. Editorial, Sept. 25, 1961.
———. Editorial, May 5, 1962.
———. Editorial, July 14, 1965.
———. Editorial, Oct. 24, 1964.
———. Letter from Professor Norman Dorsen, May 16, 1962.
———. Sept. 24–Oct. 24, 1961; April 6–Sept. 12, 1962; Oct. 22–23, 1964; July 14, 1965;
        May 2–Aug. 31, 1967; Feb. 6, 1980.
Rehnquist, William J. Remarks at the Funeral of Supreme Court Justice Thurgood Mar-
        shall, Washington, D.C., Jan. 28, 1993 (Federal News Service).
"Remembering Thurgood Marshall." National Radio's Weekend Edition, Jan. 30, 1993
        (transcript).
"Searching for Justice: Three American Stories." Hosted by Carl Rowan, WUSA-TV, Sept.
        13, 1988 (transcript).
"Thurgood Marshall the Man." WUSA-TV, Dec. 13, 1987 (transcript).
Washington Post. Editorial, "Justice Marshall," Sept. 1, 1967.

Government Publications

Congressional Record. 87th Cong., 2d Sess., 1962, vol. 108, at 16,075.
———. 87th Cong., 2d Sess., 1962, vol. 108, at 17,449.
———. 87th Cong., 2d Sess., 1962, vol. 108, at 18,357.
President. Executive Order No. 10,925, *Federal Register* 26 (1961): 1977.
———. Executive Order No. 11,246, *Federal Register* 30 (1965): 12,327.
U.S. Code. Vol. 28, § 1443 (1994).
U.S. Senate Committee on the Judiciary. *Hearings on the Nomination of Thurgood Marshall
        Before the Senate Special Subcommittee on Nomination of the Senate Committee on the
        Judiciary,* S. 1532, 87th Cong., 2d Sess. (1961).

————. *Hearings on the Nomination of Thurgood Marshall Before the Senate Committee on the Judiciary*, S-1700-2, 89th Cong., 1st Sess. (1965).
————. *Hearings on the Nomination of Thurgood Marshall Before the Senate Committee on the Judiciary*, S-1826-3, 90th Cong., 1st Sess. (1967).

Unpublished Manuscripts and Letters

Hammond Chaffetz, to author, August 30, 1988
Joseph Dolan to author, October 18, 1988
Howard C. Equitz to author, August 30, 1988
James O. Freedman to author, April 26, 1988
Brett Gerry to Randall Kennedy, July 26, 1995 (in author's possession)
Benjamin Heineman, Jr., to author, Aug. 22, 1994
Puzant Merdinian. "The Nomination and Confirmation of Thurgood Marshall as a Judge of the Second Circuit Court of Appeals in 1961–62" (undergraduate thesis, Merton College, Oxford University, 1994).
Deborah Rhode, notes of conversations with Thurgood Marshall (in author's possession)
Rebecca Mae Salokar. "The Solicitor General: Balancing the Interests of the Executive and Judicial Branches, 1959–1982," (Ph.D. diss., Syracuse University, 1988).

Books and Articles

Alexander, Janet Cooper. "TM," *Stanford Law Review* 44 (Summer 1992): 1231.
Amsterdam, Anthony. "Criminal Prosecutions Affecting Federally Guaranteed Civil Rights: Federal Removal and Habeas Corpus Jurisdiction to Abort State Court Trial," *University of Pennsylvania Law Review* 113 (April 1965): 793.
Baker, Liva. *Miranda: Crime, Law, and Politics* (New York: Atheneum, 1983).
Ball, Howard. *"We Have a Duty": The Supreme Court and the Watergate Tapes Litigation* (New York: Greenwood Press, 1990).
Berman, William C. *America's Right Turn: From Nixon to Bush* (Baltimore: Johns Hopkins University Press, 1994).
Biedemeier, Kenneth. "Frustration: Lake Dwellers Who Lost Their Lake," *Washington Post*, May 10, 1971.
Bigel, Alan I. "Justices William J. Brennan, Jr. and Thurgood Marshall on Capital Punishment: Its Constitutionality, Morality, Deterrent Effect, and Interpretation by the Court," *Notre Dame Journal of Law, Ethics & Public Policy* 8 (Issue 1, 1994): 11.
Blasi, Vincent, ed. *The Burger Court: The Counter-Revolution That Wasn't* (New Haven: Yale University Press, 1983).
Bloch, Susan Low. "Thurgood Marshall: Courageous Advocate, Compassionate Judge," *Georgetown Law Journal* 80 (Aug. 1992): 2003.
Bloch, Susan Low, and Vicki Jackson. "Marshall Papers: The Library (and Our Colleague) Got It Wrong," *Legal Times*, June 14, 1993.
Brennan, William J. "Constitutional Adjudication and the Death Penalty," *Harvard Law Review* 100 (Dec. 1986): 313.
Buchsbaum, Herbert. "The Kids on the Court," *Scholastic Update*, Sept. 17, 1993.
Califano, Joseph A., Jr. *The Triumph and Tragedy of Lyndon Johnson: The White House Years* (New York: Simon & Schuster, 1991).

Canon, Bradley C. "Justice John Paul Stevens: The Lone Ranger in a Black Robe," in *The Burger Court: Political and Judicial Profiles,* Charles M. Lamb and Stephen C. Halpern, eds. (Urbana: University of Illinois Press, 1991).

Caplan, Lincoln. *The Tenth Justice: The Solicitor General and the Rule of Law* (New York: Alfred Knopf, 1987).

Carter, Stephen L. "Thurgood Marshall," *Valparaiso Law Review* 26 (Fall 1991): xxxv.

Cook, Beverly B. "Justice Sandra Day O'Connor: Transition to a Republican Court Agenda," in *The Burger Court: Political and Judicial Profiles,* Charles M. Lamb and Stephen C. Halpern, eds. (Urbana: University of Illinois Press, 1991).

Davis, Martha. *Brutal Need: Lawyers and the Welfare Rights Movement, 1960–1973* (New Haven: Yale University Press, 1993).

Davis, Sue. *Justice Rehnquist and the Constitution* (Princeton: Princeton University Press, 1989).

———. "Justice William H. Rehnquist: Right-Wing Ideologue or Majoritarian Democrat?" in *The Burger Court: Political and Judicial Profiles,* Charles M. Lamb and Stephen C. Halpern, eds. (Urbana: University of Illinois Press, 1991).

de Grazia, Edward. *Girls Lean Back Everywhere: The Law of Obscenity and the Assault on Genius* (New York: Random House, 1992).

Devins, Neal. "*Adarand Constructors, Inc. v. Pena* and the Continuing Irrelevance of Supreme Court Affirmative Action Decisions" *William & Mary L. Rev.* 37 (Winter 1996): 673.

Domnarski, William. *In the Opinion of the Court* (Urbana: University of Illinois Press, 1996).

Douglas, Davison M. *Reading, Writing, and Race: The Desegregation of the Charlotte Schools* (Chapel Hill: University of North Carolina Press, 1995).

Drummond, Roscoe. "The Race Revolution: Marshall—A Symbol of Change," *Washington Post,* June 17, 1967.

Duggan, Paul. "Mourners Reflect Breadth of Marshall Legacy, *Washington Post,* Jan. 28, 1993.

D'Zurilla, William T., ed. "Directory of Law Clerks of the Justices of the United States Supreme Court" (mimeographed, Sept. 19, 1994).

Eastland, Terry. "While Justice Sleeps," *National Review,* April 21, 1989.

Edsall, Thomas Byrne, with Mary D. Edsall. *Chain Reaction: The Impact of Race, Rights, and Taxes on American Politics* (New York: W. W. Norton & Co., 1991).

Ferguson, Thomas, and Joel Rogers. *Right Turn: The Decline of the Democrats and the Future of American Politics* (New York: Hill & Wang, 1986).

Fisher, Anne. "Businessmen Like to Hire by Numbers," *Fortune,* Sept. 16, 1985.

Fiss, Owen. "Thurgood Marshall," *Harvard Law Review* 105 (Nov. 1991): 49.

Fox, James Alan, Michael Radelet, and Julie Bonsteel. "Death Penalty Opinion in the Post-*Furman* Years," *New York University Review of Law & Social Change* 18 (1990–91): 499.

Frank, John P. *Clement Haynsworth, the Senate, and the Supreme Court* (Charlottesville: University Press of Virginia, 1991).

Fraser, Steve, and Gary Gerstle, eds. *The Rise and Fall of the New Deal Order, 1930–1980* (Princeton: Princeton University Press, 1989).

Garrow, David J. *Liberty and Sexuality: The Right to Privacy and the Making of* Roe v. Wade (New York: Macmillan, 1994).

Gellhorn, Gay. "Justice Thurgood Marshall's Jurisprudence of Equal Protection of the Laws and the Poor," *Arizona State Law Journal* 26 (Summer 1994): 429.

Goldman, Albert. From the journalism of Lawrence Schiller. *Ladies and Gentlemen: Lenny Bruce!!* (New York: Random House, 1974).

Gordon, Robert. "The Independence of Lawyers," *Boston University Law Review* 68 (Jan. 1988): 1.

Graham, Hugh Davis. *The Civil Rights Era: Origins and Development of National Policy, 1960–1972* (New York: Oxford University Press, 1990).

Griggin, James H., Jr. "Case Comment," *Boston University Law Review* 46 (Spring 1966): 260.

Gross, Samuel, and Robert Mauro. *Death and Discrimination: Racial Disparities in Capital Sentencing* (Boston: Northeastern University Press, 1989).

Gunther, Gerald. "The Supreme Court, 1971 Term—Foreword: In Search of Evolving Doctrine on a Changing Court: A Model for a Newer Equal Protection," *Harvard Law Review* 86 (Nov. 1972): 1.

Guthman, Edwin O., and Jeffrey Shulman, eds. *Robert Kennedy In His Own Words: The Unpublished Recollections of the Kennedy Years* (New York: Bantom Books, 1988).

Halpern, Stephen C. *On the Limits of the Law: The Ironic Legacy of Title VI of the 1964 Civil Rights Act* (Baltimore: Johns Hopkins University Press, 1995).

Harris, Richard. *Justice: The Crisis of Law, Order, and Freedom in America* (New York: E. P. Dutton, 1970).

Harvard Law Review. "The Supreme Court, 1967 Term," 82 (Nov. 1968): 93.
———. "The Supreme Court, 1968 Term," 83 (Nov. 1969): 60.
———. "The Supreme Court, 1969 Term," 84 (Nov. 1970): 30.
———. "The Supreme Court, 1970 Term," 85 (Nov. 1971): 38.
———. "The Supreme Court, 1971 Term," 86 (Nov. 1972): 50.
———. "The Supreme Court, 1972 Term," 87 (Nov. 1973): 55.
———. "The Supreme Court, 1973 Term," 88 (Nov. 1974): 41.
———. "The Supreme Court, 1974 Term," 89 (Nov. 1975): 49.
———. "The Supreme Court, 1975 Term," 90 (Nov. 1976): 56.
———. "The Supreme Court, 1976 Term," 91 (Nov. 1977): 70.

Human Events. "LBJ Packs the Court," June 24, 1967.

Iowa Law Review. "Comment on Recent Case," 52 (Aug. 1966): 109.

Jacobsohn, Gary. *The Supreme Court and the Decline of Constitutional Aspiration* (Totowa, N.J.: Rowman & Littlefield, 1986).

Jeffries, John C., Jr. *Justice Lewis F. Powell, Jr.: A Biography* (New York: Scribner's, 1994).

Kagan, Elena. "For Justice Marshall," *Texas Law Review* 71 (May 1993): 1125.

Kalman, Laura. *Abe Fortas: A Biography* (New Haven: Yale University Press, 1990).

Kennedy, Anthony. "The Voice of Thurgood Marshall," *Stanford Law Review* 44 (Summer 1992): 1221.

Kennedy, Randall L. "Doing What You Can with What You Have: The Greatness of Justice Marshall," *Georgetown Law Journal* 80 (Aug. 1992): 2081.

———. "*McCleskey v. Kemp:* Race, Capital Punishment, and the Supreme Court," *Harvard Law Review* 101 (May 1988): 1388.

Kilpatrick, James J. "Marshall's Appointment Upsets Court Balance," *Washington Sunday Star,* June 18, 1967.

———. "Term's End," *National Review,* July 25, 1967.

Kohlmeier, Louis. *"God Save This Honorable Court!"* (New York: Scribner's, 1972).

Kraft, Joseph. "Hung Court," *Washington Post,* June 15, 1967.

Kramer, Victor. "The Road to *City of Berkeley:* The Antitrust Position of Justice Thurgood Marshall," *Antitrust Bulletin* 32 (Summer 1987): 335.

Kronman, Anthony. *The Lost Lawyer* (Cambridge: Harvard University Press, 1993).

Kurland, Philip, and Gerhard Casper, eds. *Landmark Briefs and Arguments of the Supreme Court of the United States: Constitutional Law,* vol. 62 (Arlington, Va.: University Publications of America, 1975).

Labaton, Stephen. "Thousands Fill Cathedral to Pay Tribute to Marshall," *New York Times,* Jan. 29, 1993.

Lamb, Charles M., and Stephen C. Halpern, eds. *The Burger Court: Political and Judicial Profiles* (Urbana: University of Illinois Press, 1991).

Lawrence, Susan. *The Poor in Court: The Legal Services Program and Supreme Court Decision Making* (Princeton: Princeton University Press, 1990).

Le Duc, Don. "Note," *Wayne Law Review* 12 (Spring 1966): 685.

Levy, Leonard. *Original Intent and the Framers' Constitution* (New York: Macmillan, 1988).

Lewin, Nathan. "The Justice and the Hairpiece," *Washington Jewish Week,* July 4, 1991.

Lewis, Anthony. *Gideon's Trumpet* (New York: Random House, 1964).

Mann, Jim. "Prepping for the Justices," *American Lawyer,* New. 1982.

Marshall, Thurgood. "Address," *Texas Southern Law Review* 4 (Special Issue 1977): 171.

———. "Address to the Judicial Conference of the Second Circuit," *Federal Rules Decisions* 115 (1987): 349.

———. "Commentary: Reflections on the Bicentennial of the United States Constitution," *Harvard Law Review* 101 (Nov. 1987): 1.

———. Extraordinary Session of the Court of Appeals for the Second Circuit, "In Memoriam: Honorable Henry J. Friendly," *Federal Reporter* 2d 805 (1986): lxxxvii.

———. "Remarks on the Death Penalty Made at the Judicial Conference of the Second Circuit," *Columbia Law Review* 86 (Jan. 1986): 1.

———. "Remarks at the Judicial Conference of the Second Circuit," Federal Rules Decisions 125 (1989): 197.

Massaro, John. *Supremely Political: The Role of Ideology and Presidential Management in Unsuccessful Supreme Court Nominations* (Buffalo: State University of New York Press, 1990).

Mauro, Tony. "Courtside: Reading Between Blackmun's Lines," *The Recorder,* March 2, 1994.

———. "Files Shed Unflattering Light on Fortas," *Legal Times,* Feb. 5, 1990.

———. "Honoring Thurgood Marshall, the Advocate," *Legal Times,* Nov. 22, 1993.

———. "Marshall Nugget," *Legal Times,* April 25, 1994.

———. "Preserving Marshall's Greatness," *Legal Times,* Feb. 8, 1993.

Mayer, Michael. "Eisenhower and the Southern Federal Judiciary: The Sobeloff Nomination," in Shirley Anne Warshaw, *Reexamining the Eisenhower Presidency* (Westport, Conn.: Greenwood Press, 1993).

McFeeley, Neil. *Appointment of Judges: The Johnson Presidency* (Austin: University of Texas Press, 1987).

Meese, Edwin. "The Law of the Constitution," *Tulane Law Review* 61 (April 1987): 979.

Meltsner, Michael. *Cruel and Unusual: The Supreme Court and Capital Punishment* (New York: Random House, 1973).

Michigan Law Review. "Recent Development," 63 (Feb. 1965): 720.

Mendelson, Wallace. "Brennan's Revolution," *Commentary* 91 (Feb. 1991): 36.

Minow, Martha. "Thurgood Marshall," *Harvard Law Review* 105 (Nov. 1991): 66.

Minow, Martha, and Randall Kennedy. "Thurgood Marshall and Procedural Law: Lawyer's Lawyer, Judge's Judge," *Harvard Blackletter Journal* 6 (Spring 1989): 95.

Moreno, Paul. "Direct Action and Fair Employment: The *Hughes* Case," *Western Legal History* (forthcoming).

Murphy, Bruce Alan. *Fortas: The Rise and Ruin of a Supreme Court Justice* (New York: William Morrow, 1988).

Navasky, Victor. *Kennedy Justice* (New York: Atheneum, 1971).

Newman, Roger K. *Hugo Black: A Biography* (New York: Pantheon, 1994).

Newsweek. "Marshall: Speaking Ill of the Dead," Aug. 6, 1990.

O'Brien, David. *Storm Center: The Supreme Court in American Politics,* 3d ed. (New York: W. W. Norton & Co., 1993).

O'Connor, Sandra Day. "Thurgood Marshall: The Influence of a Raconteur," *Stanford Law Review* 44 (Summer 1992): 1217.

Overby, L. Marvin, Beth M. Henscher, Julie Strauss, and Michael H. Walsh. "African-American Constituents and Supreme Court Nominees: An Examination of the Senate Confirmation of Thurgood Marshall," *Political Research Quarterly* 47 (Dec. 1994): 839.

Piven, Frances, and Richard Cloward. *Poor Peoples' Movements: Why They Succeed, How They Fail* (New York: Pantheon, 1977).

Post, Robert. "William J. Brennan and the Warren Court," in *The Warren Court in Historical and Political Perspective,* Mark Tushnet, ed. (Charlottesville: University Press of Virginia, 1993).

Rehnquist, William H. "Tribute to Justice Thurgood Marshall," *Stanford Law Review* 44 (Summer 1992): 1213.

Reider, Jonathan. "The Rise of the 'Silent Majority,'" in *The Rise and Fall of the New Deal Order, 1930–1980,* Steve Fraser and Gary Gerstle, eds. (Princeton: Princeton University Press, 1989).

Revesz, Richard. "Thurgood Marshall's Struggle," *New York University Law Review* 68 (May 1993): 237.

Reynolds, William Bradford. "In Honor of *Brown v. Board of Education:* Individualism v. Group Rights: The Legacy of *Brown,*" *Yale Law Journal* 93 (May 1984): 995.

Rosen, Jeffrey. "Court Marshall," *The New Republic,* June 21, 1993.

Rowan, Carl T. "Library of Congress Betrayed Marshall," *Washington Post,* May 26, 1993.

Sachs, Andrea. "Laurence Tribe," *Constitution* 3 (Spring–Summer 1991): 24.

Schick, Marvin. *Learned Hand's Court* (Baltimore; Johns Hopkins University Press, 1970).

Schwartz, Bernard. *The Ascent of Pragmatism: The Burger Court in Action* (Reading, Mass.: Addison-Wesley Publishing Co., 1990).

———. *Behind Bakke: Affirmative Action and the Supreme Court* (New York: New York University Press, 1988).

———. *Super Chief* (New York: New York University Press, 1983).

———. *Swann's Way: The School Busing Case and the Supreme Court* (New York: Oxford University Press, 1986).

———. *The Unpublished Opinions of the Burger Court* (New York: Oxford University Press, 1988).

———. *The Unpublished Opinions of the Warren Court* (New York: Oxford University Press, 1985).

Shogan, Robert. *A Question of Judgment: The Fortas Case and the Struggle for the Supreme Court* (Indianapolis: Bobbs-Merrill, 1972).

Simon, James F. *The Center Holds: The Power Struggle Inside the Rehnquist Court* (New York: Simon & Schuster, 1995).

Steiker, Carol. "'Did You Hear What Thurgood Marshall Did for Us?'—A Tribute," *American Journal of Criminal Law* 20 (Winter 1993): vii.

Steiker, Jordan. "The Long Road Up from Barbarism: Thurgood Marshall and the Death Penalty," *Texas Law Review* 71 (May 1993): 1131.

Stern, Mark. *Calculating Visions: Kennedy, Johnson, and Civil Rights* (New Brunswick, N.J.: Rutgers University Press, 1992).

Stone, Geoffrey. "Marshall: He's the Frustrated Conscience of the High Court," *National Law Journal,* Feb. 18, 1980.

Stone, Geoffrey, L. Michael Seidman, Cass Sunstein, and Mark Tushnet. *Constitutional Law* (Boston: Little, Brown, 1986).

Sullivan, Kathleen M. "Marshall, the Great Dissenter," *New York Times,* June 29, 1991.

Sunstein, Cass. "On Marshall's Conception of Equality," *Stanford Law Review* 44 (Summer 1992): 1267.

Symposium. "The Role and Function of the United States Solicitor General," *Loyola of Los Angeles Law Review* 21 (June 1988): 1047.

Taper, Bernard. "A Reporter at Large: A Meeting in Atlanta," *The New Yorker,* March 17, 1956.

Taylor, Stuart, Jr. "Glimpses of Thurgood Marshall," *The American Lawyer,* March 1993.

Theoharis, Athan, and John Stuart Cox. *The Boss: J. Edgar Hoover and the Great American Inquisition* (Philadelphia: Temple University Press, 1988).

Tushnet, Mark. *Constitutional Issues: The Death Penalty* (New York: Facts on File, 1994).

———. *Making Civil Rights Law: Thurgood Marshall and the Supreme Court, 1936–1961* (New York: Oxford University Press, 1994).

———. "Mr. Justice Marshall: A Tribute," *Black Law Journal* 6 (Fall 1978): 142.

———. *The NAACP's Legal Strategy Against Segregated Education, 1925–1950* (Chapel Hill: University of North Carolina Press, 1987).

———. "The Supreme Court and Race Discrimination, 1967–1991: The View from the Marshall Papers," *William & Mary Law Review* 36 (Jan. 1995): 473.

———. "The Supreme Court, the Supreme Law of the Land, and Attorney General Meese: A Comment," *Tulane Law Review* 61 (April 1987): 1017.

———, ed. *The Warren Court in Historical and Political Perspective* (Charlottesville: University Press of Virginia, 1993).

Von Drehle, David. *Among the Lowest of the Dead: The Culture of Death Row* (New York: Random House, 1995).

Wasby, Stephen L. "Justice Harry A. Blackmun: Transformation from 'Minnesota Twin' to Independent Voice," in *The Burger Court: Political and Judicial Profiles,* Charles M. Lamb and Stephen C. Halpern, eds. (Urbana: University of Illinois Press, 1991).

White, Byron. "A Tribute to Justice Thurgood Marshall," *Stanford Law Review* 44 (Summer 1992): 1215.

White, G. Edward. *Earl Warren: A Public Life* (New York: Oxford University Press, 1982).

Wilkinson, J. Harvie. *From Brown to Bakke: The Supreme Court and School Integration, 1954–1978* (New York: Oxford University Press, 1979).

Williams, Juan. "Marshall's Law," *Washington Post Magazine,* Jan. 7, 1990.

Woocher, Elliott D. "Case Comment," *Boston University Law Review* 45 (Spring 1965): 283.

Woodward, Bob, and Scott Armstrong. *The Brethren: Inside the Supreme Court* (New York: Simon & Schuster, 1979).

Zion, Sidney. "Thurgood Marshall Takes a New 'Tush-Tush' Job," *New York Times Magazine,* Aug. 22, 1965.

Table of Cases

Ake v. Oklahoma, 470 U.S. 68 (1985),
156–58
Alexander v. Holmes County Board of
Education, 396 U.S. 19 (1969), 70–
74, 75, 76
Alvord v. Florida, 428 U.S. 923 (1976),
189
Amalgamated Food Employees v. Logan
Valley Plaza, 391 U.S. 308 (1968), 33
Andrews v. Shulsen, 485 U.S. 919
(1988), 159–60, 222n37
Barefoot v. Estelle, 463 U.S. 880 (1983),
171–72, 224n28
Barnes v. Glen Theatre, 501 U.S. 560
(1991), 48–49
Batson v. Kentucky, 476 U.S. 79 (1986),
65–67, 184
Beal v. Doe, 432 U.S. 438 (1977), 4, 197
Bellis v. United States, 417 U.S. 85
(1974), 62, 211n23
Benton v. Maryland, 395 U.S. 784
(1969), 15, 32–33, 175
Berkemer v. McCarty, 468 U.S. 675
(1986), 62
Bethel School Dist. v. Fraser, 478 U.S.
675 (1986), 40, 205n41
Black v. United States, 385 U.S. 26
(1966), 20–21, 201n42
Board of Education of Oklahoma City
v. Dowell, 498 U.S. 237 (1991), 90
Booth v. Maryland, 482 U.S. 496 (1987),
176

Bowsher v. Synar, 478 U.S. 714 (1986),
40–41
Brown v. Board of Education, 347 U.S.
483 (1954), 3, 9, 68, 78, 81, 88, 92,
101, 102, 116, 120, 132, 144, 176,
191, 194
Brown v. Board of Education II, 349 U.S.
294 (1955), 71, 72, 86, 145
Buck v. Bell, 274 U.S. 200 (1927), 94,
215n1
Caldwell v. Mississippi, 472 U.S. 320
(1985), 155–56
California v. Rooney, 483 U.S. 307
(1987), 50, 208n71
California Federal Savings & Loan Ass'n
v. Guerra, 479 U.S. 272 (1987), 62,
211n24
Carella v. California, 491 U.S. 263
(1989), 50, 208n71
Casteneda v. Partida, 430 U.S. 482
(1977), 59, 210n13
City of Richmond v. J. A. Croson Co.,
488 U.S. 469 (1989), 137, 139–43
Cleburne v. Cleburne Living Center, 473
U.S. 432 (1985), 112–15
Coates v. Cincinnati, 402 U.S. 611
(1971), 61, 211n22
Coleman v. Balkcom, 451 U.S. 949
(1981), 165–66, 223n4
Committee for Public Education v. Nyquist, 413 U.S. 756 (1973), 60,
210n16

Cooper v. Aaron, 358 U.S. 1 (1958), 72, 175, 176, 177

County of Los Angeles v. Davis, 440 U.S. 625 (1979), 61, 211n21

County of Riverside v. McLaughlin, 500 U.S. 44 (1991), 51–52

Craig v. Boren, 429 U.S. 190 (1976), 105–6

Dandridge v. Williams, 397 U.S. 471 (1970), 98–100, 115

Darden v. Florida, 430 U.S. 704 (1977), 167, 223n10

Darden v. Wainwright, 477 U.S. 168 (1986), 167–68, 169, 223n11

Dayton Board of Education v. Brinkman I, 433 U.S. 406 (1977), 89–90

Dayton Board of Education v. Brinkman II, 443 U.S. 526 (1979), 90

Department of Justice v. Tax Analysts, 492 U.S. 136 (1989), 51, 208n75

Dobbert v. Florida, 432 U.S. 282 (1977), 172

Dugger v. Adams, 489 U.S. 401 (1989), 169–71, 224n25

Dunn v. Blumstein, 405 U.S. 330 (1972), 98, 99

Ephraim v. Safeway Trails, Inc., 341 F.2d 815 (2d Cir. 1965), 17

Estelle v. Gamble, 429 U.S. 97 (1976), 62–63, 211n25

Estes v. Metropolitan Branches of Dallas NAACP, 444 U.S. 437 (1980), 84–85

Fifth Avenue Coach Co. v. New York, 221 U.S. 467 (1911), 94, 215n3

Flagg Bros. v. Brooks, 436 U.S. 149 (1978), 183, 226n15

Florida v. Bostick, 501 U.S. 429 (1991), 8

Ford v. Wainwright, 477 U.S. 399 (1986), 156, 157

Frank v. United States, 395 U.S. 147 (1969), 32

Franks v. Bowman Transportation Co., 424 U.S. 747 (1976), 135–36

Frontiero v. Richardson, 411 U.S. 677 (1973), 104–5

Fullilove v. Klutznick, 448 U.S. 448 (1980), 132–35, 139, 140, 142, 143

Furman v. Georgia, 408 U.S. 238 (1972), 150–53, 158

Gideon v. Wainwright, 372 U.S. 335 (1963), 175

Gilliard v. Mississippi, 464 U.S. 867 (1983), 65, 212n32

Goldman v. Weinberger, 475 U.S. 503 (1986), 42, 57, 206n46

Gray v. Lucas, 463 U.S. 1237 (1983), 159

Green v. New Kent County, 391 U.S. 430 (1968), 69–70, 74, 75, 76, 77, 78, 82

Gregg v. Georgia, 428 U.S. 153 (1976), 153–55

Gwaltney of Smithfield v. Chesapeake Bay Found'n, 484 U.S. 49 (1987), 51, 208n75

Hamilton v. Texas, 498 U.S. 908 (1990), 173

Harper v. Virginia Board of Elections, 383 U.S. 663 (1966), 23–24

Harris v. McCrae, 448 U.S. 297 (1980), 102–3

Healy v. James, 408 U.S. 169 (1972), 42, 206n48

Hewitt v. Helms, 459 U.S. 460 (1983), 46, 207n59

Holland v. Illinois, 493 U.S. 474 (1990), 49, 208n70

Hughes v. Superior Court, 339 U.S. 460 (1950), 117–19, 141, 144, 217n11

Illinois v. Andreas, 463 U.S. 765 (1983), 40, 205n41

In re Whittington, 391 U.S. 341 (1968), 33–34

INS v. Pangilinan, 486 U.S. 875 (1988), 50, 208n72

Jacobs v. Wainwright, 469 U.S. 1062 (1984), 189

Kadrmas v. Dickinson Public Schools, 487 U.S. 450 (1988), 101–2

Kentucky v. Whorton, 441 U.S. 786 (1979), 41

Keyes v. School Dist. No. 1, 413 U.S. 189 (1973), 82–84, 85, 90

Kissinger v. Halperin, 452 U.S. 713 (1981), 44–45, 60, 206n56

Kolender v. Lawson, 461 U.S. 352 (1983), 57, 209n3

Kremens v. Bartley, 431 U.S. 119 (1977), 48, 207n63

Lankford v. Idaho, 500 U.S. 110 (1991), 189–91

Larkin v. Grendel's Den, 459 U.S. 116 (1982), 63, 211–12n28

Lee v. Washington, 390 U.S. 333 (1968), 7, 198n17

Lemon v. Kurtzman, 403 U.S. 602 (1971), 40

Linn v. United Plant Guard Workers, 383 U.S. 53 (1966), 23

Lloyd Corp. v. Tanner, 407 U.S. 551 (1972), 39, 205n34

Local 28, Sheet Metal Workers v. EEOC, 478 U.S. 421 (1986), 137–38, 139

Local 93 v. Cleveland, 478 U.S. 501 (1986), 138–39

Lochner v. New York, 198 U.S. 45 (1905), 95, 215n4

Lockhart v. McCree, 476 U.S. 162 (1986), 222n36

Loretto v. Teleprompter Manhattan CATV Corp., 458 U.S. 419 (1982), 185

Lowenfield v. Phelps, 484 U.S. 231 (1988), 158–59

Mapp v. Ohio, 367 U.S. 643 (1961), 14

Massachusetts Board of Retirement v. Murgia, 427 U.S. 307 (1976), 108–12, 115

Maxwell v. Bishop, 398 U.S. 262 (1970), 148–49

McCleskey v. Kemp, 481 U.S. 279 (1987), 160–61, 163

McCleskey v. Zant, 499 U.S. 467 (1991), 162

McCray v. New York, 461 U.S. 961 (1983), 65, 212n31

McDonald v. Santa Fe Trail Transportation Co., 427 U.S. 273 (1976), 138

McDonough Power Equipment v. Greenwood, 464 U.S. 548 (1984), 61, 211n21

McGautha v. California, 402 U.S. 183 (1971), 149–50, 221n12

Mempa v. Rhay, 389 U.S. 128 (1967), 32, 204n13

Memphis v. Greene, 451 U.S. 100 (1981), 91–93

Metro Broadcasting Inc. v. Federal Communications Comm'n, 497 U.S. 547 (1990), 143–44, 220n79

Milliken v. Bradley I, 418 U.S. 717 (1974), 85, 87–88, 90, 93

Milliken v. Bradley II, 433 U.S. 267 (1977), 88–89

Miranda v. Arizona, 384 U.S. 436 (1966), 24, 26–27, 43

Moore v. City of East Cleveland, 431 U.S. 494 (1977), 7–8

Morrison-Knudsen Constr. Co. v. Director, 461 U.S. 624 (1983), 48, 207n64

Nassau Lens Co. v. Commissioner, 308 F.2d 39 (2d Cir. 1962), 14, 200n16

Neitzke v. Williams, 406 U.S. 319 (1989), 47, 207n63

New York v. Galamison, 342 F.2d 255 (1965), 16–17

Nixon v. Fitzgerald, 457 U.S. 731 (1982), 44–45, 206n55

NTEU v. Von Raab, 489 U.S. 656 (1989), 49, 207n69

O'Connor v. Ortega, 480 U.S. 709 (1987), 49, 208n70

Palko v. Connecticut, 302 U.S. 319 (1937), 15, 200n21

Patterson v. McLean Credit Union, 491 U.S. 164 (1989), 53–54, 208n84

Payne v. Tennessee, 501 U.S. 808 (1991), 173–75

Penn-Central Merger Case (Baltimore & Ohio R. Co. v. United States), 386 U.S. 372 (1967), 22–23

Pennhurst State School v. Halderman, 451 U.S. 1 (1981), 59, 210n14

Pennsylvania v. Muniz, 496 U.S. 582 (1990), 43, 206n50

Penry v. Lynaugh, 492 U.S. 302 (1989), 223n1

Plessy v. Ferguson, 163 U.S. 537 (1896), 92, 129, 131, 132

Police Department of Chicago v. Mosley, 408 U.S. 92 (1972), 97–98, 101

Powell v. Texas, 392 U.S. 514 (1968), 181–83, 192

Quern v. Jordan, 440 U.S. 332 (1979), 48, 207n65

Railway Express Agency v. New York, 336 U.S. 106 (1949), 95, 215n5

Ralston v. Robinson, 454 U.S. 201 (1981), 62, 211n23

Reed v. Reed, 404 U.S. 71 (1971), 103–4, 105, 215n23

Regents of University of California v. Bakke, 438 U.S. 265 (1978), 122–32, 133, 134, 135, 137, 139

Rhodes v. Chapman, 452 U.S. 337 (1981), 6, 198n14

Richmond School Board v. Bradley, 412 U.S. 92 (1973), 85–87, 93

Roberts v. Louisiana, 428 U.S. 325 (1976), 154, 221n24

Robinson v. California, 370 U.S. 660 (1962), 181, 182, 226n10

Roe v. Wade, 410 U.S. 113 (1973), 6–7, 37–38

Rostker v. Goldberg, 453 U.S. 57 (1981), 106–8

Rudolph v. Alabama, 375 U.S. 889 (1963), 147, 221n4

San Antonio Independent School District v. Rodriguez, 411 U.S. 1 (1973), 100–101, 102, 103, 106, 115, 216–17n52

Sawyer v. Smith, 497 U.S. 227 (1990), 221–22n26

Schmuck v. United States, 489 U.S. 705 (1989), 51

Selective Service Sys. v. Minnesota PIRG, 468 U.S. 841 (1984), 57, 209n3

Skinner v. Oklahoma, 316 U.S. 535 (1942), 95–96, 97, 101

Slaughterhouse Cases, 83 U.S. 36 (1873), 94, 215n1

Solem v. Helm, 463 U.S. 277 (1983), 63, 211n28

South Carolina v. Gathers, 490 U.S. 805 (1989), 174, 224n38

Stanford v. Kentucky, 492 U.S. 361 (1989), 223n1

Stanley v. Georgia, 394 U.S. 557 (1969), 33

Strickland v. Washington, 466 U.S. 668 (1984), 187–89

Swain v. Alabama, 380 U.S. 202 (1965), 64, 65, 66

Swann v. Charlotte-Mecklenburg School District, 402 U.S. 1 (1971), 74–82, 85, 86, 90, 120, 139

Texas v. Williams, 484 U.S. 816 (1987), 172, 224n30

Thornton v. Caldor, 472 U.S. 703 (1985), 40

Torres v. Oakland Scavenger Co., 487 U.S. 312 (1988), 185

Trop v. Dulles, 356 U.S. 86 (1986), 147, 221n3

Truesdale v. Aiken, 480 U.S. 527 (1987), 172, 224n31

Turner v. Murray, 476 U.S. 28 (1986), 173

United States ex rel. Angelet v. Fay, 333 F.2d 12 (2d Cir. 1964), 14, 27, 200n19

United States ex rel. Hetenyi v. Wilkins, 348 F.2d 844 (2d Cir. 1965), 14, 32, 33, 43

United States Postal Service v. Aikens, 460 U.S. 711 (1983), 61, 211n21

United States v. Brignoni-Ponce, 422 U.S. 873 (1975), 44, 206n53

United States v. Carolene Products, 304 U.S. 144 (1938), 95, 215n6

United States v. Kras, 409 U.S. 434 (1973), 5–6, 59

United States v. Montgomery County Board of Education, 395 U.S. 225 (1969), 79

United States v. Nixon, 474 U.S. 683 (1974), 39, 205n37

United States v. Seckinger, 397 U.S. 203 (1970), 39, 205n33

Vorchheimer v. School Dist., 430 U.S. 703 (1977), 41

Wainwright v. Adams, 466 U.S. 964 (1984), 166–67, 223n8

Wallace v. Jaffree, 472 U.S. 38 (1985), 63, 211n28

Weems v. United States, 217 U.S. 349 (1910), 147, 221n3

Welch v. Texas Dept. of Highways, 483 U.S. 468 (1987), 41–42, 206n45

Williams v. Illinois, 466 U.S. 981 (1984), 65, 212n33

Witherspoon v. Illinois, 391 U.S. 510 (1968), 147–48, 149

Witters v. Washington Dept. of Services for the Blind, 474 U.S. 481 (1986), 63, 211n25

Wooley v. Maynard, 430 U.S. 705 (1977), 61, 211n22

Wright v. City of Emporia, 407 U.S. 451 (1972), 82

Wygant v. Jackson Board of Education, 476 U.S. 267 (1986), 136–37, 138, 139

Zablocki v. Redhail, 434 U.S. 374 (1978), 103, 215n22

Index

Abortion cases, 6–7, 37–38, 97
Abortion finance case, 102–3
Accommodation of religion, 40
Affirmative action, 116–45; in desegregation cases, 120; in employment, 135–39; origins of, 117; public views on, 121
Age discrimination, 108–12
Ali, Mohammed, 68
Amsterdam, Anthony, 147, 148
Avins, Alfred, 26, 27

Balanced budget case, 40–41
Baldus, David, 160
Bickel, Alexander, 130
Black, Fred, 21
Black, Hugo, 27, 28, 32, 35, 45; on death penalty, 148; in desegregation cases, 70, 71, 72–73; in obscenity cases, 177; on overruling cases, 36
Blackmun, Harry, 4, 5–6, 8; on abortion, 6–7, 38; on affirmative action in *Bakke* case, 129–30; in *Bakke* case, 128; on Burger, 37, 39; in Charlotte busing case, 77; on death penalty, 148; early slowness at work, 45–46; on gender discrimination, 106; on Marshall, 63; on rational basis review, 109; in Richmond desegregation case, 85–86; on Scalia, 50, 52
Bork, Robert, 191; nomination of, 53

Brandeis, Louis, 58, 64
Brennan, William J., 6–7, 28, 194; on affirmative action in *Bakke* case, 122, 126–27; on affirmative action in *Fullilove* case, 133, 134; and assignment of opinions, 61; in *Bakke* case, 129; on Burger, 39, 72; in Charlotte busing case, 78, 81; on death penalty, 150; in desegregation cases, 72–73, 74, 75, 89–90; on discrimination against whites, 135; on employment discrimination, 139; on gender discrimination, 104–5, 105–6; on race discrimination in death penalty cases, 161; relations with colleagues, 41–42; relations with Marshall, 42–43, 66; relations with Powell, 42; retirement of, 54; on rational basis review, 108–10; role of, 41–43; on set-asides, 143; on stays of execution, 168–69, 171; use of law clerks, 58
Brown, Ernest, 14
Brownell, Herbert, 20
Bruce, Lenny, 17–18
Burger Court, and relation to Warren Court, 31
Burger, Warren, 28; in abortion cases, 37–38; on affirmative action in *Bakke* case, 123–24; on affirmative action in *Fullilove* case, 133–34; appointment to Supreme Court of, 35; and assignment

Burger, Warren (*continued*)
   of opinions, 60–61; in Charlotte busing
   case, 76, 77–82; on Chief Justice's
   role, 39; colleagues' reactions to opinion drafts by, 61–62; in Dallas desegregation case, 84; on death penalty,
   153, 154; in Denver desegregation
   case, 83; in desegregation cases, 70–
   74, 75, 76, 82; in Detroit desegregation case, 85, 87; effect of appointment, 36; equal protection theory of,
   102, 112; evaluation of performance
   of, 41; on gender discrimination, 104,
   106; as manager, 56; in Nixon tapes
   case, 39; opinion assignment practices
   of, 39; performance of, 36–41; on psychiatric experts in death penalty cases,
   157–58; in Richmond desegregation
   case, 86; relations with Marshall, 37;
   relations with Brennan, 169; retirement of, 36; on stays of execution,
   170–71; use of law clerks, 58
Busing, 74–88, 89–90
Butterfield, Alexander, 44
Byrnes, James F., 37

Capital punishment. *See* Death penalty
Carswell, Harrold, 35
Carter, Jesse, 118–19
Carter, Jimmy, 106
Carter, Stephen, 45, 60, 183n
Charlotte, N.C., busing case, 74–82
Civil Rights Act of 1964, 69, 123
Civil rights cases, at Second Circuit, 16–
   17
Claiborne, Louis, 22–23
Clark, Ramsey, 25, 202–3n55
Clark, Tom, 25
Coleman, William T., 9, 13–14, 196
Communist party, 117
Confessions, 24, 43
Court-packing plan, 95
Cox, Archibald, 18
Cox, Harold, 13
Craven, J. Braxton, 76
Crawford, George, 146, 178

Dallas school desegregation case, 84–85
Davis, John W., 10
De facto segregation, 83–84

Death penalty, 64, 65, 146–78; constitutionality of, 150–55; 1972 decisions,
   150–53; 1976 decisions, 153–55; public
   views on, 147; race discrimination in,
   159–62; standards for administering,
   148–49, 153–55; strategy for challenging, 163–64; "troika" in 1976 decisions, 154
Death-qualified juries, 147–48
Denver school desegregation case, 82–84
Desegregation, 68–93; in North, 82–84,
   89–90
Detroit desegregation case, 85, 87–88, 88–
   89
Devins, Neal, 121
Dirksen, Everett, 11
Dodd, Thomas, 11
Double jeopardy clause, 15, 32–33, 175
Douglas, William, O.,28, 35, 46; on Burger, 36–37, 38, 39; on death penalty,
   148, 150; on equal protection clause,
   95–96; on gender discrimination, 105;
   on Marshall, 34
Draft registration case, 106–8

Eastland, James, 9, 12
Eastland, Terry, 63
Employment discrimination cases, 53–54,
   116–19
Episcopal Church, 180
Equal protection clause, 94–95, 115; and
   age discrimination, 108–12; and discrimination against mentally retarded,
   112–15; and education cases, 100–102;
   and gender discrimination, 97, 103–8;
   rational-basis review in, 95, 113–14;
   sliding-scale theory of, 100, 114–15;
   strict scrutiny in, 95–96; two-tier
   theory of, 100, 102, 104, 121–22
Equal Rights Amendment, 104, 105
Ervin, Sam, Jr., 26
Establishment of religion, 40, 60
Evidence, illegal seizure of, 14
Exclusionary rule, 14

Faubus, Orval, 176, 177
Federal Bureau of Investigation, 20–21,
   24
First Amendment, 97–98
Fitzgerald, Ernest, 44

Ford, Gerald, 46, 53
Fortas, Abe, 15, 22, 28, 32, 182; on death penalty, 148, 149; losing Court majority, 182; on Marshall, 202n45; on Marshall's nomination, 25; resignation of, 35; nomination as Chief Justice, 34–35
Frankfurter, Felix, 68, 119; comments on Marshall, 13–14
Free speech, 97–98
Freedom-of-choice plans, 69–70
Friendly, Henry, 14, 16–17, 18

Galamison, Milton, 16–17
Gewirtz, Paul, 55
Ginsburg, Douglas, 53
Goldberg, Arthur, 147
Gordon, Robert, 4
Great Society, 96–97
Greenberg, Jack, 118
Gunther, Gerald, 108, 110, 132

Habeas corpus, 163
Halperin, Morton, 44–45
Harlan, John Marshall, 28, 31, 35; in Charlotte busing case, 78, 81; on death penalty, 148, 149–50; in desegregation cases, 71, 73, 74
Harlow, Bryce, 44
Hart, Philip, 11–12
Hastie, William, 25
Haynsworth, Clement, 35
Hein Park, 91–92
Hershey, Lewis, 20
Holding cases, 164, 165–66, 169–70
Holmes, Oliver Wendell, 94, 192
Hoover, J. Edgar, 21, 201–2n43
Houston, Charles Hamilton, 3, 31, 146, 181, 186
Hruska, Roman, 10, 35
Hyde Amendment, 102, 103

Incorporation controversy, 15
Insane prisoners, 156
Interdistrict desegregation cases, 85–88

Jackson, Andrew, 176–77
Javits, Jacob, 12
Jefferson, Thomas, 176–77
Jeffries, John, 93, 110–11

Johnson, Lyndon, 3–4, 34–35; and appointment of Marshall as Solicitor General, 18–19; and intention to nominate Marshall to Supreme Court, 19; nomination of Marshall to Supreme Court, 25
Johnston, Olin, 10, 11

Kagan, Elena, 101
Katzenbach, Nicholas, 12, 19, 21, 24, 25
Keating, Kenneth, 10, 11, 12
Kefauver, Estes, 12
Kennedy, Anthony, 5, 36; appointment of, 53
Kennedy, Edward M., 27
Kennedy, John F., 4, 12; and appointment of Marshall to Second Circuit, 9–10
Kennedy, Randall, 67, 161, 186
Kennedy, Robert F., 12, 13, 22; and appointment of Marshall, 9–10, 201–2n43; and wiretapping controversy, 20–21
Kilpatrick, James Jackson, 25–26, 31
King, Martin Luther, Jr., 68
Kissinger, Henry, 44
Knox, Simmie, 180
Kraft, Joseph, 25
Kronman, Anthony, 4, 181

Law clerks, 53; criticisms of use of, 63; of Marshall, 209n4, 209–10n5; role of, 46, 57–60
Legal services programs, 97
Levi, Edward, 46
Little Rock school case, 72, 175, 176, 177
Lumbard, Edward J., 10
Lyons, W. D., 146

Mansfield, Mike, 11
Marshall, Burke, 10
Marshall, Cecilia (Cissy), 25, 116, 179
Marshall, John (son), 179
Marshall, Thurgood, on abortion, 6–7, 38; in abortion finance case, 102–3; on affirmative action, 144–45; on affirmative action in *Bakke* case, 125, 127–28, 128–29, 131–32; on affirmative action in *Fullilove* case, 134; on age discrimination, 111–12; in antitrust cases, 183; appointment to Second Circuit,

Marshall, Thurgood (*continued*)
9–10, 198–99n2; appointment to Supreme Court, 3–4; and assignment of opinions to, 60–61; Bicentennial speech on constitutional interpretation, 191–92, 195–96; on black power, 68; on Bork nomination, 53, 191; and business cases, 13–14; and changing votes as justice, 32, 190–91; in Charlotte busing case, 76–77, 80; church activities of, 180; on civil disobedience, 180; and civil rights cases at Second Circuit, 16–17; and civil rights cases as Solicitor General, 23–24; colleagues' views of, 64; comments on nominations to Supreme Court, 25–26; on Court at his retirement, 55; on death penalty, 67, 149, 151–53, 154–55, 158–59, 162, 178; departure from NAACP, 3; in desegregation cases, 71–72, 74, 82, 84; in Detroit desegregation case, 87–88, 89; on double jeopardy clause, 15, 32–33; on drafting opinions, 183–84; on education, 101–2; on employment discrimination, 135–36, 138; equal protection theory of, 30, 94, 97–98, 99–100, 102–3, 111–12, 114–15, 121; evaluation of performance as Solicitor General, 20, 21–22; on executing insane prisoners, 156; on expediting death penalty cases, 171–72, 173; on families, 7–8; first Supreme Court opinions of, 32; on gas chamber, 159; on gender discrimination, 104, 107–8; general perspective of, 31; hearings on nomination to Supreme Court, 26–27; on his life style, 179; on image of judge, 64; and implementation of Warren Court precedents, 14–15; on ineffective assistance of counsel, 187–89; insistence on procedural regularity, 185–86; on instructing juries in death penalty cases, 155–56; on Anthony Kennedy, 54; as lawyer-statesman, 191–92; on lawyers in death penalty cases, 146, 158, 187–91; and Lenny Bruce case, 17–18; on Martin Luther King, Jr., 68; Masonic activities of, 180; on merit, 119–20; as New Deal liberal, 180–81; nomination to Supreme Court, 25; and obscenity cases, 33; on O'Connor, 46; participation in oral argument, 8; performance in business cases as Solicitor General, 21–22, 23; personality of, 4–5; on poverty, 5–6; practices in death penalty cases, 175–78; pragmatism of, 33–34, 183, 192–93; preparation for Court discussions, 56; and presidential immunity case, 44–45; on private property, 185; on professionalism, 187–88; on psychiatric experts, 156–58; on quotas in hiring, 118; on race discrimination, 7, 91–93, 116; on race discrimination in death penalty cases, 159–60, 161; recusal policy of, 84; on Rehnquist, 47, 48; relations with Brennan, 42–43; relations with Burger, 37; relations with Henry Friendly, 14; relations with J. Edgar Hoover, 21; relations with law clerks, 59–60, 191; relations with Powell, 44; relation with Warren, 31; as republican lawyer, 4; reputation as Second Circuit judge, 18; response to Rehnquist on death penalty, 166; retirement of, 3, 54; and revising drafts to accommodate colleagues, 62–63; in Richmond desegregation case, 86–87; on right to job, 30; role in Court discussions, 56–57; and role of judge, 13; role in peremptory challenge cases, 64–67; on Scalia, 51–52; as Second Circuit judge, 13–18; Second Circuit nomination hearings, 10–13; on seniority systems, 136–37; on set-aside programs, 141–43; as social engineer, 182–83; as Solicitor General, 19–24; on Souter, 191; on stare decisis, 174–75, 175–78; and state action doctrine, 33; on stays of execution, 167, 170; on Stevens, 46; as story-teller, 5; Supreme Court papers of, 195n; traditionalism of, 59–60, 61, 64, 184–86; use of law clerks, 57–60; on victim impact statements, 174–75; on Vietnam war, 68; views in general, 4
Marshall, Thurgood Jr., 179
Martin, Louis, 9–10
Maryland, University of, 7

McClellan, John, 10, 12, 25
McCleskey, Warren, 160, 162
McMillan, James, 76, 78, 79, 80
Mehrige, Robert, 85, 86
Memphis school desegregation case, 75
Minow, Martha, 59, 186
Mitchell, John, 44–45

National Lawyers Guild, 11
New Deal coalition, 28–29
Nickerson, Eugene, 65
Nixon, Richard, 35, 44–45; administration position on desegregation, 70–71
Nixon tapes case, 39
Nude dancing case, 48–49

Obscenity cases, 33
O'Connor, Sandra Day, 5, 8, 36, 43, 51–52; appointment to Supreme Court of, 46; equal protection theory of, 101–2; on residential segregation, 91; role of, 46; on set-aside programs, 140–41

Parker, John, J., 69, 77, 88
Patterson, Brenda, 53–54
Penn-Central merger controversy, 22–23
Peremptory challenge cases, 64–67, 184
Perry, Marian Wynn, 117
Poll tax case, 23–24
Poole, Cecil, 117–18
Powell, Lewis F., 6, 35, 56, 82; on abortion, 6–7; and abortion cases, 97; on affirmative action in *Bakke* case, 125–26, 127–28, 130–31; on affirmative action in *Fullilove* case, 133, 134; on Burger, 37, 40; in Dallas desegregation case, 84–85; in Denver desegregation case, 83–84; in Detroit desegregation case, 89; on discrimination against whites, 135; on drafting opinions, 184; on employment discrimination, 137–38, 138–39; equal protection theory of, 100–101, 102, 112–13, 115; on executing insane prisoners, 156; on gender discrimination, 105, 106; on Marshall, 63; opinion in peremptory challenge case, 66; on psychiatric experts, 157; on race discrimination in death penalty cases, 160–61; on rational basis review, 108, 109–11; relations with

Marshall, 44; retirement of, 53; role of, 43–45; on Scalia, 49; on seniority systems, 136; on stays of execution, 166, 168, 170; use of law clerks, 58; on work of Court, 45
Presidential immunity case, 44–45, 60
Prisoners' rights, 6, 62–63
Progressive party, 117
Proxmire, William, 56n

Rape, death penalty for, 148
Reagan, Ronald, 36, 46, 53
Rehnquist, William H., 35, 36; on affirmative action in *Bakke* case, 123, 124; and aggressive opinion drafts, 61; appointment as Chief Justice of, 36, 46–47; on Burger, 37; colleagues' views of, 47; on death penalty, 165–66; in Denver desegregation case, 83–84; in desegregation cases, 89–90; on gender discrimination, 106–7; as manager, 56; on Marshall's retirement, 3; opinion assignment practices of, 190; on race discrimination in death penalty cases, 161; on rational basis review, 108–10; relations with Marshall, 47–48; on residential segregation, 90–91; on Scalia, 62; on scheduling death penalty cases, 173; on stays of execution, 168; use of law clerks, 58
Religion clauses, 63; interpretation of, 40
Relisting cases, 169
Removal statute, 16–17
Republican party, and challenge to New Deal coalition, 29; constitutional theory of, 29
Richmond desegregation case, 85–87
Richmond, California, 117
Roosevelt, Franklin D., 95
Rowan, Carl, 195
Rule of four, 164

Scalia, Antonin, 36, 46–47; colleagues' views of, 49–50; on race discrimination in death penalty cases, 161; role of, 49–52; and statutory interpretation, 50–51
School finance case, 100–101
Schwartz, Bernard, 126, 129
Search and seizure cases, 40, 44

Segal, Bernard, 10
Segregation, on interstate buses, 17; residential, 90–91
Seniority systems, 136–37
Separate but equal education, 41
Set–aside programs, 139–44
Shopping mall cases, 33
Sobeloff, Simon, 12
Social engineer, lawyer as, 31, 181
Solicitor general, description of job, 19
Souter, David, 191
Spritzer, Ralph, 21
State action doctrine, 33
Statutory interpretation, 50–51
Stays of execution, 164, 170, 173
Steiker, Jordan, 176
Stevens, John Paul, 7, 35; on affirmative action in *Bakke* case, 125, 128; on Burger, 37, 46; in Dallas desegregation case, 84–85; on death penalty, 153; in desegregation cases, 89–90; equal protection theory of, 112; on fairness in death penalty cases, 190; on race discrimination, 91; on Rehnquist, 47; response to Rehnquist on death penalty, 166; role on Court of, 46; on Scalia, 49
Stewart, Potter, 5, 28, 31–32, 64n; on affirmative action, 120; on affirmative action in *Bakke* case, 127; on affirmative action in *Fullilove* case, 133; on Burger, 36; in Charlotte busing case, 78–79, 80; in death penalty cases, 147–48, 149; on death penalty, 150–51, 153, 154; in desegregation cases, 73, 89; on gender discrimination, 104, 105, 106; in Richmond desegregation case, 85; use of law clerks, 58
Stone, Geoffrey, 60, 94

Stone, Harlan Fiske, 95
Sunstein, Cass, 101, 116
Supreme Court, and assignment of opinions, 60; discussions among justices, 56; general operation of, 56; internal practices of, 164–65, 166, 169; political context of, 96–97
Sweatt, Heman, 11

Thornberry, Homer, 34
Thurmond, Strom, 25, 26, 27
Traynor, Roger, 118, 119
Tribe, Laurence, 58

Victim impact statements, 173–74
Voting rights, 98

Warren, Earl, 28, 182; and relation to Marshall, 31; retirement of, 34
Warren Court, 54–55; constitutional theory of, 29–30; political context of, 28–31
Welfare rights, 98–100
White, Byron, 5, 28, 32, 64, 182; on affirmative action in *Bakke* case, 123; on death penalty, 151, 153, 154; equal protection theory of, 112, 113–14; on gender discrimination, 104; on overruling cases, 36, 55; on residential segregation, 91; in Richmond desegregation case, 85–86; on Scalia, 50; on set-asides, 143
White, Walter, 117
Wilkinson, J. Harvie, 43
Winter, Ralph, 14
Wiretapping, 20–21

Yarborough, Ralph, 12
Yarmulke case, 42